Y0-BYA-077

TEACHING GIFTED STUDENTS

A Book of Readings

Edited by

James J. Gallagher

Professor of Education
Institute for Research
on Exceptional Children
University of Illinois

1965 ALLYN AND BACON, INC. BOSTON

LIBRARY OF CONGRESS CATALOG CARD NUMBER: 65-19243

Grateful acknowledgment is hereby made for permission to reprint the following:

GUILFORD, J. P. Three faces of intellect, *American Psychologist*, 1959, 14, 469–479.

MARTINSON, RUTH, & LESSINGER, L. Problems in the identification of intellectually gifted children. *Exceptional Children*, 1960, 26, 227–231.

PEGNATO, C. V. Identifying mentally gifted in junior high school. *Pittsburgh Schools*, 1959, 33, 215–223.

TERMAN, L. M. Are scientists different? *Scientific American*, January 1955. Reprinted with permission. Copyright © 1955 by Scientific American, Inc. All rights reserved.

TAYLOR, C. W. Who are the exceptionally creative? *Exceptional Children*, 1962, 28, 421–431.

LUCITO, L. J. Independence-conformity behavior as a function of intellect: bright and dull children. *Exceptional Children*, 1964, September, 5–13.

BONSALL, MARCELLA R., & STEFFLRE, B. The temperament of gifted children. *California Journal of Educational Research*, 1955, 6, 162–165.

FINLAY, G. C. The Physical Science Study Committee. Reprinted from *The School Review*, 1962, 70, 63–81, by permission of The University of Chicago Press. Copyright 1962 by The University of Chicago.

SUPPES, P., & HILL, SHIRLEY. Set theory in the primary grades. *The Mathematics Teacher*, 1963, 13, 46–53.

SUPPES, P. Mathematical logic for the schools. *The Arithmetic Teacher*, 1962, 9, 396–399.

UICSM Project Staff, University of Illinois. Arithmetic with frames. In 27th Yearbook, Council of Teachers of Mathematics, Washington, D.C., 1963, 64–72.

OJEMANN, R. Basic approaches to mental health: the human relations program at The University of Iowa. *Personnel and Guidance Journal*, 1958, 37, 199–206.

SENESH, L. The organic curriculum: a new experiment in economic education. *The Councilor*, 1960, 21, 43–56.

ATKIN, J. M. Some evaluation problems in a course content improvement project. *Journal of Research in Science Teaching*, 1963, 1, 129–132.

HENDRIX, GERTRUDE. Learning by discovery. *The Mathematics Teacher*, 1961, 54, 290–299.

TABA, HILDA. Learning by discovery: psychological and educational rationale. Reprinted from *Elementary School Journal*, 1963, 63, 308–316, by permission of The University of Chicago Press. Copyright 1963 by The University of Chicago.

ATKIN, J. M., & KARPLUS, R. Discovery or invention? *The Science Teacher*, 1962, 29, #5.

UCHMAN, J. R. Inquiry and education. Adapted from a speech given at an Association for Supervision and Curriculum Development, Anaheim, California, December, 1962. All of the papers presented at that institute are published in an ASCD booklet entitled: *Intellectual Development: Another Look.*

ORRANCE, E. P. Curriculum frontiers for the elementary gifted pupil–flying monkeys and silent lions. *Exceptional Children*, 1961, 28, 119–127.

PAULDING, R. L. What teacher attributes bring out the best in gifted children? *The Gifted Child Quarterly*, Winter 1963.

OLDBERG, MIRIAM L., & ASSOCIATES. A three year experimental program at DeWitt Clinton High School to help bright underachievers. *High Points*, 1959, 5–35.

SHAW, M. C., & MCCUEN, J. T. The onset of academic underachievement in bright children, *Journal of Educational Psychology*, 1960, 51, 103–108.

BAYMUR, F. B., & PATTERSON, C. H. Three methods of assisting underachieving high school students. *Journal of Counseling Psychology*, 1960, 7, 83–90.

RIESSMAN, F. *The Culturally Deprived Child*, Chapter VII, "The Slow Gifted Child." Copyright © 1962 by Frank Riessman. Reprinted with the permission of Harper & Row, Publishers, Incorporated.

GALLAGHER, J. J., GREENMAN, MARGARET, KARNES, MERLE, & KING, A. Individual classroom adjustments for gifted children in elementary schools. *Exceptional Children*, 1960, 26, 409–422, 432.

REYNOLDS, M. C., BIRCH, J. W., & TUSETH, ALICE A. Review of research on early admission. In M. C. Reynolds (Ed.), *Early School Admission for Mentally Advanced Children*, Washington, D.C.: Council for Exceptional Children, 1962, 7–17.

PREFACE

WHILE INTEREST in the problems of educating gifted children has been evidenced by educators for half a century, it is only in the last decade that the problem has become of general interest to the American public. The dramatic challenge to the American society of the Soviet Union and communist nations in the late 1950's had an equally dramatic response in terms of increased public concern for the education of gifted students. Prior to that time, concern for the effective education of gifted youth was received with varying degrees of indifference, and even shades of hostility and suspicion. The public has long made clear its desire to avoid an intellectual aristocracy which might become synonymous with privileged social classes. However, the clear need for the development of intellectual talent for self-protection appears to have overwhelmed the old fears.

It would be wrong to conclude, however, that the need for special attention and concern for talented students relates solely to the international conflicts, important though they may be. In their own ways, the rapid development of technology and the dramatic increase in new knowledge have probably produced a permanent influence on the educational system by accentuating differences and diversities in our society. Modern society has often been portrayed as the developer of conformity. The grey flannel suit became a symbol of the lack of diversity in the suburbanite, managerial class. This regrettable stereotype however, should not blind us to the essential conclusion that technology, in reality, creates huge differences within the society rather than similarities.

Consider the intellectual differences between two natives (chief and follower) in a primitive tribe. The distance does not seem too great nor does there seem to be a need to provide differential education for whatever simple tasks need to be accomplished in this society. In the agricultural or pioneer society, which represents much of our own educational heritage, the difference between occupations and thus educational needs was greater. However, the one-room school or the self-contained country classroom could still impart enough past wisdom to allow the student to perform comfortably, if not outstandingly, in his society.

In the complex modern society, however, based on continuing research and development, the differences between the uneducated person, the slightly educated person, and the highly educated individual such as the nuclear physicist, the microbiologist, or the medical specialist is a phenomenal one. When these great differences are matched against another cherished American goal, that of universal education, the pressures for differential education within the system becomes manifest.

The set of articles collected here have been chosen to supplement a recent text, *Teaching the Gifted Child*, by the compiler, also published by Allyn and Bacon. The general sections of this book parallel those in the text. As in *Teaching the Gifted Child*, the emphasis is placed on classroom environment, new curriculum movements, and special teaching methods as opposed to administrative provisions. However, the compiler fondly believes that these articles, representing the frontier of educating the gifted, stand on their own as an interesting and provocative collection of ideas, proposals, and current operations in this area.

J.J.G.

CONTENTS

Part Three
Teaching Method Changes 157

Part Four
Special Problems 235

Part One

DEFINITION, IDENTIFICATION, AND CHARACTERISTICS

THE FIRST QUESTION usually asked when a school system is interested in embarking on a program for gifted children is, "How can we find the gifted children in our schools?" The second question often is, "What are gifted children like?" Behind these seemingly innocuous questions lie other questions of deep philosophical importance which strike at the heart of the values of our society.

Each culture and era defines giftedness to suit its own particular needs and values. Until recently, high performance on IQ tests has been accepted as the most effective yardstick of intellectual giftedness. This acceptance was furthered by Terman's classic longitudinal study, *Genetic Studies of Genius*, which set the style for much of the research that followed. The acceptance of the IQ score was based also on the well-established relationship between IQ scores and achievement in the educational program.

Changes in the focus and orientation of educational programs during the past decade have already brought suggested changes in identification procedures for the gifted. Thus, we can see a tendency to expand the concept of giftedness beyond what the educator has become accustomed to over the last few decades.

The idea that the IQ test is not measuring everything that we know as "intellect" is hardly new. The defects of the standard measures, particularly in their inability to reach such obviously important characteristics as creativity, originality, and foresight, were well known to psychologists and educators. Yet one does not give up old tools that have served a useful purpose unless they can be replaced or improved by a new model. One such theoretical model for potential improvement has been provided by Dr. Guilford as outlined in his paper.

The present article represents the product of a decade and a half of research on cognitive abilities. Much of the emphasis in psychology during and immediately following World War II was devoted to emotional problems and personality development, and little attention was paid to cognition. Many persons were satisfied to accept, what now seems to be a totally unacceptable proposition, that "intelligence is what an IQ test measures."

Guilford's three-dimensional model of intellectual processes clearly implies that there are a number of cognitive processes that are not measured in conventional tests and provides the basis for additional research into such areas as divergent thinking and problem solving. It is likely that Guilford, as much as any one single person, is responsible for the rebirth of interest in cognitive processes that has been evidenced in both psychological and educational circles during the past decade.

This article has particular relevance to gifted children in that it calls into question the IQ criterion which has been used for identifying the gifted student. Giftedness assumes multifaceted dimensions with attention being paid to such exotic and unusual areas as intellectual flexibility and originality.

In a stable and unchanging culture where the present is but a mirror of the past and the future a replica of the present, the intellectual characteristics that would be valued would be those of a competent memory and a desire to conform to established practice.

In contrast, in a dynamic culture where change is the norm and adaptability the desired characteristic, the skills of memory and of social conformity do not seem as important. The role of the creative person and the productive thinker in a changing society is crucial.

Professor Taylor in his article does not believe that creative abilities are being measured effectively by current tools. He points out that the measurement of remembered knowledge may be a necessary, but it is not a sufficient, condition for creative performance. Something more is required than the usual IQ test. He indicates that there is a generally low or nonexistent relationship between "creative abilities," as currently measured, and scores on intelligence tests. Rather than recommend that the intelligence tests should be scrapped, Taylor is suggesting that the concept of intelligence be expanded to include broader dimensions.

Many still believe that the gifted child identifies himself through his behavior and that one only needs to be a reasonably alert and intelligent observer in order to find him. The article by Martinson and Lessinger should provide a necessary antidote to such beliefs. To a large extent, the problem of screening intellectually gifted youngsters in the schools is one of economics rather than psychology. If one were able to give individual intelligence tests, such a matter would be solved to a large extent (even though one may miss those whose special skills are noted by Guilford). But we must depend on other much less reliable indicators, such as group intelligence tests or teacher ratings. Martinson and Lessinger point out the imperfect relationship between group intelligence test scores and individual test results, although the authors concluded that it was possible to screen gifted children effectively at the kindergarten level through the use of a combination of teacher judgment and group tests.

Apparently the relationship between the group IQ test scores and the individual IQ test scores depends to a large extent on the upper test limits. For tests such as the Stanford–Binet, an IQ score of over 200 is possible for a young child, whereas for the same child on some group intelligence tests the maximum score would be only 140 or less.

Also in the individual examination, the youngster receives the close attention and praise of the individual examiner, and it is difficult for any youngster to resist giving a reasonably good performance. Under the conditions of the group intelligence test, when it is given in a class of 30, 40, or more, it is possible for the disinterested student to perform lackadaisically and thus give a sizable underestimation of his aptitude. It is always wise to hold a healthy disrespect for such tools so that we do not become their slaves rather than their masters.

How many youngsters of high intellectual talent are identifiable by their teachers? Pegnato's report will not serve to calm the suspicions of those who have felt that a number of talented students might be missed through casual teacher nomination methods. The need for more thorough training of teachers in recognition of the crucial factors of intellectual superiority seems called for. It should be noted also that the standard of intellectual giftedness in Pegnato's paper was a high score on the Stanford–Binet IQ test. A student with unusual creative gifts but limited interest or skill on the intelligence test items could have been nominated by the teacher as "highly intelligent."

In this case, who is more correct—the teacher or the test? More disturbing is the large number of students who appeared to possess high intellectual credentials but who were overlooked. Despite the relatively poor performance of teachers in this carefully done study, it seems unlikely that any other group of professional people faced with the same situation, but without adequate tools of measurement, could do much better. Since intellectual ability represents a *rate* of growth, measuring it is difficult without tools and standards of average performance.

To return to the first question, it should probably be best answered by asking some other questions. For what purpose does the school wish to make the identification? Is it idle curiosity? Is it to facilitate the beginning of a new accelerated curriculum program for gifted youngsters? Is the program limited to a specific content area? The answers to all of these questions will help shape the identification procedures used in a particular instance.

What are gifted children like? It depends on who we include as gifted for one thing. For another, we must be aware of how our own presuppositions play a role in what we think. At one time, it was a commonly held view that mentally retarded individuals were supposed to be very strong physically. This represented a type of compensation theory so that a person would have good points to balance off the bad. As a part of this compensation idea, gifted children were supposed to be either physically weak or mentally unbalanced. If true, this would tip the scales back into proper balance.

Lewis Terman needs no introduction to those who have been interested in the field of gifted children. His contributions are widespread and have a permanence that resists time. Out of his particular interest in gifted children came the monumental *Genetic Studies of Genius*. A sample of 1,500 students has been studied over three decades to see what type of academic and life adjustments were made by students with high IQ scores as they were followed through their adult life. The results which showed that the gifted sample (identified by IQ test scores) were superior to the average in almost every dimension and remained so throughout life did much to destroy the validity of the "compensation theory."

The article by Terman included here presents some data from that study and attempts to answer the question which is quite relevant to our age—are scientists different from others in our society? The stereotype of the introverted, absent-minded, amoral scientist who may, in the end, destroy us has invaded our popular literature and entertainment media. This study of the interests and values of gifted men in a variety of occupations provides some necessary data to supplement and adjust the overgeneralizations that have caused admiration for the scientist to exist side by side with a disinclination to encourage one's children to choose this occupation.

Ever since Terman's study on the characteristics of gifted children found its way into the educational textbooks, there has been a marked tendency to present the gifted as persons who, on the average, are moderately superior in many different avenues of adjustment or development–social, emotional, and physical.

Nevertheless, the evidence, as presented, still did not give a clear-cut indication whether intellectual ability was responsible for, or just an associated condition to, better social and emotional adjustment. It would be possible to develop an elaborate rationale explaining how advanced intellect made social perception easier and helped the individual to a better understanding of self and others. But is this really the case? Most investigators also found superior family background and a stable family structure were also usually associated with gifted children.

What would happen if one equated for the family background? Would the gifted youngster still seem so superior to those of average ability in social and emotional adjustment? This is the question proposed by Bonsall and Stefflre. While their small sample leaves conclusions less decisive than one would like, there is some evidence to suggest that it is the superior home background, more than the superior intelligence, influencing the favorable social and emotional development of these children.

One of the more specific characteristics that has received some scrutiny during the past few years has been tendencies toward conformity and noncomformity. The paper by Lucito is interested in exploring whether gifted youngsters will give up their own personal perception in deference to a group decision that he must see as manifestly incorrect.

As might be expected, the youngsters of high ability showed a greater tendency towards resisting conformity and held some confidence in their own beliefs even when these beliefs ran contrary to the group decision. While the groups differed, the range of conformity and nonconformity within the group of gifted youngsters is worthy of attention. Some of the gifted youngsters appeared to be every bit as conformist to the group judgment as were the slow learners, whereas others seemed to be remarkably independent.

Too often our research reports concentrate on group differences when the *range* of responses really has greater educational significance. It is one thing to find that the average height of American men is 5 ft. 10 ins., and it is quite another to design cars precisely to that height or physical build. No car manufacturer would be so foolish as to ignore the variations in height in favor of the central tendency. So another crucial aspect of characteristics of a group is their variation on a given characteristic, as well as their average.

For an educator, it is important to know not only whether gifted children have a better than average social adjustment but to know what proportion of the youngsters have unfavorable social adjustment or to be aware of the total range of social adjustment. It is as important to know how many gifted youngsters are performing poorly in academic achievement as it is to know that the average of the gifted youngsters is well above the norm. Too often educational policy seems to be directed toward rather exclusive consideration of averages, and this results in the consequent construction of a program that would be like the car designed solely for the man of 5 ft. 10 ins. in height. It is variation of characteristics that should determine our attitude and educational approach as well as the average.

❦ 1

Three Faces of Intellect[1]

J. P. Guilford
University of Southern California

MY SUBJECT is in the area of human intelligence, in connection with which the names of Terman and Stanford have become known the world over. The Stanford Revision of the Binet intelligence scale has been the standard against which all other instruments for the measurement of intelligence have been compared. The term IQ or intelligence quotient has become a household word in this country. This is illustrated by two brief stories.

A few years ago, one of my neighbors came home from a PTA meeting, remarking: "That Mrs. So-And-So, thinks she knows so much. She kept talking about the 'intelligence *quota*' of the children; 'intelligence *quota*'; imagine. Why, everybody knows that IQ stands for 'intelligence *quiz*.' "

The other story comes from a little comic strip in a Los Angeles morning newspaper, called "Junior Grade." In the first picture a little boy meets a little girl, both apparently about the first-grade level. The little girl remarks, "I have a high IQ." The little boy, puzzled, said, "You have a what?" The little girl repeated, "I have a high IQ," then went on her way. The little boy, looking thoughtful, said, "And she looks like such a nice little girl, too."

It is my purpose to speak about the analysis of this thing called human intelligence into its components. I do not believe that either Binet or Terman, if they were still with us, would object to the idea of a searching and detailed study of intelligence, aimed toward a better understanding of its nature. Preceding the development of his intelligence scale, Binet had done much research on different kinds of thinking activities and apparently recognized that intelligence has a number of aspects. It is to the lasting credit of both Binet and Terman that they introduced such a great variety of tasks into their intelligence scales.

1 The Walter V. Bingham Memorial Lecture given at Stanford University on April 13, 1959.

Two related events of very recent history make it imperative that we learn all we can regarding the nature of intelligence. I am referring to the advent of the artificial satellites and planets and to the crisis in education that has arisen in part as a consequence. The preservation of our way of life and our future security depend upon our most important national resources: our intellectual abilities and, more particularly, our creative abilities. It is time, then, that we learn all we can about those resources.

Our knowledge of the components of human intelligence has come about mostly within the last 25 years. The major sources of this information in this country have been L. L. Thurstone and his associates, the wartime research of psychologists in the United States Air Forces, and more recently the Aptitudes Project[2] at the University of Southern California, now in its tenth year of research on cognitive and thinking abilities. The results from the Aptitudes Project that have gained perhaps the most attention have pertained to creative-thinking abilities. These are mostly novel findings. But to me, the most significant outcome has been the development of a unified theory of human intellect, which organizes the known, unique or primary, intellectual abilities into a single system called the "structure of intellect." It is to this system that I shall devote the major part of my remarks, with very brief mentions of some of the implications for the psychology of thinking and problem solving, for vocational testing, and for education.

The discovery of the components of intelligence has been by means of the experimental application of the method of factor analysis. It is not necessary for you to know anything about the theory or method of factor analysis in order to follow the discussion of the components. I should like to say, however, that factor analysis has no connection with or resemblance to psychoanalysis. A positive statement would be more helpful, so I will say that each intellectual component or factor is a unique ability that is needed to do well in a certain class of tasks or tests. As a general principle we find that certain individuals do well in the tests of a certain class, but they may do poorly in the tests of another class. We conclude that a factor has certain properties from the features that the tests of a class have in common. I shall give you very soon a number of examples of tests, each representing a factor.

The Structure of Intellect

Although each factor is sufficiently distinct to be detected by factor analysis, in very recent years it has become apparent that the factors them-

[2] Under Contract N6onr-23810 with the Office of Naval Research (Personnel and Training Branch).

selves can be classified because they resemble one another in certain ways. One basis of classification is according to the basic kind of process or operation performed. This kind of classification gives us five major groups of intellectual abilities: factors of cognition, memory, convergent thinking, divergent thinking, and evaluation.

Cognition means discovery or rediscovery or recognition. Memory means retention of what is cognized. Two kinds of productive-thinking operations generate new information from known information and remembered information. In divergent-thinking operations we think in different directions, sometimes searching, sometimes seeking variety. In convergent thinking the information leads to one right answer or to a recognized best or conventional answer. In evaluation we reach decisions as to goodness, correctness, suitability, or adequacy of what we know, what we remember, and what we produce in productive thinking.

A second way of classifying the intellectual factors is according to the kind of material or content involved. The factors known thus far involve three kinds of material or content: the content may be figural, symbolic, or semantic. Figural content is concrete material such as is perceived through the senses. It does not represent anything except itself. Visual material has properties such as size, form, color, location, or texture. Things we hear or feel provide other examples of figural material. Symbolic content is composed of letters, digits, and other conventional signs, usually organized in general systems, such as the alphabet or the number system. Semantic content is in the form of verbal meanings or ideas, for which no examples are necessary.

When a certain operation is applied to a certain kind of content, as many as six general kinds of products may be involved. There is enough evidence available to suggest that, regardless of the combinations of operations and content, the same six kinds of products may be found associated. The six kinds of products are: units, classes, relations, systems, transformations, and implications. So far as we have determined from factor analysis, these are the only fundamental kinds of products that we can know. As such, they may serve as basic classes into which one might fit all kinds of information psychologically.

The three kinds of classifications of the factors of intellect can be represented by means of a single solid model, shown in Figure 1. In this model, which we call the "structure of intellect," each dimension represents one of the modes of variation of the factors.[3] Along one dimension are found the various kinds of operations, along a second one are the various kinds of products, and along the third are various kinds of content. Along the dimension of content a fourth category has been added, its kind of content being designated as "behavioral." This category has been added on a

[3] For an earlier presentation of the concept, see Guilford (1956).

purely theoretical basis to represent the general area sometimes called "social intelligence." More will be said about this section of the model later.

In order to provide a better basis for understanding the model and a better basis for accepting it as a picture of human intellect, I shall do some exploring of it with you systematically, giving some examples of tests.

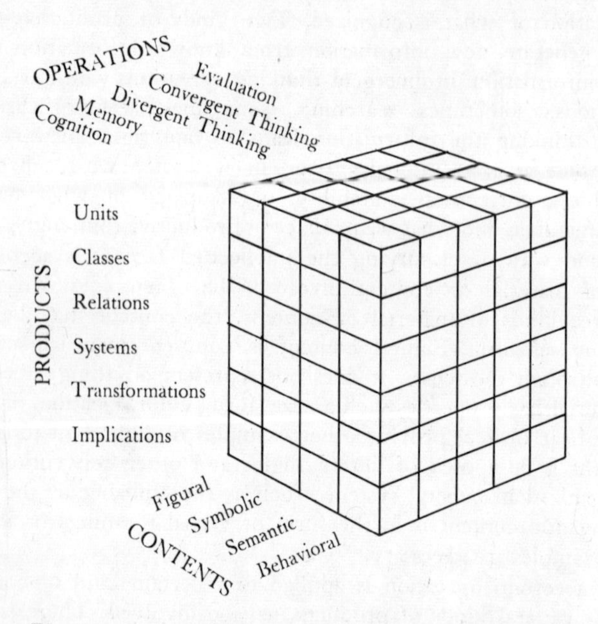

Figure 1. A cubical model representing the structure of intellect.

Each cell in the model calls for a certain kind of ability that can be described in terms of operation, content, and product, for each cell is at the intersection of a unique combination of kinds of operation, content, and product. A test for that ability would have the same three properties. In our exploration of the model, we shall take one vertical layer at a time, beginning with the front face. The first layer provides us with a matrix of 18 cells (if we ignore the behavioral column for which there are as yet no known factors) each of which should contain a cognitive ability.

The Cognitive Abilities

We know at present the unique abilities that fit logically into 15 of the 18 cells for cognitive abilities. Each row presents a triad of similar abilities, having a single kind of product in common. The factors of the first row are concerned with the knowing of units. A good test of the ability to cognize figural units is the Street Gestalt Completion Test. In this test, the recognition of familiar pictured objects in silhouette form is made difficult for testing purposes by blocking out parts of those objects. There is another factor that is known to involve the perception of auditory figures–in the form of melodies, rhythms, and speech sounds–and still another factor involving kinesthetic forms. The presence of three factors in one cell (they are conceivably distinct abilities, although this has not been tested) suggests that more generally, in the figural column, at least, we should expect to find more than one ability. A fourth dimension pertaining to variations in sense modality may thus apply in connection with figural content. The model could be extended in this manner if the facts call for such an extension.

The ability to cognize symbolic units is measured by tests like the following:

Put vowels in the following blanks to make real words:

P___W___R
M___RV___L
C___RT___N

Rearrange the letters to make real words:

R A C I H
T V O E S
K L C C O

The first of these two tests is called Disemvoweled Words, and the second Scrambled Words.

The ability to cognize semantic units is the well-known factor of verbal comprehension, which is best measured by means of a vocabulary test, with items such as:

GRAVITY means ________
CIRCUS means ________
VIRTUE means ________

From the comparison of these two factors it is obvious that recognizing familiar words as letter structures and knowing what words mean depend upon quite different abilities.

For testing the abilities to know classes of units, we may present the following kinds of items, one with symbolic content and one with semantic content:

Which letter group does not belong?
XECM PVAA QXIN VTRO

Which object does not belong?
clam tree oven rose

A figural test is constructed in a completely parallel form, presenting in each item four figures, three of which have a property in common and the fourth lacking that property.

The three abilities to see relationships are also readily measured by a common kind of test, differing only in terms of content. The well-known analogies test is applicable, two items in symbolic and semantic form being:

JIRE : KIRE : : FORA : KORE KORA LIRE GORA GIRE
poetry : prose : : dance : music walk sing talk jump

Such tests usually involve more than the ability to cognize relations, but we are not concerned with this problem at this point.

The three factors for cognizing systems do not at present appear in tests so closely resembling one another as in the case of the examples just given. There is nevertheless an underlying common core of logical similarity. Ordinary space tests, such as Thurstone's Flags, Figures, and Cards or Part V (Spatial Orientation) of the Guilford-Zimmerman Aptitude Survey (GZAS), serve in the figural column. The system involved is an order or arrangement of objects in space. A system that uses symbolic elements is illustrated by the Letter Triangle Test, a sample item of which is:

```
            ___
          d     ___
      b      e      ___
  a      c      f      ?
```

What letter belongs at the place of the question mark?

The ability to understand a semantic system has been known for some time as the factor called general reasoning. One of its most faithful indicators is a test composed of arithmetic-reasoning items. That the phase of understanding only is important for measuring this ability is shown by the fact that such a test works even if the examinee is not asked to give a complete solution; he need only show that he structures the problem properly. For example, an item from the test Necessary Arithmetical Operations simply asks what operations are needed to solve the problem:

A city lot 48 feet wide and 149 feet deep costs $79,432. What is the cost per square foot?

A. Add and multiply
B. multiply and divide
C. subtract and divide
D. add and subtract
E. divide and add

Placing the factor of general reasoning in this cell of the structure of intellect gives us some new conceptions of its nature. It should be a broad ability to grasp all kinds of systems that are conceived in terms of verbal concepts, not restricted to the understanding of problems of an arithmetical type.

Transformations are changes of various kinds, including modifications in arrangement, organization, or meaning. In the figural column for the transformations row, we find the factor known as visualization. Common measuring instruments for this factor are the surface-development tests, and an example of a different kind is Part VI (Spatial Visualization) of the GZAS. A test of the ability to make transformations of meaning, for the factor in the semantic column, is called Similarities. The examinee is asked to state several ways in which two objects, such as an apple and an orange, are alike. Only by shifting the meanings of both is the examinee able to give many responses to such an item.

In the set of abilities having to do with the cognition of implications, we find that the individual goes beyond the information given, but not to the extent of what might be called drawing conclusions. We may say that he extrapolates. From the given information he expects or foresees certain consequences, for example. The two factors found in this row of the cognition matrix were first called "foresight" factors. Foresight in connection with figural material can be tested by means of paper-and-pencil mazes. Foresight in connection with ideas, those pertaining to events, for example, is indicated by a test such as Pertinent Questions:

> In planning to open a new hamburger stand in a certain community, what four questions should be considered in deciding upon its location?

The more questions the examinee asks in response to a list of such problems, the more he evidently foresees contingencies.

The Memory Abilities

The area of memory abilities has been explored less than some of the other areas of operation, and only seven of the potential cells of the memory matrix have known factors in them. These cells are restricted to three rows: for units, relations, and systems. The first cell in the memory matrix is now occupied by two factors, parallel to two in the corresponding cognition matrix: visual memory and auditory memory. Memory for series of letters or numbers, as in memory span tests, conforms to the conception of memory for symbolic units. Memory for the ideas in a paragraph conforms to the conception of memory for semantic units.

The formation of associations between units, such as visual forms, syllables, and meaningful words, as in the method of paired associates, would seem to represent three abilities to remember relationships involving three kinds of content. We know of two such abilities, for the symbolic and semantic columns. The memory for known systems is represented by two abilities very recently discovered (Christal, 1958). Remembering the arrangement of objects in space is the nature of an ability in the figural column, and remembering a sequence of events is the nature of a corresponding ability in the semantic column. The differentiation between these two abilities implies that a person may be able to say where he saw an object on a page, but he might not be able to say on which of several pages he saw it after leafing through several pages that included the right one. Considering the blank rows in the memory matrix, we should expect to find abilities also to remember classes, transformations, and implications, as well as units, relations, and systems.

The Divergent-Thinking Abilities

The unique feature of divergent production is that a *variety* of responses is produced. The product is not completely determined by the given information. This is not to say that divergent thinking does not come into play in the total process of reaching a unique conclusion, for it comes into play wherever there is trial-and-error thinking.

The well-known ability of word fluency is tested by asking the examinee to list words satisfying a specified letter requirement, such as words beginning with the letter "s" or words ending in "-tion." This ability is now regarded as a facility in divergent production of symbolic units. The parallel semantic ability has been known as ideational fluency. A typical test item calls for listing objects that are round and edible. Winston Churchill must have possessed this ability to a high degree. Clement Attlee is reported to have said about him recently that, no matter what problem came up, Churchill always seemed to have about ten ideas. The trouble was, Attlee continued, he did not know which was the good one. The last comment implies some weakness in one or more of the evaluative abilities.

The divergent production of class ideas is believed to be the unique feature of a factor called "spontaneous flexibility." A typical test instructs the examinee to list all the uses he can think of for a common brick, and he is given eight minutes. If his responses are: build a house, build a barn, build a garage, build a school, build a church, build a chimney, build a walk, and build a barbecue, he would earn a fairly high score for ideational fluency but a very low score for spontaneous flexibility, because all these uses fall into the same class. If another person said: make a door stop, make a paper weight, throw it at a dog, make a bookcase, drown a cat, drive a nail, make a red powder, and use for baseball bases, he would also receive a high score for flexibility. He has gone frequently from one class to another.

A current study of unknown but predicted divergent-production abilities includes testing whether there are also figural and symbolic abilities to produce multiple classes. An experimental figural test presents a number of figures that can be classified in groups of three in various ways, each figure being usable in more than one class. An experimental symbolic test presents a few numbers that are also to be classified in multiple ways.

A unique ability involving relations is called "associational fluency." It calls for the production of a variety of things related in a specified way to a given thing. For example, the examinee is asked to list words meaning about the same as "good" or to list words meaning about the opposite of "hard." In these instances the response produced is to complete a relationship, and semantic content is involved. Some of our present experimental tests call for the production of varieties of relations, as such, and involve figural and symbolic content also. For example, given four small digits, in how many ways can they be related in order to produce a sum of eight?

One factor pertaining to the production of systems is known as expressional fluency. The rapid formation of phrases or sentences is the essence of certain tests of this factor. For example, given the initial letters:

with different sentences to be produced, the examinee might write "We can eat nuts" or "Whence came Eve Newton?" In interpreting the factor, we regard the sentence as a symbolic system. By analogy, a figural system would be some kind of organization of lines and other elements, and a semantic system would be in the form of a verbally stated problem or perhaps something as complex as a theory.

In the row of the divergent-production matrix devoted to transformations, we find some very interesting factors. The one called "adaptive flexibility" is now recognized as belonging in the figural column. A faithful test of it has been Match Problems. This is based upon the common game that uses squares, the sides of which are formed by match sticks. The examinee is told to take away a given number of matches to leave a stated number of squares with nothing left over. Nothing is said about the sizes of the squares to be left. If the examinee imposes upon himself the restriction that the squares that he leaves must be of the same size, he will fail in his attempts to do items like that in Figure 2. Other odd kinds of solutions are introduced in other items, such as overlapping squares and squares within squares, and so on. In another variation of Match Problems the examinee is told to produce two or more solutions for each problem.

A factor that has been called "originality" is now recognized as adaptive flexibility with semantic material, where there must be a shifting of meanings. The examinee must produce the shifts or changes in meaning and so come up with novel, unusual, clever, or farfetched ideas. The Plot Titles Test presents a short story, the examinee being told to list as many appropriate titles as he can to head the story. One story is about a missionary who has been captured by cannibals in Africa. He is in the pot and about to be boiled when a princess of the tribe obtains a promise for his release if he will become her mate. He refuses and is boiled to death.

In scoring the test, we separate the responses into two categories, clever and nonclever. Examples of nonclever responses are: African Death, Defeat of a Princess, Eaten by Savages, The Princess, The African Missionary, In Darkest Africa, and Boiled by Savages. These titles are appropriate but commonplace. The number of such responses serves as a score for ideational

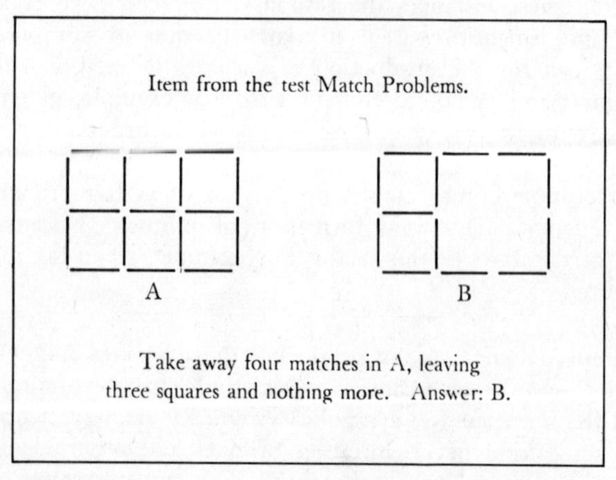

Figure 2. A sample item from the test Match Problems. The problem in this item is to take away four matches and leave three squares. The solution is given.

fluency. Examples of clever responses are: Pot's Plot, Potluck Dinner, Stewed Parson, Goil or Boil, A Mate Worse Than Death, He Left a Dish for a Pot, Chaste in Haste, and A Hot Price for Freedom. The number of clever responses given by examinee is his score for originality, or the divergent production of semantic transformations.

Another test of originality presents a very novel task so that any acceptable response is unusual for the individual. In the Symbol Production Test the examinee is to produce a simple symbol to stand for a noun or a verb in each short sentence, in other words to invent something like pictographic symbols. Still another test of originality asks for writing the "punch lines" for cartoons, a task that almost automatically challenges the examinee to be clever. Thus, quite a variety of tests offer approaches to the measurement of originality, including one or two others that I have not mentioned.

Abilities to produce a variety of implications are assessed by tests calling for elaboration of given information. A figural test of this type provides the examinee with a line or two, to which he is to add other lines to produce an object. The more lines he adds, the greater his score. A semantic test gives the examinee the outlines of a plan to which he is to respond by stating all the details he can think of to make the plan work. A new test we are trying out in the symbolic area presents two simple equations such as $B - C = D$ and $z = A + D$. The examinee is to make as many other equations as he can from this information.

The Convergent-Production Abilities

Of the 18 convergent-production abilities expected in the three content columns, 12 are now recognized. In the first row, pertaining to units, we have an ability to name figural properties (forms or colors) and an ability to name abstractions (classes, relations, and so on). It may be that the ability in common to the speed of naming forms and the speed of naming colors is not appropriately placed in the convergent-thinking matrix. One might expect that the thing to be produced in a test of the convergent production of figural units would be in the form of figures rather than words. A better test of such an ability might somehow specify the need for one particular object, the examinee to furnish the object.

A test for the convergent production of classes (Word Grouping) presents a list of 12 words that are to be classified in four, and only four, meaningful groups, no word to appear in more than one group. A parallel test (Figure Concepts Test) presents 20 pictured real objects that are to be grouped in meaningful classes of two or more each.

Convergent production having to do with relationships is represented by three known factors, all involving the "education of correlates," as Spearman called it. The given information includes one unit and a stated relation, the examinee to supply the other unit. Analogies tests that call for completion rather than a choice between alternative answers emphasize this kind of ability. With symbolic content such an item might read:

pots   stop   bard   drab   rats   ?

A semantic item that measures eduction of correlates is:

The absence of sound is ________.

Incidentally, the latter item is from a vocabulary-completion test, and its relation to the factor of ability to produce correlates indicates how, by change of form, a vocabulary test may indicate an ability other than that for which vocabulary tests are usually intended, namely, the factor of verbal comprehension.

Only one factor for convergent production of systems is known, and it is in the semantic column. It is measured by a class of tests that may be called ordering tests. The examinee may be presented with a number of events that ordinarily have a best or most logical order, the events being presented in scrambled order. The presentation may be pictorial, as in the Picture Arrangement Test, or verbal. The pictures may be taken from a cartoon strip. The verbally presented events may be in the form of the various steps needed to plant a new lawn. There are undoubtedly other kinds of systems than temporal order that could be utilized for testing abilities in this row of the convergent-production matrix.

In the way of producing transformations of a unique variety, we have three recognized factors, known as redefinition abilities. In each case, redefinition involves the changing of functions or uses of parts of one unit and giving them new functions or uses in some new unit. For testing the ability of figural redefinition, a task based upon the Gottschaldt figures is suitable. Figure 3 shows the kind of item for such a test. In recognizing the simpler figure within the structure of a more complex figure, certain lines must take on new roles.

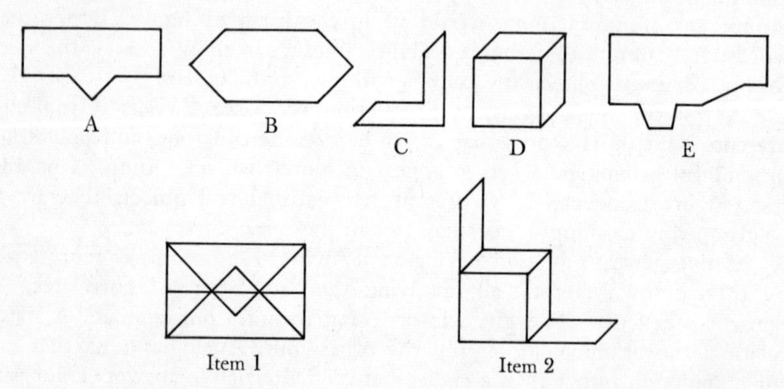

Figure 3. Sample items from a test Hidden Figures, based upon the Gottschaldt figures. Which of the simpler figures is concealed within each of the two more complex figures?

In terms of symbolic material, the following sample items will illustrate how groups of letters in given words must be readapted to use in other words. In the test Camouflaged Words, each sentence contains the name of a sport or game:

I did not know that he was ailing.
To beat the Hun, tin goes a long way.

For the factor of semantic redefinition, the Gestalt Transformation Test may be used. A sample item reads:

From which object could you most likely make a needle?

A. a cabbage
B. a splice
C. a steak
D. a paper box
E. a fish

The convergent production of implications means the drawing of fully determined conclusions from given information. The well-known factor of numerical facility belongs in the symbolic column. For the parallel ability in the figural column, we have a test known as Form Reasoning, in which rigorously defined operations with figures are used. For the parallel ability in the semantic column, the factor sometimes called "deduction" probably qualifies. Items of the following type are sometimes used.

Charles is younger than Robert
Charles is older than Frank
Who is older: Robert or Frank?

Evaluative Abilities

The evaluative area has had the least investigation of all the operational categories. In fact, only one systematic analytical study has been devoted to this area. Only eight evaluative abilities are recognized as fitting into the evaluation matrix. But at least five rows have one or more factors each, and also three of the usual columns or content categories. In each case, evaluation involves reaching decisions as to the accuracy, goodness, suitability, or workability of information. In each row, for the particular kind of product of that row, some kind of criterion or standard of judgment is involved.

In the first row, for the evaluation of units, the important decision to be made pertains to the identity of a unit. Is this unit identical with that one? In the figural column we find the factor long known as "perceptual speed." Tests of this factor invariably call for decisions of identity, for example, Part IV (Perceptual Speed) of the GZAS or Thurstone's Identical Forms. I think it has been generally wrongly thought that the ability involved is that of cognition of visual forms. But we have seen that another factor is a more suitable candidate for this definition and for being in the very first cell of the cognitive matrix. It is parallel to this evaluative ability but does not require the judgment of identity as one of its properties.

In the symbolic column is an ability to judge identity of symbolic units, in the form of series of letters or numbers or of names of individuals.

Are members of the following pairs identical or not:

825170493________825176493
dkeltvmpa________dkeltvmpa
C. S. Meyerson________C. E. Meyerson

Such items are common in tests of clerical aptitude.

There should be a parallel ability to decide whether two ideas are identical or different. Is the idea expressed in this sentence the same as the idea expressed in that one? Do these two proverbs express essentially the same idea? Such tests exist and will be used to test the hypothesis that such an ability can be demonstrated.

No evaluative abilities pertaining to classes have as yet been recognized. The abilities having to do with evaluation where relations are concerned must meet the criterion of logical consistency. Syllogistic-type tests involving letter symbols indicate a different ability than the same type of test involving verbal statements. In the figural column we might expect that tests incorporating geometric reasoning or proof would indicate a parallel ability to sense the soundness of conclusions regarding figural relationships.

The evaluation of systems seems to be concerned with the internal consistency of those systems, so far as we can tell from the knowledge of one such factor. The factor has been called "experiential evaluation," and its representative test presents items like that in Figure 4 asking, "What is wrong with this picture?" The things wrong are often internal inconsistencies.

A semantic ability for evaluating transformations is thought to be that known for some time as "judgment." In typical judgment tests, the examinee is asked to tell which of five solutions to a practical problem is most adequate or wise. The solutions frequently involve improvisations,

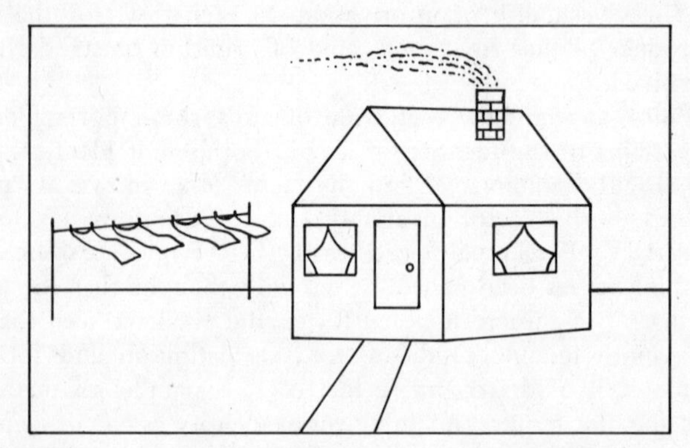

Figure 4. A sample item from the test Unusual Details. What two things are wrong with this picture?

in other words, adaptations of familiar objects to unusual uses. In this way the items present redefinitions to be evaluated.

A factor known first as "sensitivity to problems" has become recognized as an evaluative ability having to do with implications. One test of the factor, the Apparatus Test, asks for two needed improvements with respect to each of several common devices, such as the telephone or the toaster. The Social Institutions Test, a measure of the same factor, asks what things are wrong with each of several institutions, such as tipping or national elections. We may say that defects or deficiencies are implications of an evaluative kind. Another interpretation would be that seeing defects and deficiencies are evaluations of implications to the effect that the various aspects of something are all right.[4]

Some Implications of the Structure of Intellect

For Psychological Theory

Although factor analysis as generally employed is best designed to investigate ways in which individuals differ from one another, in other words, to discover traits, the results also tell us much about how individuals are alike. Consequently, information regarding the factors and their interrelationships gives us understanding of functioning individuals. The five kinds of intellectual abilities in terms of operations may be said to represent five ways of functioning. The kinds of intellectual abilities distinguished according to varieties of test content and the kinds of abilities distinguished according to varieties of products suggest a classification of basic forms of information or knowledge. The kind of organism suggested by this way of looking at intellect is that of an agency for dealing with information of various kinds in various ways. The concepts provided by the distinctions among the intellectual abilities and by their classifications may be very useful in our future investigations of learning, memory, problem solving, invention, and decision making, by whatever method we choose to approach those problems.

For Vocational Testing

With about 50 intellectual factors already known, we may say that there are at least 50 ways of being intelligent. It has been facetiously suggested that there seem to be a great many more ways of being stupid, unfortunately. The structure of intellect is a theoretical model that predicts as many as 120 distinct abilities, if every cell of the model contains a factor. Already we know that two cells contain two or more factors each, and there

[4] For further details concerning the intellectual factors, illustrative tests, and the place of the factors in the structure of intellect; see Guilford (1959).

probably are actually other cells of this type. Since the model was first conceived, 12 factors predicted by it have found places in it. There is consequently hope of filling many of the other vacancies, and we may eventually end up with more than 120 abilities.

The major implication for the assessment of intelligence is that to know an individual's intellectual resources thoroughly we shall need a surprisingly large number of scores. It is expected that many of the factors are intercorrelated, so there is some possibility that by appropriate sampling we shall be able to cover the important abilities with a more limited number of tests. At any rate, a multiple-score approach to the assessment of intelligence is definitely indicated in connection with future vocational operations.

Considering the kinds of abilities classified as to content, we may speak roughly of four kinds of intelligence. The abilities involving the use of figural information may be regarded as "concrete" intelligence. The people who depend most upon these abilities deal with concrete things and their properties. Among these people are mechanics, operators of machines, engineers (in some aspects of their work), artists, and musicians.

In the abilities pertaining to symbolic and semantic content, we have two kinds of "abstract" intelligence. Symbolic abilities should be important in learning to recognize words, to spell, and to operate with numbers. Language and mathematics should depend very much upon them, except that in mathematics some aspects, such as geometry, have strong figural involvement. Semantic intelligence is important for understanding things in terms of verbal concepts and hence is important in all courses where the learning of facts and ideas is essential.

In the hypothesized behavioral column of the structure of intellect, which may be roughly described as "social" intelligence, we have some of the most interesting possibilities. Understanding the behavior of others and of ourselves is largely nonverbal in character. The theory suggests as many as 30 abilities in this area, some having to do with understanding, some with productive thinking about behavior, and some with the evaluation of behavior. The theory also suggests that information regarding behavior is also in the form of the six kinds of products that apply elsewhere in the structure of intellect, including units, relations, systems, and so on. The abilities in the area of social intelligence, whatever they prove to be, will possess considerable importance in connection with all those individuals who deal most with other people: teachers, law officials, social workers, therapists, politicians, statesmen, and leaders of other kinds.

For Education

The implications for education are numerous, and I have time just to mention a very few. The most fundamental implication is that we might well undergo transformations with respect to our conception of the learner and of the process of learning. Under the prevailing conception, the learner is a kind of stimulus-response device, much on the order of a vending machine. You put in a coin, and something comes out. The machine learns what reaction to put out when a certain coin is put in. If, instead, we think of the learner as an agent for dealing with information, where information is defined very broadly, we have something more analogous to an electronic computer. We feed a computer information; it stores that information; it uses that information for generating new information, either by way of divergent or convergent thinking; and it evaluates its own results. Advantages that a human learner has over a computer include the step of seeking and discovering new information from sources outside itself and the step of programing itself. Perhaps even these steps will be added to computers, if this has not already been done in some cases.

At any rate, this conception of the learner leads us to the idea that learning is discovery of information, not merely the formation of associations, particularly associations in the form of stimulus-response connections. I am aware of the fact that my proposal is rank heresy. But if we are to make significant progress in our understanding of human learning and particularly our understanding of the so-called higher mental processes of thinking, problem solving, and creative thinking, some drastic modifications are due in our theory.

The idea that education is a matter of training the mind or of training the intellect has been rather unpopular wherever the prevailing psychological doctrines have been followed. In theory, at least, the emphasis has been upon the learning of rather specific habits or skills. If we take our cue from factor theory, however, we recognize that most learning probably has both specific and general aspects or components. The general aspects may be along the lines of the factors of intellect. This is not to say that the individual's status in each factor is entirely determined by learning. We do not know to what extent each factor is determined by heredity and to what extent by learning. The best position for educators to take is that possibly every intellectual factor can be developed in individuals at least to some extent by learning.

If education has the general objective of developing the intellects of students, it can be suggested that each intellectual factor provides a particular goal at which to aim. Defined by a certain combination of content, operation, and product, each goal ability then calls for certain kinds of practice in order to achieve improvement in it. This implies choice of curriculum and the choice or invention of teaching methods that will most likely accomplish the desired results.

Considering the very great variety of abilities revealed by the factorial exploration of intellect, we are in a better position to ask whether any general intellectual skills are now being neglected in education and whether appropriate balances are being observed. It is often observed these days that we have fallen down in the way of producing resourceful, creative graduates. How true this is, in comparison with other times, I do not know. Perhaps the deficit is noticed because the demands for inventiveness are so much greater at this time. At any rate, realization that the more conspicuously creative abilities appear to be concentrated in the divergent-thinking category, and also to some extent in the transformation category, we now ask whether we have been giving these skills appropriate exercise. It is probable that we need a better balance of training in the divergent-thinking area as compared with training in convergent thinking and in critical thinking or evaluation.

The structure of intellect as I have presented it to you may or may not stand the test of time. Even if the general form persists, there are likely to be some modifications. Possibly some different kind of model will be invented. Be that as it may, the fact of a multiplicity of intellectual abilities seems well established.

There are many individuals who long for the good old days of simplicity, when we got along with one unanalyzed intelligence. Simplicity certainly has its appeal. But human nature is exceedingly complex, and we may as well face that fact. The rapidly moving events of the world in which we live have forced upon us the need for knowing human intelligence thoroughly. Humanity's peaceful pursuit of happiness depends upon our control of nature and of our own behavior; and this, in turn, depends upon understanding ourselves, including our intellectual resources.

References

Christal, R. E. Factor analytic study of visual memory. *Psychol. Monogr.*, 1958, 72, No. 13 (Whole No. 466).

Guilford, J. P. The structure of intellect. *Psychol. Bull.*, 1956, 53, 267–293.

Guilford, J. P. *Personality*. New York: McGraw-Hill, 1959.

❦ 2

Problems in the Identification of Intellectually Gifted Pupils

Ruth A. Martinson
Leon M. Lessinger

MANY PROBLEMS beset the educator who recognizes the importance of providing for individual learning ability at the upper end of the ability scale. He is plagued by a number of questions and a considerable amount of confusion. Much of the confusion, though certainly not all, is related to the problem of identifying the intellectually gifted pupils.

Questions which arise concerning the identification of the intellectually gifted may be classified principally as follows:

1. Who are these persons? What should we call them?
2. What kinds of measures should be employed in the identification process? At what age should they be used?
3. Should criteria other than tests determine whether special provisions are needed?

In attempts to answer the questions satisfactorily, schools have developed a bewildering array of methods for selecting their gifted. The "New Deal" for the gifted has also produced a "New Deal" assortment of initials for designating the group. Witness the HAPs (high academic potential), HEPs (high educational potential), and HIPs (high intellectual potential), or the MRL (more rapid learner) and MCL (more capable learner).

The problem of proliferating percentages also confronts the educator. Should he include one or two percent of the total population, or would it

RUTH A. MARTINSON is Director of Teacher Education, California State College at Palos Verdes.
LEON M. LESSINGER is Assistant Superintendent, Grossmont Union High School District, Grossmont, California.

be better to consider the upper 15 percent in this category? The larger percent is favored by some on the grounds that identification of the gifted will then be certain and comprehensive. In the extension of the group size the pupil with special needs again may become lost in the press for providing for large numbers.

A third concern is that of complete identification. How can we be sure that we have identified all of the intellectually gifted? Should the identification process begin at the third-grade level, or should it be confined to certain other selected grade levels?

Another important problem is that of adequate measurement. The question of whether group or individual tests should be used, in what ways they should be used, and the proper context for their use is perplexing. The problem of teacher judgment, and administrator judgment as part of the identification process also enters here.

The problems already mentioned are compounded when consideration is given to special provisions for the identified intellectually gifted pupil. Should provisions be made for the person with extremely high ability but with poor motivation and achievement? What of the child with personality problems? On what basis should we select from the selected?

The result of the dilemma, in some schools, may be obscure identification policies and procedures. A *range* of scores may include the exceptions within a given school district. IQ cutoff points may be given for group tests without specification of the test. Qualifications for admission may insure that only the high achieving well-behaved gifted child who needs the program least of the gifted will be admitted to it. Or partial and limited identification facilities may cause the gifted child to remain unidentified.

It is the conviction of the writers that much of the success of a program for the intellectually gifted is based upon sound identification procedures. So much of educational planning depends upon adequate knowledge of pupil potential that necessary time and expense should be invested to determine as accurately as possible what the potential is.

The problems outlined above are not simple. Some of them can be considered on the basis of evidence while others must be met through the application of common sense. That some will be dismissed more briefly than others does not make them less important within the present context.

Questions: Who Are These Persons? What Should We Call Them?

The term *intellectually gifted* relates to the kinds of abilities which are measured by individual intelligence tests. The term has the connotation of a small fraction of the total population who have exceptionally high learning ability. These children constitute the group of up to three percent of the population who, because they are exceptionally high in learning ability, have exceptional educational needs. On individual tests, they measure at two standard deviations or more beyond the mean. In measured general intelligence, they differ as much from the average as do the mentally retarded. In studies of intelligence levels within the general population, the mentally retarded and the intellectually gifted have been found to include approximately the same percent of the total population.[1]

It is important to think of the intellectually gifted, while a small percent, as including a *range* of potential. The following table shows the number of pupils within the total population who might be found at various IQ levels on the basis of expectancy. All of these pupils would be classified as intellectually gifted, yet the differences among the members of this group are exceedingly complex and diverse.[2]

TABLE 1. NUMBER OF PUPILS FROM GENERAL POPULATION AT VARIOUS IQ LEVELS

No. of Pupils	*IQ Level*
3 per 100	130
1 per 100	137
1 per 1000	150
1 per 10,000	160
1 per 100,000	168
1 per 1,000,000	180

The fallacy of employing grade-level materials or of applying age-norms to the intellectually gifted is apparent when the mental age is considered. If educational provisions are made which are consonant with the potential of the child, the usual materials and experiences are inappropriate. The intellectually gifted child is capable of learning at an accelerated rate which should *widen* the differences between his attainment and that of the average child as he progresses in school. The hypothetical table which follows indicates the expanding differences as the child grows older, and as the IQ difference increases.

The higher the IQ, the wider the gap. The six-year-old with an IQ of 150 has the mental age equivalent of a beginning fourth-grader. At the age of 10 as a beginning fifth-grader, he has the mental age equivalent of a high school sophomore. It is clearly obvious that his needs cannot be met through the usual curriculum provisions.

[1] Thompson, George C., *Child Psychology*. New York: Houghton Mifflin Company, 1952, p. 387.

[2] Carter, Harold D., *Cut-off Points for Securing Groups of Pupils at Various Levels of Superiority as Indicated by 1937 Stanford-Binet IQ's*, (mimeographed).

Questions: What Kinds of Measures Should be Used for Identification? At What Age?

Part of these questions relate to the age selected for identification of the gifted. Obviously, certain preliminary screening devices which are appropriate at one age level are not appropriate at another. And—those designated for certain age levels within the general population also may not be appropriate for this group. Another part of this question is whether identification is a single or multi-step process.

In deciding the age of identification and resultant special provisions for the gifted, it is well to recall that the educational needs of the intellectually gifted are not limited to certain grade levels, but that they exist throughout the grades. Hollingworth[3] and others have pointed out that the early grades are actually the time of greatest need for the gifted child.

Table 2. Mental Age Equivalents of Various Chronological Ages and IQ Levels

Actual Chronological Age	*Corresponding Grade*	*M.A. at 130 IQ Level*	*Corresponding Grade*	*M.A. at 150 IQ Level*	*Corresponding Grade*	*M.A. at 170 IQ Level*	*Corresponding Grade*
6	1	7.8	2	9.0	4	10.2	5
8	3	10.4	5	12.0	7	13.6	8
10	5	13.0	9	15.0	10	17.0	12
12	7	15.6	10	18.0	13	20.4	**
14	9	18.2	13	21.0	**	*	**
16	11	20.8	**	*	**	*	**

* Beyond test level
** Beyond normal school range

Questions sometimes arise whether tests with primary-age pupils possess sufficient reliability to allow decisions. It may be worthwhile again to think of the intellectually gifted pupils in relation to his potential. He is mature far beyond his chronological age, when one considers his mental and intellectual development. It is more realistic, for example, to think of him as an upper-primary grade, or middle-elementary grade child than as a first-grader. In many schools, the age for first identification of mentally retarded children is set at third-grade level, because of the problem of test reliability. Yet the mentally retarded child with an IQ of 70 who is

[3] Hollingwood, Leta, *Children Above 180 IQ*. New York: World Book Company, 1942, p. 282.

eight years of age is not as mature intellectually as the five-year-old child with an IQ of 130. It is reasonable, therefore, to continuously identify gifted children throughout the grades, including kindergarten.

Another question relating to early identification is whether the costs are prohibitive. This must be weighed against evidence, and against the value accruing to the child who through identification may be given the basis for a total school experience which is appropriate for him. The dollars invested then assume less importance.

To identify gifted kindergarten children for participation in a research study,[4] a multiple screening process was used. The screening included teacher judgment, a teacher identification form, the Pintner-Cunningham Intelligence Test, and the Goodenough Draw-A-Man Test. On the basis of the multiple screening criteria, 127 out of 1084 kindergarten children were referred for individual testing with the Revised Stanford-Binet Scale. Of the 127, 62 were identified as intellectually gifted on the criterion of a minimum IQ of 130.[5] Therefore, the group screening procedure was effective in nearly 50 percent of the cases. It seems legitimate, then, since we are responsible for educating gifted children from the time when they enter kindergarten, to identify them early.

The problem of identification changes from the lower primary grade level to upper grades with the increasing use of group tests. The problem becomes one of a differentiated process of identification in several steps. The first step is *screening*, which involves the use of carefully selected group tests and other devices. The second is *identification*, which is based upon preliminary screening, and which involves the establishment of the true potential of the pupil. This potential is determined by the use of individual tests in the hands of a specialist, given in such a way as to permit assessment of the level and quality of the pupil's ability to learn. The third step is *program planning*, an outgrowth of proper identification based upon thorough knowledge of pupils, their abilities, achievement levels, and personal attributes. All three of the steps listed precede any educational provisions.

The group test is suggested as a screening method rather than as an identification point for several reasons. One of these is the problem of group test ceiling. Group tests do not give the same kind of measure as the individual test when extremes at either end of the ability scale are considered. Evidence to this effect was found in the California Study[6] in which scores for the same group and individual tests were available for 332 gifted

[4] California Study Project on Programs for Gifted Pupils.

[5] This study was done by Margery P. McIntosh, Director of Guidance, La Mesa-Spring Valley Schools.

[6] California Study Project on Programs for Gifted Pupils.

pupils. All of the pupils rated 130 or more on the Revised Stanford-Binet Scale.

If a criterion score of 125 or above on a group test (a score which is commonly designated for screening) had been used for selecting the gifted pupils, 82 of the 332 would have been eliminated. If the criterion score of 130 (the same as that for the individual test) had been applied, 51.5 percent of the gifted group would have been eliminated.

Essentially the same findings occurred within the context of a study of the entire population of a junior high school.[7] If a cut-off point of 125 on the group test had been employed, 49 out of 84 gifted pupils would have failed to qualify, including nine whose actual scores on the Binet ranged from 146 to 161.

The effect of test scores on curriculum planning requires sound planning of identification procedures. The sometimes vast discrepancy between group and individual scores causes educators to look upon the abilities of the gifted erroneously. In the Pegnato study, 45 pupils had Binet scores which were higher than the group test scores by 20 points or more, and 15 lost at least 30 points in the group test scores. The implications for educational planning are quite different when one considers the group test score of 134 and an individual test score of 178 for the same person, or a group test score of 115 and an individual score of 149, to cite two examples from this study.

Further evidence of the problem of differences between group and individual tests with the higher intelligence levels was subjected to study by a test publisher.[8] At the upper Binet levels, it was found that the group test scores were lower. Test scores within the average range were comparable, and below the average range, the group test scores tended to be higher. The group test, therefore, gave the gifted pupils lower test scores, with algebraic differences of 33 points at the upper ranges. The discrepancy within the gifted group would actually make a difference in the kinds of curriculum experiences which were planned for these pupils.

The following partial table was adapted from the test publisher's report to show the algebraic differences between group and individual tests for pupils with IQ's above 130. The individual test score is consistently higher at each interval, with an increase at higher ability levels.

An analysis of group test manuals reveals the problems of applying a group test score criterion to a selected population. Three group tests, all

[7] Pegnato, Carl V., "Identifying Mentally Gifted in Junior High Schools." In James J. Gallagher (Ed.), *Teaching Gifted Students: A Book of Readings* (Boston: Allyn and Bacon, Inc., 1965), pp. 34–42.

[8] Data through courtesy of California Test Bureau.

widely used, were subjected to examination from the standpoint of adequacy for gifted pupils:[9]

TABLE 3. DIFFERENCES IN TEST SCORES BETWEEN GROUP AND INDIVIDUAL TESTS AT VARIOUS IQ LEVELS

IQ Range	*Number of Pupils*	*Algebraic Difference**
160–169	6	33.833
150–159	11	18.273
140–149	11	13.909
130–139	28	10.607

* In favor of the Binet

TEST A required that the second-grader succeed on 77 percent of the items in order to attain an IQ of 125, and that the third-grader succeed on 84 percent for the same IQ. The third-grader would have to succeed on 138 out of 164 items. At the next level, the percent of success required is 63 percent for grade four; 72 percent for grade five; 81 percent for grade six; 89 percent for grade seven; and 94 percent for grade eight. Thus it is evident that the total number of items available for the measurement of pupil potential is low, and decreases at each succeeding grade level.

TEST B is designed for grades 7–12. One form of this test does not yield an IQ of 125 or more beyond the ninth-grade level. The other form of the test requires success on 96 percent of the items in order to attain a score of 125. Therefore, although this test is used extensively in the high schools, it does not measure the potential of the gifted pupil.

TEST C is a primary level test. To attain a score of 125 on this test, the kindergarten child would have to succeed on 76 percent of the items, and the first-grader on 90 percent. The second-grader could not make a score of 125, although the test is designed to include this age level.

The advanced level of Test C shows the same pattern. This test, for ages 7–11, would not measure a sixth-grader with an IQ of 125 or over.

The implications regarding the use of group tests in the identification process are clear. They should be used for screening purposes, and should be followed by measures which show the kinds of abilities and true potential of the gifted pupil. The group tests which are used for screening should be selected so that they possess adequate content of appropriate difficulty for the gifted pupil. On many occasions, group tests at an advanced grade level would be more useful for screening purposes than those of the child's actual grade level.

[9] Data available in *Technical Supplement, California Study of Programs for Gifted Pupils.* Bureau of Education Research, California State Department of Education, Sacramento.

At the identification stage, the individual intelligence test is used to give trained examiners, under standardized conditions, a reliable assessment of the subject's responses to items which are important in school learning and performance. The items evaluate such abilities as memory, verbal skill, comprehension, generalization, and synthesis, among others.

Individual administration of the test means that the ability of the gifted pupil is measured more directly and effectively than in a group situation. The group test is built upon items designed for the entire population, and therefore contains a number of items which serve no function in measuring the ability of the gifted pupil. In the individual test, on the other hand, the examiner is able to estimate the level at which he should begin testing, and thus save pupil energy, prevent frustration, and insure interest and motivation.

The individual test also must be evaluated from the standpoint of ceiling. One widely used individual test yields an IQ of 154 or less. Reference to Table 1 shows that certain individuals would be identified erroneously at less than true potential. *These are the individuals who most need special provisions.* Every effort should be made to utilize an individual test which will enable the gifted child to reveal his true ability. Curriculum planning otherwise would be unsoundly based.

QUESTION: SHOULD CRITERIA OTHER THAN TESTS DETERMINE WHETHER SPECIAL PROVISIONS ARE MADE?

The purpose of multiple screening, followed by individual testing, is to locate and study those pupils whose learning abilities are exceptional. Any administrative planning and structuring of programs should *follow* the identification process, and should include whatever plans seem best for each individual.

Every intellectually gifted pupil, regardless of problems, ought to have an educational program planned to meet his needs. Identification does not assure achievement or motivation.[10] A "program" which includes only part of the identified gifted and excludes others is only a partial service. The intellectually gifted child who is excluded from special opportunities because he is poorly motivated, physically handicapped, or withdrawn may be the individual who could profit most from proper attention. Individuals with long histories of difficult behavior can make remarkable adjustments, and have, because they are given meaningful learning experience. The individuals with special problems will require special and skilled help, but his should be given, as it is with other types of exceptional children.

[10] Jacobs, Norman, "Formal Recognition of Mentally Superior Children; Its Effect on Achievement and Achievement Motivation." Unpublished Doctor of Philosophy dissertation, Stanford University, January, 1959.

Summary

The problem of identification is one of using the best available measures in order to arrive at an assessment of pupil potential which is as accurate as possible. Screening should be thought of as a preliminary step toward identification, in which multiple measures including group intelligence and achievement tests, teacher judgment, teacher check lists, and others are used. The final assessment of potential should be made with a measure which permits the pupil to perform at this true level and not with one which imposes ceiling limitations. This insures a proper basis for adequate curriculum planning.

Identification should begin at the kindergarten level, and should be a continuous process extending throughout the grades. The process should be aimed toward the identification of all intellectually gifted pupils, including those with special educational problems.

3

Identifying Mentally Gifted in Junior High Schools

Carl V. Pegnato

One of the major concerns of our educational system is the identification and education of our mentally gifted children. Essential to any program of educating mentally gifted is the proper identification of those to be included in the program. With a reasonable degree of certainty, the identification of the intellectually gifted student is now possible through the use of individual intelligence examinations administered by psychologists.[1]* Ideally, sufficient psychological service for individual examinations of all children should be provided by each school district, but it is very rarely the case. In fact, it is the very shortage of the psychological staff which makes it so necessary to find ways of choosing some small group of children from the total student body to refer for individual evaluations.

It was the purpose of the author of this study to evaluate in terms of relative efficiency and effectiveness the various methods of selecting junior high school pupils for referral to the psychologist to be identified as mentally gifted. The major purpose of the investigation was to discover which commonly used procedure or which combination of procedures would prove best. In the process data were collected making it possible to present some conclusions in response to several subordinate questions.

1. Do teachers recognize the mentally gifted in their classes?
2. Can group intelligence tests be relied upon in the identification of mentally gifted children?
3. Are group achievement test scores useful in selecting gifted children?
4. What is the magnitude of the problem of underachievement among gifted children?

* See Bibliography.

5. Are the children who win honor roll status the gifted of each class?
6. Can gifted children be located by evaluating mathematical aptitude?
7. Do some mentally gifted children prefer to exercise their abilities in the areas of art and music?
8. To what extent are students who are recognized by their peers as social and political leaders also intellectually gifted?

This study was concerned with the gifted only in terms of intellectual ability at the upper end of the intelligence scale, rather than those with exceptional talents or aptitudes in other areas. For the purposes of this inquiry, mental giftedness was defined as scoring a Stanford-Binet Intelligence Quotient of 136 or higher as determined from an examination by a school psychologist. This definition includes the most intelligent one per cent of the general population, and, to that extent, is consistent with a number of current and widely used definitions.[2]

The procedure was planned to have the psychologist give mental evaluations to as many students as necessary to identify all of the mentally gifted in a particular junior high school. A combination junior-senior high school providing for an approximate total of 3,600 pupils was selected. The study was confined solely to the junior division with the enrollment of 1,400 students in grades seven through nine. In order to improve the prospect that a fairly large proportion of gifted children would be available for the study, the school chosen was not only a large one, but it was situated in and drew upon a very favored neighborhood from a socio-economic standpoint.

Methods of Screening for Referral

Four basic methods generally used for screening purposes in identifying mentally gifted children were utilized. The methods were teacher selection, group intelligence test scores, standardized achievement test results, and honor roll lists. In addition, methods were devised to locate the intellectually gifted children by evaluating those with special abilities in mathematics, art, music, and social leadership. To be certain that all of the mentally gifted were located, the counselor was asked to refer those students who were known to be socially maladjusted or emotionally disturbed but who gave some evidence of being superior in intellect.

Teacher Selection

The first step in the investigation was to find which pupils the teacher considered mentally gifted. Before any mental evaluations were administered at the school, a simple inquiry form was submitted to the teachers. They were requested to list the names of any students they considered mentally gifted. In addition, they were asked to give reasons why they felt each of the students was gifted. No information concerning exceptional abilities was provided. Except that the teachers had been informed in a general faculty meeting that their help would be enlisted in finding all the gifted children in the school, no further orientation was furnished. Teachers were left to their own devices to define mental giftedness, to use subjective judgment, or to search out objective evidence from records. The forms returned by the teachers contained 154 names.

Group Intelligence Test Results

In the Pittsburgh school system the Otis Quick-Scoring Mental Ability Test, Beta Form, is administered at the end of the sixth grade and again at the end of the eighth grade, depending upon the type of organization. Scores were available on all the children at the school. The most recent group test data were used to list all of the children who earned I.Q.'s of 115 or better. This screening procedure produced 450 pupils who qualified as to the criterion.

Group Achievement Test Results

In the junior high school the Metropolitan Achievement Tests, Advanced Battery, are administered at the close of the seventh and eighth grades. From the most recent test results, an average reading score in grade equivalent was obtained for each student. In the same manner an average arithmetic score was determined on the basis of two subtests–arithmetic fundamentals and arithmetic problems. A list was compiled of those students who had average scores in the basic skill subjects, reading and arithmetic, and who scored three years above grade placement. Since the ceiling of the Metropolitan is the 11th grade, the ninth-graders who scored at the ceiling level were included. This list contained 334 names.

Honor Roll Listing

The names of the students who had made the honor roll at the time of the most recent report period were provided by the 39 homeroom teachers. An honor-roll student was one who averaged a B grade or better in all of his subjects. The teachers involved placed 371 children on the honor roll.

Special Abilities

Based on the premise that individuals who have outstanding special aptitudes or abilities are also generally intellectually superior, it was decided to evaluate measures of special abilities as a possible screening method for identifying the mentally gifted. Since mathematical skill is considered closely associated with mental giftedness, the most promising method appeared to be the selection of students known to be outstanding in mathematical ability. The fact that the school had advanced classes in algebra and geometry for eighth- and ninth-grade students made the selection of those with the best mathematical ability convenient. Outstanding students in the seventh-grade arithmetic classes were rated by teachers on the basis of achievement test results, homeroom work, and subjective judgment. The names of 179 children were compiled.

Art teachers were requested to consider their students in terms of creative ability and to submit names of the most talented. In selecting those with exceptional musical talent, teachers of vocal music as well as those instructing instrumental music were requested to rate their students. The teachers involved contributed a list of 137 children, 71 from music and 66 from art.

To avoid the possibility that some intellectually gifted children preferred to use their abilities in the areas of social and political leadership and would thereby not be identified, an additional screening method was devised. An assumption was made that these students would be recognized and accorded a role of leadership. Therefore, the 82 representatives to the Student Council were also referred for possible identification as mentally gifted.

Other Aspects of Screening

The significance of the study depended on the fact that all of the mentally gifted children attending that particular junior high school would be identified. It was believed that by administering the Binet Intelligence Scale to over half of the school population that all of the mentally gifted would be located. The possibility that some of those not evaluated would be mentally gifted, but not adequately adjusted in school for emotional or social reasons, was investigated. The counselor reported that all of the students who would fit in that category had been screened by other methods.

Procedure

When the lists from all the various screening methods were combined and analyzed, 781 students were referred for individual intelligence examinations and possible identification as mentally gifted. Although the number of boys and girls varied proportionately at the different grade levels, the total referred was close to an even distribution (394 boys and 387 girls). The 781 students to whom the individual intelligence scale was administered represented more than half of the student body.

Binet I.Q.'s were available for 368 children who were examined in the elementary grades. On the basis of scoring an I.Q. of 136, or better, 68 of these children had been classified previously as intellectually gifted. At the junior high school, 413 other students were given individual intelligence examinations. From this group, 23 students were identified as mentally gifted, making a total of 91 gifted children (55 boys and 36 girls).

With the identification of reasonably all of the mentally gifted children at the junior high school level, it was then possible to evaluate the effectiveness and efficiency of the various screening methods.

Effectiveness of a screening method is defined by the percentage of gifted children it correctly locates. A screening procedure which includes all the gifted children among those it selects for referral to the psychologist is 100 per cent effective. If it fails to refer one-half of the gifted children, it is 50 per cent effective.

Efficiency of a screening method is defined by the ratio between the total number of children it refers to individual examination and the number of gifted children identified. If the screening procedure refers ten children and nine of them are then identified as mentally gifted by the psychologist, its efficiency is considered to be 90 per cent.

The best screening method is one which combines high effectiveness and high efficiency, for that would result in most of the mentally gifted being identified with the minimum amount of psychological service. However, if the main objective is to identify as many of the mentally gifted as possible, it would be necessary to use a highly effective screening method with less importance being placed on its efficiency. The effectiveness and efficiency of the various screening procedures can be evaluated by reference to the material in Table I.

Results

Of the 781 children selected by screening methods, 91 had Stanford-Binet I.Q.'s of 136 or higher. The fact that 91 were identified as mentally gifted, 6.5 per cent of the school population, indicated that the school had more than six times the normal expectancy.

Following the order of first examining the children selected on the basis of group intelligence tests, out of the 450 referred, 84 were identified as mentally gifted. This group of gifted students represented 92 per cent of all of the intellectually gifted in the school. The three other major screening methods, teacher selection, group achievement, and honor roll, requiring an additional 190 individual intelligence examinations, contributed only five other names to the mentally gifted group. Therefore, 89 or 98 per cent of the gifted were screened by four of the procedures.

Additional screening methods based on special aptitudes failed to locate any of the gifted not previously screened. The remaining two gifted children had been identified earlier in the elementary grades and did not appear

TABLE I. EFFECTIVENESS AND EFFICIENCY OF SCREENING METHODS

Screening Methods	*No. Selected by Screening Methods (N = 781)*	*No. Identified as Gifted by Stanford-Binet (N = 91)*	*Effectiveness (Per Cent of Gifted Located)*	*Efficiency (Ratio of No. Selected to No. Identified as Gifted)*
Teacher selection	154	41	45.1	26.6
Group intelligence tests				
Cut-off I.Q. 115	450	84	92.3	18.7
Cut-off I.Q. 120	(240)	(65)	71.4	27.1
Cut-off I.Q. 125	(105)	(40)	43.9	38.1
Cut-off I.Q. 130	(36)	(20)	21.9	55.5
Group achievement tests	335	72	79.2	21.5
Honor roll	371	67	73.6	18.0
Mathematical ability	179	50	56.0	27.9
Special talent	137	14	15.5	10.2
Art	(66)	(6)	6.6	9.1
Music	(71)	(8)	9.9	11.2
Student Council	82	13	14.3	15.8

on any of the referral lists. As far as the screening methods were used, it would appear that two per cent of the gifted would be identified only by chance.

In terms of effectiveness (refer to Table I), a screening procedure depending on group intelligence test scores would be the most effective single screening measure. Approximately 92 per cent of gifted children could be located in this manner. The second best single procedure would be group achievement test results. This would be followed by honor roll lists, and the least effective of commonly used screening procedures—teacher selection. Considering children for referral according to mathematical aptitude is more effective than relying on teachers' judgment.

If efficiency is to be the only consideration, again, the group intelligence test procedure should be utilized. By using cut-off I.Q.'s from 120 to 130, efficiency ratios from 27 per cent to 55 per cent can be obtained. Although lowering the limit to I.Q. 115 involves a considerable number of individual examinations, the locating of at least 20 per cent more of the gifted children makes its use advisable. Some of the other screening procedures are as efficient as the group intelligence test method using the cut-off I.Q. of 115, but the fact that they locate one-half or less of the gifted children questions the advisability of their use.

To find all of the gifted at a school, a combination of procedures should be utilized. Children who do not score high on group intelligence tests, but rate high according to teacher judgment and with objective evidence of superior achievement should be referred for identification. It should be noted, however, that after using the group intelligence test method, 30 per cent additional individual examinations are required to identify less than six per cent more of the gifted children.

Some of the subordinate questions involved in the investigation can now be answered in quantitative terms.

1. Teachers do not locate gifted children effectively or efficiently enough to place much reliance on them for screening. Teacher referrals in Table I accounted for only 45.1 per cent of the gifted children. In the surveying procedure not only were more than half of the gifted overlooked but analysis revealed that almost a third of those selected by the teachers were neither gifted nor superior but merely average in intelligence. Out of the 50 children they had failed to refer, 37 of them had been previously identified and had Binet I.Q.'s of 136 or better on their permanent record cards. This certainly was evidence of a lack of awareness on the part of teachers of the mentally gifted in their classes.

2. Group intelligence tests cannot be relied upon in the identification of gifted children in the junior high school grades. The Otis Quick-Scoring Mental Abilities Test has the disadvantages inherent in most group intelligence tests, one of which is readily apparent–a limited ceiling. Reference to Table I indicates that when a cut-off I.Q. of 130 is used, only 21.9 per cent of the gifted are located. Almost four out of five are missed. Similarly, with a cut-off point of I.Q. 125 used, more than half are missed. Also note that sixteen scoring above an I.Q. of 130 were not found to be gifted. This lack of discrimination among brighter children makes the use of group intelligence tests as a means of identification inadvisable.

3. The achievement test results as used in the study contributed the second largest number of children properly selected as mentally gifted. Although it runs a fairly close second to group intelligence tests as a screening procedure, over 20 per cent of the gifted were overlooked. It is evident that many average and superior children are also achieving at comparably high levels.

4. An analysis of the records of the mentally gifted children who were located gave some information as to the problem of underachievement. Six of the 91 gifted children appeared only on the referral list of Otis I.Q. of 115. In addition, four others were on neither the honor roll nor achievement referral lists. There is good reason to think, therefore, that ten of the 91 gifted children might be underachievers. The implication is strong that perhaps more than one out of ten is achieving considerably below expectancy for mental level.

5. Almost three-fourths of the 91 gifted children were on the honor roll. However, 304 other children were rated honor roll status. Not only is it an inefficient screening procedure, but many factors other than a high level of mental ability are involved.

6. When considering mathematical aptitude as a screening procedure, the relative efficiency can be considered as good. However, almost half of the

mentally gifted will not be located, and for every mentally gifted child referred, more than two who are not gifted will be on the referral list.

7. Some mentally gifted children display exceptional talent in music and art. However, they are too few in numbers to consider talent in these areas as a possible basis for a screening procedure to locate children high in general intellectual potential. All of the children referred in the study by this method appeared on at least two other referral lists.

8. The few children listed as members of the Student Council were among those already included by the group intelligence screening, as well as several other referral methods. A screening procedure based on recognition by peers for social and political leadership appears to have little promise in locating mentally gifted children.

Summary

The recognition and education of mentally gifted children is a major concern of school systems at this time. Proper identification of those who are mentally gifted would be an essential first step in any program of enrichment or advanced education. This identification is now possible through individual intelligence examinations administered by psychologists. The limited psychological services provided by most school districts makes it necessary to have effective and efficient screening methods for proper referrals to the psychologist.

An evaluation of various commonly used screening procedures is presented. The use of group intelligence test results for screening is found to have advantages over other methods both in effectiveness and efficiency. To use group intelligence tests as a means of identification rather than screening would be poor practice because of limited ceilings and the lack of discrimination among students of better than average mental ability. A screening measure based on achievement test results less effectively duplicates the efforts of the group intelligence test method. Teachers' judgment cannot be relied upon as an effective screening procedure. To attempt to locate mentally gifted children because of special aptitudes or talents would be difficult; however, to refer children with mathematical ability would be efficient but not effective. Combining other screening procedures with the group intelligence test method would lead to the possible identification of an additional six per cent of the mentally gifted, but 30 per cent additional individual intelligence examinations would be required.

Bibliography

1. Educational Policies Commission, *Education of the Gifted*, Washington, D.C., National Education Association, 1950.
2. Hildreth, Gertrude H., *Educating Gifted Children*, New York, Harper and Brothers, 1952.

3. Pegnato, Carl V., *An Evaluation of Various Initial Methods of Selecting Intellectually Gifted Children at the Junior High School Level*, Doctoral Thesis, Pennsylvania State University, 1958.

4

Are Scientists Different?

Lewis M. Terman

Of the many reasons why we need to know more about scientists than we do, two are particularly important at this time. One is the current shortage of scientists, especially in the physical sciences and engineering. This shortage exists despite the rapid rise in the numbers trained in recent decades, and the ratio of supply to demand promises to become less rather than more favorable. To develop more fully the scientific resources of our population will require the identification of potential scientists at a reasonably early age, and this in turn calls for more specific information than we have about the "earmarks" of scientific talents.

The second reason we need more information about scientists is the tension that is building up between them and important segments of the general public. The scientist is looked upon by many as an object of suspicion, and he in turn is irked by the distrust he senses and by the restrictions government work imposes upon him.

Suspicion of scientists has a long history. In the Middle Ages their works were easily confused with black magic and sorcery. Later they came to be looked upon as enemies of the Church; some were tried and condemned for heresy. Even as recently as 75 years ago a scientist (especially a biologist) who proclaimed a new theory was likely to be met with angry vituperation. By 1900 scientists had won the freedom to explore and to publish in all but the most backward areas of the western world. They were free to work at problems of their own choosing and to discuss them freely with one another. Their research was inadequately supported, but they were beholden to no government.

The fission of the atom changed all that. Scientists suddenly found themselves strait-jacketed by security regulations which limited severely their contacts with fellow scientists, their freedom to publish, their right to work on specific problems, even their right to travel abroad. Although these limitations were often carried to unnecessary lengths, during the war the great majority of scientists patriotically acquiesced in them. It is hardly surprising that now, in the current climate of suspicion and fear, more and more of them are reluctant to work for a government which does not protect them from harassment and unjust accusations.

It is not our purpose to apportion blame for the misunderstandings but rather to try to identify some of the human factors that contribute to them. If scientists are frequently misunderstood by nonscientists, the converse also is true, and information capable of throwing any light on the differing attitudes of the two groups ought to be welcomed.

For the double purpose, then, of trying to learn how to detect specific scientific talents and of understanding the differences between scientists and nonscientists, we undertook, with financing from the Office of Naval Research, a comparative study of the men in the well-known group of gifted persons whose careers we have followed for more than 30 years.

Our entire group consists of 800 males and 600 females who were selected in 1921 when they were students in the top 1 per cent of the school population in general intelligence, as measured by mental tests. The careers and development of all these persons have been followed almost continuously, through questionnaires mailed to them from time to time and by four detailed field studies (in 1921, 1927, 1939 and 1950). The group is the only one of its kind that has been studied so intensively over so long a period.

For the comparative study of scientists and nonscientists we confined ourselves to the 800 men, because only a few of the women have pursued scientific careers. We classified the men into seven groups:

Physical Science Research–workers in basic physical science or engineering research. This group of 51 includes 18 engineers, 17 chemists, 9 physicists and 7 in four other fields.

Engineers–practicing engineers and those who have done some applied research. The group totals 104.

Medical-Biological–workers in biological research or in medicine. Of the 61 members of this group, 26 are researchers and 35 practicing physicians.

Physical or Biological Science, Nonresearch–men who majored in a science as undergraduates but have mainly gone into other fields of work. Of the 68 in the group, 11 are science teachers.

Social Science–men who majored in a social science. Most of these persons are in business occupations. Those who became research social scientists, mostly psychologists, were omitted from our comparisons because they seemed not to belong with the business group and were too few in number (19) for statistical treatment as a separate group. The SS group totals 149.

Lawyers–a group totaling 83.

Humanities–men who majored in a field of the humanities in college. They have gone into a great variety of occupations, with teaching and business predominating. The group totals 95.

To uncover differences among these groups, information about the individuals under several hundred headings was analyzed by means of IBM cards and a sorting machine. The method used in assessing the differences for a given variable was the chi square technique. Of the many variables on which these groups were compared, 108 yielded significant differences. We shall consider here only those in three categories: (1) scientific interests evidenced, (2) interests in business occupations, (3) social traits and social adjustment.

Let us see first how the groups compare in scientific interests. For rough purposes of comparison we can class as scientists the workers in physical sciences, the engineers, the workers in biology and medicine and the men who majored in science in college; the nonscientists include the lawyers, the majors in the humanities and the majors in social science. The reader should bear in mind that the three categories based on majors in college (in science, social science or humanities) are heterogeneous groups embracing a wide variety of occupations in each case.

Eleven items of information relating to scientific interests or ability yielded highly reliable differences between scientists and nonscientists. The first five of these items represent the early interests and talents of the subjects as youngsters; the information was obtained in 1922, when the average age of the subjects was close to 11 years. The remaining six items report their interests 18 years later in 1940, when they were grown men and launched on their careers. The ratings of the groups on these 11 items, in terms of the percentage of persons who exhibited interest or talent on each variable, are summarized in the table on the opposite page.

Even as children those who later fell in the four science groups showed a far higher tendency to aptitude in science than those in the three nonscience groups. This is in accord with studies of the early mental development of eminent scientists, which have shown that often their bent is foreshadowed by their interests and preoccupations in childhood. Apparently the same is true of scientists whose achievement to mid-life is much less distinguished. It is especially significant that aptitude for science is so often detected by parents and teachers with little or no professional training in psychology, and even more often by the children themselves.

It might be supposed that the interests of our subjects in 1940, when their average age was about 30, would not reflect natural bents so much as the effects of educational concentration and vocational experience. That such experience is far from being the sole factor in shaping interest patterns is indicated by the fact that the intergroup differences in 1940 were

	VARIABLE TESTED	PHYSICAL SCIENCES (RESEARCH)		ENGINEERING		MEDICAL-BIOLOGICAL SCIENCES		PHYSICAL-BIOLOGICAL SCIENCES (NONRESEARCH)		SOCIAL SCIENCES		LAW		HUMANITIES		TOTAL	
		Number	*Per Cent*	*Number*	*Per Cent*	*Number*	*Per Cent*	*Number*	*Per Cent*	*Number*	*Per Cent*	*Number*	*Per Cent*	*Number*	*Per Cent*	*Number*	*Per Cent*
1922	A science named as suitable occupation for the child by the parent	27	59	49	59	25	40	24	58	50	14	40	10	46	20	261	34
	A science named as suitable occupation for the child by the teacher	12	67	39	49	16	56	21	43	43	23	36	14	32	25	199	34
	Child named a science as his occupational preference	34	74	76	62	45	58	46	52	109	31	67	21	64	28	441	43
	Child named engineering as his occupational preference	34	38	76	58	45	20	46	33	109	13	67	9	64	14	441	25
	High on mechanical ingenuity: composite of parent and teacher ratings	45	47	94	63	50	34	64	52	137	28	77	31	82	33	549	40

1940	Interest in science above average on self-rating	45	98	89	88	53	96	58	86	130	36	73	32	83	49	531	63
	Interest in mechanics above average on self-rating	45	64	89	82	53	34	58	60	130	24	73	21	83	30	531	43
	Score of B+ or better for chemist on vocational interest test	44	98	82	83	44	73	55	64	116	25	61	28	78	41	480	53
	Score of B or better for engineering on vocational interest test	44	95	82	87	44	64	55	75	116	32	61	31	78	33	480	55
	Score of B or better for math-science teacher on vocational interest test	44	77	82	78	44	66	55	64	116	40	61	41	78	46	480	56
	Score of B or better for physician on vocational interest test	44	75	82	49	44	86	55	62	116	24	61	38	78	62	480	51

SCIENTIFIC INTERESTS of men in the group studied by Terman are correlated with their present occupations (upper right). Engineering is combined with the other sciences in the first three items of the table and is also treated separately as the fourth item.

in most cases very similar to those in 1922. Indeed, scores on the Strong vocational interest test are surprisingly constant. Of 250 men who took the Strong test as college freshmen and again 20 years later, few showed appreciable changes in their scores, and such changes as occurred bore little relation to the kind or amount of educational or vocational experience in the interim.

It can be seen in the table that the groups with the most consistently low percentages on scientific interests are the social science majors (mainly businessmen) and the lawyers. The humanities group is fairly high on one item but is relatively low on all the others. At the opposite extreme are the physical scientists, engineers and science majors, who are high to very high on at least 10 of the 11 items. The contrast between the four groups of scientists and the three groups of nonscientists in this gifted population is much the same for the childhood data as for the data obtained nearly 18 years later.

When we come to interest in business occupations, the picture is reversed, as we might expect. The nonscientist groups score highest on interest in the nine business occupations listed (the law is included among them because so much legal work is concerned with or similar to business). In contrast, the three groups of workers in science score low to very low on interest in business, and the science majors hold an intermediate position; it will be recalled that most of the latter went into fields other than science. In the exceptional cases where a science group showed high interest in a business occupation, the reason is fairly obvious. For example, the occupation of certified public accountant would be expected to have some appeal to a physical scientist, who has an interest in numbers. Similarly the interest of engineers in the jobs of purchasing agent and production manager reflects their preoccupation with "things," while their low score on interest in the occupation of life insurance salesman probably reflects ineffectiveness in person-to-person relationships.

The marked contrast between the groups of scientific workers on the one hand and the lawyer and social science majors on the other is most significant. For it is physical scientists, engineers and biologists who do most of the Federal Government's secret research, and do it under rules that are laid down by a Congress composed mainly of lawyers and businessmen. It would be an oversimplification, however, to assume that the difficulties of these contrasting groups in trying to understand each other are fully explained by their differing interests *per se*. Rather the differences in interest are symptomatic of underlying differences in personality.

This brings us to the group differences in social traits. They were expressed in terms of 15 items relating to sociability, social adjustment, interest in people and social insight. The sociability score was derived from the subjects' preferences, as children, between social play and less social or solitary activities. Some items in the table are based on self-ratings; interest in people was measured by the subjects' reactions to two occupations calling for such interest. On the next to last item of the table a high score signifies a tendency to poorer social adjustment.

The analysis leaves no doubt that nonscientists tend to score higher than scientists in social relations. The lawyers and social science majors usually rated highest; the physical science researchers, engineers and science majors generally rated lowest; and the medical-biological group and humanities majors were in between. The groups showed a consistency of scores which is remarkable when one considers the wide range of attributes, indexes and times represented by the 15 items.

Nevertheless one must guard against overgeneralization. Actually all degrees of social adjustment and social understanding are found within each of the seven groups. Everyone knows that some scientists are extremely adept in social perception and in social relations–sufficiently adept to become deans, college presidents or other administrative officials. Yet it is true that the bulk of scientific research is carried on by devotees of science for whom research is their life and social relations are comparatively unimportant.

The life histories of the physical scientists and engineers among our gifted subjects bear interesting similarities to those of the 22 eminent physicists examined by Anne Roe [see "A Psychologist Examines 64 Eminent Scientists," by Anne Roe; SCIENTIFIC AMERICAN, November, 1952]. Her physicists and our two groups exhibited the same early interest in mechanics, mathematics and science. The resemblance also holds for social traits: as a group her physicists tended to be shy, lonely, slow in social development, indifferent to close personal relationships, group activities or politics. There are also some resemblances between Roe's 20 eminent biologists and our medical-biological group: most of these individuals showed little interest in mechanics or mathematics, either in childhood or later. However, our physicians and biologists displayed more social interests than our physicists, chemists and engineers, whereas Roe described her biologists as socially very similar to her physicists. Her 22 professional social scientists are not comparable with the businessmen of our SS (social science major) group.

Are the social traits that characterize so many scientists to be regarded as defects of personality bordering on the abnormal? The answer is no. Mental or emotional breakdowns were no more common among scientists than among nonscientists in our gifted sample of the population. It appears that departures from the average personality pattern, upward or downward, may be decidedly favorable to the making of a scientist; for example, a below-average interest in social relations and a heavy concentration of interest on the objective world.

At any rate, in our gifted group the physical scientists and engineers are at the opposite pole from the businessmen and lawyers in abilities, in occupational interests and in social behavior. These basic personality differences may well account for much of the current friction between scientists and the government officials who are responsible for their security clearances and for the restrictions imposed upon them.

❦ 5

Who Are the Exceptionally Creative?

Calvin W. Taylor

For over a decade, those not hiding their heads in the sand have known that our nation has been faced with manpower problems, especially as far as the international situation is concerned. Even that long ago, it could be said that we were outnumbered in the sheer quantity of manpower available in comparison to potential international competition. Focusing solely upon manpower needs in basic and applied sciences, one could also see that we were fast becoming outnumbered in the high quality type of personnel generally required in sciences and engineering. Scientists in competing nations represented a large youth movement with a great number of students and recent graduates and also a high percentage of young teachers and professors. One of our remaining hopes was that we might be able to rely on one or more types of important high quality personnel in order to remain in competition over the long pull. One such type is the creative scientist, who is important because only a few such men could keep our scientific movement vigorously in front and render obsolete some of the current thinking, practices, and materials. The outcome of World War II might have been different except for a few creative scientists in our nation, at least two of whom (Einstein and Fermi) had moved here from the Axis countries.

For these and other reasons, we have been very interested in the problem of identifying and developing those with high potential to be creative

CALVIN W. TAYLOR is professor of psychology at the University of Utah. This paper was delivered on December 27, 1961 to the CEC section of the annual meeting of the American Association for the Advancement of Science, in Denver, Colorado. The paper is taken partly from the chapter on predictors of creative performance by Calvin W. Taylor and John L. Holland in Calvin W. Taylor (Ed.), *Creativity: progress and potential* (New York: McGraw-Hill, 1964).

in science. However, we have not limited ourselves to science since we are interested in creativity in all fields of human endeavor as one important way to surge forward to a better world on all fronts.

Predictors of Creativity and Future Success

In order to speed up research on the creative individual in science and to clear the way for rapid implementation of such research findings, it appears necessary to open up the thinking of some of those responsible for counseling, testing, educational and research programs in the nation.

From indications to date, certain widely available measures of characteristics of individuals appear to be inadequate as measures of creative potential. For example, if school grades were efficient predictors of creativity, the identification of persons with more potential to be creative from those with less potential would be a simple problem. Although certain school grades have been shown to have low validity for the prediction of creative performance, school grades in general have little validity for this purpose (C. W. Taylor, 1958b; Taylor, *et al.*, 1961). A noticeable portion of school activities may have to change in nature so that creative behavior is demanded, if grades are ever to become very useful in predicting creative performance. Essentially the same picture has been found for the sheer number of years of education.

Let me elaborate on other aspects of the relation between school achievement and on-the-job achievement. While more positive (though still not high) results have been reported over the years, we have cited two studies in which undergraduate grades correlated zero with research performance on the job. In our medical studies (Richards & Taylor, 1961), the highest correlations are always between achievement in the two most adjacent years. Thus, first year grades in medical school (almost entirely classroom and typical lab courses) are not good predictors of performance as interns, but third year grades based partly on clinical courses are fair predictors of internship performance. Interestingly enough, interviews are better predictors of grades in the clinical years than are the non-clinical first two years of medical school. In our study of Air Force scientists (Taylor, *et al.*, 1961), biographical, self-report, and motivation scores predicted creative and other performance on the job better than did grades or aptitude type of tests or the sheer number of years of education.

Next, let me speculate about the relationship between the amount of knowledge possessed and creative performance. If the sheer accumulation of knowledge were sufficient for predicting creative performance, then the problem of identifying creative potential would be near solution. But there are many signs that the sheer accumulation of knowledge does not guarantee that the remaining incubation and insight stages in the creative process will occur. In thinking about learned members of the academic world, it is easy to cite persons who are extremely well-versed in their field but who have demonstrated little creative behavior.

In creative performance one certainly needs some kind of "stuff," but the mere possesssion of large amounts of knowledge does not guarantee in any sense that the other steps in the creative process will occur in an individual. As some corroboration of my own learning experience in mathematics, I am intrigued by the non-verbal, non-verbalizing learning stressed by Hendrix (1961). One of our graduate students has just found the same thing in a typical concept formation experiment; that the verbalizing of the learning is a distinct deterrent to the learning of the concept. So maybe it really is "stuff" much more than vocabulary, verbal knowledge, and verbalizing that is needed, especially in the arts and probably also in the sciences. I recall Torrance's (1963) finding that children who manipulate toys get more ideas about them than children who do not handle them. And I recall the silkworm case that Pasteur solved. When he was recruited to work on the silkworm problem, one expert on silkworms was stunned at Pasteur's ignorance in this area, but Pasteur–not the experts–found his way through the problem, a different set of psychological processes, I contend, than mastering the existing knowledge. Perhaps, among other things, Pasteur had an ability to sift out relevant from irrelevant knowledge as he moved forward to break through the problem. My present conclusion is that the sheer mastery of knowledge is not a sufficient condition for the occurrence of creative performance.

If *traditional intelligence tests* were highly valid measures of creative potential, the prediction problem would be a small one. Unfortunately, the gradually accumulating evidence increasingly suggests that these tests suffer from the same shortcomings: at best they account for only a minor portion of the variation in creative performance. The nature of intelligence tests does not directly involve the ability to create new ideas or things. In factor analysis studies by many research workers, the factors involving the ability to sense problem areas, to be flexible in each of several ways, and to produce new and original ideas tend to be unrelated or to have only low relations with the types of tests used to measure intelligence (e.g., Guilford, *et al.* 1952; French, 1951).

The question arises about the correlation between IQ scores and creativity (*as measured by current so-called creativity aptitude tests*). From a wealth of factor studies (e.g., French, 1951; Guilford, 1952), it is well known that the parts of a creativity battery such as ideational fluency, originality, adaptive flexibility, spontaneous flexibility, etc., are sufficiently separate to require a new dimension to account for each of them–and certainly this means that they are new dimensions when compared to some of the initially found dimensions, such as V (verbal), N (number),

S (spatial), R (reasoning), M (memory), etc., which are the most usual components of a traditional intelligence test. By their being new dimensions we generally mean that they each have zero or low correlations with the previously established dimensions. These studies have usually been done on samples where there can be relatively little complaint about the question of restriction of range.

In many ways, everything else cited on this specific point is really corroboration of the above basic findings. Stein (1955), Parnes & Meadow (1959), Getzels & Jackson (1959), and Torrance (1959a) all separately find low or zero (not high in any sense) relations between IQ and creativity scores. The majority of studies suggest that the relation of intelligence tests or components of intelligence tests to creative performance is generally low (.20 to .40) in unselected populations and is .00 and even negative for homogeneous samples at high levels of intelligence (MacKinnon, 1959; Holland, 1961; Mullins, 1959; and Yamamoto, 1961). Chorness (1956) studied civilian personnel in the Air Force who had suggested ideas which were officially accepted by their organization. He obtained their approximate IQ scores (from the information scales of the Wechsler-Bellevue) and found that these suggestors of good ideas were spread out across the entire gamut of the IQ scores found for civilian personnel.

Gallagher (personal communication) reported that there were no low ceilings in the creativity test performances of a group of students selected as having I.Q. scores definitely below average. Harris (1960) reported some correlation between the AC Test of Creative Ability and the Wonderlic. With Torrance (1959a) having replicated his studies, it means that there are seven to ten studies all supporting the previous factorial findings of dimensional independence of parts as well as combinations of creativity scores with parts or with combinations of intelligence scores. The main problem I can see is that one might ask whether a so-called creativity (aptitude) battery score is related highly enough to a "true" criterion of creative performance "on-the-job." For example, Anne Roe (1951) estimates that the eminent scientists she studied had IQ scores some distance above average—but one possible interpretation is that a high profile score across the *two relatively separate dimensions* of intelligence and creativity is usually needed, not that these two are essentially highly related characteristics.

My view is that we should extend the profile beyond the IQ score. As is quite well known, Torrance (1959a)—in replicating the Getzels and Jackson study on various other less restricted groups and in more recent unpublished studies—has reported that if an intelligence test is used to select top-level talent, about 70 percent of the persons with the highest 20 percent of the scores on a "creativity" battery will be missed (80 percent would be missed if the intelligence and "creativity" scores were completely unrelated). To be highly rigorous at this early state of knowledge, their two so-called "creativity" batteries were not identical in composition and these batteries might more safely be called divergent thinking batteries until they are more adequately validated against suitable external criteria of creativity. The same type of naming problem still exists, however, for the so-called "intelligence" tests. Among the nearly 60 dimensions of the mind discovered to date, more than 50 of these dimensions would now have to be described as *non-intelligence* intellectual dimensions (C. W. Taylor, 1960), even though intelligence has often been very broadly defined verbally.

In her studies of eminent scientists, Roe (1951, 1953) reported that their intelligence scores were all distinctly above average. However, her main focus was on "non-intelligence" characteristics that apparently play a strong role in accounting for creativity and career choices. She always felt that a comparison group should be studied in the same way as her eminent scientists, with the comparison group to be matched as being equally promising, viewed from their academic career measures. Many scientists who look equally promising on achievement and intelligence measures typically available during their academic career failed to attain the eminence of the group she studied, and she wanted to check for important group differences on other psychological scores. It is unfortunate that such a well-matched comparison group has not yet been studied. It might be added that such eminent scientists had been screened through a long, formal academic program, the grades in which are usually correlated to a sizable degree with intelligence test scores. (Such academic prerequisites are required more for persons in science to move into research positions than for persons in the arts to do creative work.) However, the assumption that this long formal academic program, as now constituted, is completely relevant and prerequisite to doing research and creative work in the sciences is being challenged by some findings cited earlier that academic grades are lowly correlated or even unrelated to on-the-job performance in research work (Martin & Pachares, 1962; C. W. Taylor, *et al.*, 1961), and by the unexpected and remarkable readiness of high school students (prior to the last year in high school and also without five to eight years of college preparation) to do research work of publishable quality as found in many newly emerging research participation programs in the NSF Summer Science Program for Secondary Students (for one example, see Riley, *et al.*, 1961). And yet in some fields a large percentage, even a majority, of persons with college training through graduate research degrees do not produce any publications.

The best conclusion at present is that intelligence, as measured, accounts for only a minor portion of the variation in creative performance and by itself is not at all a sufficiently adequate measure of creativity. In fact, nearly all research designed to measure and study creativity has focused upon *non-intelligence* intellectual tests, non-intellectual tests (including biographical inventories), and environmental factors.

As for *intelligence and school environment*, let me add but a little to the voluminous results. If you examine a recent report (Harmon, 1961), you will find that many people with IQs below 100 and a few with IQs well below 100 have obtained the doctorate. As for creativity and *school* environment, Getzels and Jackson (1959) found that overachievement was not synonymous with overmotivation but was, *to a sizable degree*, accounted for by above average scores in creativity (in essence by other intellectual characteristics not measured in the IQ score).

As for *intelligence* and *on-the-job achievement*, Terman's (1925) studies indicate at least low predictive value in many things. In an oversimplified way, I sometimes think of these intelligent types of gifted as being successful in "playing the existing ropes," in adjusting to the existing environment, in contrast with adjusting the environment. Terman developed a Concept Mastery Test as a follow-up adult measure of intelligence. (See my review of it in the latest volume of Buros.) The farther one goes through school into graduate work (in science, at least), the more this test loses validity—though some competing tests outstrip it—until its validity vanishes on the job in science. And I doubt that this is all due to restriction of range by any means. C. W. Taylor (1958) found that the Terman Concept Mastery Test had no significant validities with supervisory ratings of scientists on creativity, productivity, or originality. Every other intellectual test in his study showed at least some significant validities with these criteria. While it could be argued that some restriction of range was present in his study, in contemplating what would happen to such non-significant correlations in a sample with unrestricted range, it is quite possible that more of the non-significant correlations will remain essentially zero than will become significant correlations.

One other exploratory study by Guilford and Allen (Guilford, 1959) seems relevant. They selected some 28 dimensions of the mind which they felt were relevant to success on the job in the physical sciences. Then they prepared plain-English descriptions and also a sample item of a best test for each of these 28 intellectual characteristics. A number of scientists of various types were interviewed by Allen, after which he asked them to rank these 28 characteristics in terms of their judged importance on their job. Five or six of these characteristics, such as general reasoning, vocabulary ability, number ability, memory for ideas, ability to visualize spatially, and perhaps perceptual speed, have been included in traditional intelligence tests. All but one of these traditional intelligence factors ranked below 20th in the list. In other words, 19 of the 20 intellectual characteristics ranking at the top of the job in science were *non-intelligence intellectual characteristics.*

J. M. Richards Jr., and I (1962) have just found that the farther a person goes through medical school and into internship, the more the medical selection tests of V, Q, and Premedical Achievement lose their validity until they actually have low *negative* validities in predicting performance as an intern.

Problems of Terminology

Let us examine further some of the terminology problems emerging as a result of new research findings that were not fully anticipated by those coining certain technical words nor by many now using them.

On certain terminology problems I have already taken a strong stand. As a worker in the field of measurement I feel we define by our IQ tests what we measure and mean by intelligence. I would like to keep these two tied together, and let the stretching of meaning occur in the word "giftedness." Without confusing too much past literature, we can talk about the intelligence (or IQ) type of giftedness, the creative type, the planning type, the decision-making type, etc., and thus open the way for many parallel types of giftedness so we don't fall into a trap of only two types, as so many did about one main type of giftedness. This terminology is much better than getting into the confusion of traditional intelligence versus creative intelligence, etc.

Each of these several types of giftedness has its place; in other words, no researcher in psychological measurement, to my knowledge, believes that we should ignore traditional intelligence tests and abolish testing for the IQ type of giftedness. Instead we are trying to learn how to discover and how to develop other types of giftedness largely ignored or not adequately focused upon to date. There is a real hope in the finding of several different and relatively separate types of giftedness. Already the Army researchers are capitalizing upon the great complexity in individual differences. For example, Uhlaner reported in a recent Army Reserve handout that, after several years of research, the Army now claims that 82 percent of their personnel can be placed into a type of work for which they have above-average potential.

Characteristics of the Creative

Before commenting on creative characteristics, let me mention a research result with interesting implications. Behavorial scientists have long been trying to establish standards of normality, especially in the mental illness area, for comparison purposes. A research team of Golden, Mandel, and Glueck of the American Psychiatric Association recently gave a report (1962) to the psychiatric profession on a study of the so-called "normal" man. The authors said they believed that their normal group of subjects represented as nearly as possible the "conception of the well-adjusted, average American male." The research team found that the normal man leads a contented, home-centered life, he has little imagination and has limited interests in social activities. His aspirations are not high, either for himself or for his children.

The two highest ratings in mental-status tests for the "normal" man were "contentment and compatibility with spouse." The lowest were "richness of personality and breadth of interest" (the latter two being just the opposite to those found for creatives). The researchers were asked, "Does normality as evidenced by lack of intrapsychic tension, adequate social, economic, and familial adaptation, and harmonious integration with other individuals at all levels necessarily imply *a lack of creativity*, imagination, and spontaneity?" They replied, "Our data are suggestive of this conclusion."

We are in an early state of research knowledge regarding characteristics of the creative person. From our experience, all of the research results to date (Taylor & Barron, 1963) indicate that no single characteristic by itself accounts for much of the total phenomenon of creativity; in other words, many human characteristics are usually involved in making creative contributions. No single-variable panacea and no single variable theory will serve in this area. In fact, our present theory of creativity would definitely be a multi-variable one along these lines: creative performance is dependent upon a large number of relatively separate variables, each one of which accounts generally for only a small, unique, and usually statistically almost insignificant part of the total variation in creative performance.

With this viewpoint in mind, we were frustrated in our study (Taylor, *et al.*, 1961) of Air Force scientists when it became necessary to select among a large number of intellectual and non-intellectual tests that had been reported as promising, primarily in the 1955, 1957, and 1959 Utah creativity research conferences (C. W. Taylor, 1956, 1958b, 1959). For example, Match Problems, Consequences, Word Association, Pertinent Questions, Apparatus Test, Visual Imagery, and Revision II were the only intellectual tests used, which sampled less than half of the intellectual tests felt at this early stage to be potential components of creative performance. Consequently, only 130 test scores were collected and each of these was validated against the 14 factored criteria found in the initial criterion phase of this project. The validities of the best single scores for each criterion ranged in the .40's, .30's, and .20's, with a sizable number of scores being valid for most criteria. Multiple correlational analyses suggest that on the initial sample studied, nearly half of the variance in any of 14 criteria of creative and other scientific contributions may be overlapped by a linear regression combination of 15 or more valid test predictors, although the shrinkage on cross-validation is as yet unknown.

Hopefully, on cross validation this phenomenon may parallel that found for "a large battery of biographical items" wherein the initial concurrent validities for empirically constructed keys have been typically in the .70's and .80's. The cross validities have also held up in the high .40's and .50's on different samples of NASA scientists at different geographical locations, even with a somewhat different creative criterion in the cross-validation study. Such approaches may remind one of actuarial methods in the insurance fields and may lead toward prediction of a fairly high degree of efficiency. The final check, however, of such concurrent validity studies will be predictive validity studies.

In summary, there is still uncertainty about the degree to which any currently available sets of "creativity" tests are valid predictors of important creative performances. Nevertheless, there is no reason to doubt that they are measuring other intellectual processes and non-intellectual characteristics that are not closely related to those involved in scoring high on intelligence tests and that essentially a different "gifted" group of persons will be identified as high scorers on these new tests than those selected as "gifted" by high scores on intelligence tests.

The high level aptitude (or intellectual) factors most involved are probably originality, adaptive flexibility, spontaneous flexibility, ideational fluency, expressional fluency, associational fluency, word fluency, sensitivity to problems, visualization, judgment, and redefinition (Guilford, 1959).

In turning to non-intellectual measures we should start with the most promising device, a well-developed biographical inventory measuring the relevancy of one's total experience up to a given period of time. Nearly every time that even a brief biographical inventory or biographical approach has been tried on scientists, it has been found to have promising validity in the initial sample studied (Stein, 1956; Knapp, 1956; Taylor, 1958b; Roe, 1958, 1959; Owens, *et al.*, 1958; Cattell, 1959; Ellison, 1960; C. W. Taylor, *et al.*, 1961; Holland, 1961; Smith, *et al.*, 1961; and Mullins, 1959). Although Mullins did not get good results on cross-validation, surprisingly high cross-validities between .46 and .56 against creativity criteria are being found in our current Utah studies of four samples of NASA scientists (N = 654) by C. W. Taylor and Ellison, following up the two previous biographical studies on 71 Utah scientists (Ellison, 1960) and 107 Air Force scientists (C. W. Taylor, *et al.*, 1961). In each of these six studies, alternative item analyses have been accomplished on every sample studied to formulate empirical keys to be cross-validated on other samples. Sizable cross-validities for a biographical inventory have also been found by Smith, *et al.* (1961). Admittedly, multiple biographical scores are being obtained by some investigators and these inventories usually deal with a hodgepodge of motivational and personality traits (e.g., work habits, attitudes, interests, values, family and academic history, and several personality characteristics).

Some motivational characteristics suggested are a great dedication to one's work, intellectual persistence, liking to think, liking to manipulate and toy with ideas, need for recognition for achievement, need for variety, need for autonomy, preference for complex order and for challenges therein, tolerance of ambiguity, resistance to closing up and crystallizing things prematurely, coupled with a strong need for ultimate closure, need for mastery of a problem, insatiability for intellectual ordering, and a need to improve upon currently accepted systems. High energy with vast output through disciplined work habits is usually apparent.

We need to know better how to get students more deeply involved in their work, for Bloom (1958) has indicated that science students who truly become involved in research work and in the research role during graduate training, tend to become the productive researchers afterwards. The reverse may be even more generally true.

From personality evidence to date, creative persons are more devoted to autonomy, more self-sufficient, more independent in judgment (contrary to group agreement, if needed, to be accurate), more open to the irrational in themselves, more stable, low in sociability, more interested in unconventional careers, more feminine in interests and characteristics (especially in awareness of one's impulses), more dominant and self-assertive, more complex as a person, more self-accepting, more resourceful and adventurous, more radical (Bohemian), more controlling of their own behavior by self-concept, and possibly more emotionally sensitive, and introverted, but bold.

A Challenge for the Future

Five important points or questions will next be mentional briefly. (a) The first point is that real progress has been made in discovering creative characteristics and in learning how to measure them, at least crudely. (b) There are probably organizational problems in education and elsewhere pertaining to the encouragement and utilization of creative talent. Expectations are that sustained research in this area might be very fruitful. (c) There may well be multiple types of creativity, but as yet we do not know scientifically what these types are nor to what degree they cut across disciplines. (d) Early indications suggest that the education of students is a problem area, with changes needed if creative potential is to be developed in students. Much more research knowledge is needed here. The final point is raised quite appropriately in question form. (e) Are there losses in creative talent along the academic ladder? Further study is again indicated in this last point which underlies many current and projected national programs on scientific manpower and education. It is of great potential value to the nation to obtain further insights into this area in order that (a) losses of the most relevant types of manpower needed in research work in scientific laboratories and in other high level activities can be reduced, (b) the most relevant types of talent will be developed in our educational programs, and (c) such talent will be most fully utilized to speed up scientific and other progress in the nation.

We should be deeply concerned about this point because there may be an above average dropout of those with creative talent through the academic program. Since early evidence suggests that fellow students and teachers may not favor, in fact may even disfavor, more creative students and, likewise, principals and supervisors may not favor more creative teachers, *we should determine what the losses in creative talent are at each crucial level* through the present school system.

There also may be another type of loss—the decrease of creative talent within individuals as they move along the academic ladder. If this is true, as some are suspecting, we should again be deeply troubled about such losses.

In closing I want to raise some questions and challenges to educators. When I spoke previously to the CEC organization in April, 1960, I raised a series of questions under the general heading "What Type of Training for What Type of Giftedness?" A variation of this question could also be asked: "What Type of Counseling for What Type of Giftedness?" A more general question is "What Should Be Done After We Have Learned to Identify a New Type of Talent or a New Type of Giftedness?" In other words, the whole question emerges as to what changes would be needed in our educational systems as well as in our testing and counseling programs as we discover and learn to identify other types of giftedness.

We feel that a large developmental activity by specially trained "educational engineers" is needed in order that basic research findings with implications for education can be engineered and developed so that they can be rapidly installed into educational programs. The closing challenge is that the future may belong to the nation or nations that build effective R & D programs in education which lead to rapid identification and cultivation of creativity and of all other vital human resources.

References

Bloom, Benjamin S. Some effects of cultural, social, and educational conditions on creativity. In Calvin W. Taylor (Ed.), *The second (1957) University of Utah research conference on the identification of creative scientific talent.* Salt Lake City, Utah: University of Utah Press, 1958. Pp. 55–65.

Cattell, Raymond B. The personality and motivation of the researcher from measurements of contemporaries and from biography. In Calvin W. Taylor (Ed.), *The third (1959) University of Utah research conference on the identification of creative scientific talent.* Salt Lake City, Utah: University of Utah Press, 1959. Pp. 77–93.*

* Also in Taylor & Barron (Eds.), *Scientific creativity: its recognition and development.* New York: John Wiley, 1963.

CHORNESS, MAURY. An interim report on creativity research. In Calvin W. Taylor (Ed.), *The 1955 University of Utah research conference on the identification of creative scientific talent.* Salt Lake City, Utah: University of Utah Press, 1956. Pp. 132–155.*

ELLISON, ROBERT L. The relationship of certain biographical information to success in science. Unpublished Master's thesis, University of Utah, 1960.

FRENCH, JOHN W. The description of aptitude and achievement tests in terms of rotated factors. Psychometric Monogr., No. 5, Chicago: University of Chicago Press, 1951.

GETZELS, J. W., & JACKSON, P. W. The highly intelligent and the highly creative adolescent: a summary of some research findings. In Calvin W. Taylor (Ed.), *The third (1959) University of Utah research conference on the identification of creative scientific talent.* Salt Lake City, Utah: University of Utah Press, 1959. Pp. 46–57.*

GUILFORD, J. P. Intellectual resources and their values as seen by scientists. In Calvin W. Taylor (Ed.), *The third (1959) University of Utah research conference on the identification of creative scientific talent.* Salt Lake City, Utah: University of Utah Press, 1959. Pp. 128–149.*

GUILFORD, J. P., WILSON, R. C., & CHRISTENSEN, P. R. A factor-analytic study of creative thinking. II. Administration of tests and analysis of results. Reports from the Psychol. Laboratory, No. 8, Los Angeles: University of Southern California, 1952.

HARMON, LINDSEY R. High School backgrounds of science doctorates. *Science*, 1961, 133 (3454). Pp. 679–681.

HARRIS, D. The development and validation of a test of creativity in engineering. *J. appl. Psychol.*, 1960, 44. Pp. 254–257.

HENDRIX, GERTRUDE. Learning by discovery. *Math. Teach.*, 1961, 54.

HOLLAND, JOHN L. Creative and academic performance among talented adolescents. *J. educ. Psychol.*, 1961, 52. Pp. 136–147.

KNAPP, ROBERT H. Demographic cultural and personality attributes of scientists. In Calvin W. Taylor (Ed.), *The 1955 University of Utah research conference on the identification of creative scientific talent.* Salt Lake City, Utah: University of Utah Press, 1956. Pp. 204–212.*

MACKINNON, DONALD W. What do we mean by talent and how do we test for it? In *The search for talent.* College Admissions, No. 7, New York: College Entrance Examination Board, 1959. Pp. 20–29.

MARTIN, ROBERT A., & PACHARES, JAMES. Good scholars not always best. *Business Week*, 1962, Feb. 24. P. 77.

MULLINS, CECIL J. The prediction of creativity in a sample of research scientists. Technical Note, WADC-TN-59-36, ASTIA Documents, No. AD 211039. Lackland Air Force Base, Texas: Personnel Laboratory, Wright Air Development Center, Air Research & Development Command, Feb. 1959.

* Also in Taylor & Barron (1963).

OWENS, W. A., SCHUMACHER, C. F. & CLARK, J. B. The measurement of creativity in machine design. In Calvin W. Taylor (Ed.), *The second (1957) University of Utah research conference on the identification of creative scientific talent.* Salt Lake City, Utah: University of Utah Press, 1958. Pp. 129–140.

PARNES, SIDNEY J., & MEADOW, ARNOLD. University of Buffalo research regarding development of creative talent. In Calvin W. Taylor (Ed.), *The third (1959) University of Utah research conference on the identification of creative scientific talent.* Salt Lake City, Utah: University of Utah Press, 1959. Pp. 187–201.*

RICHARDS, JAMES M., & TAYLOR, CALVIN W. Predicting academic achievement in a college of medicine from grades, test scores, interviews, and ratings. *Educ. psychol. Measmt.*, 1961, 21. Pp. 987–994.

RICHARDS, JAMES M. JR., TAYLOR, CALVIN W., & PRICE, PHILIP B. The prediction of medical intern performance. *J. appl. Psychol.*, 1962, in press.

RILEY, REED F., & OVERBERGER, C. G. A summer research participation program for high school students. *J. chemical Educ.*, 1961, 38. Pp. 424–427.

ROE, ANNE. Psychological tests of research scientists. *J. consult. Psychol.*, 1951, 15. Pp. 492–495.

ROE, ANNE. *The making of a scientist.* New York: Dodd, Mead, & Co., 1953.

ROE, ANNE. Early differentiation of interests. In Calvin W. Taylor (Ed.), *The second (1957) University of Utah research conference on the identification of creative scientific talent.* Salt Lake City, Utah: University of Utah Press, 1958. Pp. 98–108.

ROE, ANNE. Personal problems and science. In Calvin W. Taylor (Ed.), *The third (1959) University of Utah research conference on the identification of creative scientific talent.* Salt Lake City, Utah: University of Utah Press, 1959. Pp. 202–212.*

SMITH, WALLACE J., *et al.* The prediction of research competence and creativity from personal history. *J. appl. Psychol.*, 1961, 45. Pp. 59–62.

STEIN, MORRIS I. A transactional approach to creativity. In Calvin W. Taylor (Ed.), *The 1955 University of Utah research conference on the identification of creative scientific talent.* Salt Lake City, Utah: University of Utah Press, 1956. Pp. 171–181.*

TAYLOR, CALVIN W. (Ed.), *The 1955 University of Utah research conference on the identification of creative scientific talent.* Salt Lake City, Utah: University of Utah Press, 1956.

TAYLOR, CALVIN W. Some variables functioning in productivity and creativity. In Calvin W. Taylor (Ed.), *The second (1957) University of Utah research conference on the identification of creative scientific talent.* Salt Lake City, Utah: University of Utah Press, 1958. Pp. 3–19. (a)

TAYLOR, CALVIN W. The creative individual: a new portrait in giftedness. *Educ. Leadership*, 1960, 18 (1). Pp. 7–12.

* Also in Taylor & Barron (1963).

TAYLOR, CALVIN W. (Ed.), *Creativity: progress and potential.* New York: McGraw-Hill, 1964. (a)

TAYLOR, CALVIN W. (Ed.), *Widening horizons in creativity.* New York: John Wiley, 1964. (b)

TAYLOR, CALVIN W., & BARRON, FRANK (Eds.), *Scientific creativity: its recognition and development.* New York: John Wiley, 1963.

TAYLOR, CALVIN W., SMITH, WILLIAMS R., & GHISELIN, BREWSTER. Analysis of multiple criteria of creativity and productivity of scientists. In Calvin W. Taylor (Ed.), *The third (1959) University of Utah research conference on the identification of creative scientific talent.* Salt Lake City, Utah: University of Utah Press, 1959. Pp. 5–28.*

TAYLOR, CALVIN W., SMITH, WILLIAM R., GHISELIN, BREWSTER, & ELLISON, ROBERT. Explorations in the measurement and prediction of contributions of one sample of scientists. Technical Report ASD-TR-61-96. Lackland Air Force Base, Texas: Personnel Laboratory, Aeronautical Systems Division, Air Force Systems Command, April 1961.

TAYLOR, CALVIN W., GHISELIN, BREWSTER, & WOLFER, JOHN A. Bridging the gap. *Natl. Educ. Ass. J.*, 1962, 51. Pp. 23–25. (a)

TAYLOR, CALVIN W., GHISELIN, BREWSTER, WOLFER, JOHN, LOY, LORRAINE, & BOURNE, LYLE. A theory of education based upon psychological and other relevant research findings. Unpublished manuscript, University of Utah, 1962. (b)

TAYLOR, DONALD W. Variables related to creativity and productivity among men in two research laboratories. In Calvin W. Taylor (Ed.), *The second (1957) University of Utah research conference on the identification of creative scientific talent.* Salt Lake City, Utah: University of Utah Press, 1958. Pp. 20–54.*

TERMAN, LEWIS M. (Ed.), *Genetic studies of genius. Vol. 1.* Stanford, California: Stanford University Press, 1925.

TORRANCE, E. PAUL. Explorations in creative thinking in the early school years: a progress report. In Calvin W. Taylor (Ed.), *The third (1959) University of Utah research conference on the identification of creative scientific talent.* Salt Lake City, Utah: University of Utah Press, 1959. Pp. 58–71. (a)*

TORRANCE, E. PAUL. Current research on the nature of creative talent. *J. counsel. Psychol.*, 1959, 6. Pp. 309–316. (b)

YAMAMOTO, KAORU. Creativity and intellect: review of current research and projection paper read at Minnesota Psychol. Ass., April, 1961.

* Also in Taylor & Barron (1963).

6

Independence-Conformity Behavior as a Function of Intellect: Bright and Dull Children

Leonard J. Lucito

Abstract: A simplified version of Crutchfield's experimental procedure was used for assessing conformity to peer-group pressure among children. In general, the data indicate that there is an inverse relationship between level of intelligence and amount of conformity. More detailed analysis suggests that bright and dull children may approach the same task with different perceptual and goal orientations.

One factor of personality structure is independence-conformity behavior. What is the relationship between the level of intellect of children and independence-conformity? It is the purpose of this study to examine this question by exploring one type of independence-conformity situation with two levels of intelligence—bright and dull sixth grade students.

The pioneer empirical studies of Asch (1956), Crutchfield (1955), and Sherif (1935) on college students and adults offer some models of the independence-conformity situation. From a theory based on the differential diets of social and objective verification due to intelligence (Lucito, 1959), three hypotheses and their accompanying assumptions were generated.

Hypothesis I: The intellectually bright group will conform less than the dull in the total independence-conformity situation. This statement is based on the assumption that bright children expect to play the role of defining social reality for themselves and for others while the dull children

LEONARD J. LUCITO is Coordinator of Special Education, University of South Florida, Tampa. This investigation was supported (in part) by a predoctoral research fellowship from the National Institute of Mental Health, Public Health Service while the author was at the Institute for Research on Exceptional Children, University of Illinois.

expect to play the role of dependency. These role expectations should exist in situations both where there are no relevant cues on which to base judgments and where there are relevant cues.

Hypothesis II: The bright group will be less conforming than the dull on both difficult and easy tasks. If generality of conformity is assumed, then the group which is less conforming on one level of task difficulty should also be less conforming on the other level.

Hypothesis III: The performance of the dull group on the two levels of task difficulty will be more similar than the performance of the bright group on the two levels of task difficulty. This hypothesis is based on inferred differences in the motivational orientations of the two groups. The bright group is more task oriented; whereas, the dull group is more concerned with avoiding group rejection or relying upon the group to obtain goals.

Description of Sample

Selected for the study were 106 sixth grade children from two Illinois elementary school districts. The total IQ score on the California Test of Mental Maturity (Short-form, Form S, Junior High level, 1957) was used to place the children into two categories–bright and dull. Inclusion in the bright class required a z score of $+1.25$ (IQ of 120) or above; for the dull category a z score of -1.125 (IQ of 82) or below was required. The mean IQ of the 55 bright children was 126.04 with a standard deviation of 5.09. The 51 dull children had a mean IQ of 76.96 with a standard deviation of 3.96. The dull group was older and had a wider range of ages–the means of the chronological ages in months were 141.07 for the bright and 154.06 for the dull, with standard deviations of 7.21 and 12.06 respectively. There were 26 females in the dull group, and 22 females in the bright. Thirty-two of the 106 subjects were Negroes.

Task and Visual Discrimination Material

Two white cards with vertical black lines were presented simultaneously. These cards were kept three feet apart and approximately 12 feet from the eyes of the subjects. The card on the left had one line, the standard. Below it was a yellow circle. The card on the right had three choice lines. Each of the choice lines had a colored circle below it, from left to right red, white, and blue respectively. The task was to select one line from the choice lines that matched the standard in length.

Lines of nonambiguous and ambiguous levels of difficulty were constructed. All nonambiguous lines were ¼″ in width. The standard lines were either 5″ or 8″ in length. One of the choice lines was the same length as the standard, and was labeled the *s* line. The other two choice lines were either both larger or both smaller in length than the correct line. The line most different in length from the correct line has been called the *e* (extreme) line; the line intermediate in length between the *s* and *e* lines was labeled the *i* line (see Figure 1). Six sets of nonambiguous cards were chosen on the bases of pilot investigations which demonstrated no significant advantage for the bright in the independence-conformity situation due to their greater ability to discriminate (Lucito, 1959).

The standard and the three choice lines of the ambiguous material were all ¼″ in length and ⅛″ in width (see Figure 1).

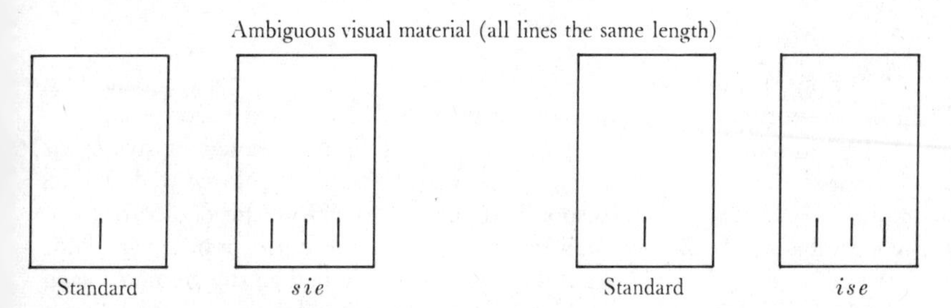

The notations *s*, *i*, *e* for the lines on the ambiguous material have no meaning in themselves. The lines are so labeled because they occupy the same spatial position on the cards as lines similarly labeled on the nonambiguous material.

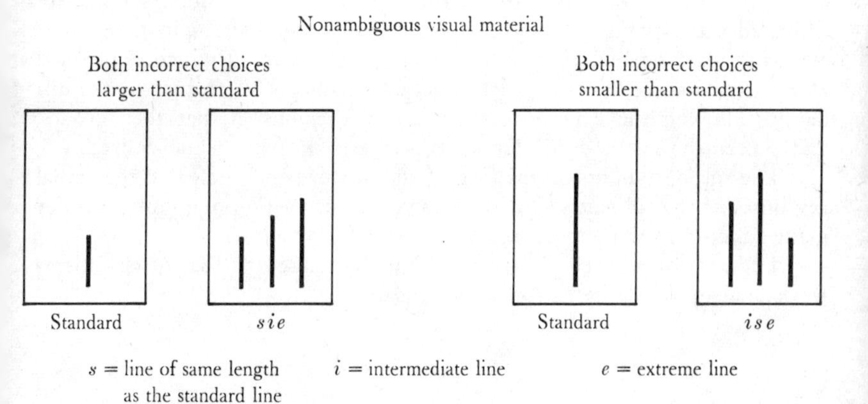

Figure 1. Samples of visual discrimination materials.

In the independence-conformity situation, the presentation of each set of nonambiguous cards was immediately preceded by a set of ambiguous cards. The subjects were led to believe the ambiguous lines were the same collection of lines as the nonambiguous, but on a smaller scale, and that the spatial position of the correct answer did not change between each pair.

With the aid of line segments, this impression was induced during a training period by demonstrating that short lines could be made proportionately larger without changing the relative size of the lines. Thus, the paired sets of ambiguous and nonambiguous cards were presented to the subjects as a single problem with two levels of difficulty—small and large drawings of the same lines. The choice lines of the ambiguous cards were labeled *s*, *i*, and *e*, in accordance with the spatial arrangement of the nonambiguous comparison lines which immediately followed them (see Figure 1).

Apparatus

The apparatus consisted of six individual panels, a master panel, an automatic polygraph recorder, and 4½′ by 3½′ cardboard partitions.

The individual panels (Figure 2) had 15 lights arrayed in five rows with three lights in each. Each column of lights was colored red, white, or blue respectively to correspond to the colors below the choice lines of the stimulus cards. Below each column was a hole corresponding in color to the column of lights above it. A stylus was attached to the frame of each individual panel. By placing the stylus in the appropriate hole the subject could indicate the comparison line he had chosen as an answer.

All individual panels were visibly connected by wires. The subjects were given the erroneous impression that they could communicate their answers to other subjects through the use of the styli which supposedly activated corresponding colored lights on all other panels. In fact, however, the master panel (Figure 2) had a set of switches which controlled all communication lights on each individual panel. This feature of the apparatus allowed the experimenter to create the illusion that the "group" had chosen the *s* (standard) line or the *e* (extreme) line as he desired.

The response lights on the face of the master panel indicated the actual responses of the subjects. Simultaneously, the automatic polygraph recorder made a record of these responses.

The 4½′ by 3½′ cardboard partitions were used to force the subjects to depend upon the lights for communication.

Procedure

Two sittings were required of each subject accepted into the study. The general approach to the first sitting is illustrated below by excerpts from the pretest instructions.

Before we start I would like to thank you for coming to help me with this experiment. You know what an experiment is; it is a way of studying how things work. I am studying how people judge the size of things from a distance. The ability to judge size is important in many jobs. For example, it would be pretty silly for a pilot to walk out of his plane with a ruler to measure the size of something he sees. He must judge the size of things just by looking. This is also true when driving a car. You can think of other times when judging the size of things without measuring them is important, such as when working in a factory or doing art work in school. We don't know enough about how people learn this; that's why you are needed to help. Because you are helping me, I want to make it fun for you. To make this experiment more fun for you, it is going to be made into a contest with prizes for the winners. I'll explain how the contest works after you understand what you are to do.

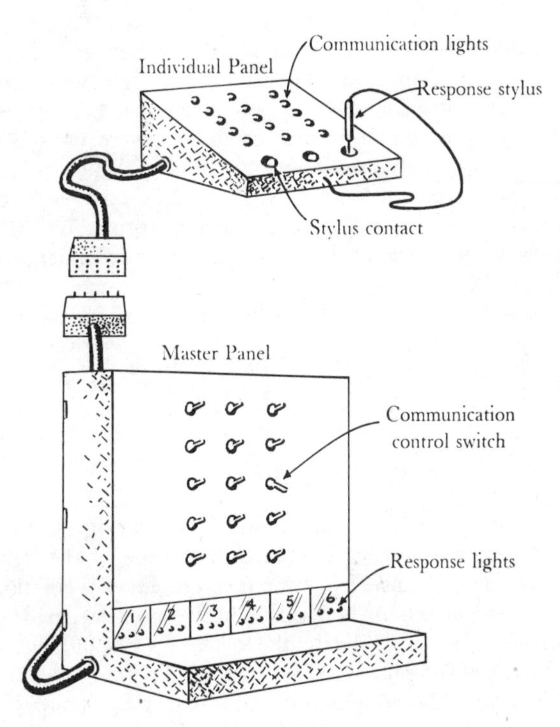

Figure 2. Apparatus.

Four training trials were conducted to familiarize the children with the task. The rules of the contest were then explained.

. . . the six of you are going to be a team. There will be about 15 or 20 teams just like this one in the contest. The team with the highest number of points will win \$6.00. This means that each one of you can win a dollar, *if your team wins*. Let me tell you how to get points for your team. For every yellow line there are three lines to choose from; if you choose the line that is the same size as the yellow line, your team will get 3 points; if you choose the next best line, your team will get 2 points (point to intermediate line); and if you choose the line most different from the yellow line, your team will get 1 point. All the points each person on a team earns will be added together and this will be the team's score. The team with the highest number of points will win the \$6.00.

The major purpose of the first sitting was to identify bright and dull children who could consistently discriminate the correct answer on the six items selected in the pilot investigation so that the presentation of these items in the second sitting might be considered a nonambiguous stimulus situation. These six items were presented three times in random order to a pool of subjects. The criterion of nonambiguity was: no more than three errors on the 18 trials, with the restriction that not more than one error be made on any one item. Those who met the criterion were organized into six-member groups so that there was a balance between the number of bright and dull subjects with respect to sex and race within each group. When necessary, children who were just outside the acceptable range for inclusion in either the bright or dull categories were used as fillers. For example, if there were only two bright children with IQ's of 120 or above available for a group, a child with an IQ of 118 or 119 was used as a filler, but was not included in the analyses. The groups formed by the above procedure were used in the second sitting to measure independence-conformity behavior.

The second sitting was introduced by these instructions:

> I want to thank you for coming back to help with another part of this experiment. To make it fun for you again, it is going to be another contest. The six of you now here are going to be a *new* team for a $9.00 contest. Among the new teams like this one, the team with the highest score will have a chance to win $9.00; therefore, each one of you can win $1.50 if this new team wins. You will get points for your team the same way as last time. . . .

The subjects were given a demonstration of the pairing of ambiguous and nonambiguous material, and were trained in the use of the lights on their individual panels as a means of communication. They were also given the impression that the numbers one through six were assigned to different members of the group to indicate the order of responding; in fact, *all members were given number six*. This offered the experimenter an opportunity to induce into the communication system the "group's" solution to the problem before any of the subjects gave their response.

Thirty-four trials were run. In each trial the ambiguous material was presented first, and then the nonambiguous material was presented as a magnification of the ambiguous. After each presentation, ten seconds were allowed for the subjects to make private judgments. Then, the "group" response was introduced through the apparatus and simultaneous responses were elicited from the subjects.

There were two types of trials, E-type and S-type. In the 21 E-type trials the "group" responses were in the spatial position of the *e* (extreme) line for both the ambiguous and nonambiguous halves. In the 13 S-type trials the "group" responses were in the spatial position of the *s* (standard) for the entire trial. The primary purpose of the S-type trials was to lend creditability to the "group" responses.

Any study involving deception runs the risk of some subjects discovering it before the appropriate time. In order to check the effectiveness of the deception, at the end of the second sitting each group of subjects was told to push back the cardboard partitions which separated them while the experimenter pretended to busy himself with the apparatus. Since each child had a card with a number which indicated the position of his turn to answer, it was possible to observe whether or not their behavior indicated prior knowledge when they discovered that everyone in the group had been answering in the sixth position. In four out of the ten groups it was necessary to ask if they noticed anything odd before they discovered everyone was number six. None of the subjects seemed to be aware of the deception immediately, and a considerable amount of discussion was required to explain the nature and purpose of the deception. Therefore, some confidence can be assumed in the naiveness of the subjects until the very end of the study.

Results and Discussions

On the ambiguous halves of all 34 trials, a response which was the same as the "group's" was operationally defined as a conforming one. By summing the number of conforming responses, a conformity score could be assigned to each subject for the ambiguous half of the trials. The lower the conformity score the more independent the subject had behaved. On the nonambiguous halves of the trials, a response which was the same as the "group's" and contrary to the answer the subject gave during the first sitting was considered conforming behavior. However, only the 21 E-type trials were used for computing conformity scores on the nonambiguous halves of the trials since it was meaningless to give a response different from the "group's" when it had chosen the correct answer.

The ranges and medians of the conformity scores for the two types of tasks and the two levels of intelligence can be seen in Table 1.

Table 1. Ranges and Medians of Conformity Scores

	Ambiguous Task		*Nonambiguous Task*	
	Bright	*Dull*	*Bright*	*Dull*
Range	9–34	24–34	0–21	0–21
Median	30	34	5	20
Combined Median	33		11	

An extension of the median test (Siegel, 1956, p. 179) was used to evaluate Hypothesis I—the bright group is less conforming than the dull in the total independence-conformity situation. Considering only the conformity scores on the ambiguous halves of the trials, the scores of both the bright and dull groups were dichotomized at their combined median. Those children scoring above the combined median were regarded as exhibiting more conforming than independent behavior; those below the combined median were judged to be more independent than conforming. The same process was used to dichotomize the scores of the children on the nonambiguous half of the E-type trials. Table 2 presents the distribution of bright and dull children scoring above and below the combined medians for both the ambiguous and nonambiguous parts of the trials.

TABLE 2. DISTRIBUTION OF BRIGHT AND DULL CHILDREN FOR THE AMBIGUOUS AND NONAMBIGUOUS PARTS OF TRIALS

			Ambiguous		
			Conforming (Above combined median)	*Independent (Below combined median)*	*Totals*
Nonambiguous	*Conforming (Above combined median)*	Bright	11	6	17
		Dull	26	11	37
	Independent (Below combined median)	Bright	10	28	38
		Dull	7	7	14
Totals		Bright	21	34	55
		Dull	33	18	51

$\chi^2 = 17.78$, $p < .005$.

Since the total independence-conformity situation also includes a dimension of ambiguity-nonambiguity, it is possible to test Hypothesis I by a four by two χ^2 as shown in Table 2. The dimensions included in this test are independence-conformity patterns, stimulus ambiguity-nonambiguity and bright-dull students. For example, Table 2 indicates that 10 bright students showed a conforming pattern (above combined median) when faced with ambiguous stimuli but showed an independent pattern when given nonambiguous stimuli. While only 11 of the bright students were found to be conforming to both ambiguous and nonambiguous stimuli, 26 of the dull students showed a conforming pattern in the same situations.

A χ^2 of 17.78 was obtained through this analysis which was significant at a probability level of .005. With three degrees of freedom, it is significant beyond the .005 level. Therefore, the null hypothesis was rejected, and it was confirmed that the bright children as a group are less conforming than the dull children in the total independence-conformity situation.

The data were reexamined for the effect of possible sex and race differences in relation to conformity behavior. First, a subsample was drawn from the total sample so that the IQ means and standard deviations of the males and females were matched. Again using the extended median technique on the composite conformity scores of the subsample, a test of sex differences was made. The χ^2 was 3.564. With three degrees of freedom, p lies between the .30 and .50 levels. A second subsample was drawn so that the means and standard deviations of the IQ's of the Negro and white groups were matched. The same statistical technique was applied to test race differences; the χ^2 was .38 (nonsignificant). With the probability of sex and race differences ruled out, the conclusion that the bright children as a group are less conforming than the dull children was strengthened.

Hypothesis II was assessed with two separate median tests (Siegel, 1956, p. 111). From the data in Table 2, the χ^2 between the bright and the dull groups on the ambiguous material (difficult task) was 4.54 with one degree of freedom. By linear interpolation from the χ^2 tables, p is approximately at the .02 level. Employing the same procedure on the data for nonambiguous halves of trials in Table 2, a χ^2 of 20.067 was obtained. With one degree of freedom, p is beyond the .005 level. Thus, it was concluded that bright children as a group are less conforming than the dull children on both difficult and easy tasks.

In Hypothesis III it was predicted that the performance of the dull group on the two levels of task difficulty would be more similar than the performance of the bright group on the two levels of task difficulty. Two types of analyses confirmed this hypothesis. Separate Spearman Rank Correlation coefficients were computed between the ambiguous and nonambiguous conformity scores of the bright and dull groups. The correlation for the dull group was +.61 (significantly different from zero); whereas, the correlation for the bright group was +.06 (*not* significantly different from zero). Further evidence was provided by noting that on all 21 E-type trials the differences between the percentage of conformity on both halves of the trials for the dull group was smaller than those for the bright. The probability associated with predicting which difference was smaller 21 out of 21 times is beyond the .001 level using the Sign Test.

Since the bright children as a group were significantly less conforming to their peers than the dull children in all of the analyses, it appears that intelligence is inversely related to conformity behavior for sixth graders. This is consistent with studies made of college students and adults by Barron (1955), Crutchfield (1955), DiVesta (1958), and Tuddenham (1958). It also suggests the possibility that the inverse relationship between intelligence and conformity to peers may hold for most of the range of chronological ages.

In developing the theory which generated the three hypotheses, Lucito (1959) made certain assumptions. Because all of the results were consistent with the theory, these results can be considered to offer *indirect* evidence to support the assumptions. The assumptions were: (a) the most probable role the bright children perceive as their own is one of defining social and objective reality for themselves and for others, while the dull play the role of accepting the definitions of others; (b) there is generality of conformity across some situations; and (c) bright children are more task oriented while the dull children are more concerned with avoiding rejection by their peer group or relying upon the group to obtain goals.

SUMMARY

The purpose of this study was to compare the behavior of intellectually bright and dull children in an experimentally designed independence-conformity situation.

Sixth grade children from the same classroom were organized into groups. Each group had six members, and was a mixture of bright and dull subjects. Fifty-five bright children and 51 dull children were used in the study.

The independence-conformity situation allowed the subjects to make two judgments of every problem—one judgment when the problem was difficult (ambiguous set of lines), and one judgment when it was easy (nonambiguous set of lines). The ambiguous set of lines consisted of a standard line and three comparison lines, all 1/4″ in length. The lines of the nonambiguous set were 20 or 30 times larger, and it was easy for the children to discriminate which one of the three comparison lines was the same size as the standard line. The ambiguous followed by the nonambiguous sets of lines were presented as pairs, and the subjects were led to believe that these pairs of lines were proportional in length so that the correct answer for the nonambiguous lines was the same as for the ambiguous.

Other deceptions were introduced into the study. Through the use of an electrical communication system, the subjects were given the erroneous impression that they could communicate their judgments to other subjects. Actually, the experimenter had a set of switches which controlled all of the signals of communication. This feature of the apparatus allowed the experimenter to manufacture an erroneous "group" response. The individual was then faced with the alternative of either conforming to the "group's" judgment or remaining independent.

Three hypotheses were tested, and the results were:

1. The bright children as a group were significantly less conforming to their peers than the dull children in the total independence-conformity situation.

2. The bright children as a group were significantly less conforming to their peers than the dull children on both difficult (ambiguous) and easy (nonambiguous) tasks.

3. The similarity between the extent of conformity exhibited by the dull group on the two levels of task difficulty (ambiguous and nonambiguous) was significantly greater than that exhibited by the bright group.

References

Asch, S. E. Studies of independence and conformity. *Psychological Monograph*, 1956, 70.

Barron, F. The disposition toward originality. *Journal of Abnormal Social Psychology*, 1955, 51, 478–485.

Crutchfield, R. S. Conformity and character. *American Psychologist*, 1955, 10, 191–198.

DiVesta, F. J. Susceptibility to pressures toward uniformity of behavior in social situations: A study of task, motivational, and personal factors in conformity behavior. Contract AF 18 (603)–20. Syracuse University, Syracuse, New York, 1958.

Lucito, L. J. A comparison of the independence-conformity behavior of intellectually bright and dull children. Unpublished doctoral dissertation, University of Illinois, 1959.

Sherif, M. A study of some social factors in perception. *Archives of Psychology*, 1935, 27, No. 187.

Tuddenham, R. D. Studies in conformity and yielding VIII: Some correlates of yielding to a distorted group norm. Technical Report No. 8, ONR Contract NR 170–159. University of California, Berkeley, 1958.

❦ 7

The Temperament of Gifted Children

Marcella Ryser Bonsall
Buford Stefflre

In the past decade there has been a revival of interest in the education of intellectually superior children. This points up the need for further study of the characteristics possessed by these children. Among the many research studies in this area are several which have produced objective testimony showing a favorable moderate divergence of gifted children from the unselected children on characteristic personality patterns in general.

The present study investigates temperament differences between the gifted and other high school senior boys to determine the extent to which previously observed temperament differences were a function of "giftedness" and the extent to which they were a function of the socio-economic background of the gifted. Comparisons were first made of gifted and others at each of the several occupational levels. Then a comparison was made of all the gifted with all others disregarding the occupational level of the home.

The sample consists of 1,359 white high school senior boys in several high schools in a metropolitan area who in the course of a vocational coun-

MARCELLA RYSER BONSALL is a consultant for Programs for the Gifted in the Division of Research and Guidance of the Los Angeles County Superintendent of Schools Office. She is a member of the American Psychological Association, American Personnel and Guidance Association, Pi Lambda Theta, Delta Kappa Gamma, and numerous professional organizations. She received the doctor of education degree from USC in 1952.

BUFORD STEFFLRE is a Professor of Education at Michigan State University, East Lansing, Michigan. He is a member of the American Psychological Association, American Personnel and Guidance Association, Phi Delta Kappa, and many other professional organizations. Dr. Stefflre received his degree in education at USC in 1953.

seling experience completed the SRA Primary Mental Abilities Test (here used as an index of giftedness) and the Guilford-Zimmerman Temperament Survey (here used as a temperament measure) and who gave enough information about the occupation of their wage earning parent (in most cases the father) to enable the occupation to be classified according to the Alba Edwards Scale.

On the basis of the total score on the Primary Mental Abilities Test students were designated as "gifted" if they were in the top 11 per cent of published norms. Parents' occupations of all students were classified according to the Alba Edwards six level scale–professional, managerial and official, clerical, skilled, semi-skilled, and unskilled. Within each of these occupational levels the gifted were compared with the others with regard to scores on each of the ten sections of the Guilford-Zimmerman Temperament Survey. These ten sections are (1) General Activity, (2) Restraint, (3) Ascendance, (4) Sociability, (5) Emotional Stability, (6) Objectivity, (7) Friendliness, (8) Thoughtfulness, (9) Personal Cooperation, and (10) Masculinity of Interest. When these comparisons were subjected to the *t* test to determine the significance of the observed differences the results were as shown in Table I.

Differences Found

Those gifted boys whose fathers were classed as professionals manifest greater objectivity at the 1 per cent level when compared to non-gifted boys having professional fathers.

The gifted boys from homes where fathers are in managerial or clerical positions demonstrate more restraint at the 1 per cent and the 5 per cent level, respectively, than do non-gifted boys from like occupational backgrounds and gifted boys from homes where the fathers are in managerial jobs are at the 1 per cent level more thoughtful than other boys from like homes. The boys classified as gifted, whose fathers were employed in semi-skilled and skilled occupations, reveal more masculinity at the 1 per cent and the 5 per cent levels than did average ability boys whose fathers are working at similar jobs.

When gifted boys are compared with all other boys, with the occupational levels of the home disregarded, they show at the 1 per cent level more thoughtfulness and, at the 5 per cent level more general activity, restraint, ascendance, emotional stability, objectivity, and masculinity.

Effect of Socio-Economic Level

This study indicates that the previously found superiority of the "gifted" as regards temperament stems much more from the socio-economic

TABLE 1. SIGNIFICANCE OF DIFFERENCES IN TEMPERAMENT TRAITS BETWEEN GIFTED AND NON-GIFTED

Home Level According to Alba Edwards Scale	*Number of Students*		*Significance of Differences in Scores on Sections of Guilford-Zimmerman Temperament Survey*[1]									
	Gifted	*Non-Gifted*	*G*	*R*	*A*	*S*	*E*	*O*	*F*	*T*	*P*	*M*
Professional	18	160	n	n	n	n	n	**	n	n	n	n
Managerial-Official	37	354	n	**	n	n	n	n	n	**	n	n
Clerical	22	266	n	*	n	n	n	n	n	n	n	n
Skilled	8	283	n	n	n	n	n	n	n	**	n	*
Semi-Skilled	7	157	n	n	n	n	n	n	n	**	n	**
Unskilled	0	37	n	n	n	n	n	n	n	n	n	n
Total	92	1257	*	*	*	n	*	*	n	**	n	*

KEY: n No significant difference.
* Gifted superior at the 5 per cent level.
** Gifted superior at the 1 per cent level.

[1] Sections are designated as follows: G–General Activity; R–Restraint; A–Ascendance; S–Sociability; E–Emotional Stability; O–Objectivity; F–Friendliness; T–Thoughtfulness; P–Personal Cooperation; M–Masculinity of Interest.

level at which most gifted children are found than from any other difference in "gifted" children as such. When socio-economic background is taken into account, relatively few significant differences are found between "gifted" and others, but when the parent background of these children is disregarded, there seem to be differences in seven of the ten areas measured and in all these areas the "gifted" child has superior temperament scores.

Research using different measuring instruments might well have resulted in different findings, and it is interesting to speculate on the influence of culture in developing or suppressing "giftedness." Certainly the incidence of giftedness is greatest among the more favored socio-economic groups, and it is these groups which exhibit the temperament traits most valued by our educational institutions. This juxtaposition of high intelligence and valued temperament is not seen as wholly a matter of background, however, since restraint and thoughtfulness seem to be generally characteristic of gifted children. There were no significant differences between the total gifted and the total average students on the following temperament traits: sociability, friendliness, and personal cooperation. Many think the development of these traits should be given special attention as it is felt that from this gifted group should come more of the future leaders and that these traits may be important in many leadership situations. In teaching these students it may be important to keep such temperament differences and similarities in mind and check the findings of studies like this one against the situation as seen in the classroom.

Since this study suggests that failure to keep constant the socio-economic level in making comparisons of the temperament of gifted and other children results in misleading assumptions about the superior adjustment of the gifted, it may be well to re-study some of the findings of Terman and others. Is it possible that Terman in *Genetic Studies of Genius* in describing the multiple superiority of the gifted child is simply describing children from the upper socio-economic levels? If this is so, many of our assumptions about the "differences" of the gifted which call for special educational approaches and methods will need to be reconsidered.

Bibliography

1. DAVIDSON, HELEN H., *Personality and Economic Background: A Study of Highly Intelligent Children.* New York: King's Crown Press, 1943. 189pp.
2. HOLLINGSWORTH, NETA S., & RUST, METTA A., "Application of the Bernreuter Inventory of Personality of Highly Intelligent Adolescents." *Journal of Psychology*, 44:287–93, October, 1937.

3. TERMAN, LEWIS M., and others, *Genetic Studies of Genius, Mental and Physical Traits of a Thousand Children*, Stanford, California: Stanford University Press, 1926, Vol. I, 648pp.

4. TERMAN, LEWIS M., and ODEN, MELITA H., *The Gifted Child Grows Up. Twenty-five Year Follow-Up of a Superior Group*, Stanford, California: Stanford University Press, 1947, Vol. IV, 448pp.

❦❦ Part Two

CURRICULUM CHANGES

DURING THE PAST FEW YEARS a dramatic change has taken place in the literature and meetings dealing with gifted children. We have been mercifully released from repeated and repetitive discussions of identification, definition, acceleration, and the effects of ability grouping. It is not that these topics do not hold interest, or are not of some importance, but rather that we more clearly realize that all of such discussions are preliminary; they do not strike at the heart of the issue.

What is the keystone issue? If gifted children need special education what changes should take place in the methods of presenting material and what changes should take place in the curriculum itself? After all, if something dramatically different is not going to take place in the school program why go through the bother of identification and definition of gifted students in the first place? Thirty years of research has made it crystal clear that ability grouping by itself is not a crucial variable. It is what happens after the grouping that determines whether the program justifies itself with positive results.

The great current interest in creativity and productive thinking has sharpened our concern for how material can best be presented to students in order to stimulate advanced thought processes. This too, while extremely desirable, is not enough in planning a program for the gifted. One cannot simply stimulate productive thinking in the classroom without being concerned about the structure of the content matter to be presented. Without such concern, the teacher, educated in methods to stimulate creative thinking, is literally all dressed up without anywhere to go.

It is the systematic organization of such content matter that has excited the interest of educator and scholar alike. Some of the projects reported here are heavily financed while others are not. They have in common an attempt to center on important issues in specific disciplines and in abandoning a child-centered, conceptually shallow approach. They represent a bracing dose of fresh air for teachers and educators who have been disenchanted by "enrichment."

The field of mathematics was one of the first to feel the impact of a new philosophy. Uncounted unhappy generations of gifted students had come to believe that mathematics was unexciting intellectually and totally irrelevant to their own lives. Except for the rare person with mathematical talent who refused to be bored or derailed by inadequate teaching, few gifted students emerged from secondary classes in algebra and geometry with a feeling that mathematics was an alive and exciting field of interest.

Under the direction of Dr. Max Beberman, the University of Illinois Committee on School Mathematics (UICSM) has been developing dramatic modifications of both the curriculum content of mathematics courses and also a thorough revision in the way in which mathematics is taught. The student becomes an inquirer searching after ideas instead of an unwilling calculator of a series of routine problems.

They have pioneered the teaching pedagogy known as the discovery method. A later article in these readings by Hendrix describes more thoroughly the procedure followed to foster this student discovery.

The articles by Suppes represented an adventurous step into the teaching of advanced mathematics concepts to intellectually superior children. Set theory as illustrated in the first article has now become widely accepted as one of the basic elements of much of the new mathematics curricula. Professor Suppes was one of the first to experiment with such curriculum and has spent a number of years devising the curriculum material now available.

The article on the use of the mathematical logic for the schools implies, in some ways, even a more drastic revision since it has rarely been taught below the university level. In demonstrating that it is possible, with proper organization of materials and choice of problems, to introduce such ideas to fifth and sixth grade gifted children. Suppes shows again that we have been unduly pessimistic about how much children can learn given proper motivation and a well-organized curriculum.

While mathematics was the first field in the new curriculum, the physical sciences were not far behind. The historian of American education will no doubt look at the present era in education as one deeply influenced by the activities of the Physical Science Study Committee and its financial angel, the National Science Foundation. Through funds from this foundation, a large number of major curriculum projects were started or encouraged. The first of these was the Physical Science Study Committee. These projects are important not only for their content but also because they brought into liaison internationally known content-area specialists and educators who had for a long time been facing each other somewhat antagonistically.

Another important change illustrated by this project was a dramatic change in curriculum emphasis. The goal is to teach for basic principles and concepts and to discard a curriculum based on children's interests or on haphazard attempts to add new segments of knowledge as new discoveries become known. In the opinion of these groups, such planning led to trivial, if interesting, science.

The third goal noted in the Finlay article is the deliberate attempt to encourage the student to act like a scientist by providing experimental kits, reference shelves of monographs, and other devices designed to enhance the development of scientific attitudes in the student.

While the past decade has seen numerous curriculum adventures in the field of the physical sciences and mathematics, the social sciences have been much slower in the development of broad new curriculum approaches for elementary and secondary students. This was due partly to the lack of available funds, a circumstance not faced by the physical sciences, and also to a lack of a sense of urgency in doing something about the curriculum and textbooks in this field.

The article by Senesh represents one of the more imaginative departures in the development of a curriculum in economics beginning at the first grade level to provide basic concepts in economics to youngsters of quite immature mental development. Senesh places a particular emphasis on what he calls the basic contour of economics and the necessity to build the curriculum around these contours. In this regard, the curriculum has a striking similarity to attempts in the areas of science and mathematics to provide the basic structure of key concepts that would reflect the major ideas in the content field.

It is something of a paradox that man, either individually or collectively, seems to be a stranger to much of the social studies curriculum below the university level. The rapidly expanding and maturing fields of psychology and sociology are conspicuous by their absence in many social studies programs. Curricula now in use stress physical geography, with some emphasis on the role physical geography plays in modifying the environment that man lives in. Since the gifted child is destined, from what we know of past research, to fulfill leadership roles in business, politics, scholarly work, science, and so on, it would seem to be a rather logical extension of the other curriculum ideas presented in this volume to suggest that more about *man* be inserted in the curriculum to help these youngsters grasp some of the important relationships about human behavior at a younger age than now possible.

The article by Ojemann represents an attempt to provide youngsters with the attitude of searching for causal relationships in human behavior. Ojemann points out that many youngsters are operating on purely surface phenomena dealing with human behavior and rarely consider the dynamic factors which may well lie beneath the surface, but which are crucial to the understanding of man in individual or in group settings. We can hardly allow new generations of leadership potential to be so limited in knowledge in these areas vital to human development or human survival.

The great thrust forward in curriculum development provided by the many new and extensive curriculum projects has been received favorably and with much tolerance for initial pilot planning and program tryouts. Eventually, each person, or group of persons, proposing a new curriculum must be called upon to subject his program to evaluation. The evaluation of a new curriculum, however, has many pitfalls that were only dimly seen when the first attempts were made. How does one determine whether a curriculum is effective or more effective than the one that has been replaced?

The initial temptation is to give achievement tests and compare differences between experimental and control classes. But what achievement tests are to be used? Certainly not the achievement tests based on the old curriculum which includes only a fraction of the knowledge and goals of the new. On the other hand, one cannot use the achievement test built to establish the goals of the new curriculum since this would be quite unfair to those students using the old program.

In short, achievement tests do not exist independent of the curriculum. They are useful only to the degree that they can measure the extent to which a curriculum meets its own goals. If the goals differ, as in the current instances, how does one then go about making some judgment or evaluation?

The article by Professor Atkin deals directly with these issues. His conclusions are fairly representative of those who have struggled with this problem and have attempted to produce a meaningful response.

Many of the consequences of these broad curriculum movements are yet to be determined. One clear change that is marked is the tendency to move away from curriculum development solely by educators at the state and local level.

For gifted children they provide, at least, the concrete statement as to what "enrichment" should be. The coherent presentation of the conceptual framework of a content field fits well into the goals of the educator for gifted children, and it is no surprise that they respond well to these efforts.

Another consequence is the tendency for these curriculum projects to lead to greater acceptance for ability or aptitude grouping. The higher the level of conceptualization that is being demanded in this variety of curriculum projects, the more prior knowledge and competence is demanded of the student. To be competent in concepts of the relationship between space and time, or to grasp the general historical concept of revolution, requires an extended foundation of previous knowledge. This, in turn, forces the educational program, sometimes against its will, to group the youngsters in terms of their various levels of background and sophistication in these content fields.

It is going to be interesting to follow the further development and influence of these projects on American education. The only prediction which would seem to be reasonable right now is that their influence will not be small.

❦ 8

The Physical Science Study Committee

Gilbert C. Finlay

THE PHYSICAL SCIENCE STUDY COMMITTEE was formed in 1956 as a group of university and secondary-school physics teachers working to develop an improved introductory physics course. The committee is developing interrelated teaching materials for physics in the secondary school. Materials intended for direct instructional use include a textbook, laboratory apparatus and a laboratory guidebook for students, motion picture films, and a set of ten achievement tests. Supporting materials include a four-volume teacher's guide and resource book, and a series of paperback books that provide authoritative science literature for students and adults.

To help teachers who are considering the use of these materials, the committee has encouraged the development of instructional programs that enable teachers to study the new course in detail.

For its various activities, the committee organized teams of university and secondary-school physics teachers. These teams blended teaching experience at several levels with deep insight into the nature and meaning of physics. The materials developed by these teams were used in classes and subjected to close scrutiny by the teachers who used them and by the committee's staff observers. The course materials were tried, evaluated, and revised for three years before they were released for general use in the fall of 1960.

The committee, in the course of its work, thought it wise to establish a permanent organization to provide for revision and related development. A non-profit corporation, Educational Services Incorporated, was formed. This corporation now administers the program of the Physical Science Study Committee.

GILBERT C. FINLAY, now deceased, was a professor of education at the College of Education, University of Illinois.

Science is becoming an increasingly consequential factor in the affairs of man. There are the practical goods: the hand-in-hand advance of science and technology continuously increases human potential for producing, transporting, communicating, healing. The attendant problems of social control and adaptation are pervasive and complex. In business, legislation, and statesmanship, the scientist increasingly is called upon to help unravel the social and economic implications of science. But beyond its technological goods and meanings, science as a humanistic study stands on its own terms as a dynamically stable system with its own ends and procedural styles. As a form of human expression, it is one of the triumphs of the intellect. It lends perspective and direction to other aspects of life. It is a system one can ill afford to ignore if one is to become a whole man in a world of whole men.

Physics, as a parent discipline, stands close to the center of our scientific milieu. What instruction in physics is appropriate for secondary-school students in the mid-twentieth century? The work of the Physical Science Study Committee is an attempt to answer this question operationally.

As an initial target, the committee chose to design a new course to fit into the current pattern of school curriculums. Physics is usually offered as a separate, elective subject for students in the eleventh or twelfth grade. In terms of prior measures of ability, these students are drawn mostly from the upper half of their classes, with the distribution of their abilities skewed toward the top levels. Some of these students will follow careers in science or science-related fields, and further work in science will be a part of their higher education. However, the careers of many secondary-school physics students will be in fields other than science, and they will do no further formal work in physics. The committee judged that the needs of both groups of students could be served with a single course.

The committee chose to plan a course dealing with physics as an explanatory system, a system that extends from the domain inside the atom to the distant galaxies. The course tells a unified story—one in which the successive topics are chosen and developed to lead toward an atomic picture of matter, its motions and interrelations. The aim was to present a view of physics that would bring a student close to the nature of modern physics and to the nature of physical inquiry. Finally, the committee sought to transmit the human character of the story of physics, not simply an up-to-date codification of the findings. The student should see physics as an unfinished and continuing activity. He should experience something of the satisfaction and challenge felt by the scientist when he reaches vantage points from which he can contemplate both charted and uncharted vistas.

Achieving these aims in a one-year course meant that coverage of the field of physics had to be sharply restricted in favor of a deeper development of ideas that are central to a comprehension of the fundamentals of contemporary physical thought. This deeper development meant carrying key concepts to higher levels than have been ordinarily reached in secondary-school courses. Deeper development also meant a more extensive exploration of the substructure of experiment and thought that underlies the basic physical principles.

The student is expected to be an active participant in this course. The textbook, laboratory experiments, and films were developed in a way that reflects this expectation. The course materials do not assert the ideas of physics, then illustrate their utility by exemplifying them in problems and in laboratory exercises. Instead, the student is expected to wrestle with a line (or with converging lines) of inquiry, including his own laboratory investigations, that leads to basic ideas. The power of the fundamental ideas is brought out partially in the student's work on carefully chosen end-of-chapter problems, but more important, the intellectual thrust of the basic ideas is brought out sequentially through using those which are introduced early to illuminate other ideas in a chain that comprises an introductory view of the structure of physics.

As one examines the changes that have occurred in secondary-school physics courses during the past few generations, one is likely to get the feeling that modern technology has found its way into the courses almost to the exclusion of modern physics. Such modern physics as has been worked into many courses is often limited to statements of some of the conclusions. There is little other choice without a preceding development of such subjects as dynamics, wave behavior, and fundamental electricity that is sufficiently penetrating to permit seeing modern physics as a logical synthesis of ideas emerging from a related structure of experiment, principle, and theory.

No one-year course can give an adequate account of both an expanding physics and the related technology. Planning a course that concentrates on either of these subjects still poses a selection problem of large proportions. As the magnitude of what might be learned grows rapidly, it becomes increasingly clear that the school at any given level, indeed in its entirety, can do little more than provide a base for further learning. The development of a mind is never ending. The function of the school is to provide a fertile start—such a start that the end of formal schooling does not mark the end of further learning. The central problem is to transmit those ideas and styles of thought that have the broadest applicability, the greatest power for further thought and activity. To this end, the Physical Science Study Committee judged it wise to shift the emphasis in secondary-school physics away from technology toward a deeper exploration of the basic ideas of physics and the nature of inquiries that can lead to these ideas. This choice was based on the premise that, for the future scientist as well as for the non-scientist, an introductory course that provides a grasp of the central ideas of physics and the kind of thought that lies behind them is more useful and rewarding than a course that emphasizes a somewhat more ephemeral technology. Technological applications have not been eliminated from the course. But they have been cut back sharply from the role they play in many secondary-school courses. While the course was not specifically developed with college preparation in mind, the course is regarded as providing a sound base for further work in physics.

In this course, experiments—whether they are performed by the student, analyzed in the textbook, or shown on film—are not used simply to confirm an earlier assertion. The laboratory experiments are designed to supply firm rooting for the growth of ideas by providing direct, nonverbal contact with relevant data. Hence, the most common use of laboratory experiments is to introduce a topic or to contribute to the early stages of its development. The students' laboratory guidebook keeps specific instructions to a minimum, directing the students' attention to key points by raising questions. The student is responsible for thinking out the nature and the meaning of what he is to do. The purposes of the experiments vary. Some are qualitative and give general familiarity and introductory experience with a set of phenomena. Many experiments are quantitative but differ extensively in the degree of experimental accuracy that is sought. Students should understand that prior knowledge and experimental purpose influence the precision required to secure new knowledge. Experimentation is a great deal more than establishing the third decimal place. In all cases, students are encouraged to establish or approximate their experimental error.

Clearly a student can have direct laboratory experience with only some aspects of physics. Careful selection of experimental activities can advance the student's understanding of the more important physical ideas. Moreover, presenting these activities in the spirit of experiments rather than as exercises should enhance the student's ability to analyze and appreciate experiments that he reads about or sees on film. Still further, the emphasis in the course on experiment and experimental style is meant to foster insight into the role of experiment in the generation and refinement of physical ideas. While some demonstrations are suggested, more emphasis is placed on experiments performed by students. The apparatus and the laboratory guidebook provide for more than fifty experiments, many of which include optional extensions to provide for variability among students and classes.

A great deal of what might ordinarily be called demonstration is provided by the films produced by the committee. Basically, the films are built around experiments. Films are used to bring to the classroom certain key experiments and a range of experiments that are likely to be too difficult, too time consuming, or too costly for students to perform or for teachers to demonstrate. For many experiments, films can bring the purposes, techniques, data, and analysis more directly within the students' purview than any other approach can. The films are planned with attention to the general aims of the course and to the particular choices that have been made in the development of related ideas in the students' laboratory and in the textbook. Because the films articulate closely with these resources and because most of the films assume that the viewer is familiar with earlier parts of the course, the scheduling of the films is a matter of consequence. The films are intended as take-off points for teachers and students. They are not intended to replace a teacher. As of October, 1961, forty-four films were available, and sixteen more were being completed.

Some films—such as those on the Millikan experiment, the Rutherford atom, and the Franck-Hertz experiment—are concerned primarily with the presentation and the interpretation of a complex experiment. Other films are more general in purpose and may use a dozen or more experiments or models to develop a set of related ideas. Such films are intended to help integrate and summarize a field of study. Films on crystals, on the relation between mechanical and thermal energy, and on frames of reference are examples. Finally, a few films are intended as introductions to major areas of study. Such films are meant to give the viewer perspective by taking stock of the array of phenomena that require explanation and by suggesting some of the central questions.

The films do not glitter. There is no background music, and there are no elaborate stage settings. They are frankly teaching films. It should go without saying that the experiments presented are scrupulously honest. The films are not impersonal, neither are they stylized in a personal sense. They present a number of real scientists, speaking in their individual ways to students, directing their attention to key points. In this quiet way, the films bring students into closer contact with a group of scientists as persons.

As supplementary sources of authoritative, scientific information, the committee is developing a series of paperback books. These books are appearing as the "Science Study Series." Some deal with individual topics in science or technology. Some are biographical, some historical. As of October, 1961, twenty books had been published in the series. More than thirty were in preparation, and others were planned. An interesting side light on the pedagogical application of these books is the occasional use of some of the foreign-language translations of the series as reading material for science-oriented students in language classes.

The content of the course of the Physical Science Study Committee has been described in somewhat greater detail in other sources (1, 2, 3). The course is divided into four parts. Part I is an introduction to the principal actor in the physical drama—matter—and its setting, time and space. The course begins with a consideration of the dimensions of time and space and how they are sensed. Through laboratory work the student sees how his senses can be extended by instrumentation and begins to develop a perception of the role, nature, and limitations of measurement. This perception is extended through films that go beyond the usual facilities for measurement available in school laboratories. Familiarity with techniques of defining intervals of space and time leads to a study of motion through space in the course of time. The student learns the relation between distance, velocity, and acceleration and how to move from one to another through graphical differentiation and integration. The use of vectors to represent these quantities completes this introductory view of the descriptive tools of physics. The course then turns to an introduction to matter, the substance of the universe. Here, the ideas of mass and conservation of mass are considered. The student examines experimental evidence for the existence and the size of atoms. In the laboratory he establishes an upper limit for the size of a molecule and sees how extensions of his experiment can lead to determining the size of an atom. The combination of atoms in molecules is studied, and the ideas of atomicity are extended through a consideration of the arrangement of atoms in solids (crystals) and in gases. A beginning on the molecular interpretation of a gas makes it possible to deal specifically with the idea of a physical model.

In Part II the student begins the process of observation of, and abstraction from, a family of physical phenomena; in this case, light. The natural development of the subject leads to an examination of a particle theory of light. This section of the course illustrates how models are abstracted from experimental observation, how they illuminate further investigation, and how they are established, modified, or rejected. Study shows that a simple particle model does not fit the behavior of light, and the course turns to another model, waves. Extensive laboratory experience with waves—first in one dimension on ropes and springs, then in two dimensions on the surface of water—shows similarities between wave behavior and light. A detailed study of interference establishes the wave nature of light.

Part III returns to motion, this time from a dynamical point of view. Again depending heavily upon laboratory work, and extensively reinforced with films, the course moves through the relation between force and motion, the story of the discovery of universal gravitation, and the conservation of momentum and energy. The generality of the conservation laws is stressed. The use of the conservation laws in situations where detailed observation of the motion is not possible (as in the molecular turmoil in gases) and emphasis on two-body interactions lay groundwork for exploring the atom in Part IV.

The atomistic character of matter is introduced in Part I and carried further in the kinetic theory of gases in Part III. Part IV develops the nature of electrical forces and energy; begins to bind together dynamics, electricity, and waves in a consideration of electromagnetic radiation; and returns with all these tools to an exploration of the structure of matter, atoms. Analysis of scattering experiments establishes a simple Rutherford model. Some of the inadequacies of this model are pointed out. The particle-wave nature of both light and matter is shown. Experiment discloses the internal energy states in atoms. The energy levels are explained in terms of standing wave patterns, and the course comes to a close with a quantum mechanical view in which both wave and particle characteristics are essential to an understanding of the structure of matter. In this part of the course, because of the difficulty of many of the relevant experiments, films carry a large share of the burden of presenting experimental evidence.

> The logical unity of physics has been emphasized in this course. As an alternative to covering the various fields of physics at the same level, the course employs earlier material to clarify that which follows. For example, ideas about waves and particles recur, each time to be carried further in a higher synthesis of ideas. This characteristic plus the exploration of concepts that are clearly unfinished, the tightly related student laboratory, the investigative approach in the films and the frequent analysis of experiments in the text all contribute to a perception of physics as a continuing search for order in a picture of the universe. This coherent, searching character of man's approach to building an explanatory structure of the physical world is one of the course's principal aims and chief pedagogical characteristics [1: 292].

The Physical Science Study Committee had its beginning early in 1956 in exploratory discussions, held first at the Massachusetts Institute of Technology and later at other centers. These discussions, led by Jerrold R. Zacharias of the Massachusetts Institute of Technology, established the desirability of rethinking the secondary-school physics program and made it clear that an adequate number of able secondary-school and university physics teachers would be willing to join in such an effort. In November, 1956, an initial grant from the National Science Foundation marked the official beginning of the project. The National Science Foundation has provided the principal financial support. The Ford Foundation and the Alfred P. Sloan Foundation have contributed to the support of the program.

By the time of the initial grant, informal groups had been established at Cambridge, Massachusetts; the Bell Laboratories in New York; the California Institute of Technology; Cornell University; and the University of Illinois. Several of these groups developed tentative outlines for a new physics course. A meeting of most of the people who had participated in these groups, together with other interested individuals, was held in December, 1956 (4). The proposals of the several groups were presented and discussed. General agreement was reached on a broad outline and on the major pedagogical characteristics of the course. Following the December meeting, several of the centers began to prepare detailed outlines and preliminary drafts for a work conference to be held during the summer of 1957 at the Massachusetts Institute of Technology.

About fifty people participated in the 1957 summer work session. Most of this group were high-school and university physics teachers. In addition, there were specialists in such fields as testing, film-making, educational administration, and editorial production. Work was begun on all parts of the project: textbook, laboratory experiments, films, tests, teacher's guides, the "Science Study Series," and instructional programs for teachers. The textbook and the laboratory programs were given priority so that enough material would be ready by the end of the summer to make it possible to use a preliminary version of the course in a few schools during the following year. Early use of the course in schools permitted an almost immediate application of classroom feedback to the problems of revising existing materials and helping to shape materials yet to be developed.

During the 1957–58 school year, eight teachers used preliminary versions of the course with about three hundred students. These teachers had participated in the committee's summer project, and they and their schools were in a position to work closely with other members of the committee in evaluating their teaching experience. During that first year, it was possible to supply teachers with printed versions of Parts I and II of the course, mimeographed copies of Part III, and the materials from which preliminary designs of the laboratory apparatus could be built. Formal materials for Part IV of the course were not available that year. Because of the newness and the tentativeness of the materials, few classes moved fast enough that year to get into Part IV. For those that did, the teachers improvised from their knowledge of the plans for Part IV.

This first year of experience in teaching the course was extremely fruitful. Because the number of classes was small, the committee's staff was able to work intensively with the teachers. In some cases modifications of approach were discussed and tried out on the spot. The over-all evaluation was highly favorable. Teachers and students found the course stimulating and were enthusiastic. The close relation between the laboratory and the textbook and the premium on student initiative in the laboratory were well received. The results of the preliminary achievement tests used that year indicated that students attained the desired levels. The desirability of revising the textbook and the laboratory program was pinpointed at various places in Parts I and III. Part II was judged as markedly successful. In that part of the course, teachers found that the mutual reinforcement of the textbook and the laboratory program enabled them to bring students to a deep understanding of advanced ideas on wave behavior. The year's experience also suggested the desirability of a change in the way in which the committee had expected schools to acquire laboratory apparatus. Originally the committee hoped that the use of simple designs of apparatus to concentrate on fundamentals would not only clarify the subject but make it possible for schools to acquire most of the necessary laboratory material locally with construction to be done by students. While the local acquisition of materials and local construction of apparatus were shown to be possible and instructive, shopping and construction time was costly. This excessive time burden on students and teachers was confirmed in the following year, and the committee turned to the development of easily assembled kits of pre-formed apparatus.

During the summer of 1958, five universities offered institutes on the course. The institutes were from six to eight weeks in duration. These institutes were organized under the National Science Foundation's regular program of support to institutes for teachers of science and mathematics. The institutes enrolled a few more than three hundred teachers. As a part of the experimental development of the course, the preliminary course materials were supplied without cost to any of these teachers who wished to use them during the following year, 1958–59. The course was used by about 270 teachers and 11,000 students.

The course materials available for that school year were not complete, but represented a considerable advance over the year before. The preliminary textbook included a partially revised version of Part I, and the textbook extended through the first half of Part IV. The committee was able to supply preliminary laboratory guidebooks and apparatus for Parts I, II, and III and a partial laboratory program and apparatus for Part IV. A preliminary edition of the teacher's guidebook was distributed for all portions of the course except the latter half of Part IV. A complete set of ten achievement tests was used. Although a number of films had been completed during the year, only a few were available for use in the schools at the most appropriate times.

The feedback from the larger number of schools benefited all parts of the program. Intensive feedback relations were maintained with a few schools. From the rest, information was derived from periodic reports, questionnaires, and regional meetings. Results from the administration of the series of achievement tests also contributed helpful information. In one school, a few students who had gone through the first three parts of the course in the previous year studied Part IV in the fall. This experience contributed several key ideas to the further development that winter of Part IV, which was used by a large number of students in the spring.

During the summer of 1959, about seven hundred teachers studied the course in fifteen institutes. For the 1959–60 school year, the course materials were provided at cost to schools that wished to use them and whose teachers had already taught the course or had studied in one of the institutes. That year about 560 teachers used the course with 22,500 students. Some of the teachers who had taught the course during the year before had moved to administrative positions, enrolled in graduate study, or had otherwise withdrawn (in many cases temporarily) from physics teaching. Of those who continued to teach physics, 96 per cent elected to continue with the PSSC course.

Except for the films (about thirty were available for use at the appropriate showing times), a complete set of preliminary materials was on hand. Feedback arrangements were the same as for the 1958–59 school year. The information gleaned from the use of the course in earlier years had already been used as starting points for some revisions of the textbook and the laboratory experiments, and these were tried out and studied. During the 1959–60 school year, the committee's major effort was directed to a complete revision of all printed materials and the design changes appropriate to the commercial production of kits of laboratory apparatus. By the fall of 1960 the textbook, laboratory guidebook, apparatus, tests, films, and teacher's guidebook had been turned over to commercial suppliers and were available generally.

The institute programs have continued to provide opportunity for teachers to study the course in detail. During 1960–61, the course was used by about eleven hundred teachers with forty-four thousand students. As of October, 1961, a conservative approximation of the number using the course in 1961–62 was eighteen hundred teachers and seventy-two thousand students.

Evaluation of the course has several aspects. The committee's own evaluations are directed toward the improvement of the course, not comparisons with other courses. The course differs sharply from most secondary-school physics courses both in selection of content and in style of development. Comparison with other courses is not a matter of evaluating the relative merit of different methods of teaching toward the same objectives. Rather, such a comparison involves questions as to the choice of the objectives themselves. Close scrutiny of the courses is enough to confirm this fundamental difference. Further confirmation comes from the few instances in which standard examinations have been given to PSSC students and PSSC examinations have been given to students in standard courses. The results show that the students have studied different courses. The sharp difference between the PSSC course and other courses has been recognized by the College Entrance Examination Board, which has provided separate examinations in physics for PSSC and non-PSSC students. Certainly it is possible to design an examination on which matched groups of PSSC students and students from other physics courses would achieve equivalent score distributions. This procedure would hardly provide a comparison. It would prove only that such an examination can be prepared. Comparative evaluation requires common objectives—common with reference to fundamentals of substance and intellectual style.

In terms of its own objectives, the committee judges that its present course is successful in the sense that it provides a context for teachers and students through which students have reached the desired goals. Evidence comes from several sources. Performance on the PSSC achievement tests speaks of the students' understanding of content and their power to handle ideas, to apply them broadly. In preparing the achievement tests, the level of difficulty was set so that an average performance of answering half the questions correctly would be regarded as satisfactory achievement. This goal was attained. On the qualitative side, the preponderant testimony of teachers and students who have used the course indicates that it sharply stimulates the development of more powerful styles of inquiry.

The difficulty of the course and its adaptability to students of varying abilities have been the subject of a great deal of discussion by those who have used and/or studied the course and by some who have not. The results of the analysis of achievement test performance by students from various levels of academic aptitude, as measured by conventional aptitude tests, clearly suggest that success in handling the ideas of the PSSC course is not limited to a narrow band of what, by traditional measures, might be called high-aptitude students. The testimony of a majority of the teachers who have used the course supports this view. Most teachers who have used the course feel that it is appropriate for the range of student abilities that typically has been enrolled in physics. Some teachers make the point that, for the less facile student, an exposition based on experiment rather than assertion is especially helpful. Of the teachers who have used the course, a clear minority feel that the course is too difficult for average students and prefer to restrict the use of the course to high-ability students. On the difficulty of the course, the committee is inclined to agree with the student who wrote that "the course is not for those who have difficulty tying their shoelaces." The course was intended to provide a challenging experience. Students and teachers say that it does. Most of them also say that it is highly rewarding. The committee feels that the course is close to the intended mark. Certainly other course structures could be developed that would provide a satisfactory secondary-school physics course. The present course is simply a stage in the development of one satisfactory course. Indeed, through Educational Services Incorporated, the committee expects to give continuing attention to the improvement of secondary-school physics.

The committee fell a bit short of reaching its objective of providing a one-year course. The course as it stands was prepared so that teachers could omit several sections without seriously undermining the material that follows. These are, however, omissions that most teachers will make only with regret. Without cutting, many teachers feel that the course should extend for more than a year. This problem is being met in various ways. Some teachers are making the possible cuts. Some schools are lengthening the time given to physics by teaching it for more than two semesters or by giving it more class time during the year. Some schools are trying early parts of the course in earlier science courses. The development of improved science courses at lower levels will be one of the factors influencing revision of the current PSSC course.

As of the fall of 1961, the committee has a number of on-going projects. To get information on what and when revison should occur, study of the use of the course continues. In this connection, it is now apparent that improvements in laboratory experiments for Part IV will be sought. The "Science Study Series" is being extended at the rate of nearly a book each month. The film studio of Educational Services Incorporated is continuing its work on the series of films that are a part of the course.

Another current activity is the preparation of a second battery of achievement tests to augment the existing series. In the development of these new tests, techniques are being investigated that are expected to extend the information that can be obtained on the nature as well as the over-all quality of student performance.

In the general area of evaluation, other studies are planned. While the course was not planned specifically as preparation for college work in physics, it is natural to look at students' performance in college physics for one source of evidence on the effectiveness of the course. With growing numbers of students completing the PSSC course in secondary schools and continuing physics in college, it will be possible to look more definitively than before at their performance in college physics. To the extent that certain college courses and the PSSC course share common goals, such studies should be helpful in reflecting the contribution of the secondary-school work. There have been a few preliminary studies of this kind, necessarily with small numbers of students. These studies indicated that PSSC students were at no disadvantage and in several respects (grades in one study; flexibility of thought and procedure, particularly in the laboratory, in another) were at an advantage.

Another kind of investigation that is being formulated uses the extensive element of design in the PSSC course (over-all story line with closely related textbook, laboratory, and films) to provide a context for a clinical study of learning over a year-long span. Among other things, this plan contemplates the development of non-verbal as well as verbal measures of performance.

The PSSC course was planned to fit a pattern in which physics is offered as a one-year course during the eleventh or twelfth grades. The achievement of adequate depth in a one-year course required the omission of many topics that logically could have been included and for which the course as it stands lays a powerful base. Some schools are able to offer a somewhat more advanced course either because of the time they give to physics, the ability of their students, the teaching of some of the earlier parts of the PSSC course in earlier grades, or a combination of these reasons. For such courses the committee is developing supplementary textbook material, laboratory experiments, and films for a series of advanced topics.

In the development in the PSSC course of an atomic model, some teachers have found a convenient structure for moving toward the integration of their work in chemistry and physics. Several schools have developed an integrated, two-year sequence in physical science using the PSSC course and a chemistry course, either one of their own devising or one of the chemistry courses recently developed with the support of the National Science Foundation. These activities are worth further effort and support.

The development, including trial and evaluation, of a course such as that of the Physical Science Study Committee naturally leads to suggestions on the kinds of educational experiences that might logically precede and follow such a course. A number of related activities, some of them partially stimulated by the work of the Physical Science Study Committee, have come into being. Some of those who shared in the PSSC project are now working with the Commission on College Physics, which is concerned with the improvement of physics teaching at the college level. Some are working in individual university centers on the improvement of the physics courses taught at their university. Some are turning to the problems of science instruction in elementary and junior high schools.

A great deal of interest in the work of the committee has been shown by science teachers and scientists from other countries. From the beginning, many foreign visitors have come to observe and discuss the project. This interest has led to the translation of the "Science Study Series" into other languages. Publication rights have been granted in eighteen countries. The books are now appearing in seven languages other than English. As the course materials neared completion, the interest of other countries in the use of the course (in some cases translation and use) quickened. By special arrangement, several dozen educators from abroad have attended some of the regular summer institutes of the Physical Science Study Committee. During the summer of 1961, staff members of the committee accepted three invitations to conduct intensive institute programs in other countries. These institutes enrolled secondary-school teachers, university teachers, and, in some cases, science supervisors. Two of these institutes, in Israel and in New Zealand, were national in character. One, in England, enrolled teachers from half a dozen European countries. One outcome of these institutes was that the course will be used soon in several countries. Also, during the past summer, a planning conference was held in Japan to consider the problems of translation and use of the course in that country. At the invitation of the Australian College of Education, a staff member of the committee recently spent a week in Australia discussing the course with teachers who were convened for that purpose. Similar visits have been made to India and to some of the African and South American countries. These various explorations of the applicability of the course in other countries have been supported by the governments of New Zealand and Israel; the United Nations Educational, Scientific and Cultural Organization; the Carnegie Foundation; the Asia Foundation; the Organization for European Economic Cooperation; the Office of Information Services; and the Organization of American States.

The course of the Physical Science Study Committee has proved to be rewarding to a large number of teachers and students. Clearly, its applicability is not confined to highly selected students or to a particular culture. The several hundred men and women who have contributed directly to the course have derived a great deal of satisfaction from that work. The committee looks forward to continuous improvement of the course.

Notes

1. Gilbert C. Finlay. "Secondary School Physics: The Physical Science Study Committee," *American Journal of Physics*, XXVIII (March, 1960) 286–93.
2. Physical Science Study Committee. *Physics*. Boston: D. C. Heath and Co., 1960, v–vi.
3. Stephen White. "The Physical Science Study Committee (3) The Planning and Structure of the Course," *Contemporary Physics*, II (October, 1960), 39–54.
4. This conference was reported in "Physical Science Study Committee, A Planning Conference Report," *Physics Today*, X (March, 1957), 28–29.

❦ 9

Set Theory in the Primary Grades

Patrick Suppes
Shirley Hill
Stanford University

THOSE VERY CRITICAL YEARS in learning any subject, the first three or four years of school, are now coming in for their share of the considerable attention being paid to curriculum revision in mathematics. Often ignored in revision and upgrading of mathematics teaching and materials, the primary grades are being recognized as the stage at which a strong foundation in mathematics can be and should be laid. But at this point, experimentation in new mathematics programs in the primary grades has not been as extensive as new programs at other levels of the elementary and secondary school.

One of the experimental projects that began in the first grade and has thus far concentrated attention on the primary grades is The Sets and Numbers Project in Elementary-School Mathematics at Stanford University. It is completing three years of classroom experimentation and this article presents a summary of its objectives and its progress.

OBJECTIVES AND CONTENT

In general, the major objective of the project is to develop and test a new mathematics curriculum for kindergarten through grade six. At the present time materials have been prepared for kindergarten and primary grades. Another grade is added each year in the program of classroom experimentation. The intention is to provide a program that is both mathematically sound and pedagogically simple, a program that stresses structure and foundations.

Although the major emphasis is on the development of the concepts, laws, and skills of arithmetic, considerable content from other branches of mathematics is added. For example, the inclusion of a substantial body of content from geometry is introduced by work with simple geometric constructions in the first, second, and third grades. As another example, by introducing the use of letters as variables, the program intends to include the basis for a smooth transition to the study of algebra. In presenting letters as variables in a simple context that requires no technique of solution, a familiarity with algebraic variables may be developed at the earliest stages of the child's mathematical education.

While the project takes the point-of-view that there are many sound and valid arguments for the addition of more and different content in elementary-school mathematics, and that evidence is ample that children of this age *can* learn much more mathematics than traditionally assumed, a goal of greater importance is that of providing a stronger foundation in arithmetic. It is believed that arithmetic can be taught with an emphasis on concepts, on structure and logical development, on laws, without sacrificing the development of skills. Thus the goal is to deepen as well as to extend mathematical experience of the child.

Another objective is to encourage precise and exact mathematical language. Vague and ambiguous terms are avoided, and technical vocabulary is used where appropriate. Experience has shown that technical vocabulary is easily learned by the young child when the idea represented is clear and explicit.

Particular attention is paid in the material to the sequence of development of concepts. The attempt is to move from the concrete to the abstract, from familiar ideas to new ideas in a series of small steps, each one building on the previous one.

The Concept of a Set and its Role

The central concept in the project materials developed for primary grades is that of a set. It is the foundation and unifying idea throughout. This concept is basic to the development of the idea of a number and operations on sets are introduced as fundamental to the parallel operations on number.

There are at least two major reasons to begin first-grade arithmetic with the explicit introduction of the notion of set and appropriate notation for sets and operations upon them. In the first place, sets are more concrete objects than numbers. At the same time operations upon sets are more meaningful to the child than manipulation of numbers. The putting together of sets of physical objects, for example, is a more concrete operation than the addition of numbers. The many exercises in the grouping of objects displayed in current books is in fact a recognition of the greater concreteness.

In the second place, the prior introduction of sets and additional explicit notation permits mathematically exact and precise definitions and concepts rather than the often vague and ambiguous notions encountered in explanations of relations between concrete groups of objects and the Arabic numerals. For example, students can learn a clear, simple, and meaningful characterization of numbers as properties of sets. Children who have learned the notion of a property can learn that a precise answer to the question "What is a number?" is, "A number is a property of a set."

The introduction of explicit notation is intended to make the concept of number clear. Ordinarily, we can only assume understanding of the relationship when we make the great leap in abstraction from groups of objects to numerals which name their particular number properties. The use of set notation allows the steps in abstraction to be made explicit. The first step in abstraction is describing a set in the following way:

The next step in abstraction is the N notation:

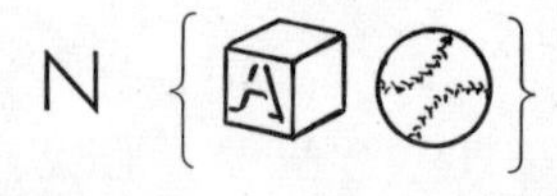

This notation names a number but at the same time it maintains the pictorial character of the set description. In this sense it may be considered a "transition" to the Arabic numerals. Here we have abstracted from the particularity of the objects in the set to the single property of number. We must assume that children understand this step if they are to have any understanding of the way a number is related to a set of objects. The notation makes the step clear and precise in a way not permitted by verbalization at the primary-grade level. The final step is to the Arabic numeral which in our example is:

2

Thus the explicit notation for sets introduces the student at the very beginning of his mathematical experience to the easily comprehended operations on sets—rather than to the more difficult and more abstract operations on numbers. Moreover the introduction of a notation for sets permits consideration of addition and subtraction of numbers without commitment to the particular notation of Arabic numerals.

Throughout the beginning materials, set operations are presented as concrete analogues to numerical operations. Union of sets and addition of numbers are presented in sequence, difference of sets and subtraction of numbers are presented in sequence, subsets and inequalities are presented in sequence, et cetera. The operations and relations of arithmetic are based upon and developed from the foundation concepts of operations on sets and relations between sets. Particular attention is given to mathematical sentences, equations, and the translation of English sentences expressing quantitative relations into mathematical equations. Introduction of commutative, associative, and distributive laws is an important part of the third-grade content.

It should be emphasized that it is not our intention to present an isolated body of mathematical content, but rather to present basic concepts and mathematical tools with which an integrated program of learning mathematical tools can be constructed.

Finally, it is believed that the introduction of such basic concepts as those of set and set operations will lead to greater understanding of the structure of the mathematics to be learned.

Background and Present Status

Classroom experimentation in the Sets and Numbers project has covered a period of three years. Prior to this, a pilot study in 1959–1960, involving four first-grade classes, was instrumental in the development of the first experimental materials.

During the academic year 1960–1961, twenty-five first-grade classes in the San Francisco Bay Area were included in the experimental program. Each of the classes used two workbooks, *Sets and Numbers, Book 1A* and *Sets and Numbers, Book 1B* as the total arithmetic program for that year.

The classes were taught by the regular classroom teachers. No special training or background in mathematics was presupposed. The teachers met for a general orientation at the beginning of the school year and approximately monthly thereafter for a discussion of progress and for purposes of introducing new materials to be covered. On the basis of the first year's results and, in particular, the comments and suggestions of participating teachers, the first-grade books were revised for use the following year.

During the academic year 1961–1962, the same classes continued as experimental groups in the second grade and twenty new second-grade classes were added. Two books were developed for these classes to test. They were *Sets and Numbers, 2A* and *Sets and Numbers, 2B*.

The program for first grade was considerably expanded. Eighty first-grade classes tested the revised Books 1A and 1B during 1961–1962.

The teacher training program again consisted of general orientation meetings at the beginning of the school year and monthly meetings thereafter. A major portion of each meeting was devoted to discussion of the materials with particular attention to suggestions for improvement. This resulted in revised versions of each of the second-grade books.

During the current academic year, 1962–1963, the program has included first-, second-, and third-grade classes. In addition, a basic book for kindergarten was prepared and is being used experimentally. At the present time, the experimental project involves 110 first-grade classes, 102 second-grade classes, 68 third-grade classes, and 20 kindergarten classes.

The usual teacher training program of orientation meetings and workshops, and meetings throughout the year has been supplemented by a course in background mathematics for teachers given at Stanford University as a part of the project.

Evaluation

One of the most difficult tasks of experimental projects in curriculum revision in mathematics is that of evaluating results. Many of the predicted and hoped-for outcomes are long-term objectives not necessarily immediately apparent. More critical to a program of evaluation, perhaps, is the difficulty in finding appropriate standardized achievement tests. With new content and new objectives, the available tests simply do not provide evidence concerning many of the goals of modern mathematics programs. This problem is greatly increased at the primary-grade level where it is underscored by the usual difficulty in measuring achievement in the absence of completely adequate skills of reading, writing, and comprehending verbal instructions.

Yet any experimental project must evaluate by objective measures. As valuable as the subjective evaluations of experienced teachers are (and these may well be the most important evaluation at this stage), they should be supplemented by objective measurement where possible.

The program of testing in the Sets and Numbers Project has consisted of a variety of types of tests. First, achievement tests are given all experimental classes at the completion of each book in the series. These tests assess the ability of the children to learn content covered in the materials and also provide evidence as to specific difficulties in learning particular concepts and skills.

Detailed results will not be given here but in general the achievement level on these tests is quite high. Table 1 gives the mean of scores on tests covering Books 1A and 2A. Specific analysis indicated that concepts of set and set operations are less difficult than number and number operations.

TABLE 1. ACHIEVEMENT TESTS ON BOOKS 1A AND 2A, 1960–61, 1961–62

Year	*Test*	*N*	*Total Possible*	*Mean*
1960–61	1A	620	73	61.40
1961–62	1A	1803	80	68.44
1961–62	2A	893	140	120.90

Although considerably more mathematics was presented to and, as evidenced by the test described, learned by children in experimental classes, the question reasonably is raised "Does the addition of content and emphasis on concepts mean a sacrifice in skills and techniques which have been traditionally the goals of arithmetic teaching?" To determine how well experimental classes can perform on traditional content, standardized achievement tests were administered to a group of randomly selected experimental classes and to matched control classes within the same districts. Classes were matched by administrators within each district on the basis of known variables such as student ability level, socio-economic level of neighborhood, staff capabilities. Children in control classes had been in a traditional program all year. The test was the arithmetic portion of the Metropolitan Achievement Test, Primary I battery (1st grade) and Primary II battery (2nd grade).

Tables 2 and 3 give results of the two tests and the significance of difference between means.

TABLE 2

Grade 1	*Exp. Group*	*Control Group*
Number	316	311
Mean Score	58.74	54.96
Median Score	60	56

Difference of Means Significant Beyond .001 Level in Favor of Experimental Group
t value = 5.50

TABLE 3

Grade 2	*Exp. Group*	*Control Group*
Number	287	208
Mean Score	55.7	56.0
Median Score	55.8	56.0

Difference of Means *Not* Significant
t value = .38

The standardized test results indicate that children using the *Sets and Numbers* materials scored at least as well or better on the traditional content as children who had been in traditional programs. In addition, a considerable body of content not tested by standardized tests was taught.

The relatively better results for the experimental group in the first grade appear to the project staff to be due primarily to two factors. One is the greater experience of the first-grade teachers in presenting project material to their classes. The other is the greater emphasis in the second-grade *Sets and Numbers* books on mathematical content and concepts not examined in the Metropolitan or other standard Achievement Tests. This means that the second-grade children in the project spent a relatively larger amount of time learning material on which they were not tested.

Future Plans

Our future plans call for continued experimental pedagogical experimentation with the concept of set theory in the primary grades. For the coming academic year we are planning to produce augmented editions of the Sets and Numbers books in order to test the efficacy of presenting primary-grade children with a very much enlarged body of curriculum materials. (The present books for the first-grade program contain 336 pages. In the augmented edition we are planning on a minimum of 600 pages.) We shall be able to report in the future whether or not considerable augmentation of curriculum materials have a significant effect on learning.

The second idea we would like to attempt to implement during the coming academic year is the idea of having the children make continual active behavioral responses during the usual period the teacher is introducing a new concept. Two kinds of observations and conclusions lead to this suggestion. The one is that with primary children the introduction of new concepts is very heavily dependent upon interaction of an extensive kind with the teacher. The second kind of observation is that in the ordinary discussion activity carried on by the primary teacher it is easy for a small percentage of the students in the class to dominate the discussion with their verbal responses. The aim of this part of our program is to see to what extent the introduction of new concepts in the mathematics curriculum can be facilitated by the use of rather carefully constructed response systems of the following sort. As part of her introduction to new concepts the teacher would use a slide projector. Each child would have on his desk a response panel consisting of three or four buttons, and he would be required to select the appropriate answer as shown on the slide. The elicitation of a response would be called for by the teacher with the beginning initial discussions of any new concepts, whether it be identity of sets, union of sets, difference of sets, addition of numbers, multiplication of numbers, etc. The teacher would have beside her on the table with the slide projector a panel that would show the response of each child together with a totalizer indicating how many children had answered the question correctly. Her own progress through the introduction of the concept and the widening of the basis of the discussion would depend on the class as a whole reaching a certain criterion of performance. What is particularly interesting to us is the possibility of the teacher's being able to control her own movement from one stage of the introduction of a concept to another on the basis of the class as a whole showing the criterion mastery of the concept. If our plans for the construction of such student response systems are successful, we hope to be able to report on their evaluation in the next year.

It should be mentioned that the writing of the workbooks has been supported by the Carnegie Corporation of New York, and the program of classroom evaluation by the National Science Foundation.

Finally, another related program of research is perhaps worth mentioning here. It is a program of psychological research on mathematical concept formation in young children being conducted under the sponsorship of the Office of Education. Much of this research is closely geared to the experimental teaching program in arithmetic. We have been particularly concerned to make a detailed analysis from the standpoint of learning theory of how children of ages 5 and 6 acquire, in a highly structured psychological experiment, the concepts of two sets being identical in the sense of ordered sets, the concept of two sets being identical in the sense of unordered sets, or the concept of two sets being equipollent, that is, having the same number of elements. An overview of some of the psychological experiments conducted during the past three years may be found in an article by Patrick Suppes and Rose Ginsberg in *Science Education*, Vol. 46 (1962), pp. 230–240.

❦ 10

Mathematical Logic for the Schools

Patrick Suppes
Stanford University

Statement of Project Goals

In general terms the aim of the program is to deepen and extend the mathematical experiences of the able elementary-school child at the broadest level of mathematics, the level of methodology and the theory of proof. The approach is through a study of modern mathematical logic, in particular that portion of it which is concerned with the theory of logical inference or the theory of deduction.

In modern times logic has become a deep and broad subject. Only in recent years have systematic relations between logic and mathematics been established and a completely explicit theory of inference formulated which was adequate to deal with all the standard examples of deductive reasoning in mathematics and the empirical sciences.

The concept of axioms and the derivation of theorems from axioms is at the heart of all of modern mathematics. The purpose of this project is to introduce the academically gifted elementary-school child to modern mathematics and mathematical methods at a level which is rigorous but simple enough in presentation and context to permit relatively easy comprehension.

Specifically, the objective of the project is to experiment in the teaching of mathematical logic to classes of academically talented fifth- and sixth-grade children. Thus it is considered a program in enrichment for the more able mathematics student and a supplement to the elementary-school mathematics curriculum. Questions of particular interest involve the capacity of children of the fifth- and sixth-grade age level to do the kinds

Editor's note. This material is adapted from a report prepared by Professor Suppes.

of deductive proof which are characteristic of modern mathematics, specific factors of difficulty, and the possible transfer of skills of analysis and correct reasoning to other subject-matter areas.

In the study of logic, the child may be introduced to a way of using language and ideas precisely. The emphasis is upon clarity and precision in thinking, upon rigor and consistency. The introduction of the concept of form and structure in language, and analysis of structure are integral parts of the child's study. Thus it is clear that while this project is considered a supplement to the program in mathematics in the elementary school, the application of the concepts and skills learned is not limited to this subject. The principles of logical inference are universally applied in every branch of systematic knowledge.

Logic has always been considered a college-level subject. The belief has been that it is too abstract for the understanding of the elementary-school student. Evidence is mounting that logic is not too abstract for the elementary-school child of age 10, 11, or 12, but on the contrary, that this age may represent the most propitious time for the introduction of abstract concepts.

The importance of the theory of proof and of the methodology of deriving theorems from axioms in modern mathematics cannot be questioned. Yet, development of the skills of deductive reasoning has been left largely to incidental learning in the school mathematics curriculum. The point of view represented in this program is that deliberate and well-planned teaching of mathematical logic will enlarge the scope of the able student of mathematics in the elementary school, and will provide a background for a deeper and more penetrating study of mathematics.

Pilot Study: 1960–61

A pilot study in teaching mathematical logic to a group of selected fifth-grade students from a public school near Stanford University was carried on during the academic year 1960–61. The class consisted of twenty-five students who were selected from the several fifth-grade classes in the school on the basis of their arithmetic achievement scores. The children were given the arithmetic achievement test during the seventh month of the fourth-grade year. All students selected for the logic programs scored at the sixth-grade level or above. The class comprised approximately 27 percent of the total fifth grade in the school.

The class met three or four days per week throughout the school year for periods of about thirty or thirty-five minutes each. It was taught by Dr. Shirley Hill, a member of the Stanford Project staff. Textbook material, composed of explanatory material and practice exercises, was written for and used by the class. Experimentation with this material and subsequent revisions resulted in a textbook in mathematical logic for the schools.

This book and its contents will be discussed in detail later in this report. The content covered by the pilot class is that which is contained in the first five chapters of the textbook.

Achievement tests given periodically indicated that this material is well within the capacity of the able fifth-grade student. Although the class proceeded much more slowly than the usual undergraduate class in college mathematical logic, the results indicate that children of this age are able to achieve a level of accomplishment comparable to college students in the skills of deduction essential to mathematical reasoning when instruction is geared to their level of experience.

Experimental Program: 1961–62

Eleven experimental classes of selected fifth-grade students began the work in mathematical logic in September, 1961. These classes represented eleven different schools in six school districts in the San Francisco Bay area. In each school approximately 25 to 30 percent of the fifth graders were selected by the administrators on the basis of general ability and high achievement in mathematics.

Each of the classes met three days a week for a period of between thirty and forty minutes. The groups were taught in each case by a classroom teacher from the staff of the school. During the summer of 1961, these eleven teachers completed a four-week intensive course in logic at Stanford University. The course was an introduction to mathematical logic with special emphasis on problems of teaching the subject matter to elementary school students. The book, *Mathematical Logic for the Schools*, was used in the summer course and was distributed to all experimental classes.

The organization of the work in the experimental classes followed the sequence presented in the textbook. There was, however, no effort to maintain a uniform rate of progress in all classes. The teachers were not committed to covering any specific body of content during the first year, but were encouraged to proceed at the pace they felt to be most appropriate for their classes.

For the academic year 1962–63, it is planned to continue the program in mathematical logic with this same experimental group at the sixth-grade level. In addition, a new group of fifth-grade experimental classes will begin the program. The plan is to continue to train teachers for the experimental classes during both 1961–62 and 1962–63. During the school year 1961–62, the original pilot class continued in the sixth-grade portion of the program as a pilot group. Additional materials were developed for this class, and this experimentation will lead to the second book in the series, *Mathematical Logic for the Schools*. Book 1 is a self-contained body of content, but at this point it is impossible to ascertain whether the experimental classes will be able to cover the entire book in a single year. The sixth-grade classes will simply carry on where the fifth-grade classes end.

In order to evaluate the achievement level of the experimental classes, a series of tests will be given to the experimental group and results compared with those from the same test given to the regular undergraduate college classes in mathematical logic at Stanford University. These tests will be examinations of achievement in the subject matter of mathematical logic. Evidence from the pilot class indicates that its level of accomplishment was comparable to that of a college class in mathematical logic, although its pace was much slower. It is suggested that the two groups, experimental and control, may be considered comparable in that both represent a selected group in terms of the general population. It is understood that this comparison of achievement will not be at comparable time periods but at comparable points of accomplishment in covering the systematically organized body of course content.

In addition to the achievement tests in the subject matter itself, general achievement tests will be given at the end of the first and second years. The purpose of the general achievement tests is to test for transfer and generalization, and these will be given to the experimental group and a matched control group of the same age and general intelligence from the same or similar school districts.

Textbook

The textbook used by all classes is *Mathematical Logic for the Schools* by Patrick Suppes and Shirley A. Hill. It contains explanatory material with an emphasis on exercises and examples. The organization of the book and its content is given below.

Part I: Sentential Theory of Inference

Chapter 1: *Symbolizing Sentences*—analysis of compound sentences; sentential connectives; symbolization.

Chapter 2: *Logical Inference*—rules of sentential inference; proofs, including conditional and indirect proofs; validity and invalidity; sentential interpretations; consistency and inconsistency.

Chapter 3: *Truth Tables and Tautologies*—truth-functional analysis; tautological implications and equivalences.

Part II: Logic of Quantification

Chapter 4: *Terms, Predicates, and Universal Quantifiers*—analysis of atomic sentences; symbolization of terms and predicates; atomic formulas; universal quantification.

Chapter 5: *Universal Specification and Law of Identity*—specification; derivations; logic of identity.

Chapter 6: *A Simple Mathematical System: Axioms for Addition*—derivation of theorems from axioms and definitions; commutative axiom for addition; associative axiom for addition; axiom for zero; axiom for negative numbers.

Chapter 7: *Universal Generalization*—derivation of general theorems with variables.

Teacher Training

The teachers for the experimental classes received a four-week intensive course in mathematical logic at Stanford University. For those teachers who continued into the sixth-grade portion of the program an additional course in mathematical logic was offered in 1962. At that time another course was offered for teachers who wished to begin the fifth-grade program.

Close contact is maintained between the members of the project staff and the teachers of the experimental classes. In order to achieve this objective, monthly meetings are held with the group, and a member of the staff consults with the individual teachers periodically.

11

Arithmetic with Frames

UICSM Project Staff
University of Illinois

The following article is based on work undertaken by the Project of the University of Illinois Committee on School Mathematics, a project which is primarily concerned with students in grades 9 through 12. Frequently the project staff is asked if its work with high school students has implications for students in earlier grades, that is, if in attempting to work out better ways of presenting material to high school students, ideas have occurred for better ways to present mathematics to elementary school students. It should be pointed out that the authors have not tested these proposals in grade school classes as they have their ideas for high school students. However, they have done some informal experimenting with groups of two or three children ranging in age from 4 to 11 years. The authors offer the following suggestions not as a comprehensive new program nor as answers to any specific problems, but rather as informal notes for those teachers who are interested in trying new ideas.

Although the ideas presented here were developed for use with all children, many teachers will find them particularly useful for enriching the program for the talented.

Arithmetic and Algebra

At each stage in their learning of arithmetic, children should be taught to do some of the corresponding kinds of "algebra." In this way, algebra grows naturally out of arithmetic and will not be viewed in high school

The ideas expressed in this article are derived from the experimental textbooks developed by the University of Illinois Committee on School Mathematics, published in 1955. Revised editions for students and for teachers are available from D. C. Heath & Company, Boston.

This article originally appeared in the April 1957 issue of the *Arithmetic Teacher* 4:119–24, published by the National Council of Teachers of Mathematics, a department of the National Education Association. It was reprinted with minor changes in the *27th Yearbook* of the *NCTM*.

as an entirely new subject in which, as too often happens, the student thinks he "adds and subtracts letters." If a student knows that

$$5 + 3 = 8,$$

then he is ready to be asked to replace the question mark by a numeral[1] in each of the following three sentences so that in each case the resulting statement is true:

$$? + 3 = 8$$
$$5 + ? = 8$$
$$5 + 3 = ?$$

Also, the student should be asked to make other replacements for each question mark so that the resulting statement is false. In an attempt to teach students correct arithmetic facts, many teachers make students feel that the writing of a statement such as:

$$5 + 6 = 8$$

is an immoral act. Rather than this, a student should examine such a statement and simply declare that it is false (or "not-true," as some children prefer to say). When the student gets to high school mathematics, he will no longer be able to live in a Utopia where false statements are never allowed to occur. Even in grade school work, he should be encouraged to make estimates and enlightened guesses; and when he checks such a guess, he must be prepared to find that he obtains a false statement which tells him that his guess was not good enough.

* * *

An early elementary school student becomes too accustomed to the pattern:

Add:

$$\begin{array}{r} 2 \\ \underline{3} \end{array}$$

and should work with, at the same time, the pattern:

$$2 + 3 =$$

[1] For a discussion of the use of the word 'numeral' as distinguished from the word 'number' and of the use of semi-quotation marks, see *High School Mathematics, 1st Course* (Boston: D. C. Heath & Company, 1964) or the article "Words, 'Words', "Words" " in the *Mathematics Teacher*, April 1955. p. 213.

and should also work with the pattern:

$$= 2 + 3$$

One of the authors asked several second and third graders if the following statement is true:

$$2 + 2 + 2 = 2 + 8$$

A surprising fraction of them, "knowing that only one numeral can follow an equals sign," transformed it mentally into '$2 + 2 + 2 + 2 = 8$' and said it was true. Students need to learn the symmetry of the use of '$=$' from the very outset of their work with it.

Using Frames

Rather than using question marks to give open sentences such as '$3 + ? = 5$', we propose the use of large frames. Thus, students might be told to first complete the following sentences, so that each of them becomes true, and then so that each of them becomes false.

Add:

$$\begin{array}{r} 3 \\ \square \\ \hline 10 \end{array} \qquad 4 + \triangle = 9$$

$$\diamond + 6 = 13 \qquad 10 = 2 + \hexagon$$

After students have carried out these exercises, ask them to tell for a given exercise how many choices for replacement there are which will give true statements. If you want to introduce a bit of philosophical discussion in the arithmetic class, ask them to support the answer that there is only one number such that replacement of the '$\triangle$' in '$4 + \triangle = 9$' by a name for this number makes a true statement. (A clever student may say that either a '5' or a '$2 + 3$' can go in the box to give a true statement. In this case he is giving two names for one number, just as 'William' and 'Bill' may be two names for one boy.) Also, ask them how many choices they have for replacements which give false statements. Accept answers such as "many," or better yet "as many as you please"; or "so many you couldn't even write them all down"; but do *not* introduce the word 'infinity'.

At a later stage, students can be introduced to sentences which contain more than one frame, for example:

$$\square + \square = 12$$

When more than one frame occurs, the student must learn an important rule of the game. Whatever numeral he puts in one of the two boxes above, he must put a copy of it in the other box. Thus, if he writes a '3' in one of the boxes, to follow the rule, he must write a '3' in the other box; he must not write a '3' in one of the boxes and, say, a '9' in the other. (This rule of "like" replacements holds only for frames having the same shape.) Again, ask students to consider how many choices they have for making '$\square + \square = 12$' into a true statement, and how many choices they have for making it false.

When students have had considerable experience in playing the "replacement game," they will find it convenient to use the word *satisfy* in such cases as:

the number 6 satisfies the sentence '$\square + \square = 12$'

and:

7 does not satisfy '$\triangle + 3 = 11$'

Notice that only one number satisfies '$\square + \square = 12$' although any one of that number's names could be used in changing the open sentence into a true statement. For example, if a student writes a '$5 + 1$' in each box, he has followed the replacement rule correctly and has found that the number 6 satisfies the sentence. At various stages of his work in arithmetic, it would be appropriate for a student to be confronted with a problem such as the following.

Find all numbers which satisfy each sentence given below.

$$⬡ + ⬡ = 16$$

$$\square + \square = 15$$

$$1 = \diamond + \diamond + \diamond$$

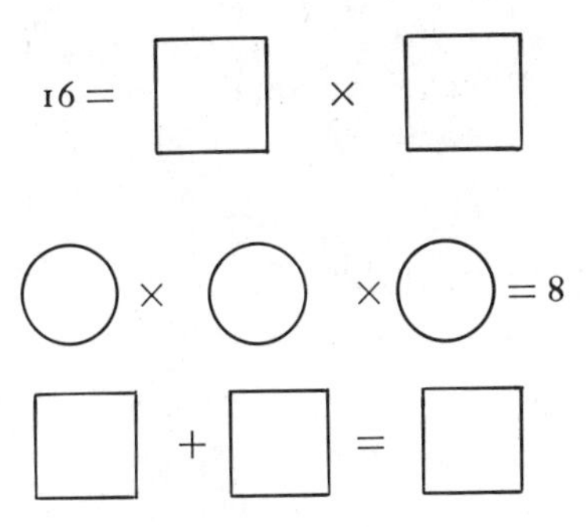

Such a list can be extended indefinitely and as much difficulty as is appropriate can be introduced using fractions, decimals, and "big numbers." Mixed in with such exercises should be some, such as:

$$5 + \diamond = 2 + \diamond + 3$$

which are satisfied by every number. The student has solved the problem when he points out that every number satisfies it (or that no number fails to satisfy it). The fact that every number satisfies such a sentence can be disguised as intricately as you please by increasing the complexity of the sentences. For example:

$$16.2 + \square + 8.3 + \square = \square + 36.9 + \square - 12.4$$

Also, among such problems should be some like this:

$$\hexagon + 3 = \hexagon$$

Here, the student should observe that there is no number which satisfies this sentence and, correspondingly, every number will make it false.

Another interesting exercise is:

$$\diamond \times \diamond = \diamond$$

Here, the student should observe that each of the numbers 0 and 1 satisfies the sentence and that no other numbers do. Encourage students to do a considerable amount of thinking in support of such a conclusion. Look for statements such as, "Well, if you multiply any number bigger than 1 by itself, you get an even bigger number. If you multiply a number between 0 and 1 by itself, you get a smaller number." Arrival at such conclusions can be promoted through questions such as:

> If you multiply 8 by a number larger than 1, what do you know about the answer?
> If you multiply 1,632 by a number less than 1, what do you know about the answer?

In fact, as soon as a child can tell *without computation* which of the numbers $\frac{981}{972}$ and $\frac{981}{972} \times \frac{981}{972}$ is the greater, and whether $\frac{2355}{2356}$ is greater or less than $\frac{2355}{2356} \times \frac{2355}{2356}$, you know he has discovered the important ideas mentioned above, whether he can give precise statements of them or not.

USING FRAMES OF DIFFERENT SHAPES

If you give the student an exercise such as:

$$10 = \square + ⬡$$

then, since you are using differently shaped frames, the agreement is that he may refer to different numbers in making the replacements. Now candidates for replacement are *ordered pairs* of numbers rather than single numbers. You might speak of candidates for the box as *first numbers*, and candidates for the hexagon as *second numbers;* since in left-to-right order the box appears first and the hexagon appears second. Thus, the pair of numbers with first number 7 and second number 3 satisfies the given sentence. Students will soon discover that, for every pair which satisfies the sentence, the pair obtained by interchanging first and second numbers also satisfies the sentence. They have discovered the *commutative principle for addition*, one of several fundamental laws of the number system.

Many first grade children through working with, say, parts of 5 as being 3 and 2, 2 and 3, 4 and 1, 1 and 4 have intuitively discovered the commutative or order property. (Students do not need to learn the word 'commutative' but they ought to be aware of the principle.)

If you give students a sentence such as:

$$10 = [4 \times \square] + ⬡$$

they will quickly find that it is not true that, for every pair that satisfies this sentence, the "reverse" also does. (But you can ask them to find a pair such that it and its reverse both satisfy the sentence. The pair (2, 2) is the only such pair.) Again, ask students to give pairs which "work"—that is, which satisfy the sentence—and pairs which do not work, and discuss the number of choices they have for pairs which do and for pairs which do not work. Problems of this type can be constructed with any desired degree of computational complexity.

Using Frames in More Places

Once students are familiar with the ideas of working with these differently shaped frames and when they understand the replacement rule, you can use frames in many more places. For example, when introducing students to the ideas of rational numbers, you can make precise the idea of, say, ⅓ by telling them that this is *the one number* which satisfies the sentence:

$$\square + \square + \square = 1$$

This is a step toward a mathematically sound formulation of the intuitive idea of cutting a pie into three pieces of the same size. (We are not recommending that the pie idea be dropped but rather that it be used to support the statement above.)

Frame-notation provides a convenient tool for the introduction of *inverse operations*. Students can learn that the number

$$5 - 3$$

is the number which satisfies the sentence:

$$5 = \hexagon + 3$$

Thus, students come to realize that two ways of setting the same problem, or, more precisely, two sentences which are satisfied by the same number are

$$5 - 3 = \diamond \quad \text{and:} \quad 5 = \diamond + 3$$

Similarly, when students are introduced to division, they can learn that the number $6 \div 3$ is the number which satisfies the sentence:

$$6 = 3 \times \square$$

When you present the idea of square root, students can learn that $\sqrt{9}$ is the number which satisfies the sentence:

$$\hexagon \times \hexagon = 9$$

You may move in another direction which is not common in grade school but which we think might be profitably undertaken, particularly in the later grades. You can give students problems which become more difficult, as indicated by the following sequence. Of course, you would give many more problems than those listed, taking several days in going from problems like the first one to problems like the last one.

$$5 + \square = 13$$

$$10 = \hexagon + \hexagon + 3$$

$$\frac{1}{2} = \left[2 \times \diamond\right] + \frac{1}{4}$$

$$\left[2 \times \square\right] + 6 = 12$$

$$\left[\frac{1}{3} \times \diamond\right] - 4 = 1$$

$$\frac{\left[2 \times \square\right] + 3}{5} = 3$$

$$\left[2 \times \square\right] + 1 = \square + 4$$

You will realize, of course, that students are solving equations in one variable. Students enjoy solving these equations as straight puzzle problems, asking themselves, "Can I find a number which satisfies it?" *Do not spoil their fun by giving rules for solving equations.* Let each student work out his own methods, and discourage attempts to give procedures for obtaining answers, such as transposing or dividing both sides, etc. Tell students that a method which they work out for themselves will be more meaningful and longer remembered than one which they are told by teacher or classmate. Again, it should be noticed that here is another method for giving practice in computation as well as preparing a student for a real understanding of algebra.

Frame-notation[2] is suggestive of many game-type activities which should appeal to elementary school children. Here is one which includes a self-checking feature. The student is given a list of "equations" such as:

$$\begin{aligned} &(1) \quad 4 + \triangle = 7 \\ &(2) \quad (9 \times \triangle) + (2 \times \square) = 37 \\ &(3) \quad 4 \times \square = (6 \times \square) - \diamond \\ &(4) \quad (3 \times \diamond) + 12 = (4 \times \diamond) + 2 \end{aligned}$$

His first task is to find a number which satisfies (1). He discovers that such a number is 3. So, he writes a '3' in the '△' of (2) and obtains:

$$(2') \quad (9 \times \boxed{3}) + (2 \times \square) = 37.$$

Next, he must discover a number which satisfies (2'); 5 satisfies (2'). So, he writes a '5' in each '□' in (3) and obtains:

$$(3') \quad 4 \times \boxed{5} = (6 \times \boxed{5}) - \diamond$$

10 satisfies (3'). Sentence (4) is so constructed that it is satisfied by 10.

Conclusion

As indicated in our opening remarks, the suggestions made in this article do not prescribe a new mathematics curriculum for the elementary school. But they do reflect the belief that children are willing to spend time on mathematics for the sheer intellectual challenge it can be made to offer. Such challenge is present whenever a child is encouraged to use his imagination and intuition. Games which are rich in mathematical (and not necessarily complex computational) content almost always contain challenges to which children respond.

[2] In preparing lists of exercises in duplicated form (by spirit or stencil duplicating processes) you will find it convenient to use a template containing various sizes of frames (circular, triangular, square, and hexagonal). You can make such a template out of stiff cardboard or obtain one from a drafting supply house.

❦ 12

Basic Approaches to Mental Health: The Human Relations Program at The University of Iowa

Ralph H. Ojemann

SOME YEARS AGO when we were making observations of parental and teacher behavior toward children, it was observed that parents and teachers tended to deal with child behavior as a surface phenomenon instead of taking account of the factors underlying or causing the behavior. Observation also tended to indicate that such an approach to behavior tended to produce conflicts and emotional strains in both adult and child.

For example, if a child attempted to overcome a feeling of inadequacy by "pushing" to be first so often that it interfered with class activity, the teacher who approached this behavior as a surface phenomenon would try to stop it by such methods as reprimanding the child, making him go to the end of the line, or sending him out of the room. She tended to do this without thinking about or inquiring as to the causes of the behavior. Since the feeling of inadequacy remained in spite of the scolding, going to the end of the line, or leaving the room, the child would still be under a strain and would attempt more vigorous action or a different approach. The teacher would soon observe that her attempts to stop the behavior were not successful. She would tend to intensify her attempts to stop the pupil's interfering behavior and the whole round of strains would rise to a new level.

Observation of the behavior of parents toward children tended to reveal a similar situation. Analyses of parental behavior often revealed a sequence somewhat as follows. In the early years of the child's life, parents

RALPH H. OJEMANN is Director of the Preventive Psychiatry Research Program of The University of Iowa, Iowa City.

would try to control him by telling him what to do, punishing him, coaxing him, and so on. When these procedures failed after years of trial some parents would give up. This left the child to his own devices for meeting problems, and he often failed to find satisfying and cooperative solutions. Other parents would doggedly persist, only to meet with increasing resistance and conflict.

What the Early Observations Suggested

An analysis of such behavior on the part of parents and teachers suggested that if they could extend their insight into an appreciation of the causes of behavior and change from a surface approach to an approach that takes account of the dynamics of behavior, the chances of blocking strong motivations in the child (and also in themselves) would be lessened and the chances for cooperative or mutually satisfying interaction would be increased.

A test of this hypothesis was made in the case of teachers in a study by Wilkinson [*13*]. Through the use of an experimental and control group it was shown that as the teacher acquired more insight into the backgrounds, ambitions, worries, and concerns of pupils, conflict between teacher and pupil tended to lessen and the pupils' attitudes toward school tended to change in a more favorable direction.

A close examination of the idea that teachers and parents can guide children more effectively and produce less emotional conflict if they approach the child's behavior in dynamic terms suggested that we were dealing with two cases of the larger problem of the relation of one person to another. The reactions of a teacher toward a child or a parent toward a child are essentially reactions of one person toward another. This observation suggested the question, will the hypothesis hold in any human relationship? If we change children to approach behavior dynamically, will that help them in getting along with adults and with their associates?

When we examined the whole problem still more closely we noted another aspect. After a child learns about the factors that underlie behavior, theoretically he could apply this learning not only to the behavior of others but also to his own actions and to the guiding of his own development. For example, if he learned that over-aggressive behavior is often motivated by a feeling of inadequacy, and if he learned something about how feelings of inadequacy develop and how they can be overcome, he would have something to help him interpret his own over-aggressive behavior or his own feelings of inadequacy. The question then became, if we change children so that they appreciate the differences between the surface and dynamic approaches to behavior, will that affect their relationships with others and their relationship to themselves?

This question had two parts. (1) Can children acquire an appreciation of the differences between the surface and dynamic approaches to behavior and apply the dynamic approach in their relations with their parents, teachers, other adults, in their relations with their associates, and in guiding their own development? (2) If they can learn and can be motivated to apply, will that reduce the emotional conflicts and increase the amount of mutually satisfying interaction in these relationships?

This question, with varying emphases on the several aspects, was studied in the investigations by Morgan [*6*], McCandless [*5*], Bate [*1*], and Stiles [*11*]. In summary, these investigations showed that children in the elementary and secondary grades can learn the beginnings of the dynamics of behavior, that they can learn to apply this knowledge in their relations with others, and that the process of learning about human behavior can be greatly extended on the school level.

The Place of Education in Human Relations in the School

When it became fairly clear that children can learn to approach behavior in terms of its causes, considerable thought was given to the next problem that suggested itself, namely, how can the material about behavior be inserted into the school curriculum?

Two approaches could be made. One would be to introduce a separate course on human relations. This is perhaps the first suggestion that occurs. When we studied the problem, however, several questions arose.

When we looked over the various "core" areas in the school curriculum we noted several that dealt rather directly with human behavior. Examples are social studies, English (human behavior in literature and writing), home economics (family relationships), and guidance. How did it happen that in spite of these opportunities to study human development people grew up with a surface approach to behavior as in the case of the parents and teachers we had observed? Why is the surface approach so apparent in our culture?

A careful study of this question led to an examination of the content and method of the several subjects as now taught in school, and this revealed an interesting situation. It can perhaps best be described by an example from community civics. When we examine the discussion in the ordinary civics book of such a problem as crime, for example, we find a discussion of how the police force is organized, its function as prescribed by law, methods for detecting and apprehending the criminal, and the system of courts, training schools, and prisons that have been developed. We may find a short discussion of the fact that crime is somewhat associated with economically underprivileged conditions.

But all of this approaches crime as a "surface" phenomenon. We can show this by considering the questions we would ask if we approached criminal behavior in terms of its causes. If we do that we would ask such questions as these: Are the ways in which the police and the courts handle a criminal such that after they apprehend him they try to find out what caused the behavior and then take the causes into account in their reactions toward him? Do they try to find out in a given case whether the causes are such that the criminal can be rehabilitated into a self-respecting cooperating citizen and not be a constant threat to other members of society, or if he cannot be rehabilitated is he then effectively isolated? In other words, do the present systems that society has set up study the criminal to find out the causes of his behavior and base their treatment of him on those findings?

Furthermore, if criminal behavior is caused, then real protection from the criminal requires that the community find out and change those conditions that produced him. Real protection—both in the sense of protection from direct damage to life and property which the criminal may inflict and also in the sense that taking care of criminals is a drain on the other citizens—comes when people in the community are aware of the forces that tend to produce crime and seek to change those forces.

In considering what the forces are we will have to go beyond the observations that poverty and similar conditions are somewhat correlated with crime and ask the more penetrating question—How does it happen that some persons living in a given environment become criminals, while other persons living in the same home and same neighborhood do not? But these questions are not considered in the usual text. The treatment is largely surface in character.

We could give other examples illustrating the same point. In short, much of the treatment of human problems in civics teaches the "surface" approach. What is true for civics also tends to hold true for the other social studies. Stiles [*10*], for example, found in analysis of the material on human behavior in 15 social studies readers used in the elementary school that less than one per cent of the selections treated human behavior in the dynamic way. Much of the treatment is of the surface variety.

The question now becomes—Under what arrangement do we have the most effective learning conditions? Do we have it if (a) we have a surface approach to behavior in the usual school subjects and a dynamic approach in a separate course on human behavior, or (b) if we have a dynamic approach wherever human behavior is discussed?

It is well known from studies on learning that changes are made most effectively when that which the child learns is applied consistently in a variety of situations. This suggested to us that we may profitably experiment further with the possibility of changing the content of school subjects from a surface to a dynamic treatment. Accordingly, studies were undertaken to determine how the material on the dynamics of behavior could be integrated into such areas as social studies, English, guidance, home economics, and others. Also, studies were undertaken to see how and to what extent the child could apply the dynamic approach in his relations with his associates and in guilding his own development.

In addition to school influences, there are the home influences. A child learns from the way his parents act toward him. Just as in the case of the teacher, the parent can work with the child using a surface approach or a more causal approach. If he uses principally a surface approach he is demonstrating to the child a non-causal method of working with others which the child will also tend to adopt. We have evidence [7] that children learn early in life a surface approach to behavior.

Such an analysis of the problem indicated to us that if we wanted to develop causally-oriented children, we needed classrooms equipped with teachers who both teach causally-oriented content materials and practice the causal approach in the daily relations with pupils. It would also help if the home environments of these children practiced the causal approach at least in some measure. We have attempted to develop such classrooms and homes.

Under our general plan, the program, by arrangement with a school system, provides summer fellowships so that selected teachers can attend an intensive training program. This program is designed to familiarize the teacher-students with the differences between surface and causal approaches, to help them apply the causal approach to the daily activities in the classroom, and to develop skill in teaching causally-oriented materials.

A supervisor of teachers, on the Preventive Psychiatry staff, works with the teachers throughout the year, holding a series of conferences with each. During the summer training program, each teacher assists in the preparation of teaching materials for his own classroom. With the supervisor's help he continues this adaptation of materials for classroom purposes throughout the year. We thus obtain a group of classrooms for our laboratory, each equipped with a causally-oriented teacher and appropriate curricular content.

Examples of Curricular Experiences

To provide a more detailed picture of the integrated program as presently conceived, it may be helpful to examine some of the actual learning experiences that are provided at several age levels. Examples for this purpose will be drawn from two age levels, namely, primary and intermediate.

1. *Examples of Experiences at the Primary Level*

A. Demonstrations furnished by the teacher's behavior. At each age level, as has been indicated, the child is influenced by the behavior of the teacher as well as by what he hears or reads. How the teacher handles the day-to-day social situations that arise in the classroom and on the playground, the extent to which the teacher seeks to know the child's ambitions, concerns, and abilities and makes use of this information in planning his program of work and understanding his behavior before dealing with it, are examples of experiences that affect the growth of a causal orientation.

This training of the teacher to practice the causal approach is an important part of the program at all age levels and the primary level is no exception.

Furthermore, as soon as the child has some appreciation of why a situation has to be understood before it can be reacted to logically, the teacher can take the simpler situations that arise and work them out with the class to involve the children in a practical application of a causal orientation. It is important that the teacher choose only the simpler situations at the beginning, for a careful grading as to difficulty is as important in learning human behavior concepts as it is in learning other concepts.

B. Use of narratives. To help the primary child develop an appreciation of the differences between the non-causal and causal approaches (at the primary levels the teachers have labeled the approaches the "non-thinking" and "thinking" ways), a variety of materials have been developed which can be read to the child and discussed with him. One type of material consists of stories in which the non-causal and causal procedures are contrasted. Listening to the narratives and discussing them provide vicarious experiences for learning the differences between the two ways of living.

Each narrative describes some behavior situation. After the situation has been set forth, some character in the story begins to make a surface approach to it, then rethinks his proposed reaction and makes a more causal approach. Some of the ways in which the behavior may have developed come out and one of the characters in the narrative acts in the light of these data. The situation has a reality about it in that someone begins to make a surface approach which children in our culture experience quite frequently. But, it also introduces a new way of living—a way that takes account of the meaning or the causes of behavior instead of its overt form.

For example, in one situation a boy gets into so many fights that something has to be done. The teacher in the story is about to deal with this in the usual way when he recalls that such things do not occur of their own accord. He does a little probing and before long it comes to light that this boy has been teased a great deal because he had to go home immediately after school each day to help take care of his baby sister and didn't have time to play with the other children. When the teacher learns this, he takes measures to work out this basic problem.

To help the child develop a more generalized conception and to prevent him from thinking only of incidents involving himself, situations were developed involving children older and younger than himself and children from quite different environments. There is some observational evidence that situations involving people different from the child tend to be less emotionally charged and therefore less difficult for the child to consider causally in the early discussions.

Each narrative is preceded by a short introduction for use by the teacher. After the reading of the story there is a discussion. The purpose of this discussion is not only to recall the incidents of the story, but also to bring out the differences in procedure when one thinks of causes as contrasted with principal attention to the overt form of behavior. The discussion is also designed to consider alternative ways of meeting situations and some of the probable effects of these alternatives.

It is suggested to the teacher that this material furnish part of the offering in the regular "story period." Under usual school conditions, the material read in the story period deals with various objects and events in the child's environment. Some of it deals with physical objects, some of it deals with people. It is suggested that material dealing with people be heavily weighted with the causally-oriented materials described. The causally-oriented stories are thus part of the primary child's story period content.

C. Use of expositions to help understand and appreciate the work of the teacher and other persons with whom the child interacts directly. An example of this type of material is a leaflet entitled "The Work of the Teacher." This is a simplified discussion contrasting the conception of the teacher as "someone whose main job is to check up on you" with the conception of "a guide to help you learn." This material is designed to be read by the teacher to the class and talked over with them. The logical implications of the "guide to help you" concept are described, including what alternatives are available to the child and their respective probable consequences when he finds his learning experiences not challenging. Included also is a discussion of how it may help the teacher to "tell her when something is worrying you."

The purpose of the material is to help the child gain some understanding of the behavior of the teacher, her feelings, and her methods. It is also designed to help the child begin learning that he has a part in arranging his social environment.

Similar material has been prepared to help the child gain some appreciation of the work of parents and other adults in his social environment.

2. *Examples of Experiences at the Intermediate Level*

A. The behavior of the teacher. Since pupils at the intermediate levels can read, syllabi, work sheets and other material to be read by pupils can be prepared. However, at this level as at the primary level, the pupil also learns from what he observes of the behavior of the teacher in the daily interactions with the class. Hence, it is recognized in the integrated program that the teacher's daily behavior is an important part of the learning experience at the intermediate level as well as at the primary level, and the plan includes training of teachers at this level also in practicing the causal orientation. A pamphlet prepared for the National Education Association for use by teachers reflects this recognition.[1] In its full development, the integrated plan expects that all teachers will apply the principles of human development in their daily work in the classroom.

At this level there is also the opportunity to help the pupil take some responsibility for his own development. The discussion of the work of the teacher, referred to in the description of sample materials at the primary level, is extended to include a consideration of how the pupil can help to build up his cumulative record for the school, in what areas he can keep the teacher informed about his attitudes and feelings, and how he can apply what he is learning to his own behavior.

At this level also there is the possibility of using the room council as a laboratory in which the child can apply the causal orientation in a real life situation. Since in the integrated plan the subject matter areas of social studies, health, and reading incorporate material designed to enrich a pupil's conception of the dynamics of behavior, and since he is encouraged to apply the enriched conception to situations arising in the room council, it will be helpful to indicate how the subject matter areas make their contribution before describing the use of the room council in detail.

B. Teaching causally-oriented social studies. In elementary social studies each of the major topics can be developed in terms of the basic factors operating in the behavior of the people involved.

The following examples will illustrate this. As an introduction to 5th grade social studies, two teachers[2] prepared the following introduction:

I. Introduction
to
Fifth Grade Social Studies

This year we are going to try to look at Social Studies in a little different way. In Social Studies we discuss problems about people. It will help us to understand these problems more fully if we know something about why people act as they do.

This little booklet is to be used with your textbook in Social Studies to make it possible for you to learn more about the behavior of people and what the effects of their behavior are.

We will want to find out how situations come about that cause people to act the way they do.

1. What are the needs the people are trying to satisfy?
2. What methods are they using to work out their feelings?
3. What are the effects on other people as a result of the methods chosen to work out those needs or feelings?
4. What might happen if other methods were used?

[1] Ojemann, Ralph H. Personality adjustment of individual children. #5 *What Research Says to the Teacher*, NEA, Oct., 1954.

[2] Appreciation is expressed to Ann Pavlovsky and Marian Kennedy.

These questions are then developed in the discussion of historical events in subsequent units.

Attitudes of Participating Teachers

Our program brings up two groups of questions. The first group relates to procedures: How does the plan work? What is the attitude of the teacher toward it? Can teachers be interested in cooperating in such an enterprise? Do the teachers resist training in mental health principles?

Thus far, we have worked with primary, intermediate, and secondary school teachers. At the present writing, we have a group of 15 primary, 15 intermediate, 11 secondary teachers, and 3 counselors drawn from three school systems. They have participated in the summer program and have helped to revise various aspects of the curriculum to develop in the child a sensitivity to the causes and consequences of behavior. For instance, instead of being content with the usual textbook statement that, unlike boundaries between many European countries, the United States–Canadian border has never been fortified, they prepared a discussion, based on available studies of conflict and cooperation, on some of the probable underlying factors in producing the United States–Canadian relationships. The counselors have helped the secondary teachers extend their knowledge of the children in their classes.

The fact that we have had more requests for inclusion in the program than we can accommodate indicates that the teachers on the whole have a positive attitude toward it. Those who have been accepted have cooperated enthusiastically.

Something we learned in our early work may provide a clue to at least part of this cooperation. While most presentations of mental health for teachers today stress the motivating forces operating in the child, little emphasis is given to the problem of how these forces can be expressed constructively under classroom conditions and how the teacher can accept her past mistakes. One of the hypotheses underlying the approach in our program is that much of the resistance appearing in work with teachers arises from the frustration a teacher feels when she learns about a child's needs but does not see how she can meet them under classroom conditions. In our work with teachers we point out these problems early in the program, on the theory that if the teacher realizes we are aware of his problems and are interested in helping him resolve them he will feel less frustrated. As the program has progressed we have found this to be true. Always we attempt to increase the security and self-respect of each individual member of the program by working *with* the teachers rather than telling them.

Can a teacher help children in elementary and secondary schools take a more understanding approach to social situations? If so, what effect does this have on the children? Does it make them more, or less, secure? More, or less, able to develop satisfying relations with others? We have evidence that significant changes have been produced throughout the primary and intermediate grades. This evidence has been reported in several studies [*3*, *9*, *12*].

A typical example may be found in some of the data obtained from our experiments with the 4th, 5th, and 6th grades. At each level a causally-trained teacher was matched with a teacher without such training from a nearby school, who served as a control. The matching was according to sex, age, training, and years of experience. Similarly, the children in the respective classes were equated as to intelligence. The experimental group was like the control group except that the control teacher did not participate in the summer training program and did not use causally-oriented curricular materials.

At the beginning of the school year all the children were given two causal-orientation tests. In one of the tests, the child was presented with a series of social situations to which he was asked to suggest a solution. The possible reactions ranged from arbitrary, judgmental, and punitive, such as: "It serves him right—he should be made to stay in"; to an awareness of possible complexity, such as: "The teacher should find out more about this."

In the second test, another series of social situations was presented, each followed by a series of statements with which the pupil was asked to indicate agreement or disagreement. Some examples are: "It wouldn't make much difference what method the teacher used to make him stop (bothering others) so long as he stopped bothering others." "Since these boys do the same things (described in the situation) they are probably all alike in most ways. If another boy disobeyed his father the same way, his reason would be the same as Jack's."

The children were given tests again in the spring and the results of the experimental and control classes compared. In all grades a statistically significant change appeared in the experimental group but not in the control group.

Thus it appears that our laboratory, which consists of a teacher trained to be sensitive to the dynamics of behavior and to demonstrate this sensitivity in the daily living in the classroom and using a curriculum which incorporates these principles, is producing a degree of causal orientation among children.

Does the new orientation help causally-oriented children make more satisfying adjustments to their environment? We have various kinds of data to throw light on this question. For example, children from both the experimental and control groups were given the anti-democratic tendency scale test developed by Gough, Harris, Martin, and Edwards [*2*]. This is essentially a measure of authoritarianism.

A detailed analysis of the results [3] obtained from the experimental and control groups showed a significant difference between the two groups on both scales. The causally-oriented children showed significantly less authoritarianism. It thus appears that as children become more aware of the dynamic complexities of human motivation and behavior, their attitudes toward others begin to change from an authoritarian relationship to a more democratic relationship. In all of the analyses the effects of intelligence were eliminated by various statistical procedures.

Role of Causal Orientation in Mental Health

A great many questions need answering before we can determine what role a causal orientation toward behavior plays in the prevention of mental illness and development of mental health. For example, we want to know what happens in later years to the child oriented causally through his school experiences. We want to know what kinds of behavior disturbances an "inoculation" with a causal orientation will prevent, if any, both during school age and in later years. Already, our laboratory enables us to study the relationships that develop between teachers and pupils in the causally-oriented classroom as compared to the relationships in a non-causally-oriented classroom. It also points the way for a study of a host of questions that arise in the investigations of the causes of emotional breakdowns and the avenues by which mental health in its full measure may be achieved.

Assumptions Underlying the Program

As we look over the whole program, what are the assumptions that underlie it? It seems that there are two or perhaps three. The first is that we can describe the differences between a surface and a causal approach to behavior. From the numerous occasions in which we have attempted to communicate the meaning of these concepts, it appears that it is possible to distinguish these approaches in their major aspects. We expect that a gradual refinement in meaning will take place [4].

A second assumption is that a careful study using methods that can be duplicated and repeated by others so that the results can be checked is the only way in which we will be able to discover what degree of causal orientation can be developed at the various age and intelligence levels and what the effect is when a thorough going causal orientation appears. It will be noted that we are not assuming that a causal orientation will relieve all mental strains or prevent all mental breakdowns. Rather we are asking the question, to what extent will an "inoculation" with a causal orientation prevent various types of mental illness and increase the amount of emotionally satisfying and creative uses of human energy? In our tests of the effects of the causal orientation, we are interested not only in measuring degree or extent of prevention but we are also interested in measuring degree or extent to which human energies are released in "creative" and "satisfying" achievement.

Finally, in the early stages of our work we had to assume that learning a causal orientation was not so incompatible with the individual goals of the teachers, children, and parents with whom we worked that it produced long-enduring conflict and frustration. Both observation and test results have indicated that this is no longer entirely an assumption but may be considered a generalization that has a degree of support.

Our program, which goes under the title of The Preventive Psychiatry Research Program, is an example of teachers, guidance workers, and other school personnel joining hands with research investigators to study not only whether changes in learners can be made but also what the effects are of these changes in the lives of the learners. Teaching is viewed as a way of creating a new pattern or way of living, the effects of which can then be studied [*8*].

References

1. Bate, Elsa B. The effect of especially prepared materials in a learning program in human growth and development on the tenth grade level. Unpublished doctoral dissertation, University of Iowa, 1948.
2. Gough, H. G., Harris, D. B., Martin, W. E., & Edward, M. Children's ethnic attitudes: I. Relationship to certain personality factors. *Child Develpm.*, 1950, *21*, 83–91.
3. Levitt, Eugene E. Effect of "causal" teacher training program on authoritarianism and responsibility in grade school children. *Psychol. Reports*, 1955, *1*, 449–458.
4. Levitt, Eugene E., & Ojemann, Ralph H. The aims of preventive psychiatry and "causality" as a personality pattern. *J. Psychol.*, 1953, *36*, 393–400.
5. McCandless, Boyd. A study of selected factors affecting radio listening behavior. Unpublished doctoral dissertation, University of Iowa, 1941.
6. Morgan, Mildred I., & Ojemann, Ralph H. The effect of a learning program designed to assist youth in an understanding of behavior and its development. *Child Develpm.*, 1942, *13*, 181–194.
7. Ojemann, Ralph H. The effect on the child's development of changes in cultural influences. *J. educ. Res.*, 1946, *40*, No. 4, 258–270.
8. Ojemann, Ralph H. Research in planned learning programs and the science of behavior. *J. educ. Res.*, 1948, *42*, No. 2, 96–104.
9. Ojemann, Ralph H., Levitt, Eugene E., Lyle, William H., Jr., & Whiteside, Maxine F. The effects of a "causal" teacher-training program and certain curricular changes on grade school children. *J. exp. Educ.*, 1955, *24*, No. 2, 95–114.

10. Stiles, Frances S. A study of materials and programs for developing an understanding of behavior at the elementary school level. Doctoral dissertation, University of Iowa, 1947.

11. Stiles, Frances S. Developing an understanding of human behavior at the elementary school level. *J. educ. Res.*, 1950, *43*, 516–524.

12. Snider, Bill C. F. Relation of growth in causal orientation to insecurity in elementary school children. *Psychol. Reports*, 1957, *3*, 631–634.

13. Wilkinson, Frances R., & Ojemann, Ralph H. The effect on pupil growth of an increase in teacher's understanding of pupil behavior. *J. exp. Educ.*, 1939, *8*, 143–147.

❦ 13

The Organic Curriculum: A New Experiment in Economic Education

Lawrence Senesh

Current Economic Education Programs

Recently our public schools have grown conscious of the significance of economic education. Many of them have organized workshops and in-service training programs, and committees have been appointed to study the curriculum all for the purpose of increasing the students' awareness of the nature and character of the American economic system. Unfortunately, many of these actions are motivated by our fears of the Russian economic system. In such courses the teachers are more preoccupied with proving that the American economic system is superior to the Russian than they are with analysis and critical thinking.

Many of the programs now available to public school teachers and intended to improve their economic competence are not broad enough to meet the educational objectives of economic education: the acquaintance of students with the structure and functioning of the American economic system, with the underlying economic theory, with the problems growing out of the dynamics of economic change, and with structure and functioning of other economic systems. Some programs now available emphasize family security and life insurance, others consumer economics, and still

The author is Professor of Economic Education at Purdue University. Prior to his appointment at Purdue he served as Economist for the Joint Council on Economic Education. As a Regional Representative of the Joint Council his contributions to the Council's program have been continued. He has been in active contact with every phase of the economic education movement. Professor Senesh is the author of materials on economics for teachers. He has worked with teachers and in classroom situations to produce many interesting and exciting pilot projects dealing with economic topics.

others utilization of community resources. Although each of these areas falls under the general heading of economics, each is too narrow to help teachers organize an economic program around economic processes and problems.

Beyond doubt the most significant contribution to economic education has been made by the Joint Council on Economic Education. For over ten years the Joint Council has served as a motivating agent to public schools and universities all over the country. As a result of the Joint Council's intensive effort on the national scene, workshops have been organized, regional councils established, and many public schools have accepted the responsibility of surveying the economic content of their curriculum and how it might be improved.

Despite these impressive accomplishments, lasting results will not be achieved until universities and colleges become active supporters of the public schools in their efforts to improve economic education and until the college economists experiment with new approaches in economic education.

Professional economists can assist the schools in three areas. First, they can help social studies teachers understand the scope of economics so that they will realize that watching stock quotations for a whole academic year, playing bank with students' savings, or learning about the political actors of the various booms and busts, are far from teaching economics.

Secondly, college economists should acquaint themselves with the teaching problems of the public school teachers who need more help than a few formal lectures on "What Economics Is All About." If economists understand that children's experiences are potentially meaningful, they can point out to the social studies teachers the underlying economic ideas behind these experiences. College economists have an important stake in the quality of the social studies curriculum. They do themselves as well as students a disservice when they discourage the study of economics for grades below the secondary school level, and when they insist that economics in the high school be of a descriptive order. If their arguments that secondary school students are not mature enough to cope with analytical thinking, why is it that college level economics leaves an intellectual mark on so few students?

College level teaching in economics is usually good, but unfortunately, it falls like seed on unprepared soil. Unless students are exposed systematically in their earlier years to analytical thinking, theory in the college years will have little meaning for most students. Conditioning for economic analysis is a long and tedious process.

Thirdly, college economists should give more attention to the development of training programs for social studies majors which will incorporate the latest findings on the psychology of learning and which will build the bridge between economic subject matter and the classroom needs of social studies teachers. College economists should try to develop in social studies majors the ability to adapt complex economic concepts to the maturity level of public school students. Without proper help social studies majors will see only a remote relationship, if any, between the principles course and the public school curriculum.

Purdue University is aware of this, and its School of Industrial Management and Economics is undertaking experimental programs on the campus and in the public schools of Indiana. On the campus it has organized two specially designed economics courses for majors in social studies. These courses present not only the subject matter but its applicability in the classroom. Both courses are organized around the following question: "What do the American people want their economic system to accomplish?" The content of these courses evolves from attempts to answer problems posed by questions regarding the social goals of economic growth, economic stability, economic security, economic freedom, and economic justice. The first course deals largely with the theoretical background necessary to understand the nature of these five social goals. In the second course students read and discuss pertinent Congressional hearings and studies prepared by economists which relate to the same five social goals. Since the objective of both courses is to improve the economic competence of social studies teachers, classroom situations are reconstructed and demonstrations continually presented by economists and students as a constant reminder of the teachers' obligation to make complex ideas communicable.

The Elkhart Project

The University also conducts with various public schools throughout the state experimental projects to find out how much economic theory children on the different grade levels are able to learn. Among these projects the most ambitious is a twelve-year experimental program being undertaken in Elkhart. The purpose of this experiment is to develop a new dimension in the social studies curriculum, an *organic curriculum.* The experiment rests on the hypothesis that children on every grade level, with proper motivation, can become excited about the abstract ideas underlying their experiences, and that these ideas can be presented in such a way as to reflect the basic structure of the body of economic knowledge.

Philosophy of the Organic Curriculum

Children, even at the beginning of the first grade, can see the great contours of the economic world. As their reading and writing skills develop and their experiences become more complex, the outlines will take on sharper focus. The outlines will be filled in with more complex patterns and details, always related to the basic contours. What are the basic contours of the economic world? With the help of the teacher, children can discover in their experiences at home, school, and in the playground that:

1. All people and all nations are confronted with the conflict between their unlimited wants and limited resources. The degree of the conflict may vary, but the conflict is always present.
2. From the beginning, men have tried new ways and means to lessen the gap between unlimited wants and limited resources. Their efforts to invent new machines and improve production processes are evidences of the desire to produce more, better, and faster.
3. In all countries the basic questions to be answered are: what goods and services will be produced; how much of these will be produced; how will they be produced—that is, with more men or more machines or more raw materials; and who will receive the goods and services?
4. In the United States what and how much will be produced, how it will be produced, and for whom are largely determined by the free choices of the American people, either as consumers or participants in the production process.
5. Through their political process the American people sometimes limit their individual free choices in order to increase the general welfare.

Such a projection of the economic world can serve as a basic frame of reference that will be useful from the earliest school days throughout adult life. This framework opens such broad horizons that teachers in succeeding grades can build on it.

How can children's experiences even in the first grade be related to this larger framework? Children and teacher, for example, may discuss what they would like to have for Christmas and how these choices have to be limited because of the size of the family income and because of the desires of other members of the family. Through a series of exercises in choice-making, children can discover that individuals, neighborhoods, cities, and nations all have to make choices for the same reasons. Watching machines work, or observing the efforts to initiate space travel, are good experiences to dramatize the role of invention and technology in closing the gap between unlimited wants and limited resources. The fact that homes run better when certain members of the family are responsible for certain duties and that school affairs operate more smoothly when certain persons are responsible for particular duties (such as principals, teachers, and janitors), are examples of the division of labor and specialization. This shows how the division of labor and the organization process increases productivity. First graders may discuss how they will use their allowances and how prices and the size of their allowances affect their decisions of what to buy and how much. They can grasp that their decisions to buy hula hoops instead of candy bars, along with the decisions of other people, will decide how many hula hoops will be produced, how many candy bars, and in the same way, how many automobiles, and how many houses. The children's recognition that certain members of the family have to support other members of the family who are too young or too old, or who are sick or unemployed, can help children to understand that the same principle is at work in government programs. Also, as the first graders become acquainted with their school building, their teacher, and the principal, they can be led to discover the need and function of taxes for certain purposes which individuals are not able to fulfill, i.e., such as education, roads, national defense, public health, conservation of resources, and relief.

To approach economic education in this way the curriculum has to discard the unrelated fragments of information that are currently offered as economics. Many of these are dull; others are so distorted that teachers in succeeding grades are preoccupied with unlearning what previous grades have taught. It is highly unimaginative to identify money management as economics. Surely it is important that every high school graduate know how to use his income, how to spend, save, and invest it, but the price of over-emphasis on this area of economics is the ignorance of youth in economic analysis and unawareness of national and international issues. This ignorance a democratic society cannot afford. The identification of the raw material program with conservation overlooks the dynamic nature of our economy where the discovery of new resources, new uses of existing resources, and the more efficient use of low-grade resources make meaningless certain conservation practices. Teaching children that banks exist for the purpose of safekeeping of money is misleading as to the true nature of the banking system. Encouraging youth to establish and manage business enterprises while in school may stimulate initiative, but it is no substitute for the study of economics. Often, students who have participated in such business projects are unable to explain the role of the market in our economy, nor can they describe the characteristics of our free enterprise system.

Organization of the Project

To avoid such pitfalls in economic education the first grade teachers of Elkhart, altogether thirty-five in number, started the project by defining the scope of economics. They wanted to know the basic ideas on which economics as an academic discipline rests. They discovered that the underlying problem of every economic issue is rooted in the basic conflict between unlimited wants and limited resources: too many desires but not enough resources to satisfy them. Therefore, all remaining problems stem from this basic one—how to allocate our resources in such a way that they assure optimum satisfaction and lessen the gap between the desire for and the availability of goods and services. The teachers learned that we solve our allocation problems largely through the interaction of decisions by consumers, producers, and resource owners within a framework of interrelated prices and markets. The interaction of their efforts and desires determine what our economy produces, how we produce the goods and services, and who will receive the fruit of the efforts. The teachers also discovered that sometimes our society is not satisfied with the outcome of the consumers' and producers' efforts. Through the political process our society defines certain goals which range from economic growth to welfare objectives and it formulates public policies designed to achieve these objectives.

The intent of the Elkhart experiment is to incorporate the study of these economic relationships into the public school curriculum regardless of grade level. In this way Elkhart youth will be exposed to the most important economic relationships in the first grade. As the pupils move from grade to grade they will encounter the same network again and again, but always relating to it their more mature experiences, thus adding depth and complexity to the basic relationships. On every grade level the allocation problem, the functioning of a free market, and the effect of public policies on the market will be projected.

In the lower grades students may discover these relationships when they study "My Home," "My Neighborhood," or "The Grocery Store"; in the higher grades when they study international trade in World Geography, or economic growth and stability in the period following the Civil War or the critical years 1837, 1873, 1907, and the 1930's in the United States History course.

Although the thesis sounds reasonable, it takes a long time to condition the public school teacher to accept the philosophy of an *organic curriculum.* The reason is that he does not have the necessary knowledge of economics to be aware of the network of relationships underlying the children's experiences.

Many of the teachers over-protect their pupils when they argue that children in the lower grades are not ready to cope with large idea relationships, and that such relationships should be postponed to later grades. The Elkhart experiment is showing that children in the first grade enjoy the discovery of the unknown when teachers motivate them properly. Motivation creates a spark and enthusiasm which can lift the children outside the range of the objective classifications of learning readiness. Classroom experience demonstrates that improvement of teaching techniques and increased emphasis on motivation negates the concept that the child is a purely biological entity.

After the Elkhart teachers defined the scope of economics, they developed additional understandings to carry out the experiment successfully.

1. They found it necessary to distinguish clearly between analysis and value judgment. Economic education need not exclude values from the classroom since the success of our economic system is measured by the extent to which it fulfills our social values.
2. The teachers viewed the economic world in process to see how science and technology affect economic institutions and to recognize the problems which such changes create.

3. Once they recognized these problems, the teachers learned the various steps of the problem approach. These steps include:

   a. The discovery of the symptoms of the problem; that is, the expression of concern of the various segments of American society for the problem.

   b. Recognition of the many aspects of the problem. Different individuals and groups, depending on their backgrounds or social status, look on the problem differently. Recognition of the many aspects of the problem is important because it affects the quality of the solution.

   c. The definition of the problem. The proper definition expresses the conflict between societal desires and existing institutional arrangements.

   d. The scope of the problem. At this step, the teachers were acquainted with various statistical measurements, such as, gross national product, national income, unemployment, income distribution, balance of payments, population statistics, all of which throw light on the magnitude of the problem.

   e. The causes of the problem. At this point the various economic theories which explain the causes were considered.

   f. The solution of the problem. In the solution phase the teachers discovered that most solutions rest on the cooperative efforts of individuals, voluntary groups, and of government. To what extent one group or another carries responsibility for the solution depends on the nature of the problem and upon the political interaction of the various pressure groups. As an outcome of the problem approach teachers became aware that no problem is ever solved once and for all, and that every effort and every new measure create new dislocations out of which new problems emerge. Teachers also realized that with every effort to solve a problem opportunity costs are involved. The solution of a problem may or may not increase total welfare.

Although the teachers participating in the Elkhart experiment attended one or two summer workshops sponsored by Purdue University, experience has shown that the competence they gained in the subject matter did not enable them to discover the economic concepts underlying conventional social studies units of the curriculum. For this reason the decision was made that the teachers would not be exposed to more formal presentations of the subject matter, but that they would learn the economic concepts which relate to their social studies units with the help of a professional economist and educator.

The first and second grade teachers in Elkhart organized into curriculum committees, each having the responsibility of incorporating economic understandings into their conventional social studies units. Each committee has developed economic concepts which are incorporated into their units. These concepts represent the basic economic relationships. At first the teachers regarded the concepts as formidable, but as they discovered the relationship between them and the children's experience, they came to respect economic theory. Their change in attitude demonstrates vividly the need for specially designed courses in teacher education.

Committees were then established to work with the social studies curriculum supervisor to translate these concepts into the curriculum. This was a tedious job because the teachers, believing that the concepts had to be simplified for the children, frequently damaged the integrity of the concept. More was accomplished when emphasis was placed on better methods of communication rather than on simplification.

These committees also developed student activities which integrate the economic concepts with the other social studies and with the skills of reading, writing, arithmetic, and the arts. Here again it was necessary to convince the teachers that the new subject matter could be used to develop skills.

A testing committee has been organized, comprised of some of the participating teachers, the head of the Department of Testing and Measurement of the Elkhart Public Schools, the curriculum director of social studies for the elementary grades, the art teacher, and an economist. The committee has studied the economic concepts included in the first and second grade teaching units from which it has formulated pictorial multiple choice questions. Examples are given later in this article. The teachers conducting the tests will read the test questions and the children check the pictures which they think show the proper answers. Tests will be given at the beginning and end of each academic year.

The Organic Curriculum: an Illustration

At present, the Elkhart project is in its second year. The first grade committee has developed two units: *My Home* and *What My Father Does.* The second grade committee also has completed two units: *My Neighborhood* and *My School.* Since the test forms will not be ready before the fall of 1960, the Elkhart experiment, complete with testing, will not start until the fall of 1960. The following are examples of economic concepts which appeared in the unit on *My Home.*

A Division of Labor Takes Place within the Family which Increases the Efficiency of the Family.

Curriculum interpretation. Work in the home is done more efficiently when each member of the family does what he is best fitted to do.

Student activities. Children draw pictures or tell stories showing how the various members of the family help in the home. The children may play "A Morning at Home," with the mother preparing breakfast and putting up father's lunch, with father getting ready for work and the children getting ready for school. A second scene will show mother preparing dinner, father returning home to do repair jobs about the house, and the children running errands for the parents and feeding their pets. After the play children discuss or draw pictures about what would happen if everyone in the family tried to cook the meals at the same time: father would be late for work, children late for school, everyone annoyed, repair jobs and errands neglected.

Within the Home All Members of the Family Are Consumers, but Only Some Are Producers.

Curriculum interpretation. In the home parents, grandparents, children, healthy and sick, young and old, use or consume durable goods, non-durable goods, and services. Only certain members of the family produce inside and outside the home.

Student activities. The students draw pictures showing the family's consumption needs: food, clothing, shelter, electricity, automobiles, furniture, air, sunshine, water. Another drawing shows those members of the family who are consumers only: the very young and the very old. A third picture shows those members of the family who are producers at home only: mother doing house chores, a retired man working in the garden. In a fourth picture are those members of the family who are producers inside the home as well as outside the home: father working at the office and also cutting grass at home; mother working in a store and also at home cooking meals. These drawings can be an outgrowth of a classroom discussion of what the family's needs are and how certain members of the family provide those needs.

All Producers Produce Goods and Services in Order to Earn Incomes. In Many Cases Members of the Family Produce Goods and Services at Home for Their Own Use in Order to Save Money. With Every Choice Another Opportunity Is Sacrificed.

Curriculum interpretation. In most families there are breadwinners who earn incomes by working in factories, offices, stores, fields, mines, on the ocean, and in the air. Their incomes are earned as a reward for producing goods and services useful to other people. When members of the family produce goods and services at home, the money saved is the same as if earned. If the members of the family had not produced these goods and services for themselves, they would have had to hire some one else to do the job.

When one works at one job, he cannot work at another at the same time; therefore, he may not be earning as much as he could at another job.

Student activities. Students can find out at home what their fathers do, and explain to the class the importance of the goods and services they produce. The class may prepare a mural showing the role of father (representing the father of all the children) as a producer. Picture 1: Father leaves home for work. Picture 2: Father shown at work. Picture 3: Father returns home with income. Picture 4: Mother goes shopping. Picture 5: The goods which father produced are shown in big trucks leaving the factory for the stores. Picture 6: Many people go to the store to buy the goods which father helped to produce.

Each child may prepare a picture showing father, mother, and children at work at home, and explain to the class how much the family may save on each occasion by doing the work themselves.

Sometimes the members of the family do not save money by doing work at home. When mother is at home doing the cooking and washing, she cannot be working away from home and earning a salary. Father may have asked to stay away from his job without pay to paint the house. The child may carry newspapers to earn money, but he deprives himself of time for studying and preparing for his future. The children may draw pictures showing how each member of the family could have other choices of work than those they are doing now.

In an Agricultural Economy, Most of the Productive Activities Are or Were Performed on the Farm, Largely Satisfying the Family's Needs. In an Industrial Market Economy, the Work-Place Has Shifted to Outside the Home, and Most of the Production Is for the Market.

Curriculum interpretation. In pioneer days, members of the family produced most of the goods they needed, and the family grew its own food, spun its own wool, made its own clothing, built its own home, and often provided education and recreation. With the development of industries, specialization of labor increased, and people began to produce for other people. Those who produced for others earned income.

Student activities. From pioneer stories, the children may reconstruct in their own stories or in table models the relative self-sufficiency of family life. As a contrast they may prepare another story or model showing that today the home is served largely by institutions outside the home: churches, schools, factories, barber shops, restaurants, dentists' offices, meat-packing plants, super markets, and power plants.

Income Earned by Families May Be Spent or Saved. Decisions to Spend or Save Affect What and How Much Our Economy Will Produce of Each Commodity.

Curriculum interpretation. Families usually want more goods and services than they can buy with their incomes; therefore, they have to make choices. Any choice they make has an impact on the types of goods and services our industry produces.

Student activities. Children may act out a family scene and may express all the things they want and then through discussion establish priorities. They will compromise.

If the children in their play decide to give up buying something which they have bought in the past, due to change of tastes or high prices, and decide to purchase another thing, the children may draw pictures showing that the shift of demand from one good to another affects the two industries. For example, if they decide to abstain from the purchase of candy to buy ice cream, the teacher may discuss with them what will happen to the business of the candy manufacturer and the ice cream manufacturer if lots of children should make similar decisions. The drawings could show the following sequence:

1. Lots of children's heads and above each a cloud showing a candy bar cancelled out and an ice cream cone remaining.
2. Children lining up in front of an ice cream store, and no one at the candy store next door.
3. The ice cream factory expands and a sign is visible—"Workers Wanted." The candy factory is closed down, and a sign is visible—"Closed," and unemployed workers are walking out.

The teacher may discuss how the children's savings may help the entire country. This can be shown through drawings. Picture 1: Johnny puts his money in the bank. Picture 2: Ice cream manufacturer goes to bank to get a loan to build a bigger business. Picture 3: Ice cream manufacturer with borrowed money purchases building material, hires labor, buys equipment to build a bigger ice cream factory. Picture 4: Factory produces and sells ice cream to a large group of children lined up in front of the factory. Picture 5: Factory takes money to bank to repay loan with interest.

After discussing these pictures, the teacher may discuss what would happen if the children of this country would decide not to buy either candy or ice cream. The discussion would lead to the recognition that savings would be unused and both candy and ice cream factories would close down. The same relationship could be developed as it applies to adults.

The study of *My Neighborhood* for the second grade introduces similar relationships in a new light.

The Needs of a Neighborhood Are Fulfilled by Means of Economic, Social, Cultural, and Political Institutions Producing Goods and Services.

Curriculum interpretation. Within the neighborhood there are homes, grocery stores, barber shops, drug stores, schools, libraries, factories, and churches. These we call institutions. They satisfy people's varied needs.

Student activities. Children may be taken on a walk around the vicinity of the school building, and on their return they may draw pictures of some of the places they have seen. From this walk and from their walks to and from school, the children may prepare a table model of their neighborhood, locating their homes, factories, banks, stores, churches, playgrounds, the school libraries, busy streets, and other institutions of the neighborhood.

All the Institutions in the Neighborhood Are Built and Maintained from Compulsory Savings or from Voluntary Savings.

Curriculum interpretation. Homes, schools, roads, stores, churches, hospitals, factories, and libraries are built from the savings of individuals. For the most part the savings which build and maintain these institutions come voluntarily from people. The number of homes built, stores opened, and churches and hospitals built depends on how many of these the individuals want and will save for. Sometimes, roads, schools, and libraries are paid from compulsory savings; that is, through taxes which government collects from us, and which we have agreed to by our votes. Sometimes, roads, schools, and libraries are built from our voluntary savings which we lend to the government when we buy government bonds.

Student activities. After the construction of the neighborhood model, children will locate the places built by voluntary individual savings, by voluntary community savings, and by compulsory community savings. Students may draw a picture series. Picture 1: How people pay money to City Hall in the form of taxes. Picture 2: How City Hall buys a piece of land with tax money for a school building. Picture 3: City Hall hires an architect to make blue prints. Picture 4: City Hall orders building materials. Picture 5: City Hall hires workers. Picture 6: City Hall brings cement mixers, trucks, and other equipment. Picture 7: City Hall buys furniture for school. Picture 8: City Hall hires teachers for school. Picture 9: Children are seen coming to new school.

Such a picture series could be adapted for building of homes or churches, showing the different methods and sources of savings.

Some Institutions Are Established to Make Profit.

Curriculum interpretation. Such business places as stores, dentists' offices, beauty parlors, gas stations must make enough money to pay their bill, to pay adequate wages to the workers and the owners, and in addition to his wage, a reward, or profit, to the owner for risking his savings in the business.

Student activities. The children may make a trip to a neighborhood grocery. The teacher will encourage them to note what is needed to open and operate the grocery store. After the field trip, the children may discuss where the grocer got his savings to open his store. To further dramatize the relationship between prices, costs, and profits, the teacher may develop a series of games for the students to play.

The Improvement of the Neighborhood Is Restricted by the Lack of Financial Resources and by the Size of the Opportunity Cost.

Curriculum interpretation. Everyone in the neighborhood cannot be satisfied with his expectations of the neighborhood because of the lack of available funds and because the financial sacrifice may be greater than the advantages gained.

Student activities. The class may discuss how they would like to improve their neighborhood in terms of more playgrounds, better housing, broader streets, more trees, better business districts, and more schools. They will compare these proposed changes with their neighborhood model, and they may discuss the following questions: 1. How can each improvement be paid for? 2. What does the neighborhood have to sacrifice (playgrounds for a store, a pretty residential district for a highway, a swimming beach for a harbor) to fulfill the various desires? Is it worth the sacrifice?

The Neighborhood Is Interdependent with the Rest of the Economy.

Curriculum interpretation. Members of the neighborhood may make their livelihood by working in stores, factories, and offices located outside the neighborhood. Many families prefer to go to stores downtown or even to other cities. Businesses and stores located in the neighborhood buy from and sell to other regions or even other countries.

Student activities. Children may visit a store in the neighborhood to find out all the goods which the store buys from other parts of the city, country, and world. They may also visit a factory in the neighborhood to find out where it gets the raw materials and where it sells its products, and how the sales affect the number of people hired.

Evaluation

At present the first and second grade committees are developing evaluation tools. The first grade committee bases the tests on multiple choices combined with cartoons. Here are some random examples: (The tests are given orally by the teacher.)

1. One cartoon shows food cooking on the stove, the water faucet leaking, the cat sitting next to his empty dish meowing. Under the cartoon will be the following question: How can the family accomplish these jobs most efficiently? 1. Mother does everything. 2. Mother feeds the cat; children repair the plumbing; father does the cooking. 3. Mother does the cooking;

father repairs the plumbing; the children feed the cat. (Check the right answer.)

2. There are two drawings—one a wealthy family, and the other of a poor family of the same size. 1. Check which one of these two families will spend more.

3. A drawing shows a clothing store on three consecutive days. In the window on Monday is a coat for $30.00. On Tuesday the coat is marked $28.00. On Wednesday there is a sign in the window, "Big Sale," and the coat is marked down to $20.00. When would you buy your coat? Monday_____ Tuesday_____ Wednesday_____.

4. Which member of the family is producing goods? Under the question is a series of cartoons showing: Mother baking a cake, small girl dusting the table, father washing the car, boy mowing the lawn.

5. Which member of the family is producing a service? Under the question is a series of cartoons showing: Mother baking a cake, mother sewing a dress, father building a dog house, child mowing the lawn.

6. Read carefully the column of needs satisfied in the home, and find the place in the neighborhood where those needs can be satisfied. Put the proper numbers in the blanks in the right column.

FAMILY NEEDS

Satisfied in the home	*Satisfied in the neighborhood*
(1) Mother cuts Tom's hair.	_____ Grocery Store
(2) Mother cooks the meals.	_____ School
(3) Father grows carrots in the garden.	_____ Bank
(4) Family holds prayer meeting at home.	_____ Restaurant
(5) Nancy and Peter learned their alphabets at home.	_____ Barber Shop
(6) David saves his money in the piggy bank.	_____ Public Library
(7) Betsy spent her birthday money for books.	_____ Church

7. Some of the things listed below are paid for from charity, some from taxes. Write in T (for taxes) and C (for Charity) in the proper blanks. Leave space open if money does not come from taxes or charity.

_____ Building a factory	_____ Building a hospital
_____ Putting a new roof on the house	_____ Building a church
_____ Building a playground	_____ Building a school

These samples of concepts, students' activities, and tests illustrate the framework of economic knowledge which is being built in the primary grades of the Elkhart Public Schools. As the pupils move into the intermediate and upper grades the framework will gather more detail. In the fourth or fifth grades, pupils will play *The Grocery Store* again. By this time the class will construct simple arithmetic tables showing how, at different price levels, the grocer may sell a certain commodity and how the numbers sold affect the cost per unit and the profit. In the sixth grade the children will study economic geography and will again meet the principle of division of labor. Added to this principle discovered in the unit on "My Home" will be the theory of comparative advantage. In the study of "My Neighborhood" the child was introduced to the role of government and how it relates to the private sector of the economy. This relationship together with the relationship of income, employment, and production discovered in the unit, "What My Father Does," results in greater depth of understanding when the child learns later about deflationary and inflationary periods in United States history.

Summary

Although the Elkhart experience has not yet undertaken objective testing, and test forms are still in the process of being developed, observers cannot avoid being impressed with the spontaneity with which the first and second graders talk about their fathers as producers of goods and services, the way they translate the circular flow of income and production into simple picture series, or the enthusiasm with which they consider the economic aspects of neighborhoods. A few weeks ago the Elkhart Local Council for the Social Studies invited a first grade group to their monthly meeting. The children explained the role of their fathers as producers, as income earners, as consumers and savers, and the impact of their decisions as consumers and savers on the total level of our economy. During the discussion the senior high school teachers expressed the thought that they could hardly wait until these first graders become their students. If the concept of the *organic curriculum* is widely adopted by the nation's public schools, it is safe to say that many of the seemingly hopeless teaching problems which college economists face will be resolved. High school graduates will come to college receptive to analytical thinking, and many may even choose economics as their profession.

The success of the Elkhart experiment, like other experiments undertaken in the public schools, hinges on three factors:

1. *The attitude of the school administration toward curriculum change.* The superintendent of the Elkhart Public Schools, together with his staff, has established an intellectual climate in the school system which stimulates and encourages professional contributions from the faculty. Discussion meetings promote exchange of ideas among the classroom teachers. Teachers are encouraged to attend summer workshops and professional meetings.

2. *The cooperation of the community.* In 1958 when the experiment began, a number of the larger civic organizations allocated one of their meetings to getting acquainted with the experiment. The Rotary Club proclaimed one of its luncheons, "The Rotary Honors the Elkhart Schools," in connection with this experiment.

3. *The attitude of the University toward public school education.* The American public school curriculum, being largely a grass roots product of its

community, suffers chronically from the lack of assistance from college specialists in the various content areas. In the area of economic education assistance has had to come from those members of economics departments of colleges and universities who will consider economic education a worthy outlet for their talents. While scientists are now intensely interested in the learning process of children from kindergarten on, most economists and foundations are still convinced that training in economics cannot and should not be started below the senior high school level. It has been this writer's observation that the first graders' curiosity is sharper than that of first year college students. Economics departments of universities should undertake programs specifically directed to the aid of public schools and social studies teachers. Purdue University and its School of Industrial Management and Economics are committed to such assistance.

The Elkhart experiment is an ambitious project. It moves slowly because as teaching units are developed, teachers have to be trained in economics, and they have also to be motivated to accept new ideas. Teaching units cannot be written by the professional economist because he is unaware of the multitude of problems which the public school teachers face in the classrooms. On the other hand, he must protect zealously the integrity of the subject matter, even if it creates conflict between the classroom teacher and himself. Out of this conflict of interest a unique creative process frequently evolves where both method and subject matter are consciously fused. As a result, college and public school educators participating in the experiment become better teachers.

ఔ 14

Some Evaluation Problems in a Course Content Improvement Project

J. Myron Atkin
University of Illinois

THOSE WHO SUGGEST that curriculum be modified have the responsibility for demonstrating the desirability as well as the feasibility of the modifications they suggest. This truism, to the extent that it is accepted, protects the schools from poorly conceived innovations, from dealing with each and every fashionable novelty. Thus those who aspire to influence curriculum decisions broadly are expected to report suitably objective evidence about the effectiveness of their work. But it is possible that this expectation, while essential, sometimes may be limiting.

It is not the purpose here to deprecate the standards that have come to be accepted for educational evaluation. Few would deny their usefulness for many educational purposes. Rather it is the contention here that inadequate attention has been given to certain evaluation problems in the broad area of curriculum development, particularly in a period of radical modification of course content such as we see today in mathematics and science, and that a few of the problems are only dimly recognized.

Specialists in evaluation may detect traces of pre-knowledge bias in what follows. The paper makes no pretext of being authoritative. However, certain evaluational rubrics seem deeply ingrained in educational practice, and if a small body of researchers is challenging some of the older guide-

DR. ATKIN, who is Co-Director of the Illinois Elementary-School Science Project, has long been interested in the evaluation of learning materials and, in particular, the evaluation of the new curricula in science. In this article he brings into sharp focus one of the important issues of the day: the related questions of when, how, and by whom learning goals should be stated in curriculum building and the suitability of traditional procedures for evaluating them.

lines, their influence is not yet broad enough to have had an appreciable impact on curriculum evaluation.

It is hoped that some of the evaluation problems can be delineated in this paper, and they will be outlined in the context of a single course improvement activity, the University of Illinois Elementary-School Science Project. This Project, which received its initial support from the National Science Foundation in September, 1960, has had as its major purpose from the inception the production of astronomy materials for children—materials that are sound astronomically, that reflect the structure of the subject as it is viewed by astronomers of stature, and that can be handled by teachers and children in actual classrooms. Thus, the Project reflects a trend characteristic of several of the current mathematics and science curriculum activities: a delineation of content is required that reveals a potent hierarchy of conceptual schemes, a few ideas with considerable intellectual mileage that help the learner understand in the most economical manner possible a given discipline as it is perceived by its senior practitioners.

Hence "new" content must be identified. It must be presented effectively to the children and teachers. It must be revised based on field trial. The revisions must conform to the content standards established by the scientists while they are adapted to the abilities of children and teachers. For such evaluation in the early stages of a curriculum project, there is usually heavy reliance on opinion. Teacher comments are solicited. Extensive observations are made of student and teacher behavior. Scientists instrumental in the development of the new curriculum materials typically work with children themselves. This semi-systematic type of evaluation is thought to be appropriate in the early stages of a course improvement activity. Feasibility, after all, is a necessary condition for curriculum innovation. A multitude of evaluation problems are still present in these early stages, problems that can and should occupy scores of well-trained people. Sampling questions and feedback procedures are just two examples of areas that need further work.

But it is in the intermediate stages of curriculum development that evaluation problems are most obvious. It is a fact, and to this writer a fortunate one, that prime movers in the large high school curriculum projects have moved ahead with a certain brashness in suggesting curriculum modifications. They have insisted on working on new curriculum and its implementation in its entirety and immediately, often recognizing but choosing to postpone some tough evaluational questions rather than to accept a reductionist approach and work primarily on the more readily solvable subsidiary problems. The scientists and mathematicians in these projects seem to have had few doubts about their ability to recognize valid curriculum materials and effective teaching. However, few curriculum developers schooled primarily in elementary and secondary education feel confident enough about their own taste to place strong reliance on rather "unsystematic" attempts at evaluation once feasible materials have been produced. There exists a pronounced expectation for the accumulation of objective evidence to ascertain the success of the materials in achieving specified aims.

The comprehension of content *per se* by the children represents one type of evaluation problem. Generally, curriculum developers are aware of a range of possible outcomes other than recall of specific information, e.g., application, comprehension of major principles. Test makers, among others, have made ingenious attempts to construct methods of measuring a multitude of content outcomes.

A major evaluation difficulty relates to the assessment of certain outcomes that may not be specific to a particular course but the outgrowth, hopefully, of many courses. Most of those engaged in science curriculum development consider the materials they produce to influence children's attitudes about science and scientists–in addition to extending understanding of certain concepts that reflect the structure of the discipline. Further, it is the hope of some that new curriculum materials will lead to a comprehension of certain broad scientific ideas–randomness, symmetry, arbitrariness, proportionality, successive approximation, reference frame, discreteness–that are tangential to the sequence of conceptual schemes within a given discipline. Few evaluation specialists seem to have directed attention to such broad questions; yet the total effect of a sequence of courses over a number of years seems to be a rather crucial educational outcome.

Still another difficulty lies in the fact that those engaged in curriculum development are exhorted to assess learning in terms of readily observable and measurable behavioral change in the students. Since psychologists in recent decades have found it most useful to employ some sort of behavioral change model when studying human learning, and since few would want to question the effectiveness of such models as antidotes to solely verbal learning, and since the models have been markedly effective for mechanical and technical applications like learning how to operate a radar set, the models of learning as behavioral change have achieved a firm place in virtually all curriculum research. (A few extremists deny that verbal learning *is* behavioral.) However, under this rubric rather short-term behavioral change usually is identified and measured, few investigators having the patience or the inclination to plan long-term studies. In most of the curriculum projects, there is a suspicion that rather higher order intellectual abilities than those readily observable and measurable in terms of immediate behavioral change are achieved, or at least sought. There is the fear that a preoccupation with short-term goals may obscure the long-term ones.

More profoundly, it is suspected that the ability of certain senior scientists radically to restructure their disciplines in a manner that is aesthetically as well as intellectually pleasing and potent has outdistanced the ability of many educational evaluators to understand completely the import of this restructuring for purposes of curriculum. "Define your objectives," says an evaluator, "and I will help you to determine your degree of success." But there is a real danger that the objectives are not understood even when enunciated, or at least their implications not appreciated. Clever men for centuries have been helping to build our conception of science. There is some danger of achieving less than the possible in curriculum revision if insights into science must be subordinated to the state of development of the field of educational evaluation.

The curriculum developer is urged, *at the start*, to formulate clear statements of anticipated behaviors. The possibility that such behaviors may be identified *later* in a new curriculum activity seems like too slipshod a procedure to certain evaluators. Of possibly greater significance is the fact that too early a statement of objectives may obscure potentially significant outcomes that do not become apparent until later because they are seldom anticipated. This statement, of course, applies to negative outcomes as well as positive ones. Scientists, as a rule, are not particularly articulate about listing the objectives of a course of study with which they are pleased. They sense the appropriateness of the course; when they enumerate their reasons, they can be expected to overlook a few of the most significant ones.

Evaluation activity in the University of Illinois Elementary-School Science Project has centered around more readily ascertainable information such as the following:

(*1*) To what extent do children comprehend the content of the astronomy materials? We make assessments of the knowledge of astronomical ideas before and after each of the books is used. We try to avoid solely recall items. Every attempt is made to gauge the ability of the children to apply the major ideas in fresh contexts and comprehend major relationships. Here we have had assistance from able test makers, and although our problems in this realm are far from solved, we believe that patterns are apparent that will make our tests increasingly valid and reliable.

(*2*) To what extent does our delineation of content reflect a major and potent sequence of astronomical ideas? Here we rely on the community of astronomers plus certain physical scientists who work in related areas. These scientists are asked to review our materials as well as to help write them. In general, our "story line" is perceived as a potentially powerful one. Suggested modifications are sometimes crucial but seldom extensive.

(*3*) What modifications in approach are suggested by teachers? Our materials are being tried by about 350 teachers. Each teacher is asked to submit a reaction sheet on every chapter in each book. The teacher is asked to report the amount of preparation and teaching time required, his estimate of appropriateness of the content for his class, his estimate of children's interest, and his suggestions for improvement of the materials. In addition, an increasing number of teachers join our writing conference during the summer. As a further check on the validity of written teacher reactions, extensive observations of the use of Project materials are made by the central Project staff. Numerous conferences are held with participating teachers.

We also ask each participating teacher to submit a personal information sheet reporting formal science and mathematics background, age, and number of years of teaching experience.

From these data, we are able to determine a few relationships:

What is the relationship between the formal science and mathematics background of the teacher and the success of his children with our books, success as measured by our tests?

What is the relationship between success with our materials and participation by children in "new" math programs?

What is the relationship between the teacher's estimate of children's interest and success of the children with the materials?

What is the relationship between teacher estimate of children's interest and teacher estimate of appropriateness of content?

These examples indicate just a few of the potentially revealing interconnections that are being sought from the data collected. They are informative of course. They are frequently useful. Probably they are necessary.

But it is the hope of Project personnel that our goals, if not our accomplishments, transcend these more measurable outcomes, that there is a long-term intellectual and aesthetic element for which we strive that is difficult even to identify, much less measure. Such pretensions are not particularly appealing in the precise literature of educational research. Yet, as indicated, we feel that some of our more significant accomplishments potentially are in the realm of a realization of the full import of new content identification, however difficult the definitive assessment of such aims.

One approach now being developed in the Project to overcome some of the limitations of evaluational procedures used to date is to make use of a type of classroom and student observation that, in one sense, is only loosely structured. On the assumption that the books developed for children are valid astronomically–i.e., they contain an astronomical "story line" embodying a potent and carefully sequenced series of ideas, and they are teachable–but that it is difficult to anticipate *all* the outcomes that may result from the course, Project personnel are beginning a series of classroom observations in an attempt to identify unexpected behavioral changes in students. In the customary method of course development and evaluation, such a procedure seems backward. The standard practice is to identify the changes desired in the students, then see if the course is effective in producing the changes. Instead we are observing classes for the purpose of identifying changes that are not predicted or recognized at the start. A child makes a remark about an insight into equilibrium based on a particular section of one book, an insight that was not expected by the authors of the book. Another child exhibits an appreciation of symmetry embedded in the development of the concept of the median. Through such observation, though time-consuming and sometimes unproductive, we are succeeding in identifying *post hoc* some "objectives" of the astronomy materials.

It is universally accepted that evaluation should be central to course improvement. But only when evaluation is seen as a facilitating rather than as a limiting function will it be utilized more effectively by curriculum developers. To achieve this end, a flexible approach to the role of evaluation must be fostered by evaluation specialists themselves; there must be a willingness to question some of the conventional wisdom that has been accepted for decades, possibly with little analysis of the appropriateness today of the basic assumptions.

❦❦ Part Three

TEACHING METHOD CHANGES

In this second half of the twentieth century, new knowledge continues to cascade over us in an ever increasing flood. The scientific and academic community which produced this deluge appears to stand aghast at its own productivity, hardly knowing how to catalogue or to absorb this new information. The problems of how to organize the new information into a coherent curriculum for talented students, as well as for a program of general education for all students, have been considered in the preceding section. This explosion of knowledge, however, has caused other problems connected with *how* the student learns, as well as what he learns.

One obvious solution to the acquisition of new information is to attempt to jam it into an already tightly packed curriculum. This increases the amount of time the student spends on memory work and absorbing facts while delaying the time in which he begins to act productively upon the information available. But can the student, who has for 14 or 15 years managed to perform effectively in the educational program by acting as an academic sponge, suddenly divest himself of these habits and become a productive thinker?

Many educators feel that there is something nonsensical about delaying the time at which the student is expected to do some thinking for himself. If nonproductive learning habits become calcified by habitual use, and little or no emphasis is placed on rewards for original thinking from the student, it is unlikely that we shall be producing the adaptive-productive-creative student that we say is our goal.

The articles in the following section concern themselves with a variety of attempts to develop inquiry methods, search skills, discovery methods, and so on. In part, they follow a general philosophy that the best way to understand a given content field is to act like a specialist in that field. To understand mathematics, a student should act like a mathematician, not like a consumer of mathematics. The consumer is only interested in information, not in *how* this information was obtained or the problems in trying to obtain the new information.

In contrast, the student who is attempting to be a producer himself worries about such matters as the reliability of information being collected, the effect of the bias of the observer on the information being collected, the necessity for testing the validity of ideas that have been generated, and a variety of other skills which mark the scholar and the scientist.

There is a tendency in education circles to greet each new development as though it were completely novel. Such a tendency can be discerned in the current enthusiasm for the "discovery" method. The article by Taba places this movement in its proper historical perspective and relates it to similar teacher strategies, past and present.

One of the fates that awaits any new educational program that becomes popular is that its initially clear image becomes progressively distorted by well-meaning but untutored disciples. Thus "permissiveness" which originally represented an active and deliberately planned program became any type of noncoercive activity—even to chronic indecision and a lack of consistent planning. The current popularity of the "discovery method" may lead to similar distortions, and the proponents of the method must keep as clear an image as possible of the essence of the method. The article by Hendrix stresses the use of the discovery method in mathematics and the distinctions to be drawn between *discovery*, *nonverbal awareness*, and *incidental learning*.

This article stresses the importance of deliberate planning on the part of the teacher. The discovery method does not, as some appear to think, allow the teacher to relax while the students struggle to the goal. Instead, the teacher plays an active role in organizing the experiences so that the final discovery can be made.

Professors Atkin and Karplus in their article have contributed additional clarification to the role of the discovery method in the instruction of advanced science concepts at the elementary level. In this instance, they are distinguishing between *invention* which, to them, means the original introduction of a new concept and *discovery* which means verification or extension of a concept's usefulness.

The question they raise is, should the students "discover" the original theoretical model or should their discovery be focused on what the model can tell them? They emphasize, as does Hendrix, the importance of intellectual discipline and organization of ideas as well as encouraging the youngsters to consider all possible answers to a given problem.

It is relatively easy and common to give lip service to the desirability of having creative thinkers in our classrooms and to make every effort to stimulate creative ability. There appears to be a growing concern for the youngster who has a flair for original ideas and for different unusual thoughts. The desire for conformity in schools has been condemned as detrimental to the development of the original thinker.

We have not fully faced up to the unpleasant fact that other goals of the educational program may be antagonistic to the goal of stimulation of creative abilities. For example, it is difficult to think of a highly organized and structured curriculum being presented to a group of creative and original thinkers. The very social conformity that creates, on the surface, a smoothly running operation may well suppress or diminish tendencies toward original thinking. The sex roles that we impose, often deliberately, on both boys and girls in this culture may well channel and limit the range of thinking and ideas to only those that are deemed acceptable for those roles.

Professor Torrance, in his article, expresses his concern about these limitations through his clever device of asking the students to tell stories with a theme built around "animals who are different." His concern is the degree to which a student's desire for conformity has influenced his creative tendencies and he presents some suggestions on methods that might reverse this trend.

Creativity appears to involve many other things that we have said we do not like, such as sloppiness, nonconformity, unusual or divergent ideas. The presence of these otherwise undesirable characteristics is the price that has to be paid for the stimulation of these productive abilities. Torrance thinks that this price should be paid and so does this writer. It is crucial that teachers agree too, if these divergent abilities are to be enhanced in the regular school program.

How does one cover an acceptable amount of material in a curriculum and at the same time provide opportunity for creative and original thinking on the part of the students? For all of the interest that has been shown in the area of creativity, it has been relatively rare to find instances in which these concepts have been integrated into curriculum planning. Until concepts such as *divergent thinking*, or the ability to draw *implications*, became integrated into overall curriculum planning, they become little but pleasant diversions in the classroom. Students may welcome these mental activities only as games and intellectual gymnastics—a relief from the hard and rather unpleasant work they have come to know as learning.

Each teacher, unconsciously or not, formulates a model or portrait of what the teacher role in education should be. Sometimes the pressure of daily tasks forces us into a model that, upon reflection, we really do not like. Two contrasting models of operation can give an illustration of this. One teacher style pictures the student's mind as an empty bucket. The teacher's job is to pour the sands of knowledge into that bucket as fast as possible. This task is complicated by the limited time the teacher has to pour and the greatly increasing pile of knowledge continually stacking up behind the teacher demanding to be poured. There is a very special place for the knowledge to be poured—the classroom—or in that extension of the classroom—homework. While most of us would indignantly reject this model as our view of teaching, the pressure of daily affairs sometimes leads us to act as though we believed it.

An alternative teacher model to follow is to view the student as a gasoline engine ready to function independently if it can just be given the fuel and the spark. In this instance, the teacher's job is quite different from the frantic shoveling of more and more information into the student's path. Here the teacher judiciously picks out a set of relevant information, strikes the spark, and depends on the student's own motivation and interest to carry him far beyond the boundaries of the classroom in his search for knowledge.

Professor Suchman's paper describes a search for teacher methods which will encourage the student to become autonomous in his search for ideas and solutions to problems. He holds, as do the others writing in this section, that the educational goals, particularly for the gifted, should include procedures for making the student intellectually independent from his instructors, and from the instructors' own biases.

What is the impact of different teacher styles and teacher characteristics upon student performance? More folklore than facts are available because of the difficulty of measuring teacher style reliably. Dr. Spaulding through his establishment of certain teacher-pupil transactions is able to draw some interesting relationships between teacher style and student self-concept, achievement, and creative thinking abilities. The relationship between strict and repressive teaching style and the low self-concept of students fits in nicely with general assumptions on the effect of repressive treatment of children generally.

One of the Spaulding results that needs to be carefully considered by teachers of gifted children is that a supportive and accepting climate provided by the teacher does not seem to be enough to encourage the development of thinking abilities. This climate must be accompanied by teacher direction, limit setting, and effective feedback to improve the quality of student performance. Often, it has been assumed that if the teacher is permissive, this style alone will serve to release the creative abilities of the student.

We also must remember that the influence of teacher and student on one another is a two-way street. A group of children with certain characteristics can certainly modify teacher style. Consider the effect of a noisy band of exuberant and uncontrolled children on a teacher. It is easy to see how the teacher style might change from permissive to controlling for this group. This correlational type of study must therefore be followed by others before any inferences on causality can be drawn.

As the classroom environment becomes a greater source of research data than it has been in the past, we expect much more useful information to be derived that will give us more insight into the importance of various types of teacher performance.

❦ 15

Learning by Discovery

Gertrude Hendrix
Teacher Co-ordinator, UICSM Project
University of Illinois

An analysis of some methods of teaching, considering the question "What is *the* discovery method of teaching?"

THE ISSUE OF LEARNING by discovery and of teaching for learning by discovery is beclouded at present by the fact that each of *three* very different procedures is being called 'The Discovery Method'. They are the inductive method, the nonverbal awareness method, and the incidental method.

THE INDUCTIVE METHOD

Many people think that 'the discovery method' is just another name for the inductive method. The inductive method is nothing new in mathematics education. Colburn's book on teaching arithmetic by this kind of approach[1] was first published in the early 1820's. The companion volume on algebra[2] came a few years later. This method was strongly advocated in

The writer acknowledges with gratitude many helpful suggestions from the following persons who read and criticized an earlier version of this article: Max Beberman, Alice G. Hart, Kenneth B. Henderson, R. Stewart Jones, David A. Page, and J. Richard Suchman, University of Illinois; Merrill B. Hill, Utah State Department of Public Instruction; and Stanley M. Jencks, University of Utah.

[1] Warren Colburn, *First Lessons; Intellectual Arithmetic upon the Inductive Method of Instruction*, new edition, with an introduction to written arithmetic by his son, Warren Colburn, and an introduction by George B. Emerson (Boston: Hilliard, Gray, Little and Wilkins, 1863). [Original edition about forty years earlier; others in 1849, 1858.]

[2] Warren Colburn, *An Introduction to Algebra upon the Inductive Method of Instruction* (Boston: Cummings, Hilliard, and Company, 1826).

reports of the National Committee on Reorganization of Secondary School Mathematics in 1918 and 1923. That committee of the Mathematical Association of America drew heavily on earlier recommendations of E. H. Moore in the United States, Perry in England, and Felix Klein in Germany–mathematicians who were writing of these things around the turn of the century. Again in the early 1940's, the Joint Committee of the National Council of Teachers of Mathematics and the Mathematical Association of America, in a report published as a yearbook of the National Council,[3] strongly advocated the inductive method. These recommendations, however, were acted upon by such a small minority of teachers of mathematics that most people seeing the inductive method in action today think they are seeing something new. Furthermore, in clarity and productive outcome it is so far superior to an authoritarian "tell'm and drill" approach that, to someone whose school experience has been dominated by a formal approach, the inductive method seems the final answer to all pedagogical difficulties. Hence, someone just now beginning to think seriously about theory of instruction is likely to look upon the inductive method as the ultimate answer. *The fallacy in the inductive method lies in its confusion of verbalization of discovery with the advent of the discovery itself.*

The separation of discovery phenomena from the process of composing sentences which express those discoveries is the big new breakthrough in pedagogical theory. In some cases, correct verbalization of a discovery *does* emerge immediately after the dawning of awareness, but these cases are rare. They are confined to learners with unusual powers of correctness and precision in the use of a mother tongue, and they are confined to situations in which the learner happens to possess all the vocabulary and rules of sentence structure needed to formulate the new discovery. In most cases, for evidence that an inductive discovery has occurred, a teacher must be able to recognize responses or behavior other than a linguistic formulation of the discovery. The widespread confusion of sentence formation with the discovery process itself has been responsible for much of the frustration, discouragement, and ultimate abandonment of the inductive method on the part of many teachers who have attempted to master it. As one head of a teachers college department of education has put it, "But the only ones who can state a generalization from examining examples are the same exceptionally bright ones who could have learned to apply the generalization from studying someone else's statement of it in the first place!" As a matter of fact, the only teachers who have been really successful with the inductive method are the rare ones who have acquired the knack of making the learner *aware* of generalizations

[3] National Council of Teachers of Mathematics, *Fifteenth Yearbook* (New York. Bureau of Publications, Teachers College, Columbia University, 1940). Cf. item (c) p. 57.

before calling for verbalizations. They have been doing "right things for wrong reasons," and the subsequent untimely verbalizations have only partially marred the outcomes.

If the writer may be permitted so personal a statement, I should like to record here that it was while in pursuit of greater skill with the inductive method that I first became conscious of the nonverbal awareness stage in discovery learning. From concentrated work in helping student teachers to acquire skill in this method, I had become very conscious of three bad mistakes which beginners are likely to make when they plan and attempt inductive teaching:

1. They begin to call for generalizations, exerting anxious pressure on their classes, long before the students have noticed any basic similarity among the examples the teacher has presented. This discussion degenerates into a guessing contest during which the students try to find out "what it is the teacher wants me to say."
2. The teacher often calls for statements of generalizations when the students do not possess the vocabulary and rules of sentence formation necessary for a precise verbalization of the generalization, even if they have "seen it."
3. The teacher often confuses generalizations which had to be discovered in the first place and, hence, are appropriate subject matter for rediscovery with situations in which the generalization is arbitrary—something that is merely a matter of definition.

A frequent costly consequence of item 2 above is a teacher's yielding to a temptation to accept a faulty answer, an answer which is either false or nonsense. Spontaneous verbal responses at moments of discovery are usually expressive of emotion only. Often they are ejaculations, referentially haphazard. Sometimes they are in sentence form but seem to be utter nonsense if repeated and examined. Or, still worse, they may be plausible, *interpretable* sentences which state false generalizations. Spontaneous verbal fragments often provide clues from which a clever teacher can infer what is in a student's mind, and for that purpose they are valuable. But, unless the teacher is a tutor working with only one pupil, encouraging such responses can be very damaging to the learning under way in *other* members of the class. Even in the tutoring situation, an incorrect spontaneous verbalization of a discovery—a sentence which really says something else—must be ignored and forgotten as soon as possible. Accepting it as a "nice try" can cause an involuntary interpretation of the false sentence to prevail over the correct discovery. If *any* recognition is accorded to such a response, the teacher must stick with it until counter examples have revealed to the whole class that the sentence must be discarded. By this time the class has shifted to an exercise in language composition, which cannot be abandoned tactfully. Pushing on through to a correct verbalization at such a time usually demands a long, laborious digression. By the time the point is clear, most of the zest for the original learning has evaporated; and the production of the correct sentence, accepted at long last, may even destroy the anticipatory attitude with which ensuing applications of the generalization should be approached. (Experimentation has established that this effect of finality and detachment is avoided if verbalization of a generalization is postponed to a later lesson. At that time the linguistic formulation of things already "known" can be undertaken as an end in itself.)

The big problem in the inductive method has been to find some way of telling when students are far enough along in an inductive approach for it to be *fair* to ask them to state a generalization. It was while a search was under way for a criterion by which to identify this stage in each inductive lesson that an event came along which led to my identification of the nonverbal awareness stage in discoveries of concepts and generalizations. This happened in 1937.

As early as 1946, clinical experts in nondirective psychological counseling were pointing out that frequently there were very significant changes in behavior based on unverbalized insights, and that the effectiveness of an interview could be destroyed by premature pressure for verbalization. The counseling experts were *not* telling us, however, how to detect when it was *not too soon* to press for verbalizations. When I designed my first experiment[4] for research on this question, for one group of subjects the teaching was terminated at the nonverbal awareness stage simply to call attention to the fact that that stage existed, that there *was* a way to tell when a learner was aware of a generalization which he might be asked to state. At the time that I designed this part of the experiment, it did not occur to me that as far as transfer power was concerned, the *whole* thing was there as soon as the nonverbal awareness had dawned. No one was more shocked than I was to find that not only did the learners who completed correct verbalization of the discovery do no better on transfer tests than those for whom the teaching was terminated at the nonverbal awareness stage, but also that the verbalization of the discovery seemed actually to have diminished the power of some persons to apply the generalization. Charles Hubbard Judd in his conscious generalization theory of transfer had considered 'generalizing' as synonymous with 'composing a sentence which states the generalization involved'.[5] But that simply is not the case; unless Judd's definition of 'generalizing' is changed, we can no longer say that generalizing is the primary generator of transfer power.

Since 1946, the problems have become:

[4] Gertrude Hendrix, "A New Clue to Transfer of Training," *Elementary School Journal*, XLVIII (December 1947), 197–208.

[5] "The human power of generalization is so intimately related to the evolution of language that the two cannot be thought of as existing separately . . . language is the chief instrument of generalization. . . ." C. H. Judd, *The Psychology of Secondary Education* (Boston: Ginn and Co., 1927).

a) How can teaching be planned and executed so that necessary verbalizations of discoveries are accomplished *without* damage to the dynamic quality of the learning itself?

b) What is there about the nature of language and the process of acquiring a language, and what goes on when one uses language that could explain (and, hence, help us to avoid) detrimental effects of verbalization?

Very soon a tremendously important by-product of this search began to appear: The discovery process itself is so exhilarating (to both children and adults) that it becomes its own motive in academic work. As a solution to the motivation problem for children in a free society whose existence is threatened by rapidly increasing scientific and technical power in the land of an enemy, the promotion of successful learning by discovery has no parallel. But such teaching is an art with a difficult technique. Furthermore, it is dependent upon sound and clearly written textbook materials. Ambiguities, inconsistencies, "fuzzy" writing tolerated for centuries—all these must be eliminated from science and mathematics courses. (Another field in which such stumbling blocks abound is that of grammatical construction of word languages. The unifying concepts common to all languages are now revealed by developments of the last half century in symbolic logic, but as yet these developments have not been utilized in reorganization of grammar.)

The Nonverbal Awareness Method

This method has been described incidentally in the above discussion of the inductive method. It will be further explained, perhaps, in the illustration developed in the second part of this article. This is the method of teaching which has been found most successful with the UICSM Mathematics Project materials. The materials are written to promote use of the method with a minimum of difficulty for a teacher to whom both materials and method are new.

The Incidental Method

This is an approach widely promoted during the Progressive Education era.

It is the method in which the school sets the stage for many experiences, which are usually being built around some central problem or project. Those who advocated this method knew that only generalizations which emerged from experiences were likely to play a dynamic part in the learner's later behavior and problem-solving activity. But all too often they took no responsibility for seeing that instances of the same generalization came along close enough together for the learner to become aware of either concepts or principles. With no underlying explanatory theory, those educators simply did not realize that most learners under such conditions seldom "broke through" to awareness of abstractions. Such a school program was doomed to triviality, except in the hands of a teacher who did many additional things, even though he did them for unsound reasons. Many persons today associate this triviality of results from many of the so-called 'activity programs' with learning by discovery. They thus reject anything called 'discovery method'.

Illustrations

The three separate and very different teaching procedures, each referred to by its proponents as '*the* discovery method', can be illustrated by reference to ways of teaching a multiplication rule for quotients. All three of the so-called discovery techniques are in contrast to any approach through initial statement of a rule. Just to get that approach out of our minds let's examine two possible statements of such a rule, one verbal, the other mathematical:

1. For each first number, for each second number not zero, for each third number, for each fourth number not zero, the quotient of the first number by the second number multiplied by the quotient of the third number by the fourth number is the product of the first number by the third number divided by the product of the second number by the fourth number.

2. $\forall_a \forall_{b \neq 0} \forall_c \forall_{d \neq 0} \frac{a}{b} \times \frac{c}{d} = \frac{ac}{bd}$.

Such sentences are avoided in traditional textbook approaches by resorting to garbled mixtures of arithmetic and meta-mathematics–rules which abandon references to numbers and tell one how to manipulate figures to get an answer. The very existence of such language as '. . . the product of the numerators over the product of the denominators' traces to confusion between numerals and the entities which numerals represent. Mathematicians have become aware of entities and relations between the entities; they have then named, or symbolized, the entities and described the relations between them; and then they have thought that they were giving us the essence of their discoveries when they gave us the symbols and sentences. In the resulting desperation to make things clearer, they have composed verbal descriptions of *their symbols and what they do with them*, a sorry substitute for making those with whom they are trying to communicate aware of the concepts and generalizations they themselves have in mind on a nonverbal level. Stating an arithmetic generalization concerning products of quotients requires sentences about numbers. If a mathematician says what he means, he needs sentences of the types illustrated in (1) and (2). In contrast, let us see how discovery lessons based on each of the three interpretations of "discovery method" outlined above would proceed.

Prerequisite to all three of the approaches are these previous learnings:

1. When a rectangle is divided into six congruent squares, each square is called 'one-sixth of the whole'; or, in general, for each counting number n, if a rectangle is divided into n congruent squares, then each square is called 'one-*nth* of the whole rectangle'.

2. When a rectangle two units wide and three units long is divided into unit squares, the resulting six squares can be thought of as two of three, or as three of two, that is, two rows of three squares each, or three columns of two squares each. That is, for each counting number m, for each counting number n, a rectangle m units long and n units wide is made up of m of n squares or n of m squares.

3. The number of unit squares in any rectangle of the kind described above is mn, that is, multiplication is the arithmetic process by which one finds the area-measure of a rectangle when he knows its length-measure and width-measure.

Inductive Method

The class reviews the three items above, probably in the reverse order from that in which they are stated above. [It would be a more natural quasi-research approach if a problem to be solved had been stated first, for example:

$$\text{What is } \frac{1}{2} \text{ of } \frac{3}{4}\text{?}$$

Unfortunately, things are not usually done in this order. Hence, the prerequisite review is imposed authoritatively by the teacher, instead of being something thought of as a way of shedding light on a new, unsolved problem. Conducting a review before stating the problem injects a false and unnatural element into the discovery process, and robs the children of experience in an important technique of research.]

Second, if not earlier, the problem is stated, and the teacher helps the student to find an answer to the question, "What is $\frac{1}{2}$ of $\frac{3}{4}$?" by making appropriate drawings (Figures 1, 2, 3) and then counting.

First, a rectangle is divided into fourths and three of them are shaded. Next, the shaded part is divided into halves, and cross shading is used to identify one-half of three-fourths of the original rectangle. Finally, each part of the cross-shaded section is found by counting to be one-eighth of the original rectangle. Then, by counting, the children see that one-half of three-fourths of the rectangle is three-eighths of the rectangle. So,

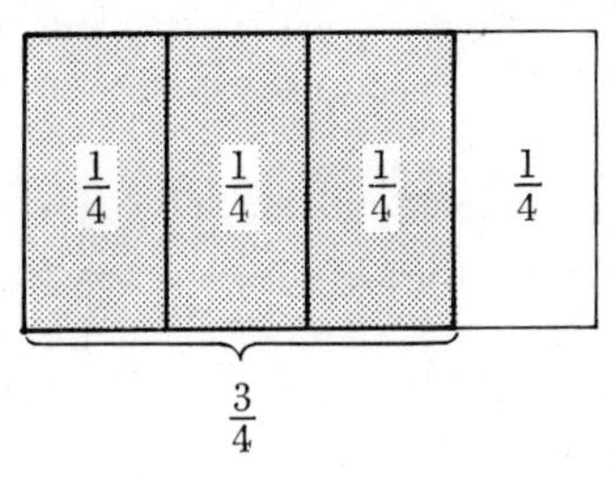

Figure 1

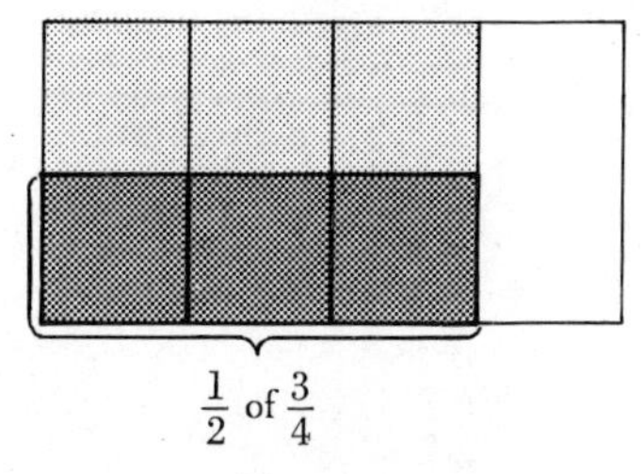

Figure 2

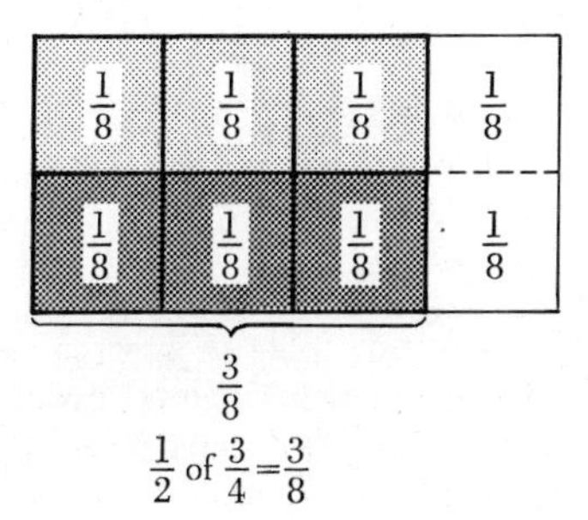

Figure 3

the teacher records on the chalkboard at one side, possibly under the heading 'Data':

$$\frac{1}{2} \text{ of } \frac{3}{4} = \frac{3}{8} \cdot$$

Referring back to 'two of three' and 'three of two' as synonyms for '3×2' and '2×3', all agree that it should be all right[6] to restate the last problem as:

[6] In the UICSM materials the "times" sign, '×,' means *multiplied by*. That is, in '$\frac{3}{4} \times \frac{1}{2}$', the number named second is the multiplier.

$$\frac{3}{4} \times \frac{1}{2} = \frac{3}{8}.$$

The period at the end of the first line of data is erased and the line is changed to this restatement of the problem:

$$\frac{1}{2} \text{ of } \frac{3}{4} = \frac{3}{8}, \qquad \text{or } \frac{3}{4} \times \frac{1}{2} = \frac{3}{8}.$$

This process of making and examining appropriate drawings is repeated for at least three more examples, but usually not more than that. By this time, the recorded data may look something like this:

$$\frac{1}{2} \text{ of } \frac{3}{4} = \frac{3}{8}, \qquad \text{or } \frac{3}{4} \times \frac{1}{2} = \frac{3}{8}.$$

$$\frac{2}{3} \text{ of } \frac{1}{5} = \frac{2}{15}, \qquad \text{or } \frac{1}{5} \times \frac{2}{3} = \frac{2}{15}.$$

$$\frac{3}{4} \text{ of } \frac{3}{5} = \frac{9}{20}, \qquad \text{or } \frac{3}{5} \times \frac{3}{4} = \frac{9}{20}.$$

$$\frac{3}{7} \text{ of } \frac{2}{3} = \frac{6}{21}, \qquad \text{or } \frac{2}{3} \times \frac{3}{7} = \frac{6}{21}.$$

A teacher alert to the structural properties of the set of numbers of arithmetic will also have, for example:

$$\frac{3}{4} \text{ of } \frac{1}{2} = \frac{3}{8}, \qquad \text{or } \frac{1}{2} \times \frac{3}{4} = \frac{3}{8}.$$

The differences between the experimental procedure for this exercise and the drawings in Figures 1 to 3 will have been illustrated on the board as follows with Figures 4 to 6:

New Problem: $\frac{3}{4}$ of $\frac{1}{2} = ?$

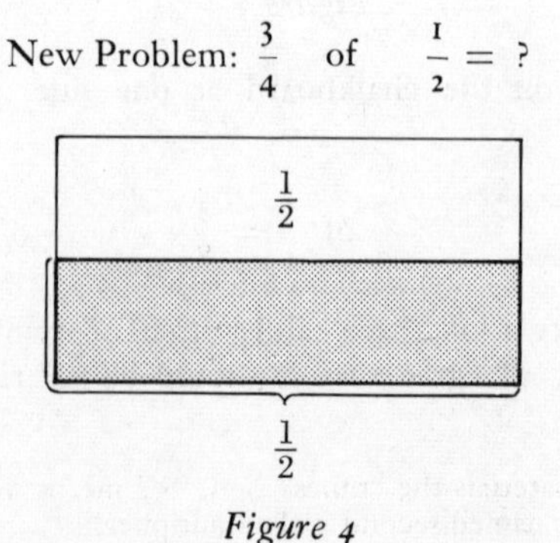

Figure 4

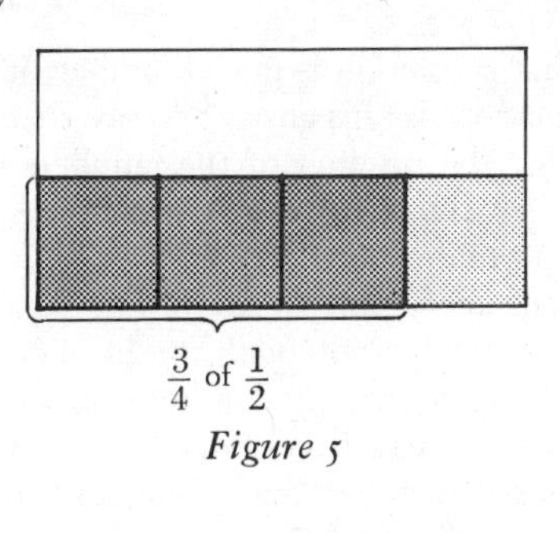

Figure 5

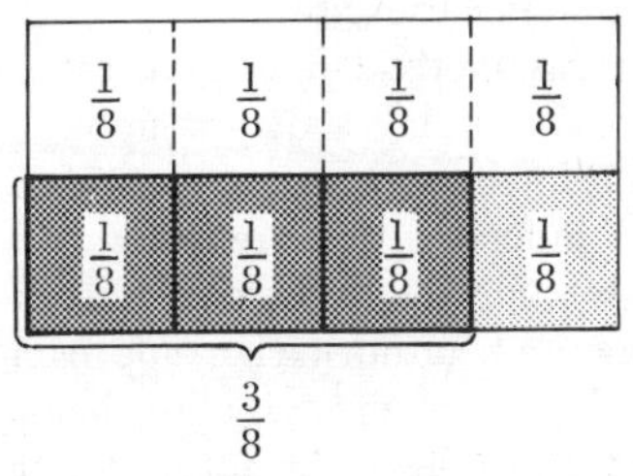

Figure 6

So $\frac{3}{4}$ of $\frac{1}{2} = \frac{3}{8}$, or $\frac{1}{2} \times \frac{3}{4} = \frac{3}{8}$, and a corresponding entry is included in the table of data.

The next part of the inductive lesson is usually introduced by the teacher with some remark, such as "Now, let's see how we could have found the answers just by looking at the fractions." The children are told to examine each pair of fractions and the fraction which names the product, and to try to tell how they could have found the product without drawing the picture. In the inductive method, *the ability to "tell how to do it" is the criterion by which the teacher recognizes that discovery has taken place.*

As a matter of fact, children at this stage in arithmetic do not have the linguistic machinery for stating precisely what they mean when they *have* discovered the rule. The inductive method forces them into saying such things as "Well, you multiply the top numbers, and you multiply the bottom numbers, and then you write the top answer over the bottom answer."

A teacher's insistence on more polished statements may call for something like "Well, to get the numerator of the answer, you multiply the numerator of the first fraction by the numerator of the second fraction; then. . . ."

If the teacher is one of those rare ones who is trying to keep clear the distinction between numbers and numerals, he must then go back and remind the student that a fraction is not a number; it is a *name* for a number. So the student must revise his answer to say that the numerator of the answer is a numeral for the product of the numbers named by the numerators of the two original fractions, etc. All this time, the teacher keeps insisting that "If you can't tell it, you don't know it."

Finally, a statement acceptable to the teacher is achieved. Each student may write the new rule in his notebook, or he may be asked to turn the page in his book, where he will find a rule already stated. (Of course, some members of the class may have looked ahead already and found out what they were supposed to be saying.) The students are then considered ready to work a set of practice exercises.

When well done, this method does give each student what is sometimes called "an intuitive crutch," a device upon which he can fall back; he can repeat the experiment whenever he finds himself in doubt about the rule. Security and independence are provided, and, in contrast to a tell-them-and-drill approach, the inductive lesson seems a revelation in pedagogy. A well-presented authoritarian approach is very satisfying to someone who *is already aware of* the ideas being presented; but for a learner to whom the ideas are new, the authoritarian method at its best is a *feeble* best in comparison with the inductive method. And *the inductive method at its best* is a feeble best in comparison with a genuine discovery approach which promotes and recognizes a nonverbial awareness stage in creative thought.

The Nonverbal Awareness Method

Let us contrast the procedure called the inductive method with a discovery lesson which follows more closely a pattern of genuine research. The goal, as in the preceding development, is the "multiplying fractions" rule.

In this approach, statement of a problem *must* precede the developmental review leading to the physical space drawing experiment by which an answer is found. From then on, the lesson may proceed exactly as in the inductive method up to a certain point. Then a highly significant, sharply defined difference appears. In *this* kind of discovery approach, as soon as each child has mastered the drawing-and-counting device for finding products of pairs of quotients, he is given a list of problems to work. As far as the student knows, he is to work every problem on the list by making an appropriate drawing. The class activity thus shifts to individual seat work. What is not done before the bell rings is to be finished for homework. The problems on the list should be arranged to promote interesting observations. The work sheet should provide a space for recording the answers to the problems. (At least two pairs of consecutive examples will illustrate the commutative principle for multiplication.)

To give pause to the conscientious little task-doer who might work the whole list by making drawings just because that is what the directions (or the teacher) said to do, examples like the one below should be included:

$$\frac{17}{21} \times \frac{11}{19} = ?$$

Students accustomed to this kind of discovery approach will, of course, be on the lookout for a short cut. Furthermore, from previous experience with the course and their teacher, pupils will know that finding and using a short cut is something that will be highly approved. Until this experience has been built up, the directions for the exercise must contain some challenge, such as "If at any time you think you know what an answer is going to be *before* you make the drawing, please write down the answer and raise your hand." When a hand goes up, the teacher should go to the student, congratulate him, or advise him to check his hunch by another experimental drawing. It must be pointed out, however, that this direction injects a false note into the stage setting for true research. It is simply a device by which a teacher helps a class to get its first experiences with this kind of learning.

In such a lesson, *how does the teacher know when a discovery has taken place?* Suppose he is walking about the class looking over shoulders. A sudden start, a flush of excitement, and a student begins writing answers almost as fast as he can put them down. When a student begins to write correct answers without making the drawings, we have evidence of the advent of awareness. Awareness of what? Awareness of the "multiplying fractions" rule.

If the child were not aware of it, he couldn't be using it. To call a halt in his progress at this point for a long, tedious verbalization attempt is damaging in several ways. In the first place, it belittles the exhilarating accomplishment of the actual discovery. Whether he can "tell it" or not, the *child* knows very well that he *has* something.

Then, in the second place, the verbalization attempt at this grade-school level is doomed to frustration. Numerical variables, universal quantifiers, and the zero restrictions on domains are all necessary to a precise formulation of the generalization the child has just discovered. The most that a teacher can do is to accept a garbled verbalization of what was at the beginning a clear, dynamic insight. The more sensitive a child is to precision in the use of his mother tongue, the more damaging this process can be to him and to the learning which a moment before was so clear on the nonverbal awareness level. The more skillful the child is in interpreting his mother tongue, the higher the probability that a literal interpretation of his own incorrect statement will impinge itself upon him. If this literal interpretation of his incorrect statement contradicts the awareness that was already there, the original learning is mutilated.[7] In a lesson of this kind, the child who notices that his neighbor is writing correct answers without making drawings is electrified into a search for "what's going on." Knowing that one of his classmates has discovered a short cut has a much more highly motivating effect upon him than a search for short cuts suggested by the teacher. The child who does not discover the rule before the end of the class period still has his chance during his homework period—if well-meaning parents do not step in and spoil it all for him!

On the following day the teacher presents other examples, such as:

$$\frac{5}{3} \times \frac{7}{8}$$

$$\frac{6}{5} \times \frac{9}{4}$$

$$\frac{6}{2} \times \frac{21}{7}.$$

In other words, *over*generalization and incomplete generalization are prevented by the introduction of *examples* which correct possible false impressions, *not* by verbalizing the rule at this stage of the game and conducting a sophisticated search for false instances. (The more sophisticated procedure is available and appropriate a few years later when these same children will have acquired the necessary linguistic equipment.)

I do not wish to belittle the tremendous improvement in instruction which results from pursuing the inductive method, in contrast to authoritarian procedures. But those who think teaching for discovery *is* the inductive method are still blinded to this second tremendous break through in theory of instruction. It is recognition of the nonverbal awareness stage in inductive learning that converts the classroom experience into that of actual discovery, the kind of thing that promotes a taste for and a delight in research.

The Incidental Method

In contrast to both of the instructional procedures outlined above, let us think about the teacher who trusts that the "multiplying fractions" rule will be discovered incidentally.

In one project a child will need to find the cost of a sheet of gold leaf to line a jewelry box, for instance, when he knows the cost per square foot and knows that the sheet must be one-half foot wide and three-fourths foot

[7] I use the word 'mutilated' deliberately and almost angrily. My feeling about this issue has been built up from several years' experience in seeing this thing happen to children over and over again.—The Author

long. He is taken through the drawing experiment until he finds an answer. No other instances of multiplying one quotient by another come along in *that* project. Six weeks later (or six months, or a year) in connection with another project, he has another occasion to find the product of two quotients. Again the physical space drawings are used, the answer is found, and the project proceeds. All pressure from teacher and group is directed toward finishing the project. (Anyone who becomes intrigued by the multiplication process itself and digresses to investigate will be frowned upon by many of the educators advocating this kind of schoolwork.) From such examples widely distributed over time and space, the probability that the generalization will emerge is almost zero. Only a little genius who has somehow escaped with his taste for contemplation undestroyed will recall such widely scattered experiences all at the same time, and hence become aware of the mathematical generalization underlying them. Critics of education who confuse this kind of school program with everything else referred to as 'learning by discovery' are justified in opposing a discovery method. Much as I, the writer, abhor authoritarian presentations of sentences which express generalizations, the words *later* to be clarified by examples, I would prefer falling back upon that relatively deadly and deadening procedure, rather than to rely upon important basic principles 'coming clear' from experiences incidental to so-called 'project activity'.

So much for the status of the discovery method in educational parlance and educational literature at the beginning of the decade to be known as 'the sixties'! It is high time, however, for another category to be added to the list when discovery in *mathematics* is under discussion. Even the instructional procedure described under the nonverbal awareness method is not properly called '*the* discovery method'. It *is* possible to arrive at discovery by pure deduction, that is, by manipulating sentences according to logical rules. It is not likely, but neither is it impossible, that the "multiplying fractions" rule would be discovered by derivation; most deductive proofs are checks for sentences first arrived at inductively; but *some* very important principles, both in mathematics and in physical science, *have* been discovered by deduction. A good example of something in secondary-school mathematics usually discovered (that is, *re*discovered) in this way is the rule for finding the measure of one side of a triangle in terms of measures of the other two sides and the cosine of the measure of their included angle. This is a case in which one begins with some sentences which express observations of a drawing. Starting with these sentences as premises, pure deduction takes over and out comes the desired formula. This last sentence, discovered deductively, is then interpreted in terms of how the variables were used in the original drawing. This interpretation of a final sentence in the deductive sequence reveals the desired geometric rule. This is a discovery process just as truly as is the inductive leap that takes place in the nonverbal awareness type of discovery. How do we know that both are discovery? Because a person can do them *all by himself*. The thing learned is not received by communication.

Much of the confusion permeating discussions of learning by discovery comes from failure to distinguish discovery from communication. One does not *discover* a concept or a principle in a book. He may discover there a *name* of a concept, a definition, a *sentence* which states a principle, etc., but before he "has" anything, he must engage himself in the process of interpreting the words and sentences of the author, that is, he must complete a communication process. Communication[8] usually plays an important part in setting the stage for discovery in the teaching of mathematics, but that part is quite different from actually communicating the new thing to be learned.

[8] A rationale of communication adequate for explaining this distinction has emerged from the nonverbal awareness research at the University of Illinois; the author hopes to make the theory available in print soon.

16

Learning by Discovery: Psychological and Educational Rationale

Hilda Taba
San Francisco State College

ONE OF THE INTERESTING phenomena in the development of ideas about learning and teaching today is the fact that the curriculum projects that were started to strengthen the role of content in the learning process have turned around and renewed the emphasis on cultivation of higher mental processes as the central outcome of learning (1).

Learning by discovery is one concept made popular by the new curriculums in mathematics and science. This concept is arousing the same kind of controversy that a few decades ago used to rage around the issue of content versus process.

THE HISTORY OF THE IDEA

Learning by discovery is not the completely new invention that some of its proponents as well as its critics seem to assume. My own explorations take me back as far as 1904.

At that time Mary E. Boole published a little booklet called *Preparation of the Child for Science* (2). Influenced by the theories of thinking developed by her husband, George Boole, and Gratry, the French priest-logician, she developed ideas about learning and thinking that are amazingly similar to the characterization of discovery learning today.

She was concerned with the laws of the sequence of thought and was trying to evolve a way of guiding the child to the "working of the scientific mind which puts itself in relation to the 'As-Yet-Unknown-Truth' " (2: 15). She was especially concerned with the ways by which children can be led to "extract the truth from a series of impressions and statements, each of which is only partially true" (2: 20).

She spoke of the need for demarcation between "what the individual child has observed and what he has learned at second hand," of the importance for children to discover the laws of nature that govern what they explore. She stressed the importance of "unconscious cerebration" and advised parents and teachers to "keep silence even from good words" (2: 25) and to refrain from pushing children into premature awareness, because this "unconscious cerebration" takes place when children are occupied with explorations that they do not perceive as something for their own instruction.

She warned that there is no such thing as "*a* right method of performing any operation in elementary mathematics; because all rightness and all mathematicalness depends on getting each operation performed by *two methods:* the first, a roundabout one, which represents and registers the conscious action of the mind during the *process of discovery* [italics mine]; the second, a short method which condenses the roundabout one, assists in stowing its results away in the memory and facilitates the using of them sub-consciously" (2: 101).

Something akin to learning set is suggested in her description of mathematical imagination, which, she wrote, "depends on the child being put into the right attitude towards mathematical conceptions in his earliest years" (2: 102).

These ideas could be matched almost point by point with current conceptions of the process of learning by discovery: helping learners get at the structure, or at the laws and principles of a subject, by allowing them to discover these laws and principles through intensive exploration of concrete instances; withholding verbalization of the basic principles until they are understood operationally and used intuitively; defining the process of learning as an active organization and reorganization of mental schemata with which to process information and to perceive relationships; strengthening the process of inference, that is, the process of going beyond that which is given (3, 4, 5).

Some elements of the current conception of discovery learning can also be found among the ideas of Maria Montessori (6), though in a more rigid form. She, too, was interested in the sequence of mental development. She maintained that abstractions were always a result of individual experience and required "pre-building" through a proper organization of these experiences.

Her mathematical games were organized to allow children to absorb impressions in their own way to promote a subconscious process of organizing, presumably independently of consciousness and will. She talked of the cultivation of the mathematical mind rather than of learning mathematics.

Inquiry as a method of learning was, of course, central to all Dewey's teaching and writing. In his *How We Think* he developed the theoretical concept of the nature of inquiry and of reflective thought. He identified learning with thinking, and thinking with active discovery of relationships and organizing principles. He considered the quality of searching to be the prime motive power of thinking and, therefore, maintained that the problem-solving processes are essential to active learning (7).

The advent of Gestalt psychology introduced a new stream of interest in learning by discovery. To describe active cognitive processes, Gestalt psychology introduced such concepts as insight, transposition, and meaning.

Insight was interpreted as the moment of discovering the organizing principle or the crucial relationship. Transposition was interpreted as an act of reorganizing one's conceptual scheme, something akin to what Wertheimer and Piaget call decentering (8, 9). These concepts are only now acquiring a firmer and a more operational definition (10: 33–36).

Several research studies have been conducted to examine the role of the discovery method and of insight in thinking. As early as 1934, T. R. McConnell conducted a study that compared discovery learning with authoritarian identification in the thinking of children (11). The volume that reports McConnell's study includes a report on a study by Lyle K. Henry (12), "The Role of Insight in the Analytic Thinking of Children."

The chief hypothesis of McConnell's experiment was that to learn is to discover. One learns through experience to discover "configurations" and to transpose them to carry out different tasks. One does not truly understand what one does not discover, and one cannot learn what one does not understand.

It was further assumed that achievement of insight involves differentiation and that habituation comes at the end rather than at the beginning of the sequence of learning acts. To test this assumption, the experimental group in McConnell's study manipulated the number relationships until they understood them before establishing or verbalizing the rules.

Henry found that insight was achieved when a correct transposition took place which enabled application. He further found that ability to apply principles meant that evidence was logically and psychologically related. Insight was characterized by suddenness of perception, a feeling of surety, and an inclination to ask heuristic questions (12). Later Swenson studied the role of organization and generalization in learning and in transfer (13).

Two Dimensions of Learning

Learning by discovery, as pursued today, pertains largely to cognitive aspects of learning: the development and organization of concepts, ideas, and insights, and the use of inference and other logical processes to control a situation. The content of these explorations is, furthermore, limited to science and mathematics.

Naturally, there are other types of learning, such as mastering the skill of typing or memorizing a poem, in which the cognitive control of the situation is at a minimum. There are also other types of content in which cognition and valuing merge. To assume that the principles of learning by discovery apply to all varieties of learning or apply to all in a similar way leads to misapprehension.

Basic to the varied and partial definitions of discovery learning by different authors is the conception of learning as a transactional process that involves at least two different aspects: the assimilation of content of some sort and operations of cognitive processes required to organize and use this content.

In most past studies these two aspects of the learning process have been separated and unevenly stressed: either one or the other was represented as the chief focus, while the other was designated as an incidental by-product.

The so-called progressive practices tended to understress the role of content, largely because the early progressive education was a reaction against rote mastery of sterile subject matter. In contrast, those who have defended the primacy of content have often overlooked the importance of cultivating active mental processes, partly because they have assumed that assimilation of well-organized content automatically produces the necessary patterns of thinking.

The recent rationale of learning by discovery seems to bring process and content into a transactional relationship. The rationale stresses the need for a strategy for cultivating autonomous mental processes in relation to the requirements of the structure or the logic of the particular content.

The learner must construct his own conceptual schemata with which to process and to organize whatever information he receives. Teaching is directed to enabling the learner to establish a relationship between his existing schemata and the new phenomena and to remake or extend the schemata to accommodate new facts and events. In doing this the learner has to decenter his current view of the situation or of the problem before him and reorganize his perception of it. He must also build a strategy of inquiry (5).

A different view of content is also involved. Content is seen not only as an array of facts to be absorbed, but as something that has structure, namely, a way of organizing detailed facts in the light of some concepts and principles.

A falling body can be viewed only as a discrete event or as an organization of gravitational forces. When one assimilates knowledge of the first sort, one has to learn each new fact anew. When one comprehends the principle of gravitation, one has hold of a more dynamic knowledge that enables one to explain and understand new phenomena and predict the consequences of events. One gets, as Bruner puts it, greater mileage from learning (3).

The act of discovery occurs at the point in the learner's efforts at which he grasps the organizing principle imbedded in a concrete instance or in a series of instances and can therefore transform this information: the learner can see the relationship of the facts before him, he can understand the causes of the phenomenon, and he can relate what he sees to his prior knowledge (4, 10). This point in the learner's efforts is also referred to as the moment of insight.

These acts of discovery are the product of the individual's intellectual effort; the nature of these acts, however, is dictated by the structure of the subject matter with which the learner deals. If the discovery is not related to the logic or the structure of the subject matter, we have what Wertheimer calls "dirty," "ugly," or "insensible" procedure (8: 24–33).

An Inductive Sequence

Learning by discovery involves an inductive sequence. This sequence starts not with the exposition of the general principle, but with exposing the learner to some concrete instances of the principle that he can analyze, manipulate, and experiment with, either symbolically or actually.

Such an instance must be studied in considerable depth to discover the rule, the idea, the principle, or the generalization that underlies it, such as the generalization behind a particular mathematical operation or the anthropological meaning of the specific way of building houses in a specific culture (14: 356 ff.). In such a sequence, an intuitive or operational grasp of the generalization precedes its verbalization.

Several proponents of this method argue that a premature verbalization of the generalization or the rule deprives the individual of the essential learning, namely, the reorganization of his own cognitive structure, and puts the student in the position of absorbing the generalization without necessarily understanding what it stands for or how to work it.

This differentiation between knowing the generalization and understanding what it stands for has led some proponents of discovery learning to insist that the subverbal or the intuitive process is the important and the essential characteristic of productive learning (4, 15).

This emphasis on intuitive learning as a prerequisite to conscious statement of the principle has often been interpreted as a negation of verbalization on any level. This interpretation does not do justice to what seem to be the actual operations in the classroom. It is only the premature verbalization of the central generalization to be learned that is delayed to allow the operational insight into its nature to take place and to permit the process of discovery to function.

The students must show operational evidence of their understanding before they are faced with formulating the rule or the principle for their operations, and the teacher must distinguish between the advent of the discovery and its verbalization. (Space does not permit me to deal with the problem of the relationship of language and verbalization to thinking.)

This distinction between the two levels of verbalization permits a clearer orientation toward the many claims made for discovery learning. The characteristics of discovery learning described here may also help to distinguish achieving meaningful learning from achieving intellectual potency. The two are often confused.

Ausubel, for example, argues that learning by the discovery method is not the necessary condition for meaningful learning, at least not for all kinds of learning or for all age levels. As the sophistication of the learner increases, the necessity for discovery learning decreases. He points out, further, that since learning by discovery is time-consuming, to use this method of learning exclusively would greatly reduce the scope of learning (16).

However, if one considers the intellectual potency or the productivity of cognitive activity as the chief outcome, one needs to redefine *meaningfulness* to include intellectual potency. Or else the effects of learning by discovery need to be considered in two different dimensions: the understanding of the meaning and the ability to use certain cognitive processes. Both need to be differentiated from mechanical or rote learning.

Hendrix, for example, differentiates knowing what a mathematical sentence stands for (meaning in the ordinary sense) from what she calls the "prerequisite for meaning" or understanding (15). For example, one can know the meaning of a geometric theorem and be able to reproduce it in a drawing, but not understand why it has to be, why certain proof can or should be employed, and how it was derived. She assumes this prerequisite to be an essentially non-verbal process that must precede verbal formulation. This "prerequisite" is very similar to what Mary Boole calls "subconscious" knowledge and to what Piaget calls "intuitive knowledge."

This intuitive or subverbal understanding is acquired by performing certain operations, such as comparing and contrasting prime and nonprime numbers until one gets the idea of what a prime number is and how it operates. This mastery can be demonstrated only by behavioral evidence. Only after the students have mastered operationally the meaning of a generalization, a principle, or a rule, are they ready for a verbal statement of it.

This distinction gives a definition of *meaningfulness* that avoids the black-and-white contrast with rote learning and admits other ways of gain-ing meaning: in other words, learning by discovery is not the only way of arriving at meaning.

Cognitive Autonomy

Learning by discovery may, then, still be considered the chief mode for intellectual productivity and autonomy. When an individual has developed an organizing scheme for his own cognitive activity, he is presumably in a position to harvest a greater amount of knowledge as well as to become increasingly autonomous and independent of all forms of authority. He is better equipped to move into unknown areas, to gather data, and to abstract from these ideas and concepts. A person who can transform what Bruner (17) calls "episodic information" into systematic knowledge is in control of organizing ideas and thereby increases his intellectual power. Further, when the learner relies on his own cognitive processes, when he is aware of the relationship of the learning tasks to his own experience, and when he has developed an attitude of search and an expectation or a set to learn under his own steam, he is in a position to continue these processes on his own.

This type of learning is more permanent and more easily transferable (17), especially when it is addressed to the structure of subject matter. A student who understands the wave theory of sound is presumably in a position to explain the phenomena of light by the same theory. Having learned to look for patterns of prime numbers, the student can use the process on content that is dissimilar to that of prime numbers.

This idea of transfer has led some experimenters to search for the generic, highly transferable skills, such as universal skills of inquiry (5) or skills in problem-solving. How generic such intellectual skills are, and how independent they are of the particular context in which they are acquired, is as yet not too clear.

It is possible that the current models of inquiry and discovery, developed almost exclusively in the neat fields of science and mathematics, may not be applicable to the untidy and multivariant field of social and human problems. This is not to deny the transfer power of generalizations, inquiry skills, searching orientation, scientific attitude, or of the method of asking heuristic questions.

Too often extrinsic rewards only–such as grades–have been used to create motivation for learning. Those concerned with active and discovery learning rightly point out that children and young people are endowed with curiosity and with what White calls "competency motive" (18) and that some approaches to learning are more capable of cultivating this motive than others. Being an active process, learning by discovery is likely to mobilize the competency motive as a drive for learning behavior, to free the learning act from the immediate stimulus control, and to establish the cognitive control of the individual.

Teaching Strategies

Learning by discovery requires a teaching-learning strategy that amounts to setting conditions to make discovery possible. All descriptions of discovery learning imply a specific teaching strategy, even though the existence of this strategy is not always so recognized.

Central in this strategy is the confrontation of learners with problem situations that create a feeling of bafflement and start the process of inquiry. Withholding certain kinds of information and certain kinds of crucial generalizations to challenge the search behavior and to preserve the opportunity for autonomous exploration and experimentation is also usually practiced. The teaching strategy is usually aimed at placing on the individual the responsibility of transforming information and reassembling it to get new insights.

So far, the experimental teaching strategies developed to foster learning by discovery are either imperceptibly imbedded in the programming of content, as in the curriculum in mathematics developed by the University of Illinois Committee on School Mathematics, or they are focused on specific tasks, as in the inquiry strategies developed by Suchman (5).

The first approach assumes that the thought processes are implicit in the sequence of the subject matter. The second approach assumes that a concentrated experience organized around selected instances suffices to produce a generic act of mental operations which, when acquired, are transferable to other settings.

Actually a bit more seems to be involved, namely, a cumulative curriculum and teaching strategy that spans time and various subjects.

When one faces the problem of providing for cumulative learning rather than training for discovery learning per se, one has to face several additional issues. Among these are the balance between assimilative or receptive learning and discovery learning, the balance between expository teaching and training in methods of inquiry, and the issue of depth study and scope. Not everything can be learned or even should be learned by the discovery method. It is time-consuming and, therefore, limits the scope of coverage. A good deal of learning must be accomplished by other means, such as deduction, logical inference, some form of exposition by the teacher, or by reading a book.

The task of organizing instruction, then, is to provide an appropriate balance between discovery learning, which requires depth study, and receptive learning to assure scope.

Depth study for discovery needs to be reserved for points at which new families of concepts or ideas are introduced, wherever or at whatever maturity level they occur. These experiences need to be alternated with intake experiences designed to extend information, generalizations, or their application to assure adequate scope.

Since the principles of depth and scope of curriculum organization are contradictory, the problem of curriculum organization is to replace the current concept of coverage with a concept of appropriate sampling of content that reduces the coverage of detail without reducing the essential idea content. This reorganization can probably be best provided by a curriculum design that focuses on fundamental ideas while judiciously sampling the detail with which to develop these ideas (14: 175–81; 352–59).

References

1. This article is based on a talk given at the symposium of the convention of the American Educational Research Association, Atlantic City, New Jersey, February 20, 1962.
2. M. E. Boole. *Preparation of the Child for Science*. Oxford: Clarendon Press, 1904.
3. J. S. Bruner. *The Process of Education*. Cambridge, Massachusetts: Harvard University Press, 1960.
4. Gertrude Hendrix. "Learning by Discovery," *Mathematics Teacher*, LIV (May, 1961), 290–99.
5. J. Richard Suchman. "Inquiry Training: Building Skills for Autonomous Discovery," *Merrill Palmer Quarterly of Behavior and Development*, VII (July, 1961), 147–69.
6. Mario M. Montessori. "Maria Montessori's Contribution to the Cultivation of the Mathematical Mind," *International Review of Education*, XVII (1961), 134–41.
7. John Dewey. *How We Think*. Boston: D. C. Heath and Company, 1910.
8. Max Wertheimer. *Productive Thinking*. New York: Harper & Brothers, 1945.
9. Jean Piaget. *The Psychology of Intelligence*. London: Routledge and Kegan Paul, 1959.
10. Allen Newell, J. C. Shaw, and Herbert A. Simon. "Elements of a Theory of Human Problem-Solving." Santa Monica, California: RAND Corporation, March 7, 1957.
11. T. R. McConnell. "Discovery vs. Authoritarian Identification in the Thinking of Children," *Studies in Learning II*. Iowa Studies in Education, Vol. IX, No. 5, Iowa City University, 1934.
12. Lyle K. Henry. "The Role of Insight in the Analytic Thinking of Children," *Studies in Learning II*. Iowa Studies in Education, Vol. IX, No. 5, Iowa City University, 1934.

13. Esther J. Swenson. "Organization and Generalization as Factors in Learning, Transfer, and Retroactive Inhibition," in Esther J. Swenson, G. Lester Anderson, and Chalmers L. Stacey, *Learning Theory in School Situations.* Studies in Education, No. 2. Minneapolis, Minnesota: University of Minnesota Press, 1949.

14. Hilda Taba. *Curriculum Development: Theory and Practice.* New York: Harcourt, Brace and World, 1962.

15. Gertrude Hendrix. "Prerequisite to Meaning," *Mathematics Teacher,* XLIII (November, 1950), 334–39.

16. David P. Ausubel. "Indications and Contributions in an Approach to Learning by Discovery," *Educational Leadership,* XX (November, 1962), 113–17.

17. J. S. Bruner. "The Act of Discovery," *Harvard Educational Review,* XXXI (Winter, 1961), 21–32.

18. R. W. White. "Motivation Reconsidered: the Concept of Competence," *Psychological Review,* LXVI (September, 1959), 297–333.

❦ 17

Discovery or Invention?

J. Myron Atkin

Professor of Science Education, University of Illinois

Robert Karplus

Professor of Physics, University of California, Berkeley

RECENTLY, THE DISCUSSION of the role of discovery in teaching has intensified. Many authors have stressed the great educational benefits to be derived if pupils discover concepts for themselves.[1] Other authors have warned that discovery teaching is so time consuming and inefficient that it should not, in general, replace expository teaching.[2]

There is a way in which autonomous recognition of relationships by the pupils; i.e., "discovery" can and should be combined with expository introduction of concepts in an efficient program. This will produce understanding rather than rote verbalization. The approach can be described more clearly, if a historical example[3] is given of how a particular scientific concept is developed.

In ancient times the sun and the planets were observed by man. These observations gave rise to various conceptual interpretations. There were the

NOTE: The experiments in this article were carried out by the authors at the Berkwood School, Berkeley, California, through the cooperation of the Director, Betty Halpern. Financial support for the project was provided by the National Science Foundation, Washington, D.C.

[1] Jerome Bruner. *The Process of Education.* Harvard University Press, Cambridge, Massachusetts. 1960.

[2] David Ausubel. *Learning by Discovery: Rationale or Mystique.* Bureau of Educational Research, University of Illinois, Urbana, Illinois. 1961.

[3] The historical development and its analysis in this illustration have been greatly oversimplified. For a fuller and more profound discussion see: Thomas Kuhn. "The Nature of Scientific Revolutions," University of Chicago Press, Chicago, Illinois. (1963)

mythological interpretations, the interpretation as "celestial matter" with certain properties, and eventually the modern interpretation of planets orbiting around the sun. With the help of each of these concepts, man could attempt to understand other phenomena besides the ones that had led him to suggest the interpretation originally. These attempts, if successful, led to a reinforcement and refinement of the concept; if they failed, they revealed limits of the usefulness of the concept or even stimulated a search for a new concept. Of the three interpretations we have mentioned, the final and currently accepted one has turned out to be much more powerful than its predecessors.

In the development of a concept, it is useful to distinguish the original introduction of a new concept, which can be called invention, from the subsequent verification or extension of the concept's usefulness, which can be called discovery. Of course, this distinction is not completely clear-cut, because the inventor must recognize that the new concept is applicable to the phenomena he is trying to interpret; otherwise he would discard the invention immediately. Return therefore to the example for determining how the distinction can be applied. Assume that the deities, the celestial matter, and the solar system were inventions. In the mythological framework, one could then discover that the deities intervened in human affairs in certain ways and refine one's idea of the characteristics of the gods. In the framework based on the existence of celestial matter, one could discover that celestial objects move in cycles and epicyles. Finally, in the framework of the solar system, one could discover additional planets.

Undoubtedly, an invention is not complete and static, but it is the germ of a concept that is developed to greater significance by the subsequent discoveries. When an invention is made, its full significance is not evident. Still, the concept must be introduced and the invention must be made, if it is to grow in meaning.

Applying this distinction between discovery and invention to science teaching, acknowledge the fact that the pupil has experience both before he enters school and also outside the school environment during the school years. He therefore makes observations all the time, and he invents concepts that interpret the observations as well. He also makes discoveries that enable him to refine his concepts. Most of the discoveries and inventions reveal a type of natural philosophy—a "common-sense" orientation popular in the culture at a given point in history.

Yet, the objective of the science program is to teach children to look at natural phenomena from the distinctive vantage point of modern science. And in the mid-twentieth century, this vantage point differs from the culturally prevalent view. In a small way the situation is analogous to that of a Copernican teacher instructing his students that the sun is at the center of the solar system while almost everyone else in the society *knows* that the earth is at the center of the universe.

In general, no results are evident if a teaching program is based on the expectation that children can invent the modern scientific concepts, because their spontaneously invented concepts, some of which even exist at the time the child enters school, present too much of a block. After all, concepts were developed to interpret their experience; why should they change these concepts on their own? Indeed, it does not seem crucial to teach the children to invent concepts, because they can and do invent concepts readily. The educational problem, rather, is to teach the children to carry out their creative thinking with some intellectual discipline. And the development and refinement of modern scientific concepts in the light of observations would seem to be one excellent vehicle for achieving this goal.

If the children are not able to *invent* the modern scientific concepts, it is necessary for the teacher to *introduce* the modern scientific concepts. During this introduction, the teacher must make clear which previous observations of the children can be interpreted (or perhaps reinterpreted) by using a concept. Further, he must follow the introduction with opportunities for the children to discover that new observations can also be interpreted by using a concept. This type of discovery is made possible by the availability of a concept to the children, because their perception is oriented by the teacher's formulation of the new idea. This type of discovery can be extremely valuable to solidify learning and motivate the children; it is essential, if a concept is to be used with increasing refinement and precision. Categorically, the teacher must not present the concept in a complete, definitive, and authoritarian way, for concepts are never final.

As an example of this teaching approach, a thirty-minute lesson will be described in which second graders discovered the usefulness of the magnetic field concept after the teacher had invented it for them. In thirteen previous sessions, a class of fifteen pupils had discussed the selection of systems by the specification of the objects in the system, and the existence of interactions among the objects, and had been introduced to the notion of the free energy of the system.

Two new concepts were introduced to the class in the lesson: the interaction-at-a-distance, and the magnetic field. These ideas were developed through a series of experiments.

Experiment 1. Two boys pulled on a rope in opposite directions. The pupils identified the system of interest as consisting of Bruce, James, and the rope. Interactions between objects in the system included the one between James and the rope and the one between Bruce and the rope. Bruce and James were considered not to interact with each other. *Invention of interaction-at-a-distance:* Next, the teacher pointed out that Bruce and James were really the important objects in the system; that the whole class could think that there was an interaction between the two boys (at a signal, Bruce yanked James with the rope); but that it was not a *direct interaction,* it was a *distant interaction.* The new term was stressed. The rope made the distant interaction possible. The teacher further asked Bruce and James to interact strongly, then weakly, then strongly again.

Experiment 2. The teacher produced two wooden balls that were held together by a strip of rubber tacked to the balls. Five objects were identified in the system: the two balls, the rubber strip, and the two thumbtacks. The pupils identified the direct interactions ball-rubber, ball-thumbtack, and rubber-thumbtack. They identified the distant interactions ball-ball, thumbtack-thumbtack, and end of rubber-end of rubber. The pupils called the interaction weak when the balls were close together, strong when they were far apart, and medium when they were somewhat separated. The strip of rubber made the distant interaction possible.

Experiment 3. The teacher put his hand on the head of one boy. The pupils correctly identified the direct interaction, teacher-boy, and the distant acoustic interactions, teacher-all pupils.

Experiment 4. The teacher repeated Experiment 2 with a long brass spring. The distant interaction between the ends of the spring and the strength of the interaction were identified. The spring made possible the distant interaction between its own ends.

Experiment 5. The teacher produced two large U-magnets mounted to attract one another on roller skates so that they could move easily. The pupils identified the distant interaction between the two magnets in the system. They also determined that the strength of the interaction decreased as the magnets were separated. The interaction was sufficiently strong for the magnets to roll toward one another at a separation of four inches. *Invention of magnetic field:* In response to the teacher's question, "Which do you like better, direct interactions or distant interactions?" The pupils expressed a strong preference for direct interactions. The teacher now told the pupils that most people prefer to think in terms of direct interactions. In the earlier experiments there had been something between the two objects that made possible the distant interaction between them. Was there something now between the two magnets that made possible the distant interaction between them? There was nothing visible. (Curiously enough, no pupil suggested that the air was involved.) Even though the magnetic field was not yet mentioned by name, the children were given the crucial idea of a mediator (an "it") for the distant magnetic interaction. This step constituted what we have called the "invention."

Experiment 6. Discovery of the significance of the magnetic field:

a. Three children came to the demonstration table to find "it" by feeling with their fingers. They did not find "it."

b. Two children came to the demonstration table to find "it" with a wooden ruler. They did not find "it."

c. One child came to find "it" with a nail held at the end of a piece of wire. The nail responded to something!

d. All pupils wanted to explore with the nail. As others had an opportunity to do so, the teacher verbally confirmed the fact that the nail indeed seemed to have responded to something. When the teacher was going to name it, he was interrupted by one pupil who said "I know what 'it' is called. 'It' is a magnetic!" The teacher agreed to the "magnetic," because it occurred in a magnetic interaction, but proposed the name "magnetic field." Thereafter, the discussion was carried out in terms of exploring to find the magnetic field–the "it" which made possible the distant interaction between the two magnets.

e. Several more pupils explored and found the magnetic field with the nail.

f. As a final step of this experiment, the teacher invited the pupils to find the magnetic field with other objects. Screws, paper, paper clips, a screw driver, jewelry, and coins were used. Some of these objects responded to the magnetic field, some did not.

It is necessary to point out here that the appeal to the children's intuitive preference that was significant in the invention of the field concept was not at all unscientific, but was the necessary first step in the adoption of a new concept. While questions of scientific observation are decided by experiment, questions of interpretation are at first decided by preference in the light of past experience and later by the usefulness of the interpretation in generating discoveries. The magnetic field is a useful *invention*, but it is not essential to describe magnetic interactions.[4] Without the invention of the magnetic field, the subsequent explorations with the nail, etc., would have resulted in the discovery of additional distant interactions between the magnets and the nail or the other objects.

There is one feature of the preparatory Experiments 1–4 which should be emphasized. These experiments had been carried out earlier in a somewhat different way, but the distant interactions and the strength of interaction were newly introduced in this lesson. The sequence in which these experiments are carried out is not important. The pupils are not led step-by-step to the magnetic field concept. Rather, they are; "led in a circle around the magnetic field concept so they may then converge on the center of the circle from several directions." This strategy offers more promise of success.

Now, the lesson described must be placed in a science course. It is essential that the discussion of magnetic fields not be terminated and wrapped-up with the discovery described. Instead, this discovery should in itself be part of a strategy of attack on another more profound concept. In teaching the second grade, the concept of energy is the next higher order of understanding. Springs, rubber bands, dry cells, candles, and air, all these had been introduced earlier. Now magnets are seen as systems

[4] J. A. Wheeler and Richard P. Feynman. "Classical Electrodynamics in Terms of Direct Interparticle Action." *Reviews of Modern Physics*, 21:425. 1949.

in which energy can be stored. The energy concept, in turn, is part of the strategy being developed for teaching about interactions among the objects in a system, a still higher order concept.

The pedagogical point to be stressed in conclusion is that this type of discovery teaching appears to be strongly motivating and rewarding. Yet, the teaching seems also to be reasonably efficient even when compared with a more verbal expository approach. The pupils come to the point where they know they will discover something, and they know what their discovery will mean. Hence, perhaps they did not invent the new concepts, but they did make discoveries.

18

Inquiry and Education

J. Richard Suchman
Professor of Education, University of Illinois

Inquiry and Learning

Inquiry is a fundamental mode of learning. Long before the process of formal education begins infants are exploring their environments, gathering data, and constructing rudimentary conceptual schemes to represent the characteristics of the world as they perceive it. The infant grasps a pot, picks it up, feels it, turns it over, puts blocks into it, dumps them out, and so on. He performs an endless series of transactions not only with his physical world but with his social world as well. He begins to store and symbolize the structural and functional characteristics of his environment. Through the use of symbols and other abstractions he extends his power to recognize, understand, interpret, and predict, control, and explain aspects of his world.

It is interesting to note that Inhelder and Piaget's (1958) investigations of the logical thinking of children were based upon learning that took place in relatively unstructured learning situations where children were given concrete tasks and were permitted to explore freely and search for ways to predict or control outcomes. They were asked to explain the reasons for the operations they performed, but were never given conclusions or explanations. Inhelder and Piaget were, in effect, studying the development of cognitive functioning as it is manifested in the inquiry process. The developmental trends they noted can be regarded as trends in the ontogeny of inquiry style. Among these are the growth of decentration, the separation of objective from subjective interpretations, and the increased use of abstract frames of reference to analyze concrete phenomena.

Infants' inquires are generally exploratory and unsystematic (sensory motor stage. The child is "playing with" the environment and in so doing is acquiring a repertoire of intuitive notions about what is related to what. Each of his actions generates some reaction. His early motivation to explore appears to be prompted largely by the activity itself rather than by its consequences. Increased familiarity through exploration of the structure and function of objects brings a sense of power and control. There is an increasing awareness of order and predictability, which is a prerequisite for being surprised and curious about discrepant events. As the child develops and matures cognitively his search for order becomes more purposeful and controlled.

The developing child repeatedly refines his strategies of inquiry. During the elementary school years he is more likely to be searching for specific end results, performing orderly manipulations of the environment, to discover systematic relationships between his operations and their respective consequences (concrete operations). He orders and groups these correspondences in an attempt to bring relationships to light.

By adolescence he becomes concerned not only with observed regularity but with the formulation of laws that embody the logical necessity of observed relationships. The child wants to go beyond the data to construct theories by which he can predict or control events. He uses empirical operations to test these theories and determine their tenability.

These changes in the developing child determine the changing strategies and schemata which characterize his cognitive attack on his environment.

As the style of inquiry changes, so does its goals and products. Through an understanding of the inquiry process educators can more effectively create the conditions in the classroom that stimulate and sustain productive inquiry. Helping children to become more productive inquirers helps them to become more independent, self-directed learners who can shape the learning situation to match their own individual cognitive styles and goals.

The Motivation to Inquire

One of the by-products of recent investigations dealing with new methods of instruction in science, mathematics, and social studies has been the recognition by researchers of a kind of motivation that is not common when teaching follows traditional didactic procedures. These new curriculum programs have typically involved a more-or-less inductive approach in which new understandings are acquired through a form of guided inquiry.

This mode of learning has a number of highly desirable consequences not the least of which is a high level of learner motivation. Self-directed data collection, theory building, and theory testing demand high levels of activity and involvement. They generate interest and a sense of intellectual power in the learner. Through his own observations and formulations he derives increased faith in the regularity of the universe. The inquiring learner comes to have a greater sense of autonomy and self-esteem which in turn leads to further inquiry and other forms of productive thinking.

It seems unwise to use the term "discovery" to describe any of the cognitive acts in inquiry. But the *sense* of discovery, the "aha" feeling, does seem to accompany the sudden attainment of meaning, understanding, or recognition. When a person is confronted by an event that is no more than partially meaningful to him he may be motivated to take some kind of action to increase the level of meaning available to him. A perceived event or object that is at odds with one's knowledge and past experience appears to fly in the face of reality. Such discrepant events put a person in the position of having to find a way to match what he perceives with what he knows. This internal pressure to "find out why" is one motivation for inquiry. When a discrepant event is suddenly rendered meaningful and assimilable with what is already known and understood there is a release of tension and a feeling of closure and satisfaction. This form of reward is directly associated with inquiry. When a child experiences the sense of discovery which can result from inquiry, he will come to value inquiry as an avenue to better understanding.

The expectation of closure is not however a *necessary* condition for the motivation of inquiry. The activity of gathering and processing information is in itself exciting and pleasurable. Pleasure can be derived from exploring or manipulating the environment without any specific goal or expectation. The inquirer is simply playing with the ideas and data and enjoying the activity. Hunt (1962) refers to this as "motivation inherent in information processing and action." It also corresponds closely to White's (1959) concept of "competence motivation." The pleasure that children derive from the intake and processing of data, the construction, testing, and application of conceptual systems supports the position that there is a motivation to inquire because inquiry is *in itself* satisfying and stimulating. This in fact seems to be the predominant motivation for exploration in the early stages of development. Later, when the individual has more differentiated conceptual structures, the need for closure also plays a role in motivating inquiry.

One might question why the schools are not filled with aggressive inquirers, gathering and processing data to satisfy their needs for closure and cognitive activity. Perhaps it is because the climate in the classroom is *hostile* to inquiry. Teachers typically capitalize on social and ego needs to motivate children to conform to fixed learning criteria. Children are expected to store and retrieve information, not to process data and build theories for themselves. The reward system converts the children into dependent learners who "play it safe" and wait for the teacher to take the lead. Where there is a premium placed on being "right," there is less willingness to run the risk of arriving at "wrong" conclusions through the independent process of inquiry. In order to tap the motivating forces inherent in the inquiry process, it is necessary to create conditions in the classroom that permit and support autonomous search, information processing, and theory building.

Inquiry and Conceptual Growth

It is well known that a child can become aware of a relationship or principle if he is exposed to enough situations where the principle is apparent. If the instances are carefully selected, one can guide or engineer the discovery of the relationships. Beberman's (1958) and Hendrix's (1961) approach to teaching algebra is based on this. They take the position that there is little point in talking about, for example, the commutative principle unless the pupils have almost an intuitive understanding of the principle. Too often this is taught through a didactic method and the pupils acquire merely a superficial, mechanistic understanding. They know what they have to do to get the answer, but they have little understanding as to *why* they get the answer they do. Beberman's method literally engineers the students into inventing the principle themselves. His pupils are given a series of mathematical operations to perform which can be done with simple arithmetic. The problems are arranged in order of increasing difficulty in that the numbers get larger and more difficult to handle arithmetically. However, it is possible to discover a short-cut that simplifies the calculations. By discovering this short-cut, the pupil has invented an algebrated principle.

Without the benefit of a carefully programmed set of experiences, one must go through a less directed series of operations to arrive at a given concept. Before arriving at such a concept it might be necessary for the learner to construct a number of intermediate solutions in a succession of conceptual reorganizations. The question arises as to what advantage might accrue from such trial-and-error thinking.

Smedslund (1961) wondered about this and tried to determine whether the emerging concept is different in the one case where it results from a simple generalization drawn from a set of positive instances; and in the other case where it is the end product of a series of conceptual reorganizations. He worked with preschool children and used the concept of the conservation of weight. He got one group of children to discover empirically that the weight of a plasticene ball does not change as its shape is modified. He contrasted this with another group who had come to internalize the concept of the conservation of weight through the unstructured, exploratory processes by which such concepts generally come internalized (Piaget, 1941). He found that concepts formed by simple generalizations are more readily discarded when data are discrepant to the concept. But when the concepts result from the resolution of cognitive conflicts through successive accommodations as in the usual trial-and-error course of conceptual growth, a concept is not easily given up, even in the face of highly discrepant data. In one experimental procedure Smedslund sneaked a little piece of clay away from the plasticene ball. He then changed the shape of the ball and weighed it for the children so that they could see "that its weight changed when the shape changed." Those children who had acquired the concept of the conservation of weight through simple generalization over several positive instances were quite ready to give up this concept in the face of *one discrepant event.* The other group, however, refused to accept the data as valid and raised rather strong doubts as to the honesty of the experimenter presenting these demonstrations.

This suggests certain weaknesses in any learning situation where the conceptual increments toward each new structure are pre-programmed for speed and ease of learning. It seems that when conceptual structures are formed by outside agents that obviate the learner's own accommodative struggles, the new concept is not fully internalized or functional and is more readily relinquished if new data challenge its validity.

The step-by-step path toward conceptual growth is typical of most teacher directed learning. The primary object is the attainment of a new concept. This attainment is engineered by starting with the familiar and moving toward the unfamiliar with the purpose of assimilating it in the framework of existing structures. The assumption is that all learners begin with conceptual structures and cognitive styles that are enough alike to permit a standard sequence of operations to bring them to the same level of conceptualization.

But children's conceptual models differ enormously in structure. Take the relatively simple phenomenon of air bubbles rising to the surface of a liquid. Some children have very diffuse notions that involve the "lightness of air" or the "tendency for gases to rise." Some believe that water pressure has something to do with it and that water pressure acts only in a downward direction. Some children understand the depth-pressure relationships in liquids, but fail to see this at all as related to gravity. If a child is going to reorganize his concepts of floating or sinking he will have to be able to proceed from where he is and not from some hypothetical points of ignorance. He must have the opportunity to try out his existing conceptual models by using them to design experiments and make predictions. He must be free to gather the data needed to test his theories and to generate events that may suggest new theories. Only through inquiry does the learner have this much autonomy.

Inquiry vs. Teacher-Engineered Learning

The distinguishing characteristic of inquiry as a mode of learning is that it is initiated and controlled by the learner. The traditional teacher engineers learning by lecturing, demonstration, and planning a sequence of experiences. The teacher tries to draw on the pupil's past experiences and focus his attention, through verbal instruction and exposition, on selected aspects of the environment. In order to be effective in doing this a teacher must be reasonably well acquainted with the conceptual systems of the learner and keep a constant check on the ways in which these systems are changing. To the extent that the teacher is deprived of this feedback he is "flying blind," since he has no way of knowing precisely what effect his teaching or any other environmental condition is having on the child at any given time. If he is to maintain optimum control over the learning process, the teacher must know what this effect is before he makes any decisions about what to do next. Adequate feedback is difficult to obtain even from one pupil. This difficulty increases sharply with the number of pupils in the class. When the mode of learning is inquiry, the process of information gathering and conceptual reorganization comes more under the control of the learner himself. He is free to reach out for information in whatever direction he chooses, and gather data in whatever sequence is most meaningful to him. He is free to obtain redundant information where he feels the need for it, and to skip over areas where he is satisfied with his level of understanding. In other words, through inquiry, the learner influences and actually programs his own learning in terms of his cognitive needs. These needs are determined in part by the information previously stored, and in part by the individual's particular style of learning.

Inquiry cannot replace didactic teaching. As children develop, and their conceptual schemes become more highly differentiated, abstract, and linked to symbolic systems, verbally mediated instruction is more and more feasible. But the danger is that teaching can become so completely verbal and teacher-controlled that the learner begins to lose his autonomy. If the pupil is given little opportunity to think his way to his own conclusions, he becomes merely a consumer of knowledge and loses touch with the ongoing processes of inquiry through which knowledge is created and organized.

The problem is to find ways of keeping inquiry alive without discarding the invaluable accumulation of knowledge and theory that is the cultural heritage of each new generation. Existing knowledge gives focus and direction to new investigations. There is no area of concern that man enters without any prior knowledge; nor is there a discipline or science that can survive without continual reorganization of its structure and body of theory.

The teacher plays many roles, and there are many times and situations when didactic instruction is appropriate and other times when inquiry will best serve the needs of the learner.

Inquiry Training: Promoting Inquiry in the Schools

There is a wide range of cognitive skills involved in the inquiry process. This process includes the gathering and organization of data, the attempt to fit conceptual models to the data, the restructuring of these models to accommodate to new data and the repeated testing of models for validity and power. At times, it is necessary to use rigorous methods of sampling, control, and analysis. At other times, a wild intuitive leap is the necessary operation. There are broad strategies and special tactics that help to make inquiry more productive. The most dependable characteristic of inquiry is that there is no one fixed method of operation. It would be difficult to identify a set of specific component skills that would have to be independently exercised and strengthened to increase the power of inquiry. Even if it were possible to make children more perceptive or flexible by giving them special exercises in this kind of activity, it is doubtful whether such a piecemeal approach would make a significant difference in the inquiry of children.

An alternative approach to teaching separate component skills is creating conditions that stimulate and sustain the inquiry process as a whole, giving the learner ample opportunity to experiment with various strategies of heuristic attack. This gives the child concrete experiences in performing the various operations involved and in combining them in a total goal-oriented activity. In a sense this trial-and-error approach becomes a kind of inquiry into inquiry where the learner finds out for himself what courses of action are best suited to him and to the various types of problems.

Two advantages accrue from such an approach: (a) The child comes to understand inquiry as a mode of cognitive activity and an intellectual orientation rather than a single strategy or method. He gains a flexible and creative mode of attack, unhampered by any rigid methodology prescribing fixed sequences of operation. (b) The learner discovers that through inquiry he has greater power to apply his existing knowledge to gain more meaning from what he perceives and to build new knowledge from his transactions with his environment. The dual function of applying knowledge and extending it takes the form of a cycle that is characteristic of all inquiry. This cycle occurs most readily when the learner is free to gather and process data, and to construct and test new systems for organizing and interpreting data (theories, models, etc.) without excessive fear of failure or pressure to attain "right" answers.

The principal goal of Inquiry Training has been to provide conditions calculated to stimulate and sustain the free functioning of this inquiry cycle. Beyond that, the child is helped to reflect upon the means by which inquiry can be made more autonomous and productive. These means can be introduced most meaningfully against a rich background of firsthand experiences in inquiry.

Inquiry Training as a learning system was developed through a series of research projects (Suchman, 1961, 1962). Preliminary studies had revealed that children in the intermediate elementary grades were engaging in virtually no inquiry in the school setting. An attitude of open-endedness toward knowledge in any content area was the exception rather than the rule. There were no instances where teachers attempted to acquaint children with the nature of the inquiry process. The "scientific method," when it was discussed, was dealt with as a fixed sequence of steps which were supposed to take the investigator from problem to hypothesis to conclusion in a precise and logical fashion. No evidence was available that the knowledge of these steps had any effect upon the children's motivation to learn, upon their autonomy as learners, or upon the productivity of their investigations.

The Inquiry Training projects have had two objectives:

1. To identify conditions that stimulate, sustain, and strengthen the process of inquiry in the school setting.
2. To develop and test materials and techniques to be used by teachers to create these conditions.

The theoretical assumptions upon which the Inquiry Training approach was based were drawn largely from the work of Piaget and his associates. The educational philosophies of Dewey, Locke, and Montessori were no doubt instrumental in their emphasis upon the importance of freedom for the learner to think and make decisions. The analyses of motivation contributed by White (1959), Hunt (1962), and Festinger (1957) shed light upon the generally untapped sources of motivation that play a central role in Inquiry Training. The analysis of concept attainment strategies developed in the Bruner, Goodnow, and Austin research studies (1958) provided an initial basis for the study of inquiry as a sequence of cognitive operations in search of extended meaning where every operation and strategy is prompted in part by the child's desire for power through knowledge and restricted by his distaste for cognitive strain.

Theory did not lead directly to the ideal conditions. There was much experimentation and in time certain requirements emerged as invariably necessary for the stimulation and support of inquiry by substantial numbers of children over an extended period.

The Primary Conditions for the Stimulation and Support of Inquiry

The following conditions were found to be necessary although not always sufficient.

1. Focus. Inquiry is rarely diffuse or nonspecific in direction. It is directed toward a goal, usually some phenomenon or problem that is disturbing to the learner because he is unable to understand or assimilate to his own satisfaction what he has perceived. Focusing marks out an area of concern, gives inquiry a direction to move in, and sets the process in motion.

2. Freedom. The inquiry process is characterized by free cognitive movement in the collection of data, the manipulation and reorganization of ideas, and the construction and testing of theory. Freedom has two dimensions: One is the freedom afforded by the environment that minimizes externally imposed constraints upon the inquirer's operations. Without freedom at this level, inquiry would be impossible.

The second dimension of freedom is internal to the inquirer. Inquiry cannot be free unless the inquirer accepts the freedom afforded by the environment and utilizes it to carry out his own self-directed searching and thinking. Autonomy cannot be developed and exercised without external freedom, but will not necessarily be exercised simply because external freedom is provided.

3. Response. Through inquiry, the learner turns to his environment to obtain the data he needs for building and testing theories. He observes, analyzes, and manipulates portions of his environment to generate data. If the environment is responsive to his probes it will yield data. Responsiveness is a function of (a) the time between probe and response and (b) the extent to which the data obtained correspond to the inquirer's quest for information.

When focus, freedom, and response characterize the learning environment, inquiry can emerge as the dominant learning mode. The influence of other conditions can generally be interpreted in terms of their interaction with these three basic dimensions. For example, knowledge can give a person resource material for constructing theories and organizing data collection. The more one knows in a given area the more intelligently he can inquire. Knowledge therefore helps to provide focus, but at the same time can interfere with freedom. Open-mindedness in theory building enhances creative thinking and makes it easier to reorganize ones conceptual schemes when data so dictate. Fixed ideas and conclusions can stand in the way of fluid accommodation and render inquiry sterile and powerless to produce new constructs or theories.

Self-esteem is closely related to internal freedom. The self-confident inquirer (confident, not in the correctness of his knowledge but in his own power to gather data, build and test theories, etc.) is freer to operate autonomously because he is not held back by the fear of being wrong or looking foolish. He is willing to try out ideas and trust in his own intuitive knowledge. He is willing to experiment to make the important leaps from data to theory.

While children do not have to be taught to inquire, they are willing and able to do so only under certain conditions. The major reason why inquiry is not the dominant mode of learning in most classrooms is that these necessary conditions do not obtain there. The typical classroom teacher makes free inquiry nearly impossible, or at best very difficult to pursue. By creating conditions that allow inquiry to occur, a teacher can provide the most important requisites for the development of inquiry skills. Children will inquire if given the means and the freedom to do so; the matter of skill development is partly a function of practice and partly a function of instruction that cannot be given until the child is actively engaged in inquiry.

Classroom Materials and Methods

The materials and techniques developed at the University of Illinois have been tested with groups of children in the intermediate grades. This does not imply that there is a fixed or total Inquiry Training method or program. Some of the materials and techniques have proven to be successful and might therefore serve as a model for future development. But, in any event, the specifics are not nearly as important as the theory and objectives underlying their use.

Problem-Focus Films

Motion picture films have been developed for the purpose of providing focus for Inquiry Training. These films (in the areas of physics, economics, and physiology) present a single event in concrete terms. The event is deliberately selected and presented to maximize its discrepant nature, that is, the event is puzzling and difficult to explain. A caption raises a focal question . . . "Why?"

The films are all in color. The physics films are silent demonstrations with various kinds of laboratory equipment. The economics and physiology films have sound and present the problems through short dramatic episodes.

A sample film in the physics series shows a demonstrator holding a narrow blade over a Bunsen burner. As the blade is heated it begins to bend downward as though it were melting. When it has bent into a distinct arc, the blade is immersed in a tank containing a clear liquid. The blade straightens out immediately. Then the blade is held over the flame a second time. This time it bends upward while the heat is applied. Once again, it straightens out in the liquid. The question asked in the caption is: "Why does the blade bend and then straighten out?"

The film, which runs for about 90 seconds, rarely fails to evoke inquiry from the children. Each film presents just enough data to pose a problem, but very little more. Additional data must be gleaned by the children through their questions. The film is used only to stimulate inquiry, but not to sustain it. The latter function is performed by the inquiry session which follows immediately after the presentation of the film.

Inquiry Sessions

Group inquiry sessions have been successfully used to introduce children to the inquiry process. The children, having seen a problem-focus film, are allowed to inquire by asking the teacher questions and verbalizing their evolving theories. In this way the freedom is extended to the children in the form of open question-asking sessions and the responsive environment is created by the teacher who attempts to answer all data-seeking questions posed by the children.

Inquiry sessions can be conducted with varying numbers of children in a single group. Within the group setting the children are free to inquire in whatever manner they wish. They may work independently or in groups, specialize in hypothesis formation or hypothesis testing, or assume the role of generalist. Inquiry sessions have been deliberately kept as unstructured as possible to give the children room to operate in ways that are best suited to their individual needs and characteristics. Inquiry sessions allow children to try out their own ideas concerning the problem at hand and the methods of attack.

Certain specific rules, although they seem to restrict freedom, actually encourage independence. The children are required to use only "Yes or No" questions as a simple barrier against the "Why?" or "How come?" question. If the latter were allowed, the children would elicit explanations from the teacher and by-pass the important task of formulating and testing their own theories and explanations.

When children offer their own theories or explanations, or ask whether such explanations are "right," they are told that they have presented a theory and that they will have to determine *for themselves* whether or not they wish to retain the theory or reject it. It is also explained that theories are useful ways of accounting for events, but can never be proven correct. Theories that have support serve as a basis for prediction, control, and explanation. Theories that find support in a wide range of events are regarded as more powerful and therefore more useful.

In the course of a series of inquiry sessions the role of theories and the means for testing them are discussed and applied to the question-asking activities of the children. In helping children differentiate the various kinds of operations used in inquiry the teacher is helping them to develop a rudimentary structure to guide them in the controlled use of inquiry. As each of the elements is used spontaneously by the children it is identified and its functions are pointed out and illustrated. The following matrix shows the principal types of inquiry operations performed by questions and the operanda upon which the operations are performed. Sample questions of each type are given in the body of the matrix.

Almost any question asked in the course of an inquiry session can be categorized in the matrix presented in Table 1. The type of question asked is of course related to the job it is supposed to perform. The choice of questions to be used will vary with the level of knowledge of the inquirer, the availability of data, the level of sophistication of theory construction, as well as the style of thinking of the inquirer.

For example, analytical children are likely to employ verification questions early in an inquiry session to pinpoint the parameters of the problem-focus event. This would involve the identification of objects ("Was the blade a knife?") or the verification of conditions ("Was the water temperature more than 50° F?"). Experimentation questions may be used in an open, exploratory manner to uncover what may be important relationships. ("Would an ordinary knife have bent the same way?")

Necessity questions are attempts to establish necessary conditions as a basis for explaining the problem-focus event. The fact that a condition is necessary for a given event can never be positively proven; only the unnecessary condition can be proven so. Thus the formulation of necessary conditions is inferential in that each individual must decide for himself what evidence he will require before he considers a condition necessary on the basis of the available data. If event *A* occurs in the presence of condition *B* and not in the absence of this condition, after *X* number of occurrences one becomes ready to infer that condition *B* is necessary for event *A*. But *X* will vary from discipline to discipline, group to group, as well as from child to child.

When the child asks the teacher whether a given condition is necessary he is requesting that the teacher evaluate the child's theory. Since in Inquiry Training the children are encouraged to evaluate their own theories such questions are not answered directly. Instead, the child is asked to decide this for himself on the basis of the data he already has or through the gathering of more data. His conclusion is always labelled as his theory to be evaluated by him empirically or in terms of its reasonableness.

Table 1. Matrix of Inquiry Operations and Operanda as Exemplified by Question Types

	Events	*Objects*	*Conditions*	*Properties*	*Variables*
Analytical					
Verification	Did she move the blade back and forth in the flame?	Was the blade a knife?	Was the water temperature more than 50°F?	Does metal contract when cooled?	
Experimentation	If she held the blade still would the same thing have happened?	Would an ordinary knife have bent the same way?	If the blade had been thicker would it have bent?	If metal contracted when heated would it have made a difference?	
Inferential					
Necessity	Did she have to put the blade in the water to make it straighten out?	Did the liquid have to be water to make the blade straighten?	Did the liquid have to be cool to make the blade straighten?	To make this work do you have to have a blade that conducts heat?	
Synthesis	Did heating the blade make it bend?	Did the water have anything to do with it?	Did the temperature of the air in the room make it straighten?	Was it because metals expand at different rates?	Does pressure have anything to do with it?

Synthesis questions deal more directly with causal relationships. Typically, they too are not given a direct answer because it is possible for children to formulate their own answers to such questions through further inquiry. The question "Did the bending have anything to do with the heat of the flame?" is an attempt to fiind teacher support for a theory. By experimenting with the effects of varying temperature a child can gather enough data to make his own inferences about the relationship between heat and bending.

Inquiry Training also leads into the discussion of the structure and function of descriptions, theories, and explanations. The children come to see the role of the hypothesis as a means of testing a theory and the role of data in the testing of hypotheses.

There are no fixed procedures for introducing these ideas. The course of events depends greatly upon the inquiry behavior of the children and manner in which the teacher chooses to respond. The common elements in all inquiry sessions are the focal point, the freedom of action, and the responsive environment. In one way or another, the teacher of inquiry must help the children begin to recognize the elements of the process and how they fit together as theories are built and tested.

Role of the Teacher

More than any other factors, those associated with the teacher will affect the outcome of Inquiry Training. His knowledge of the subject into which the children are inquiring, his understanding of the cognitive functioning and motivational characteristics of his pupils, and his skill in creating the conditions favorable to inquiry will determine the extent to which inquiry becomes a mode of learning in the classroom.

In conducting an inquiry session the teacher has four principle functions:

1. He structures the rules by which the children can gather data, present theories, exchange ideas with each other, and perform whatever other operations are required in the course of their inquiries.

2. He provides the responsive environment. At times this may be limited simply to responding to the children's questions as promptly and specifically as the questions arise. Providing opportunities for the children to conduct experiments, gather data on their own, utilize resource materials of various kinds including reference books, is also making the environment responsive. While in the early stages of Inquiry Training inquiry is kept largely at the verbal level in order to concentrate on the process itself and make it as visible as possible for everybody, in time, as inquiry is spread through the curriculum, the concept of the responsive environment becomes applicable to the total school setting. If isolated Inquiry Training periods are the only times in the program when the environment is truly responsive, the children will behave as inquirers at those times only; and it is likely that they will come to regard inquiry as some kind of game that is played to relieve the monotony of learning.

3. The teacher helps the children focus on the *process* of inquiry to heighten their awareness of the operations they are performing. This may be done at any time during an inquiry session. The teacher points out to the children what they are doing, that is, what kinds of cognitive acts they are performing. This is to help them see a structure in the inquiry process and understand how questions can clarify problems and test theories. They come to recognize the role of theories in guiding investigations and in predicting, controlling, and explaining events. They are helped to recognize the major elements of an explanation and the related roles of these elements in the analysis of events. The teacher who is well acquainted with the elements of the inquiry process and the way in which they are used can help his pupils gain more direction and control in their investigations.

4. The teacher maintains a climate in which the children are kept relatively free from external pressures to follow a given course of action or arrive at a given conclusion. To be free inquirers children must be *protected* from pressures or controls that inhibit their scope and direction of searching and thinking, and make them afraid to run the risk of being "wrong." The teacher makes room for this kind of autonomy-producing freedom by holding in check his own evaluative comments regarding the directions of the child's inquiry or the validity of his theories. In the long run the child gains more if he is allowed to think his way through to invalid theories than if he is lead to or forced to accept the theories of experts. Hopefully, the child will return to a problem and think through his theories a number of times. His first theories are rarely the same as his last ones.

Inquiry and the Curriculum

If inquiry is regarded as a game or a special kind of exercise to be inserted into the midst of an otherwise didactic and structured curriculum, the effect upon the attitudes and thinking of the children is likely to be minimal. Inquiry requires a motivation to open things up, to search, to reorganize ideas and to test them. It requires knowledge and skill in carrying out these investigations. The child who is allowed to inquire learns that he can formulate, test, and apply theories through his own planning and action. Once a person has tested the sense of power that can be derived by such self-directed learning, it is difficult to go back to accepting the preformed conclusions of others.

If inquiry is to become the fundamental orientation to learning, inquiry should be central to the organization of the curriculum. This is not to suggest that children should discover everything for themselves or that there is no room for didactic teaching or verbal learning. But one cannot expect children to develop inquiring attitudes when knowledge is passed along to them as a closed system.

The teacher who wishes to promote inquiry as the central orientation for the learner can do so only if he accepts this orientation himself. This means relinquishing a certain amount of authority on matters of knowledge and control in matters of programming pupil learning. The teacher who orients his pupils to the process of inquiry focuses first upon events and raises questions that challenge ideas, beliefs, and conclusions. Then he creates the conditions whereby the pupils can inquire freely in an effort to build and test theories. He concerns himself and his pupils as much with the process by which knowledge is produced as with the accumulation of knowledge itself. He places critical and productive thinking on a plane of value equal to or higher than the storage and retrieval of information.

The teacher must have a substantial depth of knowledge in the subject area where the inquiry is to be undertaken. In the same sense that one cannot teach from a position of ignorance, one cannot support inquiry without having the necessary knowledge to answer the questions raised by the children. Even questions in search of data alone demand a wealth of knowledge on the part of the answerer. Realistic data that lead to meaningful theory building cannot be invented out of thin air.

The teacher who undertakes the development of inquiry skill that is part of his teaching goal must be willing and able to set aside enough time for inquiry to take place. The fact that it takes less time to give a child an explanation than it does to let him find one for himself does not necessarily demonstrate that learning through inquiry is less efficient. The ultimate measure of the value of time spent must be gauged multidimensionally. What is the quality of the learning? What are the effects on the self-concept of the learner? What are the consequences for cognitive development and the motivation to learn? These and other questions must have answers before the expenditure of time in any learning activity can be regarded as efficient or exorbitant.

The child who is educated in and through the process of inquiry may cover less territory than the child taught through traditional didactics. He may have doubts about the validity of his knowledge and may regard few if any truths as absolute or final. On the other hand, he will be in a better position to know just what it is he *does* understand, how he came to understand it, and what he can do to pursue it further. Through the power to build and test his own theories and the motivation to raise new questions and open up new problems he will be more likely to continue thinking and learning productively in or out of the school setting, with or without a teacher.

References

1. Beberman, M. *An emerging program of secondary school mathematics.* Cambridge, Mass.: Harvard University Press, 1958.
2. Bruner, J. S., Goodnow, Jacqueline, and Austin, G. A. *A study of thinking.* New York: John Wiley and Sons, Inc., 1956.
3. Festinger, L. *A theory of cognitive dissonance.* Evanston, Ill.: Row, Peterson, 1957.

4. HENDRIX, GERTRUDE. Learning by discovery. *Mathematics Teacher*, 1961, 54, 290–299.

5. HUNT, J. MCV. Piaget's observations as a source of hypotheses concerning motivation. Paper read at the American Psychological Association Annual Meeting, 1952.

6. INHELDER, BARBEL, and PIAGET, J. *The growth of logical thinking from childhood to adolescence*. New York: Basic Books, 1958.

7. PIAGET, J., and INHELDER, BARBEL. *Le Développement des Quantités chez L'Enfant*. Dalachaux et Niestle, 1941.

8. SMEDSLUND, J. The acquisition of conservation by substance and weight in children. *Scand. J. Psychol.*, 1961, 2, 71–84, 85–87.

9. SUCHMAN, J. R. Inquiry training in the elementary school. *Science Teacher*, 1960, 27, 42–47.

10. SUCHMAN, J. R. Inquiry training: building skills for autonomous discovery. *Merrill-Palmer Quarterly*, 1961, 7, 147–169.

11. SUCHMAN, J. R. The elementary school training program in scientific inquiry. (Mimeo) Illinois Studies in Inquiry Training, University of Illinois, Urbana, 1962.

12. WHITE, R. W. Motivation reconsidered: the concept of competence. *Psychological Review*, 1959, 66, 297–333.

❦ 19

Curriculum Frontiers for the Elementary Gifted Pupil—Flying Monkeys and Silent Lions

E. Paul Torrance

TRADITIONALLY, it seems to me, our treatment of gifted elementary pupils has been designed "to make flying monkeys abandon such antics" and "to make silent lions roar." Today, we find the curriculum frontiers for the elementary gifted pupil leading to a reversal of this goal. I want to propose that we explore curriculum frontiers which will permit flying monkeys to fly at even greater heights and which will allow silent lions to remain silent, developing other important talents.

First, I shall try to describe some of the dynamics by which we are making flying monkeys swing by their tails and coax silent lions into roaring or be destroyed. Next, I shall identify some of the curriculum frontiers by which this process can be reversed. Finally, I shall outline some of the things which we must do in order to open up these frontiers.

Although I can support most of my ideas with research evidence from our studies of creative thinking in the early school years, the ideas which I shall present actually came from the wisdom of approximately 4000 gifted elementary pupils in Minnesota, Illinois, Oklahoma, Georgia and Massachusetts. Children express these ideas so much more eloquently and simply than research men.

The data to which I refer came from imaginative stories written by these elementary pupils. In a 20-minute period, they were asked to write imaginative stories about animals or persons with some divergent characteristics. In some cases, they were given a choice of 10 such topics, such as The Duck That Won't Quack, The Cat That Won't Scratch, The

E. PAUL TORRANCE is the Director of the Bureau of Educational Research, University of Minnesota. This article is a condensed version of a paper prepared for presentation at the annual meeting of the Association of Educators of Gifted Children in Detroit, April, 1961.

Woman Who Won't Talk, and The Boy Who Wants To Be a Nurse. In others, they were given a choice of only two titles, The Flying Monkey and The Lion That Won't Roar.

Sanctions Against Divergency

It is my hypothesis that curricular practices which seek to prevent flying monkeys from flying and make silent lions roar result primarily from society's sanctions against any kind of divergency. People have a tendency to become suspicious, anxious, even fearful of anyone who is different from most other people. The sanctions are strongest, of course, against those who are so indiscreet as to permit their differences to show.

My proposal that we seek our curriculum frontiers in a reversal of this traditional approach and free ourselves from fears is based on the belief shared by an increasing number of behavioral scientists (Barron, 1958; Kelley, 1959; Roe, 1959) that the ways in which a person is different from all others are his most priceless possession and that it is these differences which have made our country what it is and are essential to a democratic society.

Many of the coercive influences against divergency are illustrated in this story about Pepper, a Flying Monkey, by a Twin Cities girl:

> "Far into the jungle of Africa lived a flying monkey named Pepper. Pepper was a well-educated monkey and very cute. . . . Pepper was unusual too. He was not like all of the other flying monkeys. You see, Pepper didn't eat bananas like everybody else. He wanted to be different. He ate peppers!
>
> "No one ever went out of the jungle so Pepper, being different, decided to go to America! . . . When the people saw him, they began to laugh and then others began to scream. Then out of nowhere a man from a zoo came and took Pepper by surprise. . . .
>
> "Now Pepper was sad. He didn't like the cage they put him in. He made a vow that if he ever got out he would never be different again and then minutes later he saw some bent bars big enough to fly through. All of a sudden he flew out and in two days was back in the jungle. He kept his promise too. He was never different again. He was a good little flying monkey."

I suppose *he ate his bananas!*

About two-thirds of the stories about flying monkeys, thus far analyzed, tell similar tales of conformity or of destruction. Some cultures, however, are more indulgent of divergency than others. Stories written by gifted children in special classes are far more hopeful than those of gifted children in regular classes. In about 70 percent of the stories of pupils in classes for high achieving pupils, the flying monkey is in some way able to persist in his flying. The stories written by children in a small Oklahoma town composed of Indians, whites, and a few Negroes also reflect this tolerance of divergency. In 74 percent of their stories, the flying monkey succeeds.

Pressures upon gifted children who lack or are weak in some characteristic or skill regarded as highly important by society are especially severe. Since verbal skills are highly valued in our society, the stories of ducks that won't quack, lions that won't roar, dogs that won't bark, and roosters that won't crow seem to give us valuable insights into this problem as viewed by children. The relentlessness of this kind of pressure is reflected in the following story by a sixth-grade girl:

"Quack! Quack! They were after him again—the Ladies Duck Aid Society, with their hair up in pin curls and their screaming, fat ducklings swimming and holding onto their skirts. They never failed. Alas! It was getting too much for little Glob-Blob. Every day there would be quacking and screaming of ducklings while poor Glob-Blob would run as fast as he could to get away from the vicious ducks.

"The reason for this was because poor Glob-Blob could not quack. So every day the Ladies Duck Aid Society would chase Glob-Blob, for they said it was for the good of the ducks, and it was not only right but they were doing a good turn.

"It was luck for Glob-Blob that the ducks were fat and flabby, for if they were limber, I will not mention what would happen. But one day, these lazy ducks did reduce, and when chasing Glob-Blob dealt him a good many hard blows. And the next day, poor Glob-Blob, was at last doomed. The vicious quackers came and the chase was on. Glob-Blob was failing. It is a shame that so noble a duck should be doomed, but 'That is life,' said Glob-Blob to himself as, slowly but surely, failing, he dropped to the ground. The quackers, very pleased with themselves, sat down for a chat.

"But I shall always remember Glob-Blob and his death. So I shall let him finish his journey, where there will be no more quackers and chasers, and where at last, he may have passionless peace forever."

Many children see us as "quackers and chasers" when we work so hard to make them "better-rounded personalities." They might contribute far more to society and be far happier and more successful by capitalizing upon their unique strengths rather than spending fruitless energy trying hopelessly to compensate for some divergent characteristic or behavior. I would, of course, emphasize the fact that it is necessary for some of our highly creative youngsters to achieve basic skills necessary for success in their chosen areas of specialization.

Some of the Frontiers

With this introduction to the process by which flying monkeys are forced to desist and silent lions, to roar, I would like to identify some of the frontiers we discover when we reverse our goals.

Self-Initiated Learning

In my estimation, one of the most promising frontiers is to be discovered in efforts to provide for, and give credit for, self-initiated learning.

In many of our stories, the monkey learns to fly or the lion learns to roar through self-initiated learning. One of the most frequent devices is to secure the assistance of someone who is an expert. The wise old owl and the eagle are some of the favorite teachers. Some of the gifted children in our longitudinal studies of creativity are experts at self-initiated learning. One third-grade girl wanted to learn how to knit. Her mother did not know how to knit, so she started going from door to door in her neighborhood until she found someone who could knit and was willing to teach her. She mastered this skill quite readily. One fourth-grade boy, who as a second grader gave me the clearest and most accurate explanation of the principle of the magnifying glass, became interested in high speed computers. He went to the experts and is now something of an expert himself on computers.

Learning on One's Own

Another curriculum frontier is to be found in provisions which permit children to do things on their own and to learn on their own. Last year, we conducted an exciting study in which we found that children would do a great deal of writing on their own. In another (Fritz, 1958) it was found that gifted children in a split-shift school showed more growth in language development, science, and social studies than under a full-day schedule. Only in spelling was there significantly less growth among the split-shift children (seventh graders). In still another we found that children in a split-shift school engage in a large number of creative learning activities on their own.

New frontiers are bound to open up whenever we open the tops on the cages in which we imprison our flying monkeys or chase the silent lions out on their own. The following story by an Oklahoma sixth grader illustrates some important points:

> "Once there were some monkeys sitting in a group. They were all alike except three monkeys. They were very different because they could fly.
>
> "One day some men from a park zoo were looking for some monkeys because theirs had died. They came upon the three that flew. So they took them in a cage. The cage didn't have a top to it. They were in the sun one day and one monkey said to the other, 'I wish we could get out of here.'
>
> " 'Then why don't we fly out of here?' said the other.
>
> "They started to fly out. When they got about half a mile, some men came to feed them. When they couldn't find the three monkeys, they saw them flying away. One of them said, 'If we would have put them in a cage with a top, we would have had a real good thing here in the zoo.' "

I am particularly interested in the remarks of the keepers as they saw the monkeys flying away. For their own gain or their own glory, they would like to enslave the flying monkeys. It is perhaps rather brutal to suggest this, but we should perhaps examine more honestly our motives for making pupils so dependent upon us.

The Responsive Environment

Another important curriculum frontier is being opened up rapidly with experiments in creating responsive environments through which children are propelled by their curiosity. This concept of the responsive environment is illustrated in the experimental work of O. K. Moore at Yale University. Through the natural curiosity of children about electric typewriters, Moore (1961) has demonstrated that pre-school children can learn to read, write, type, and take dictation. Here we have skills being learned creatively which we have always assumed could be taught most economically by authority. In much of our own research at the University of Minnesota, I believe we have demonstrated that children can learn creatively many of the traditional educational skills.

One of the most common themes in the stories of gifted children is a failure to find a responsive environment. I am convinced that our failure to provide a responsive environment kills at a very early age much of the excitement of learning. The process by which this occurs in the kindergarten is described in a number of the letters I receive from parents. From these heart-rending accounts, we can understand why researchers such as Andrews (1930) find drops in the creative thinking of five-year-olds.

Revising Concepts of Readiness

Everywhere educators of gifted children are revising their concepts about "readiness" and what can be taught at various levels of education. This is a frontier which terrifies many however. The following recent headlines reflect this fear:

> "Caution Urged in Changing Primary into High Schools"
> "Don't Turn Grade Schools into High Schools, Educators Warn at Parley"
> "Reading for Kindergarten, Languages Too Soon Attacked"

Bruner's (1960) exciting book, *The Process of Education*, should help us chart our way through this frontier. Along with revisions about readiness, he develops the concept of structure of knowledge and interesting ideas about intuition and motivation. About readiness, he says, "Experience over the past decade points to the fact that our schools may be wasting precious years by postponing the teaching of many subjects on the grounds that they are too difficult. . . . The essential point often overlooked in the planning of curricula . . . (is that) the basic ideas that lie at the heart of all science and mathematics and the basic schemes that give form to life and literature are powerful." For this purpose, Bruner suggests "the spiral curriculum," one that turns back on itself at higher and higher levels of complexity.

A very frequent theme in our imaginative stories is related to this problem. The young animal or fowl asks, "When can I roar? When can I crow? When can I quack? When can I fly?" Almost always, the answer is, "When you are a little older." We are too afraid that the young one might not be ready to learn and that he would be forever scarred by even the most temporary failure.

A common experience in the lives of almost all highly outstanding individuals has been their ability to cope with failure and frustration. Certainly, almost all highly creative scientists, inventors, artists, and writers attempt tasks which are too difficult for them. Had they not attempted such tasks, it is quite unlikely that their great ideas would have been born.

Search for Self

Generally, people feel that the elementary period is too early for children to start developing their self-concepts, to start searching for their selves. The trouble is that the process is well underway even before the child enters school. I think children have a natural concern about this and that our failure to help them blocks access to important and exciting curriculum frontiers, especially for gifted children.

I am reminded of these things by the following story by a sixth-year boy:

> "There once was a South American monkey that didn't know what he was, who he was, or why he was even alive. He decided that he didn't know even a way to figure it out, so he thought he would make up a reason.
>
> "He had seen many airplanes fly overhead. He had seen many ferocious animals, many nice animals, and many machines. He had always thought that it would be nice to fly, so he pretended he was an airplane.
>
> "He had also heard that buzzing sound of the engines, so he called himself 'Buzz.' He also decided that he was a real fast flyer so that this was the reason he was alive.
>
> "Now we all know that monkeys can't fly, but he didn't know this. Why he didn't even know now that he was a monkey, so he kept trying and trying—and you know what? He flew!"

Perhaps this has some implications not only concerning the need for helping children discover their potentialities but for helping them achieve their self-concepts creatively rather than by authority.

We also need to help children accept themselves, remembering that children may even despise an outstanding "gift," if their giftedness makes them different from others. This makes far too many gifted children willing to emasculate themselves and consciously and unconsciously hide or destroy their talents. They prefer to be like others.

Search for One's Uniqueness

An important curriculum frontier in the education of gifted elementary pupils is to be found in helping them search for and develop their uniqueness. Such a frontier has been under exploration during the past three years in the Riverside School at Bloomington, Minnesota, through what they call their "strengths and weaknesses program." Every other week, each afternoon is devoted entirely to this program. Opportunity is given for developing further their special enthusiasms or what might otherwise be hobbies. Guidance is also given in strengthening neglected educational skills which might cause them to bog down later in the pursuit of their enthusiasms, both vocational and avocational.

Opening Up the Frontiers

I have suggested six curriculum frontiers whereby we may aid flying monkeys and silent lions realize their potentialities more fully. Now, I would like to suggest some provisions which I believe will be effective in breaking through these frontiers.

Rewarding Varied Talents

Research for years has repeatedly shown that people will develop along whatever lines they find rewarding. Thus, the need for rewarding various kinds of talents and kinds of learning should be obvious. My staff and I have conducted over a dozen experiments concerned with rewarding creative thinking (Torrance and Staff, 1961). We know now what some of the difficulties are, what some of the most effective principles and procedures are. The essence of what we know, however, is simply to be respectful of a diversity of talent.

Help Children Recognize the Value of Their Talents

We cannot open up curriculum frontiers for many children until we can help them recognize the value of their talents. Otherwise, they continue to despise their most valuable assets. Itchy, the flying monkey in the following story by a sixth-grade girl, made this discovery for himself:

"Itchy was a monkey who lived in a deep, dark jungle in Africa. He came from a very fine family, but Itchy was ashamed of himself because he didn't have a long tail like his father or curly hair like his mother. He didn't even look good at all because he had a short, wide tail and smooth hair. But what made him look real bad were two wide wings just below his shoulders.

"One day while Itchy was lying in the grass, looking up at the sky, he saw a flock of birds. . . . Then he started thinking (for he was a very smart monkey). 'If the birds can fly, why can't I?' So he climbed to the tallest tree in the jungle and jumped. Right away the wings below his shoulders started working and Itchy was flying.

" 'Why,' said Itchy, 'I shouldn't be ashamed of myself because how many monkeys can fly?'

"And off he flew to show his family that he was as good as they were."

Developing Creative Acceptance of Limitations

Inevitably there are limitations both within the environment and the individual. Both must be accepted, not cynically, but creatively. In an early study of the psychology of inventors, Rossman (1931) found that this characteristic differentiates inventors from non-inventors. Non-inventors only cuss the defects of their environment and of themselves. Inventors, however, take a more constructive approach, saying, "This is the way to do it." I like this story in which a fifth-grade boy in Massachusetts shows how the lion can accept creatively his inability to roar:

"Once there was a lion named Roary. He was the king of the beasts. But he didn't roar. Mostly every creature laughed at him and didn't listen to him. Everyone thought they should vote for another animal. They were trying to decide. Then the monkey said, 'Can't I be the king? I'm very strong.'

"The animals said, 'You'll have to prove it.' So the monkey did, but the animals weren't satisfied. . . .

". . . Then one day the animals were frightened by the hunters. They told Roary, 'Please save us!'

"But Roary said, 'I can't save you because I can't roar.'

"The animals said, 'It's no time to be joking.'

"The hunters saw Roary. They started laughing because he couldn't roar. But Roary had a record player and the record was called 'How to Learn to Roar.' So he played it. Then he opened his mouth and the roars came from the record player. And it seemed as if he was roaring. Roary scared the wits out of the hunters. They ran like lightning. The animals were saved, thanks to Roary. So they asked, 'Roary, did you really roar?'

"Roary said, 'That's my secret.' So now they wanted Roary for king even if he can't roar."

Stop Equating Divergency With Mental Illness and Delinquency

One of the big barriers to opening up the curriculum frontiers I have suggested is our practice of equating any kind of divergent characteristic or behavior with mental illness and/or delinquency. Flying monkeys in our stories are frequently thought to be crazy or to be devils or under the spell of witches. Lions that won't roar and cats that won't scratch are thought to be mentally ill. Some of the stories make us more aware of the ways by which parents intensify this problem. Others painfully show how both parents and professionals fail in understanding divergency, as is exemplified by the following story:

"Once there was a cat that could not scratch. A lady came and the cat followed her so she took the cat home with her. The cat meowed and meowed, so the lady gave him some milk and he spilt the milk all over himself. So the lady put the cat in the bath tub and gave him a bath, but the cat did not scratch her. The lady did not understand so she took the cat to the cat hospital. The veterinarian did not understand so she let the cat go and that is the end of the cat that would not scratch and the lady and the doctor that did not understand that cat."

In our studies of highly creative children, we find many evidences that they feel that their parents and teachers do not understand them. Their teachers themselves admit that they do not know these children as well as they know highly intelligent (IQ) pupils.

Changed Emphasis on Sex Roles

Our overemphasis or misplaced emphasis on sex roles is a serious block to the development of many talents, especially creative talents. It has been pointed out frequently that rarely do women become scientific discoverers, inventors, or composers. Overemphasis or misplaced emphasis on sex roles, however, exacts its toll on the creativity of both sexes and creates serious problems of adjustment to highly creative individuals of both sexes.

Creativity, by its very nature, requires both sensitivity and independence. In our culture, sensitivity is definitely a feminine virtue, while independence is a masculine value. Thus, we may expect the highly creative boy to appear to be more effeminate than his peers and the highly creative girl to appear more masculine. Roe (1959), Barron (1957), and Torrance (1959a) have all cited evidence in support of this phenomenon. In our longitudinal studies we are finding interesting examples of children who sacrifice their creativity in order to maintain their "masculinity" or their "femininity," as the case may be.

This cultural block to creativity comes out in many places. We first observed it in our Product Improvement Test in which children are asked to think of all the ideas they can for improving common toys so that they will be more fun to play with. In the first grade, boys excelled girls on the fire truck but girls excelled boys on the nurse's kit. Many of the boys refused to think of anything to make the nurse's kit more fun, protesting, "I'm a boy! I don't play with things like that!" Some of the more creative boys, however, first transposed it into a doctor's kit and as such were quite free to think of improvements. By the third grade, however, boys excelled girls even on the nurse's kit, probably because by the time girls have been conditioned to accept toys as they are and not to manipulate and change them.

The inhibiting effects of sex-role conditioning also showed up in our experiments involving small groups working with science toys (Torrance, 1960b). Girls are quite reluctant to work with these science toys and frequently protest, "I'm a girl; I'm not supposed to know anything about things like that!" Boys demonstrate and explain about twice as many ideas as girls in experiments involving these materials. We know already, however, that this situation can be modified significantly. In 1959, we found these phenomena operating quite strongly in this school. Later I had the opportunity to report these and other results to both the teachers and parents in this school. In 1960, we conducted some experiments in this same school in which we used a different but similar set of science toys. This time, we found none of this reluctance on the part of girls, there was no difference in the expressed enjoyment of the activity of boys and girls, and the mean performance of girls and boys was almost identical. In one way, however, the situation remained unchanged. The contributions of boys were more highly valued by peers than those of girls. Apparently, the school climate has helped to make it more acceptable for girls to play around with science things, but boys' ideas about science things are still supposed to be better than those of girls.

Help the Divergent Child to Become Less Obnoxious

In our studies of highly creative children, it is evident that many of them bring upon themselves many of their own woes. To open to them the curriculum frontiers I have suggested, we must help them to become less obnoxious without sacrificing their creativity.

Both our experimental and longitudinal studies and studies of outstanding creative persons reveal that highly creative individuals do, in fact, possess characteristics generally considered somewhat obnoxious. They do, in fact, create problems for their parents, siblings, peers, teachers and supervisors. Many of our young elementary school authors recognize this problem, but most, like the sixth grader who wrote the following story, feel that considerable sacrifice of creativity is necessary:

> "My brother was born a day before I was. But there was something wrong with him. He had wings! Can you imagine that? A monkey with wings!
>
> "He could fly where other monkeys couldn't get to, so they teased him. Well, he got tired of being teased and I got tired of being his brother (because of course I was teased too).
>
> "We decided to fly to some other place. So I climbed up his back and away we went.
>
> "The other monkeys were sorry then because my brother had always gotten the best bananas for them. Everyone was sad, even my brother and I. We couldn't find anywhere to go and he was getting tired. Finally, we turned around and started walking back.
>
> "When we got back, everyone was happy again! But sometimes, for spite, the 'flying monkey' wouldn't get the best bananas for them and then the teasing would start again.
>
> "Finally, he learned how to keep his 'wings' out of sight. After that he hardly ever used them and was never teased again."

We also need to help children recognize that outstanding talents may threaten others and make them uncomfortable and afraid. Our young authors recognize this and offer some interesting philosophies. The performance of important services and courageous deeds on behalf of the larger social group is seen by our juvenile authors as one way of reducing the social pressures on divergent individuals.

In conserving creative talent, the problem resolves itself into one of helping the child maintain those characteristics which are essential to his creativity and at the same time helping him acquire skills for avoiding or reducing to a tolerable level the social sanctions against him. Stein (1958) on the basis of his study of research chemists has offered a set of helpful principles whereby creative research chemists can become less obnoxious without sacrificing their creativity. I have tried to paraphrase this advice to make it apply to gifted elementary pupils, as follows:

> "Help the gifted child maintain his assertiveness without being hostile and aggressive. He must be aware of his superiors, peers, and subordinates as persons. He may work alone but he must not be isolated, withdrawn, or uncommunicative. In the classroom he must be congenial but not sociable; outside the classroom he must be sociable but not intimate. He must 'know his place' without being timid, submissive, or acquiescent and must speak 'his mind' without being domineering. As he tries to gain a point, he can be subtle but not cunning or manipulative. In all relationships, he must be sincere, honest, purposeful, and diplomatic. In the intellectual area, he must learn to be broad without spreading himself too thin, deep without being 'bookish' or 'too scientific,' and 'sharp' without being overcritical."

This model probably asks too much of the gifted child, but it at least provides a model which might guide us in making possible the exploration of the frontiers outlined.

Develop Pride in the Achievement of Gifted Pupils

It seems to me that we miss many good opportunities for developing pride in the achievement of gifted pupils. We have long done a good job of developing pride in athletic teams, bands, and the like. Much is being done now to develop pride in a school's scientific talent, especially at the high school level. Some schools are organizing elementary school art shows. Much more could be done, however, to give favorable recognition to schools for their development of intellectual and creative talents.

You may dislike the blunt exhibitionism involved in the following story by a gifted sixth-grade boy. You must admit, nevertheless, that he has the rudiments of a potentially useful idea.

> "Once there was a monkey named Business. Because this was his name and he was a monkey, all of the other animals in the jungle called him Monkey Business. Of course, Business didn't like this. Why he was the laughing stock of the whole jungle! That is, until his friend Jacko the Bird taught him to fly! Now Monkey Business was the pride of the jungle. . . . Very soon nobody made any jokes about his name. As a matter of fact, whenever they had any visitors from other jungles, the first thing they showed them was Monkey Business, the fabulous flying monkey."

Reduce the Isolation of the Gifted Child

Much attention has already been given to the problems involved in reducing the isolation of the gifted child (Kaluger and Martin, 1960). Isolation has been a favorite technique for coping with individuals having almost any kind of divergent characteristic. In the imaginative stories, the following reaction is fairly common:

". . . His mother was so surprised to see him flying. She said that she didn't want any flying monkey in her family so she sent him away to some other part of the jungle."

One of the most successful techniques in the stories of our young authors is the discovery by one divergent individual of someone with a similar divergency. This happens to both the flying monkeys and the silent lions. Several current streams of research (Drews, 1961; Torrance and Arsan, 1961; Durrell, 1961) suggest that various kinds of groupings, both within classes and into classes, may open up some exciting frontiers, especially for children with divergent characteristics.

Provide Sponsors or Patrons for Gifted Pupils

Someone has observed that almost always wherever independence and creativity occur and persist, there is some other individual or agent who plays the role of "sponsor" or "patron." The patron or sponsor is someone who is not a member of the peer group, but possesses prestige or power in the same social system. He does several things. Regardless of his own views, the sponsor encourages and supports the talented individual in expressing and testing his ideas, in thinking through things for himself. He protects the individual from the counter reactions of his peers long enough to permit him to try out some of his ideas. He can keep the structure of the situation open enough so that originality can occur. In some cases, this sponsor for the gifted elementary pupil may be a teacher, principal, an older child, an adult leader, a school social worker or counselor.

Exploit the Opportunities of the Moment

Frequently questions are asked concerning the role of chance in scientific discovery. Certainly many great discoveries have resulted because someone exploited a chance occurrence, an unexpected incident, or the like. As teachers learn to exploit such moments and train their pupils to do so, there is no question but that unpredicted curriculum frontiers for gifted elementary pupils will emerge. Many of the stories of flying monkeys and silent lions tell stories of such exploitation of the moment.

Develop Values and Purpose

Studies of outstanding individuals in various fields almost always reveal that such purposes seem to be impelled by some feeling of mission or purpose. They believe that what they are doing is tremendously worthwhile and are thereby aroused to "all-out" effort. When learning and thinking is made to be "tremendously important and worthwhile," schools will become exciting places and curriculum frontiers will unfold. Even gifted children will achieve more than we thought possible. Such is the experience of a number of the monkeys in the imaginative stories of elementary pupils.

Help Gifted Pupils Cope With Anxieties and Fears

Neither gifted children nor creative scientists (Roe, 1959) are free of handicapping anxieties and fears. Many gifted children will be unable to explore the curriculum frontiers already discussed unless they have help in coping with their anxieties and irrational fears. Not only will they fail to be fully functioning mentally; they will be afraid to break away from the safest, most frequently traveled, paths.

An unusually frequent theme in the stories of animals and persons with divergent characteristics is the fear of one's own talent or the fear that its use will bring injury or destruction. The following pathetic story by a gifted Illinois girl represents an extreme fear of one's own talent:

". . . I will tell you about a lion named Elmer who was afraid of anything. Elmer had no friends at all. In the day he laid around all the time. At night he hunted for food. He saw his shadow, he started to cry. All the animals came running. The tiger, Mr. Peabody, said, 'Why are you crying?'

"Elmer just sat there. Then an elephant, Mrs. Atlas, said, 'Why are you crying?'

"Elmer said nothing. Then the lizard, mouse, horse, cat, cow and hen tried but could not get him to answer. Then a little boy said, 'Why are you crying?'

"Elmer looked up and said, 'I saw my shadow and I'm scared of it.'

" 'I don't see it,' said the boy. The lion looked down. It was not there.

"He started to roar, then started to cry. The boy said, 'Why are you crying?'

" 'I'm afraid of my roar,' Elmer said. All the animals and the boy laughed."

In one story, a lion would not roar because he was afraid that his roar might not sound like a lion's. Another would not roar because he was afraid that a banana might fall down his throat when he opened his mouth to roar. Thus, on and on, the animals created by gifted children are shackled by some of the same kinds of fears which shackle gifted children. Quite interestingly, almost all of these handicapped animals are able to rise to the occasion and transcend their fears when some necessity arises. I feel convinced that gifted children will leap many barriers to curriculum frontiers, if we educators will learn better how to create necessities for learning and thinking.

References

Andrews, E. G. The development of imagination in the pre-school child. *Univer. of Iowa Studies in Character*, 1930, *3* (*4*).

Barron, F. Originality in relation to personality and intellect. *J. Personality*, 1957, *25*, 730–742.

Bruner, J. S. *The process of education*. Cambridge, Mass.: Harvard Univer. Press, 1960.

Drews, Elizabeth M. Recent findings about gifted adolescents. In Torrance, E. P. (Ed.) *New Educational Ideas: Third Minnesota conference on gifted children*. Minneapolis: Center for Continuation Study, Univer. of Minn., 1961.

Durrell, D. Pupil team learning: Effects of team size on retention of knowledge. Paper presented at annual meetings of AERA, Chicago, February 24, 1961.

Fritz, R. L. An evaluation of scholastic achievement of students attending half-day sessions in the seventh grade. Unpublished research paper, Univer. of Minn., August 1958.

Kaluger, G. and Ruthe Martin. The loneliness of the gifted child. *Elem. Sch. J.*, 1960, *61*, 127–132.

Kelley, E. C. The significance of being unique. In Hayakawa (Ed.) *Our language and our world*. New York: Harper, 1959. P. 152–171.

Moore, O. K. Orthographic symbols and the pre-school child—a new approach. In Torrance, E. P. (Ed.) *New ideas: Third Minnesota conference on gifted children*. Minneapolis: Center for Continuation Study, Univer. of Minn., 1961.

Roe, Anne. Personal problems and science. In Taylor, C. W. (Ed.) *The third (1959) University of Utah research conference on the identification of creative scientific talent*. Salt Lake City: Univer. of Utah Press, 1959. P. 202–212.

Rossman, J. *The psychology of the inventor*. Washington, D.C.: Inventors Publishing Company, 1931.

Stein, M. I. Creativity and/or success: A study of value conflict. In Taylor, C. W. (Ed.) *The second (1957) University of Utah research conference on the identification of creative scientific talent*. Salt Lake City: Univer. of Utah Press, 1958. P. 201–231.

Torrance, E. P. *Sex-Role identification and creative thinking*. Minneapolis: Bureau of Educational Research, Univer. of Minn., 1959. (a)

Torrance, E. P. *Personality studies of highly creative children*. Minneapolis: Bureau of Educational Research, Univer. of Minn., 1959. (b)

Torrance, E. P. *Eight partial replications of the Getzels-Jackson study*. Minneapolis: Bureau of Educational Research, Univer. of Minn., 1960. (a)

TORRANCE, E. P. *Changing reactions of girls in grades four through six to tasks requiring creative scientific thinking.* Minneapolis: Bureau of Educational Research, Univer. of Minn., 1960. (b)

TORRANCE, E. P. and Staff. *Rewarding creative thinking.* Minneapolis: Bureau of Educational Research, Univer. of Minn., 1961.

TORRANCE, E. P. and KEVSER ARSAN. Studies of homogeneous and heterogeneous groups within classes. Paper presented to Association of Educators of Gifted Children, Statler Hotel, Detroit, April 5, 1961.

❦ 20

What Teacher Attributes Bring Out the Best in Gifted Children? Affective Dimensions of Creative Processes

Robert L. Spaulding

A NUMBER OF STUDIES in the past decade have focused upon the characteristics of gifted children and effects of different types of administrative arrangements or grouping for instruction. Among these are interest grouping, ability grouping, enrichment, acceleration, ungraded or cross-graded classrooms, and early admission to school. In more recent years many researchers have turned their attention to analyses of the classroom behavior and cognitive characteristics of children as a promising field of investigation. Painstaking research projects such as the ones directed by Dr. James Gallagher (1963) and Dr. B. Othaniel Smith (1962) at the University of Illinois are cases in point.

Another facet of this recent concern with classroom process is the study of the affective dimensions of classroom transaction. Dr. Marie Hughes (1959) at the University of Utah is continuing studies of this type.

What about the affective dimensions? Are they fundamental to classroom learning? If so, what types of teacher-pupil classroom transactions are most closely related to superior creative thinking in children? What about self-esteem? Is it related to classroom teacher behavior? Is it related to processes of creative thinking?

These and other related questions have been investigated for a number of years. Many persons, among them Lewin, Lippitt, & White (1939), Anderson (1939), Withall (1952), Bush (1954), and Heil (1960), have studied

DR. SPAULDING is Associate Professor of Education, Hofstra University, Hempstead, New York. The paper was originally presented at the 1963 annual meeting of Association for Supervision and Curriculum Development, in St. Louis.

the influence of the emotional climate or atmosphere upon the behavior of the children in classes or other groups. The role taken by the teacher or leader has been found in these studies to be a critical factor in setting the classroom climate, yet the manner in which a particular teacher comes to influence the learning of a given child or the group as a whole has been found to be very complex. Each encounter of teacher and child is a unique event, with a particular *experiential* history behind it on the part of both teacher and child.

Inhelder and Piaget (1958) have traced the manner in which types of thought structures characteristically develop from childhood and adolescence and how each child comes to operate intellectually with a hierarchy of concepts and generalizations derived from his own concrete experience. Hunt (1961) has suggested that a child's functional intelligence is dependent upon "the kind of external circumstances encountered and the kind of internal organization already present . . ." (p. 357). He speaks of the "richness" of the environment and emphasizes the importance of "self-directed interest and curiosity and genuine pleasure in intellectual activity . . ." He also cautions against implying a kind of "grim urgency which has been associated with 'pushing' children" (p. 363). What might this "richness" be? How might the teacher structure the external circumstances encountered by the child in order to "enrich" it? How might "grimness" affect the child? How might it be avoided?

Teachers Influence the Child's Behavior

In order to begin to look for answers to these questions it might be profitable to examine the environment of children in classrooms from two points of view—affectively and cognitively. Each of the transactions in which the child participates has an affective as well as a cognitive component. The child stores affective information as well as cognitive parameters. Each new environmental encounter thus involves an affective loading based upon relevant past experience and this feeling state serves to guide action and modify perception.

Perception itself may be distorted if the affective properties of the encounter result in markedly increased tension or anxiety. Because children have structured for themselves, intuitively, individualistic systems of concepts and generalizations, overladen with positive and negative affect, the behavior of the teacher in the classroom can be expected to mean different things to different children. What is threat to a dependent child may be interesting and challenging to an intellectually creative child, who is generally secure as a result of successful coping in the past. Heil (1960) has found that some children (he calls them "strivers") readily adapt to almost any type of teacher classroom behavior, while others ("wavering" or anxious children) make their greatest academic progress under calm, ordered classroom conditions.

Without deprecating the importance of studying the ways in which different types of children with specific response hierarchies and thought systems transact with specific patterns or types of teacher classroom behavior, it seems important to look for components of teacher behavior which have common relationships with the attitudes and performance of children generally.

Since objective dimensions of experience are always concomitants of specific affective factors it is necessary to examine the classroom transactional process as it occurs if specific environmental antecedents of types of teacher affective response are to be noted. For example, when a teacher threatens a child it is always done in some specific setting or situation. Over the past two years I have been investigating types of teacher response to fifteen-second sequences of classroom teacher-pupil transaction. The method emphasizes the interpretation of each teacher response in terms of the context in which it was imbedded—both affectively and objectively. If the teacher were approving at the moment of analysis, questions of Who? Why? In what manner? With what publicity? and so forth, were asked. The technique provides for interpretations of teacher tone or mood, the source of authority appealed to, the publicity of transaction, the type of pupil behavior controlled or reinforced, the sex of pupil involved, the activity level of the pupils in the classroom at the moment, the nature of the information conveyed, and the presence of covert sequential positive and negative reinforcement—for each of the molar variables—approval, disapproval, instruction, and listening. The non-communicative activity of the teacher is also recorded and interpreted.

Specifically, the study was designed to test relationships predicted between variables of pupil self-esteem, academic achievement, and creative thinking, and several types or patterns of teacher-pupil interaction which have been identified in past studies—the "socially integrative" pattern discussed by Anderson (1939), the "democratic" type of leader behavior studied by Lewin, Lippitt, & White (1939), the "learner-supportive" category identified by Withall (1948), and three types of teacher behavior described by Bush (1954)—the "academic" teacher, the "counseling" teacher, and the "creative" teacher.

The research was carried out in a West Coast upper middle-class suburban city of about 50,000 population. Ten of the larger elementary schools in the city were selected to represent a cross-section of the school population. All teachers in these schools who were teaching in self-contained classrooms at the fourth and sixth grade levels were asked to participate. The twenty-one classrooms obtained in this manner were located in nine different elementary school buildings and included a sample of

507 boys and girls who were registered from October through June of the year 1960–61.

Differences between children in mental ability (SCAT), socio-economic status, sex, and chronological age were adjusted for statistically. Tests of the significance of placement of a child in one or another of the twenty-one classrooms with regard to the target variables–pupil self-concept, academic achievement, and creative thinking–indicated that "room placement" was significantly related to each of the target variables. Even within a highly selective school system, where standardized employment practices and high salaries existed, and where a large number of qualified applicants were available each year for the few positions open, there were important differences in pupil performance and self-concept which could be accounted for in terms of classroom placement.

What about the classrooms in which pupil academic or creative thinking performance was superior? What kinds of teacher-pupil transaction characterized them? What kinds of teacher behavior were to be found in the classrooms where children had higher self-concepts? In order to provide data regarding these questions the instrument of classroom analysis which I mentioned earlier was developed. It focused upon affective responses of the teacher to specific classroom situations and types of pupil behavior. An analysis of a full morning of classroom process provided data on 113 categories of teacher-pupil transaction. These basic units of transaction were combined statistically to obtain 17 components of teacher response to specific classroom situations. The seventeen components derived in this manner are described in Table 1.

Relationships of these components with the target pupil variables have been computed and the results suggest that the primary importance of the affective climate set by the teacher is to be found in terms of pupil self-concept and academic achievement. Few significant relationships with variables of creative thinking were obtained, but these few suggest some important hypotheses.

Pupil self-esteem (SC Mean) was found to be significantly related positively ($r = .39$) with one component which was common to both the "socially integrative" syndrome of Anderson (1946) and the "learner-supportive" category of Withall (1952)–this was Component 5–*Calm, acceptant transactions in general with private, individualized instruction and a concern for divergency, attention to task, and the use of task appropriate procedures and resources.* The other components of the "socially integrative" syndrome (Components 7, *9*, and *12*) and of the "learner-supportive" category (Components 7, *8*, *12*, and *13*) were not significantly related to any of the pupil target variables.

Predictions of superior reading (Read) and mathematics achievement (Math) in classrooms taught by "academically oriented" teachers as described by Bush (1954) were unsupported by the results of this study.

TABLE 1. COMPONENTS OF TEACHER-PUPIL TRANSACTION

1. Observant and small-group facilitative emphasizing appropriate task procedures and social relations through semi-autonomous, semi-private small-group process
2. Dominative through use of shame, ridicule, and threat
3. Firm, dominative control with emphasis on paying attention, proper planning, and the use of appropriate procedures and resources
4. Good natured, personalized control with concern for sources of error, character, self-control, and proper social relations
5. Calm, acceptant transactions in general with private, individualized instruction and a concern for divergency, attention to task, and the use of task appropriate procedures and resources
6. Businesslike lecture method with insistence upon attention to task and conformity to rules of procedure
7. Supportive, receptive, responsive transactions regarding pupil ideas and concerns
8. Self-centered, and judgmental transactions emphasizing acceptable skill, knowledge, and planning
9. Warm, open transactions with boys and a general avoidance of transaction with girls
10. Formal group instruction with control through shame, ridicule, or admonition
11. Observant-controlling, emphasizing attention to task and encouraging pupils' use of own abilities
12. Acceptant-supportive-evaluative, with an appeal to group authority and responsibility
13. Highly verbal and good-humored transactions with individuals or the class as a whole and an avoidance of small-group process
14. Unresponsive transactions with grim domination regarding rules (girls), skill or knowledge (boys), and paying attention (boys and girls)
15. Acceptant, controlling through standards, with appeal to convention as the source of authority, and avoiding negative evaluation
16. Cold, impersonal public instruction emphasizing knowledge and skill and the use of shame or ridicule or a means of control
17. Humorless transactions with control through threat and an appeal to outside authority in instruction

The component which most closely resembled the "academic" type of teacher as described by Bush was Component *16—Cold, impersonal public instruction emphasizing knowledge and skill and the use of shame or ridicule as a means of control.*

Predictions of significantly higher self-concepts in classrooms taught by teachers oriented toward pupil counseling were also not substantiated. Nor were pupils found to be superior in cognitive flexibility (Flex) or originality (Orig) in the classroom taught by the teacher most closely

TABLE 2. CORRELATIONS OF SEVENTEEN COMPONENTS OF TEACHER-PUPIL TRANSACTIONS WITH EIGHT TARGET PUPIL VARIABLES

	Target pupil variables							
Component[a]	*SC Mean*	*SC SD*	*Read*	*Math*	*Flex*	*Prob Solv*	*Synth*	*Orig.*
1. Observant-facilitative	48[b]	−68[c]	18	−19	11	−14	−19	16
2. Dominatve-threatening	−71[b]	49[c]	−49[b]	−10	−20	−07	02	−16
3. Firm-dominative	−40[b]	19	−27	−24	02	−03	14	18
4. Good-natured-personal	−25	33	−29	−19	−55[c]	−28	−10	−53[c]
5. Calm-acceptant	39[b]	−34	04	−38	−11	−24	−20	−01
6. Businesslike-orderly	41	−13	44[c]	39	15	37	09	10
7. Receptive-responsive	16	−17	−05	−23	−10	−36	−10	−01
8. Self-centered with concern for knowledge	−18	19	−05	07	21	20	−02	11
9. Warm, open with boys	−16	16	−37	−38	−34	−41	−22	−30
10. Formal group instruction using shame and ridicule	−46[b]	61[c]	−42[b]	−08	−49[b]	−06	05	−53[b]
11. Observant-controlling	32	−20	04	−20	−25	−14	−12	−16
12. Acceptant-supportive	09	−03	15	08	04	19	24	−12
13. Good-humored-verbose	−07	44[c]	10	30	−21	12	26	−09
14. Grim domination	−63[b]	43[c]	−34	−08	−20	06	11	−13
15. Acceptant-controlling, avoiding negative evaluation	37[b]	−48[c]	01	−29	19	−33	−26	35
16. Cold, impersonal, emphasizing knowledge	−52[b]	42	−21	04	−04	20	09	−11
17. Humorless-threatening	−37[b]	22	−03	11	06	30	06	−10

NOTE: Decimal points have been omitted.
[a] Complete descriptions of these components may be found in Table 1.
[b] Significant at the .05 level (*one*-tailed test).
[c] Significant at the .05 level (*two*-tailed test, used in testing unpredicted relationships).

resembling the "creative" type of teacher as described by Bush. In fact, the pupils in this classroom had the lowest scores on cognitive flexibility and originality.

Negative relationships in general were obtained for the two components of behavior which most closely resembled the "democratic" type of teacher behavior which Lewin, Lippitt, & White (1939) had studied. These two components are numbered 4 and 7 in Table 1. Component 4 has been described as *Good-natured, personalized control with concern for sources of error, character, self-control and proper social relations.* Component 7 is identified as *Supportive, receptive, responsive and transactions regarding pupil ideas and concerns.* In the case of Component 4 significant negative relationships ($r = -.55$ and $-.53$) were found with pupil cognitive flexibility and originality, contrary to prediction.

A third component of the "democratic" syndrome is number *15*—*Acceptant, controlling through standards, with appeal to convention as the source of authority, and avoiding negative evaluation.* Though not central to the original typology this component has been given greater emphasis in recent writings of White and Lippitt (1960):

> The most efficient procedure does appear to be, as a rule, democracy—*if* democracy is sharply differentiated from laissez-faire, with clear acceptance not only of active leadership but also of the firm use of authority when firmness is called for, and explicit delegation of authority to certain individuals when such delegation is appropriate (p. 292).

Component *15* was found to be significantly related positively (r = .37) with height of self-concept (SC Mean) and to be related at the .06 level with originality (r = .35). The teacher who uses this type of control avoids negative evaluation of pupil behavior and obtains pupil cooperation through an emphasis upon standards set by society. He appeals to convention as the source of authority rather than to peers or himself.

When the results of the study as a whole are considered there is a general support for the importance of an acceptant, supportive climate with respect to superior pupil self-esteem. Significant positive relationships with height of self-concept were obtained for Components *5* (*Calm-acceptant*), *15* (*Acceptant-controlling*), *1* (*Observant-facilitative*), *6* (*Businesslike-orderly*), and *15* (*Acceptant-controlling avoiding negative evaluation*). These last three components emphasize the importance of task appropriate procedures and a businesslike approach with control achieved through public standards applying equally to all, with convention as the source of authority.

Significant negative relationships were obtained for Components *2* (*Dominative-threatening*), *3* (*Firm-dominative*), *10* (*Formal group instruction using shame and ridicule*), *14* (*Grim domination*), *16* (*Cold and impersonal, emphasizing knowledge*), and *17* (*Humorless-threatening*).

As for reading and mathematics achievement, only one component stands out as significant—Component *6* (*Businesslike lecture method with insistence upon attention to task and conformity to rules of procedure*). Two others are significantly *negatively* related—Component *2* (*Dominative-threatening*), and Component *9* (*Warm, open with boys and a general avoidance of transactions with girls*). This last finding suggests that the "buddy-buddy" type of relationship with boys, established by some teachers as a possible means of control, vitiates the academic effectiveness of the teacher.

Very few positive relationships were obtained with dimensions of pupil creative thinking. Component *15* (*Acceptant-controlling*), which was found to be a marginal component of the "democratic" pattern of teacher behavior, was the *one* component which approached a significant level of relationship ($r = .35$, $p < .06$). Yet, the importance of the affective climate to creative processes cannot easily be dismissed since in the case of two components (Component *4* and *10*) relatively large and highly significant *negative* relationships were observed. The correlations with cognitive flexibility were $-.55$ for Component *4* and $-.49$ for Component *10*. With originality the coefficients were both $-.53$. Component *4* (*Good-natured, personalized control with concern for sources of error, character, self-control, and proper social relations*) reflects an emotional rather than cognitive encounter between the teacher and his pupils. Teachers whose behavior is reflected by this component of transaction apparently respond primarily to the social and emotional qualities displayed by pupils rather than their cognitive performance. It can be hypothesized that when teachers become overly concerned with socialization and impulse control in dealing with children, the concepts and generalizations appropriate to the subject matter at hand may frequently be neglected.

Component *10* (*Formal group instruction with control through shame, ridicule, or admonition*) appears to characterize a type of teacher who is so concerned with his own ideas and needs that he fails to provide the "climate" of support and acceptance necessary for children to venture out into the cognitive unknown to try to assimilate the new or restructure the old. Component *10*, with its loading of shame and ridicule in public as a means of control appears to destroy the personal security of the pupils.

None of the components obtained in this study were found to be significantly related to pupil problem-solving (Prob Solv) or synthesis abilities (Synth). These convergent thought processes appear to depend upon relatively stable cognitive factors within the personality structure of the child. The pattern of relationships obtained, though reasonably explained by the operation of chance alone, is similar to that found for gains in mathematics performance and suggests (a) the importance of a business-like approach on the part of the teacher, with attention to the cognitive dimensions of tasks; (b) an absence of overly supportive-responsive teacher behavior which permits and encourages tangential thinking and digression; (c) the absence of an overly familiar, "buddy-buddy" type of relationship with boys in the class; (d) the absence of threat as a means of control; and (e) the presence of a moderate degree of humor in dealing with the control problems and instruction in general.

Synthesis ability in the sample of boys and girls was found to be related significantly with differentiation of self-concept ($r = .43$). Indirectly, acceptant-supportive-controlling teacher behavior may contribute to organizational abilities by providing adequate feedback to pupils in a non-threatening climate. In such a situation pupils might be encouraged to differentiate among areas of strength and weakness without suffering a debilitating drop in height of self-concept. The one component which was significantly related to increased self-analysis (greater differentiation of self-concept) was number *13—Highly verbal and good-humored transactions with individuals or the class as a whole and an avoidance of small-group process.* This type of teacher behavior and structuring of classroom activity appears to provide a high level of feedback to pupils in an atmosphere of acceptance and support.

Summary

In summary, affective components of teacher behavior in the classroom appear important, primarily, in fostering self-esteem and providing an atmosphere in which cognitive risk-taking can freely occur. Such a supportive, acceptant climate, though apparently necessary, does not appear to be sufficient. Some teacher direction, limit setting, and feedback regarding cognitive dimensions of the subject matter at hand, structured in a businesslike, orderly manner, seems called for also. To a degree these factors appear necessary for all children.

In preliminary studies at Illinois, Dr. Suchman and I have been studying the classroom responses of five types of children in transaction with teachers and other children in their rooms. These pilot studies support the idea that the teacher must structure the curriculum differently for various types of children. The "creative intellectual," or creatively gifted appears most highly motivated and constructively occupied in settings where limits are clearly set but which permit a wide range of choice for self-direction. The creative or inventive thinker appears not so much to want to become less involved with the classroom activity but to be permitted to enter into each, with a greater degree of autonomy and responsibility.

The "conforming achiever" seems most at ease and most productive when the lines of expectation are closely drawn and the instructions clearly given. With too much latitude responses tend to become regressive and defensive. Ego concerns appear to take precedence when lines of acceptable action are ambiguous, tending to push out his efforts at assimilation or accommodation of cognitive material. Attention appears to get focused upon external parameters related to defensive coping strategies rather than internal processes of scanning for thought structures appropriate to the cognitive task at hand.

These preliminary observations of types of children lend additional support to the importance of the affective climate of the classroom, but suggest that much more is required of the teacher than to be acceptant and supportive. He must come to the point where he can not only identify the sources of motivation and anxiety in each of his pupils and provide adequate limits and structuring for each child to feel secure, but he must begin to recognize the level at which each child is operating cognitively so that he can help structure his intellectual encounters. With such skills and knowledge he can, hopefully, provide for a more frequent occurrence of the kind of *match* of which Hunt speaks.

References

1. Anderson, H. H. "The Measurement of Domination and Socially Integrative Behavior in Teachers' Contacts with Children." *Child Develpm.*, 1939, *10*, 73–89.
2. Bush, R. N. *The Teacher-Pupil Relationship*. New York: Prentice-Hall, 1954.
3. Gallagher, J. J., & Aschner, Mary Jane. "A Preliminary Report on Analyses of Classroom Interaction." *Merrill Palmer Quarterly* (in press), 1963.
4. Heil, L. M., Powell, Marion, & Feifer, I. *Characteristics of Teacher Behavior Related to the Achievement of Children in Several Elementary Grades*. Washington: U. S. Department of Health, Education, and Welfare, Office of Education, Cooperation Research Branch, 1960.
5. Hughes, Marie M. *Assessment of the Quality of Teaching in Elementary Schools*. Washington: U. S. Department of Health, Education, and Welfare. Office of Education, Cooperative Research Branch, 1959.
6. Hunt, J. McV. *Intelligence and Experience*. New York: Ronald Press, 1961.
7. Inhelder, Barbel, & Piaget, J. *The Growth of Logical Thinking from Childhood to Adolescence*. New York: Basic Books, 1958.
8. Lewin, K., Lippitt, R., & White, R. "Patterns of Aggressive Behavior in Experimentally Created Social Climates." *J. soc. Psychol.*, 1939, *10*, 271–299.
9. Smith, B. O. *A Study of the Logic of Teaching*. Washington: U. S. Department of Health, Education, and Welfare, Office of Education, Cooperative Research Branch, 1962.
10. Withall, J. "Assessment of the Social-Emotional Climates Experienced by a Group of Seventh Graders as They Moved from Class to Class. *Educ. Psychol. Measmt.*, 1952, *12*, 440–451.

❦❦ Part Four

SPECIAL PROBLEMS

FOR MANY YEARS the educator has been confronted with several standard problems dealing with gifted children. Does enrichment in the regular classroom help gifted children? Does acceleration harm gifted children? What can we do about the gifted underachiever, the student who appears to possess more aptitude than his performance would indicate? The articles in this section touch on some of these issues.

Until recently, whenever an up-to-date administrator was asked what his school district was doing for gifted children at the elementary level his answer was almost certainly that they were receiving an *enrichment* program in the regular grades. This meant that the teacher was providing stimulating and challenging projects or assignments that would help the student understand concepts and ideas at a level appropriate to his advanced mental development. Many persons have been suspicious that *enrichment* as a policy has remained more on paper than in operation.

In the article by Gallagher, Greenman, Karnes, and King an attempt was made to evaluate the strengths and weaknesses of an enrichment program developed for the self-contained classroom at the elementary level. Despite the presence of more highly trained personnel than is usually available to help the elementary teacher, no dramatic group improvements were noted. The central limitation seemed to be the limits of knowledge in specific content areas of the elementary teachers. For example, a teacher must know mathematics to enrich mathematics or must know history to enrich history, and so on. While this study does not definitely establish the limits of *enrichment* as a technique, since it was done in only two school systems, the burden of proof on the efficacy of the procedure is clearly on its proponents.

Although the topic *acceleration* of gifted students still generates much heat, it has gradually come to be recognized as a highly overrated educational issue. Whether the student is accelerated or not, there is still the problem of what to include in his educational program, and these curriculum and methods issues probably should be given greater attention. Nevertheless, the lengthening period of training that many of our young gifted students must complete before being prepared for their life work does require us to consider useful ways of reducing this period of time without inflicting problems on the student.

The article by Reynolds, Birch, and Tuseth summarizes much of the literature on early admission of gifted students (allowing a mature gifted child to enter the school program without the usual age restrictions). Early admission has much to recommend it over other types of acceleration. The youngster does not miss any of the school program, and it is not condensed or speeded up in an unfavorable fashion. As the authors point out, the evidence for this method is strongly positive, as it is with other methods of acceleration when they are executed systematically and with individual planning. Now the important problem to solve is how to make this procedure economically and professionally feasible for a school system. Many more school administrators would have adopted this, or other acceleration procedures, if they felt that it could be done without involving their program in the extensive use of psychological tests and the services of psychologists that were not available or that could not be afforded under present financing.

The gifted underachiever is a continual headache for the school administrator. The concept of underachievement itself has been subjected to extensive discussion and analysis. Is there really such a thing or is it an artifact of our tests? If there is something that can be called underachievement, how can it be measured and what can be done about it? In the set of readings in this section the emphasis has been on ways of dealing with the problem, since it is taken for granted that there *are* students who have talents and do not use them. This grievous waste of talent should be of concern to the individual and to his society.

The article by Goldberg provides us with a good picture of the type of behavioral syndrome we have come to expect from these students and also gives us one of the few written versions of a school program that was adapted to fit their particular needs. This article points out that underachievement generally represents a lifelong pattern of maladaptive behavior which will not reform itself either through casual enticement or threat. The traditional reaction of teachers and parents is that these youngsters are lazy or misbehaving and that they should be told in no uncertain terms that they have got to shoulder much greater responsibility for their own actions. The school program described by Goldberg takes a dramatically different approach—that it is the school who should adapt, as well as the student.

Since personality factors play such an important part in the life pattern of the gifted underachiever, another approach at remediation has been to place him in counseling. The article by Baymur and Patterson attempts to evaluate the relative effectiveness of three different approaches: individual counseling, group counseling, and one-session motivational counseling.

While the results of this experiment show trends in favor of counseling, these results were not enthusiastic when compared with a control population. These modest results should warn us that the chronic underachiever's difficulties are part of a total life pattern that has been developing over many years and is not easily changed.

Since much of the educational work has been tried at the secondary level with underachievers, some thoughts have been given to the possibility of identifying underachievers at an earlier age. The article by Shaw and McCuen asks, how early can one identify the youngster who is going to be a chronic underachiever? The answer is different for boys than for girls and should sensitize us to the fact that we know precious little about underachieving girls, the majority of the research having been carried out on boys.

The fact that the underachieving boys can be identified as early as the third grade points out the chronic nature of these problems. If remediation is going to be maximally effective it would seem desirable to begin while the youngsters are younger when these maladaptive patterns have not hardened into complete resistance and recalcitrance.

Another type of talent loss is obtained through inadequate educational stimulation or opportunities provided to some of the minority groups in our society. One of the great lessons to be drawn from research on talented children is that intellectual talent flourishes everywhere. It can be found in children of every race, creed, and nationality. It is not merely found in the homes of the favored in our society, although it is found there more often than elsewhere.

One of the noblest of American dreams is that of universal education in which, in theory, all children have an equal opportunity to develop their talents to the limits of their ability. This philosophy commits us to educating, not only those who are ready to learn by virtue of their able family background and a preschool life rich with opportunities for learning, but also those who are not really ready to learn. At least, they are not ready to learn in the same way as our favored youngsters.

It is this educationally deprived group that Riessman describes in his article. In many of our urban areas today there is a distinct problem of talent waste. The failure to develop the leadership potential in any segment of our society leads to inadequate spokesmen for that segment, lack of appropriate models for behavior for the next generation, lack of motivation to achieve at difficult tasks, and a descending spiral of unfavorable consequences.

There has been little recognition of the necessity to modify the school program to take into account the different backgrounds of these students–backgrounds that set them apart from both the school curriculum and their teachers. The world of the inner city child is one where words do not mean as much as action, where ideas are not as important as things, where strength and masculinity may count for more than warmth and affection. The suggestions that Reissman makes are worth careful attention of educators who wish to present an educational program which challenges and at the same time fits the needs of these talented children.

But this is not the end of the problem. There are the educationally disadvantaged students from rural areas who also have special needs which are different from those of his city counterparts. It is in this type of differential programming for special needs that the programs for the gifted will reach their full, and yet to be attained, maturity.

❦ 21

A Three Year Experimental Program at DeWitt Clinton High School to Help Bright Underachievers

Miriam L. Goldberg and Associates
DeWitt Clinton High School

SCHOOLS HAVE long been concerned with suiting programs to the ability levels of students. This has been particularly true of the New York City academic high schools, where CRMD and "modified" general non-Regents classes are available for slow-learning students, or for average students who are not college bound, with regular academic programs for the average college bound students, and honors classes for the most able groups. For the exceptionally gifted student, special scholarship classes or advanced standing courses are sometimes provided.

But there is one group in our schools which is not being adequately serviced by the broad range of offerings; a group which does not properly fit into any of the above categories: the gifted underachiever. On the basis of measured intelligence and aptitude, these students should be successful in honors and scholarship programs; on the basis of school performance, they often fail to cope adequately even with modified courses. In terms of the administrative organization of the high school they are misfits—potential giants who perform like pygmies.

Attempts to explain the discrepancy between measured intelligence and performance date back many years. There is considerable evidence to suggest that social-psychological factors such as socio-economic status, ethnic and religious background, educational level of the family, stability of family structure and the availability of educational and occupational models in the home and in the community, are related to achievement.[1, 2]

[1] Goldberg, Miriam L. Motivation of the Gifted, Chapter V in *Education of the Gifted*, Part II, NSSE Yearbook, Nelson Henry (Ed.). Chicago: University of Chicago Press, 1958.

[2] Beasley, Jane. *Underachievement: Review of the Literature*. Talented Youth Project, H.M.L.I., Teachers College, Columbia University, March 1957. (Unpublished document.)

Although a knowledge of intellectual ability and of background factors helps to predict with better than chance accuracy the achievement level of a *group* of students, such information is insufficient to predict or explain the behavior of an *individual.* One of the first formal studies of personality factors associated with achievement among gifted students, conducted in the New York City high schools,[1] did not reveal any consistent set of differences between gifted high-achieving, and failing students. In fact, background and personality characteristics were found to motivate diverse behavior in different students. This generalization has found support in subsequent research.[2] For example, from the information gathered at DeWitt Clinton a high level of anxiety was found to drive one student to perform on the highest possible level, another to become disorganized, discouraged, and eventually to give up. Or, where the family sets high achievement standards, one student appears to accept and internalize these standards, while another rebels against the family and its values and becomes a failure in the very area where the family prizes success most. What causes such diverse responses to apparently similar problems, pressures and handicaps is not yet known. Recent studies[3] have begun to explore possible differences in the self-attitudes of gifted achievers and underachievers, on the assumption that motivational differences will be observed in the individual's self-concept, especially as it relates to the assumption of responsibility and the performance of school or work related tasks.

The roots of the problems, in most instances, can probably be traced to early experiences in the family, the neighborhood or the school. Ideally, potential underachievers should be identified in the early grades and be helped to redirect their attitudes. Thus far, such identification has not been made until the child actually falls down in his work, which, for gifted children, usually does not occur until the latter part of junior high school.

But whatever the causes, and wherever the roots, the cumulative effects of underachievement become most apparent in the senior high school. If at the high school level the gifted underachiever is not helped to attain academic success, at least sufficient to enable him to go on to higher education, his potential gifts may be seriously inhibited. There is some evidence that not only the class grades of gifted underachievers become increasingly poor during the high school years, but that their performance on objective achievement and even aptitude tests shows signs of deterioration.[4]

Underachievement, at any level, respresents human waste. At the

[1] Conklin, A. M. "A Study of the Personalities of Gifted Students by Means of the Control Group." *American Journal of Orthopsychiatry* 1:178–83, 1931.

[2] Beasley, *op. cit.*

[3] Goldberg, Miriam. *Studies in Underachievement.* Talented Youth Project, H.M.L.I., Teachers College, Columbia University, 1957. (Unpublished document.)

[4] Frankel, Edward. *A Comparative Study of Achieving and Underachieving High School Boys of High Intellectual Ability.* Unpublished doctoral thesis, Yeshiva University, 1958.

gifted level, it represents serious social waste as well; the number of students who fall into this classification reveals the shocking magnitude of this *waste.* Although gifted underachievers are found in all schools, their proportion relative to the school's total high intelligence group is especially great in those high schools which draw students from the same geographic areas as does one or another of the special schools. Those gifted students who are functioning at an academic level commensurate with their intellectual endowment often find their way into the special schools; those who are equally bright, but poor school performers, either do not apply to the special schools or, if they do, are rejected. Thus, of the entering high ability tenth grade students at DeWitt Clinton High School in the last three years, about one half fit the description of underachiever.

Recognition of this problem led the administrative and supervisory staff of DeWitt Clinton High School to seek ways in which high ability students, who enter high school with low junior high school grades, could be helped to achieve at a level more in line with their ability. In the spring of 1956 the principal invited members of the Talented Youth Project of the Horace Mann-Lincoln Institute of School Experimentation, Teachers College, Columbia University, to cooperate with the school in studying the problem. As a result of preliminary discussions, DeWitt Clinton High School and the Talented Youth Project entered cooperatively upon a series of experimental studies, designed to test ways in which grouping, teacher selection, and individual and group guidance may affect the academic performance of gifted underachievers.

The studies undertaken at DeWitt Clinton High School had a dual purpose: (1) to determine, as far as possible, social and personal factors associated with underachievement, and (2) to experiment with school procedures which would provide special attention to the problems of an underachieving group.

Previous research in the nature of underachievement provided several leads for carrying out the first purpose. In planning the experimental procedures, however, there was little previous research to suggest models. There were no precedents to follow and no information on the kinds of procedures that might prove effective. We were breaking new ground and had to be prepared to experiment with a variety of procedures, without prior commitment to any one of them.

Academic, Personal and Social Characteristics of Gifted Underachievers and the Effects of Grouping Them in Homeroom and One Subject Class

The first study, initiated in the spring of 1956, was designed to (1) study the academic, personal and social characteristics of underachievers, and (2) assess the effects of grouping gifted underachievers in a homeroom section, and retaining them as a group in one subject matter class taught by their section officer. It was hypothesized that if such students could share each other's problems, so to speak, and could, at the same time, become closely identified with and receive support from a teacher, their general school attitudes and performance would improve. In order to achieve the desired relationships, the teacher selected for the task had to be vitally interested in the problem, had to be warm and outgoing, and, above all, had to combine flexibility with maintenance of high standards.

Grouping the Students

Initially, 102 entering tenth grade underachievers were identified–students with IQ's of 120 or higher and ninth year grade averages below 80%.

To verify the intelligence scores, the 102 students were brought to Clinton in June, 1956, and tested on the California Test of Mental Maturity. All students whose average score on the junior high school intelligence test[1] and the California test was 120 or higher and who did not fall below 120 on either measure were included. Seventy students met the above criteria and were paired on the basis of IQ and ninth year averages. One student from each pair was placed in the special class (designated as the S class), the other became a control (designated as C). The control students were unidentified to themselves or to their teachers and were randomly distributed in homeroom sections and subject matter classes.

In addition, a group of high ability high achievers (designated as H) was identified–students with IQ's comparable to those of the underachievers, but with ninth year grade averages above 85%. No special provisions were made for this group beyond those normally made by the school for able students.

Inspection of the junior high school records of the three groups and of the sociometric ratings made in the junior high school classes from which the underachievers came[2] showed that the Special and the Control groups did not differ significantly from each other on any of the measures on which information was available at that time (spring 1956). The Highs differed from the other two groups not only in ninth year grades–the basis

[1] The junior high test was either the Pintner General Ability Test or the Henmon-Nelson. In the case of SP students, the sixth grade Pintner scores were used, since there was no junior high retest.

[2] Each of the junior high school homeroom sections in which one or more of the selected underachievers was located was asked to complete a sociometric survey which asked for nominations of best and least liked student, the one most or least apt to be successful in later life, etc. Returns were received for 49 of the students–24 S and 25 C's. Since the highs were not identified until after they arrived at Clinton, sociometric ratings were available only on 10 students who were in classes which filled out the surveys.

upon which they were selected–but also on average IQ. However, the IQ difference, although significant, was actually not very large and all three groups fell into the "gifted" category. The only measure on which there were large differences between the highs and the underachievers was in relative number of positive and negative ratings received from classmates. The underachievers were nominated by their peers as potential failures in high school and in life, as most apt to get into trouble and as least popular, far more frequently than were the highs, whereas the highs were more often rated positively.

TABLE 1. STATUS OF THE THREE GROUPS AT THE END OF THE NINTH YEAR (JUNE 1956)

	Special Class	*Control Group*	*High Group*
Average ninth year grades	73.7	73.0	87.7
Range of ninth year grades	56–79	61–79	84–94
Number from S.P. classes	13	10	16
Average age	14.1	14.2	14.0
Average IQ[1]	131.8	131.6	136.0
IQ range	120–152	121–148	125–148
Average reading increment over grade[2]	2.24	2.56	2.51
Range of Reading Increments	1.0–4.0	.4–4.0	.5–4.6
Average Arithmetic Increment	1.4	1.5	2.0
Range of Arithmetic Increments	−1.3–4.0	−2.2–4.1	−1.3–4.5
Average positive sociometric rating	1.8	1.8	9.0
Average negative sociometric rating	17.0	19.8	4.9

[1] Where students were retested on the California or had two IQ ratings listed on their record, a composite average was used.

[2] Since the reading and arithmetic tests were given either in eighth or in ninth year, the means and ranges were calculated on the basis of increment over grade in which the student was when he took the test. For example, if a student took either of the tests in eighth grade and received a grade equivalent of 10.2, his increment score would be 2.2. If he took the test in ninth grade and received a grade equivalent of 7.8, his increment score would be −1.2.

It is noteworthy that even though the underachievers were characterized by low teacher grades, their performance on standardized achievement measures of reading and arithmetic differed but little from the performance of the bright high achievers. These findings (supported by similar findings from the junior high school records of subsequent groups) suggest that during the elementary and junior high school years most bright youngsters, regardless of classroom performance as reflected by school grades, acquire considerable mastery of basic skills and knowledge.

Organizing the Special Class

In September 1956, the experiment began. The special group was assigned to a person who was the section officer as well as the social studies teacher. The social studies class was held the first period each day, immediately following the homeroom period. The students were informed that they were a specially selected group, placed in this class because of their high level of ability and their need for help in raising the level of their school performance.

Characteristics of Underachievers

To achieve the first purpose of the project, namely to study the achievement patterns, attitudes and personality characteristics of underachievers, a testing and interview program was designed. The Iowa Tests of Educational Development were administered as a regular part of the school's testing program. Dr. Jane Beasley of the Talented Youth Project staff interviewed 26 of the underachievers (15 from the special class, 11 from the control group) and 4 of the high achievers.

In addition, objective measures of self-attitudes, attitudes toward school, family patterns, problem areas, academic aspiration levels and vocational choice were obtained from each student in the study. The parents of the involved students were invited to the school, informed of the purpose of the study and asked to fill out questionnaires which dealt with some of the same problems as did the student forms.

The Iowa Tests further supported the conclusion that achievement on objective measures of academic mastery is more closely related to intelligence than to school grades. The combined group (S and C) of underachievers did not differ significantly from the highs on any part of the test.

However, although the Special Group and the Control Group were alike on all the junior high school measures (see Table I) they differed significantly on the composite score of the Iowa tests. This finding cast some doubt on the comparability of the two groups. By chance, the control students started the tenth year with a significant edge over the Special Group.

The attitude and personality measures provided a revealing picture of bright young adolescents, and found some significant differences between the high and low achievers among them. They did not differ in the appraisal of most of their own abilities and characteristics, either as they now are or as they would wish them to be. Nor did they differ in their occupational aspirations, since most of them expressed a preference for professional careers. Their interests differed neither in kind nor in intensity. Their families were similar in occupational status, parents' educational level, number of working mothers and number of children per family. Birth order did not make a difference.

But despite the similarity of most aspects of the family picture, disruption of the normal family pattern was much more frequently observed among the underachievers. Among the 62 underachievers for whom information was available there were 15 cases (25%) of disrupted homes, in all but one case resulting in the absence of the father through death or divorce. Among the high achievers there was only one case of such disruption, and this one of recent origin. These findings lend support to the theory that underachievement among boys (which is twice as extensive as among girls[1]) may be related to inadequate identification with a father figure.

The highs were more satisfied with school and with their school performance than were the underachievers, and the difference in self-ratings was supported by the parent ratings. On a problem checklist, the underachievers checked more *serious problems,* most of which were related to school work or other tasks and responsibilities. However, the parents of highs saw as many *serious problems* in their sons as did the parents of the underachievers.

Quite different were the high school (third term) grade expectations of the high and low students. The highs expected grades in the 80's or higher in almost all subjects, and where the expectation fell below 85 they expressed dissatisfaction. When asked what grade they would "settle for" if exempt from examinations, they would rarely "settle for" anything below 90. The underachievers, however, were far less hopeful. They expected to pass everything, but, in general, did not anticipate grades beyond 75 and stated that they would be "fairly satisfied" with such grades. However, few of them were willing to "settle for" such low grades just to be exempt from tests. Test taking does not seem to be particularly threatening to these students.

Only in social studies did the grade expectations of the special exceed those of the control group and approach the expectation level of the highs. Despite the short period during which the special class had been together in social studies with the teacher (tests were administered in November 1956), they perceived greater chances of success in this subject than did the controls, or than they themselves did in any of their other classes.

The interviews were electrically recorded and analyzed for recurring themes. The underachieving boys tended to refer to themselves and their

[1] Gowan, John C. "*The Underachieving Gifted Child,* A Problem for Everyone." *Exceptional Children,* April, 1955.

ability as "all right," "average" or "fair." The general picture was one of low aspiration and satisfaction with just not failing. "I just passed my subjects, and that's all I care about" or "I just want to be an average kid, nothing special. Why should I be the smartest kid in the world? I wouldn't get anything out of that. I just want to be one of the crowd."

When asked how their teachers evaluated them, their responses were of the nature of "I wasn't trying enough," "I was a smart boy, but pretty lazy," "I'm not working up to my potentiality."

They recognize that their parents are ambitious for them to succeed in school, go to college and enter a profession, to "have the advantages they didn't have." But the extent to which parents take an interest in the boys' day-to-day school work varies from "My parents leave homework pretty much up to me. They feel if I don't want to do it, I don't have to. It's just up to yourself to learn"–all the way to "They always help me every night, both of them always help me." A feeling of being pressured at home to do better was frequently expressed: ". . . when I wasn't doing too well in Spanish they started hounding me," or "When I got a low grade in math . . . he didn't say I had to study; he just said, 'You can't go fishing, you can't do this, you can't do that.' "

Rarely did the boys report outright parental approval; even when they did well, parents felt that "it's not good enough," or "don't let up now; keep it up."

Many of the responses to questions about school success, difficulties, abilities and other topics were answered in terms of their teachers. Doing well in a subject was usually related to a "good teacher," doing poorly to an unsympathetic or unfair teacher. Their willingness to work in a subject also depended on their perception of the interest of the teacher. The students wanted teachers who merit "respect," who can "control the class," who "give you an interest in the subject," are "cheerful" and "understand the student."

The special progress classes from which over ⅓ of the underachievers came were regarded by them as a mixed blessing. Some found the SP program full of pressures, an opportunity to be singled out for criticism by teachers. "Also, I believe that teachers are continually degrading the kids in the SPs. I had an official teacher in the ninth grade, and all the time she was telling us what a lousy group of kids we were and that we think we're so smart and cocky all the time. . . . But what really stands out in my mind . . . the fact that they kept degrading us."

Others, found the added challenge of the accelerated program stimulating. "I really learned quite a bit from it," ". . . the work was more interesting because it was on a higher level."

How did the underachievers explain their difficulties? Part of the explanation was in terms of specific subjects, much of it in terms of individual teachers. But some of the reasons were of a more personal nature: "I don't know. I keep on telling myself, 'I'm going to try my best' . . . But when the time comes, I always meet some fellow at school and we kid around, and I get in trouble and there it goes, right out the window. I can't help it . . ." or "I'm lazy, I'd get better grades if I studied for tests," or "Well, I guess this conduct and things worried me" or "I had to be absent, and when I came back I was completely lost." One student said, "Well, I just feel out of place in a big group with others . . . It takes me a good time to do that." Another student attributed his failure to a need for glasses and his fear of doctors, which prevented him from informing his parents of his eye condition.

A most interesting set of responses pertained to friendships. All the students had friends and took part in various social activities. But frequently they attributed their social success to "not being a grind," to not studying too much or too hard. They expressed strong, negative feelings toward the boy who is "never downstairs or anything like that." Some felt that to gain social approval one had to "play baseball or something–it didn't matter how smart you were," or that if you "got one of the highest marks in the class–I wouldn't have very many friends . . ."

Sports activities led the list of out-of-school interests, followed by such hobbies as model building, collections, electronics or other scientific interests. Reading was rarely mentioned.

In general, the boys felt that the change from junior to senior high school had been for the better. High school provided a chance to "grow up a little," "get more freedom and be on your own . . . they're not after you all the time," "Not tied to my mother's apron strings." High school teachers were perceived as more competent in their subject field and better able to explain things.

Pervading most of the interviews with the underachievers is a recognition that they are bright and potentially capable of outstanding academic achievement; but there is an equally strong resistance against making the necessary effort. "I could get the highest marks if I tried–but why should I?" is a commonly expressed sentiment. They feel that they have been hounded to do better, and that this is of no help; even their own resolutions to "turn over a new leaf" are shortlived. Some of them attribute their poor performance to bad teaching, unsympathetic teachers and dull classes; a few blame their own "laziness"; still others rationalize their lack of study as the only way to make friends, be part of the crowd–not different or too good.

Personality Assessment

The interviews more than any other material point up the great differences among the underachievers and suggest that each of these students needs to be studied as an individual with his own motivations, his own rationalizations, his own system of defenses. However, despite the great variations among the pupils, the school felt that membership in a special class with an understanding, able teacher would provide some of them with support for their own good intentions and help them modify some of their unfavorable attitudes toward school and school work.

Evaluation—Third Term

At the end of their first semester at Clinton, the students in the special class were evaluated by their teachers and compared to their paired controls on school grades in each subject and on participation in school activities. To what extent would a semester of the kind of experiences that the students had in the special class produce positive changes in their attitudes and behaviors and result in improved school performance?

Through close daily association in homeroom, social studies class and after school conferences; through contacts with parents; and through living with the group during a weekend in the country,[1] the teacher developed close relationships with the boys and became well acquainted with the strengths and problems of each one.

His first impression was that the group was well behaved and attentive, but neither interested nor enthusiastic. While not overtly unhappy at returning to school after the summer vacation, the underachievers lacked the spark generally observed in honor students. Very few of them knew each other before coming to Clinton, but were soon drawn together into strong mutual friendship ties. In their special class they were extroverted, talkative, often boisterous; in other classes they tended to keep apart and were generally subdued in their behavior. Sharing an hour each day seemed to generate a feeling of belonging, security and warmth. While boys in other sections greeted each other happily after a holiday, these students were positively enthusiastic—almost to the point of hysteria. They continued chattering until they were called to order, and although they came to attention more slowly than other classes, they were never discipline problems; nor was the noise a sign of revolt or disobedience.

Their friendship ties strengthened as the semester progressed and gradually became inbred, in many cases precluding out-of-class associations. The boys met after school and during week-ends, looking to each other for companionship outside of school as well as in it. Each boy found support

[1] Through the efforts of the Clinton Alumni Association and Mr. Irwin Guernsey ("Doc"), DeWitt Clinton High School annually sponsored a series of "Leadership Week-ends." A selected group of boys was transported to the Hudson Guild Farm where they spent two full days discussing personal, vocational and social problems, and playing, eating and rooming together under the supervision of student counselors and school staff.

in the recognition that problems which he had felt to be uniquely his own were shared by many of his classmates.

Upon entering high school, the underachievers seemed more afraid of school than hostile toward it. They had accepted a standard of mediocrity and needed strong incentives to increase their efforts. The teacher recognized the importance of giving these students sympathy, but not pity; guidance, but not overprotection; self-confidence and a sense of responsibility, but not too early demands for independence.

By creating a climate of acceptance and support, but at the same time holding up high standards of independent achievement, the teacher hoped to improve the students in their attitudes toward school and eventually spur them to greater achievement.

Because of the fused section and social studies period, the teacher did not necessarily have to terminate homeroom guidance activities at the bell. The 8:55 signal no longer meant, "Save your problem for tomorrow; now let us study the world's problems." Even though the social studies period was sometimes curtailed by a few minutes, once the lesson began, the boys were attentive and worked with little waste of time or effort.

Since the social studies class was the "homeroom" of the group, achievement in the class meant recognition and status among one's peers. The boys wanted to do well, not only for themselves but also for the teacher. Parents reported that the boys did much studying in all subject areas, but especially in social studies. They became more willing to work toward better grades when they realized that any effort on their part would be commended and rewarded. Though standards were high, they were flexible and thus never unattainable. The teacher soon discovered that any procedure which could be perceived as rejection acted as a negative motivating force. For example, when several boys submitted poorly done homework, which received low or unacceptable grades, they felt that their efforts were being rejected; consequently their homework became progressively worse. To remedy this situation, all homework offerings were accepted, but the inferior was put aside ungraded, and the students were invited to do their assignments when time and inclination permitted. A few days before grades were to be entered on the report cards, the boys were apprised of the grades they could expect in the event that their assignments remained unimproved, and what they might receive if they reworked their assignments. Faced by the immediate goal of a higher grade, many of the boys did the work over.

Some students, who had seldom done homework in junior high school, questioned the necessity of doing written assignments. Student E, for example, argued that he had little to gain from writing homework. The teacher gave him the option of doing his homework or taking a special short quiz on the assignment each time he did not do the written work.

Faced with an unprejudiced choice, he generally preferred the written homework, but occasionally exercised his option to take the quiz.

The underachievers were encouraged to participate in school activities. Almost every boy gave some service to the school in such activities as the luncheon squad, the office squad or some special squad. They were novices at giving, but the pleasure of giving was infectious. In the section room, pupils voluntarily helped each other or studied in groups. The one area in which a boy might be proficient became his badge of distinction. There was an awakening to the pleasure and prestige which accrue from helping others.

The class climate was such that the boys felt free to come to the teacher with their personal as well as with school problems. At all times they found an attentive listener, ready to help with support and suggestions which would help the youngster gain self-confidence.

Through these personal contacts it soon became clear that, in many instances, there were serious misunderstandings and poor relationships between the boys and their parents which were related to school behavior. Y's fear of his father, for example, drove him to change four failing marks to passing ones on his first report card; G could visit his divorced father only when he had good grades. These were some of the burdens the boys brought with them to school. Conferences alerted some of the parents to their part in handling the boys' problems. For example, Y's father had never before realized the extent of his son's fears and was grateful for an opportunity to reexamine his relationship with his son. Direct contacts between the teacher and the parents resulted in greater understanding of the child at home and school.

In general, Dr. K reported that many of the boys in the special section had benefited greatly from their association with each other and their close identification with the teacher. He was confident that the semester's experience had a significantly positive effect on the boys.

Despite the teacher's conviction that the boys in the special section had benefited greatly from their membership in the group, an examination of grades at the end of the semester did not, on the face of things, support the subjective evaluation. The grades of the special students did *not* improve more than those of their control pairs. It is true that there was improvement, since both groups of underachievers did better then they had in junior high school; they did, to some extent, turn over a new leaf. But contrary to expectation, as a group, the special students showed less improvement than did the controls. A part of this discrepancy was related to the fact that only 25 of the control students, as opposed to all 31 of the special students, had taken five major academic subjects, and the lesser load made possible higher grades. But this was only a partial explanation. A far more significant part of the difference in grades was related to the higher scores that the control group had received on the Iowa Tests of Educational Development. When the student grades were analyzed "as if the two groups had had equivalent Iowa composite scores," the differences between the grades of the special and control groups disappeared.[1] It was possible to conclude that, after one semester, membership in the special class had *no effect* on the scholastic attainment of the students. The improvement that occurred was related, rather, to the generally upgrading effect of the school as a whole, which enabled many of the underachievers to function more adequately in the more adult atmosphere of the high school.

However, the special students showed a greater involvement with school service activities and exceeded the controls in participation in all school activities except publications and athletics.

Since there had been little expectation of significant effects as a result of a single semester, the special group was maintained with the same teacher for homeroom and social studies for the following term.

Evaluation—Fourth Term

At the end of the school year (June, 1957), the performance of the underachievers was again evaluated both in terms of the teacher's observation and of final grades.

After a year of close association with the special class, Dr. K was reinforced in his belief that, in most instances, the students had benefited significantly from their year's experience. The patterns of working with these students which were developed during the first semester were refined, and the warm, accepting climate of the class was retained, always balanced by constantly holding up high standards as the ultimate goal.

No single incident, such as calling in a parent to praise her son's excellent work, nor giving another boy a twenty-five cent paper-back book to which he responded, "This is the first time anybody ever gave me anything in school," can be pinpointed as decisive in changing the achievement level of any one student. It was rather the entire range of experiences, interactions and every-day relationships which the teacher saw as responsible for bringing about improvement in many of the boys. A carefully planned social studies program, an expression of interest and concern with problems of both a personal and academic nature, a friendly, and in general, more supportive and flexible teacher role, combined with the support

[1] As noted above, the Iowa tests were administered in the fall of 1956 and were thus not considered in matching the special and control students. In comparing results, therefore, analysis of co-variance was used, which makes possible the comparison of changes in two groups which at the start are not equivalent on some pertinent variable.

that students in the special group seemed to give to one another, all contributed to help many of the students gain the maturity and confidence necessary for successful school work. For example, the boy who had changed his four failing marks on his first report card achieved an average of 86% at the end of the fourth term.

Along with assessing the factors which resulted in positive change for many of the students, the teacher recognized that these methods were unsuccessful in reaching some members of the group. At the end of the year, membership in the special group had had no effect on a number of boys. They presented a variety of negative attitudes, of which the descriptions below are but two examples:

A had a record of thirty absences. His mother justified each and every one of them by telephone, in person or by letter. The excuses ran the gamut from "It was very cold" to "His eyeglasses were broken." A December "chill" prevented A from attending the special camp weekend, where many friendships were cemented. A's continual absences made him almost a stranger. He formed no relationships with the other boys and his attitude to the teacher was distant and impersonal. His work deteriorated and by the end of the year he was in trouble with the police. This excessive absence was truancy, covered up by his mother's fear of letting the school know the true cause of his nonattendance.

By unanimous consent, B was the class mime, and his stentorian bass voice did not increase his popularity with the teachers. His widowed mother reported that he had shown poor effort and had learned very little in junior high school. His high school grades were very poor. When questioned about his poor performance level, B stated: "It's too late to start learning now." Despite personal conferences and discussions, the teacher saw that he was not reaching this boy and could not find a way to help him change his negative attitudes.

However, Dr. K felt that most of the boys had begun to move in a positive direction both in their attitudes toward school and in their work patterns.

When the academic achievement of the special and control students was again assessed at the end of the year, the picture looked quite different from what it had at the end of the first semester. The grades of the special group reflected the positive attitude changes which Dr. K had observed developing during the year. An analysis of final third and fourth term marks showed that the special group improved in all subjects, except social studies where they remained the same (this may have reflected the teacher's reluctance to be too lenient in grading his special class), while the control group went down in all subjects. The differences were most striking in math, science and total average. In fact, the special group made up its third term deficit, and in all subjects but English equalled or exceeded the final fourth term marks of the controls.

TABLE 2. END OF THIRD TERM AND END OF FOURTH TERM GRADE AVERAGES FOR THE THREE GROUPS

Group	*Mean of Averages*	*Range of Averages*
	End of Third Term	
High	87.3	95 – 60
Special	75.5	90 – 63
Control	79.0	92 – 66
	End of Fourth Term	
High	84.7	94 – 69
Special	78.2	89 – 65
Control	75.9	86 – 63

Had the analysis taken the discrepancy of the Iowa scores into consideration, as was done the previous term, the superiority of the special group's averages over those of the controls would have appeared even more striking. Thus, the effects of membership in the special group were sufficiently marked to overcome the handicap of initially lower general attainment (as measured by the Iowa composite score), and to move them ahead of the originally superior group.

Plans for the Eleventh Year

In view of Dr. K's conviction that the special class had been a valuable aid to the underachieving students, and in view of the objective evidence that membership in such a class resulted in greater improvement in academic achievement than would otherwise occur, it was decided to retain the group as a unit, both in homeroom and in social studies. Although Dr. K remained their section officer, he was unable to continue as their social studies teacher, and the contact between Dr. K and the group was limited to 20 detail-loaded minutes per day. Several students were permitted to transfer to "squad" sections in order to encourage their interest in special service activities. Thus the section did not remain completely intact.

On the basis of the evaluation of the year's work, the special group appeared ready for regular honor work in social studies. Such a program would test them in a situation where they could expect no special support or consideration other than what is normally afforded honor students. The teacher selected for the group was one who for many years had been eminently successful in working with honor classes. The teacher was not encouraged to modify her usual procedure of holding the students to a consistently high level of performance and making no allowances for failure to meet the high standards.

Evaluation at End of Fifth Term

Analysis of fifth term results showed clearly that the new arrangement for the special class had not proved satisfactory. The boys and the teacher were in conflict throughout the semester. The teacher, expecting high quality performance, was unable to accept the erratic, tardy and often slipshod work of the students. The techniques which she had found eminently successful with honor classes over the years were completely ineffectual in this situation. Insistence on "toeing the mark" led to ever greater resistance which expressed itself in poor work, disturbing behavior in class, "collaboration" on assignments and constant chatter and giggling.

By the end of the semester she was convinced that the group should not be kept together, contending that the close relationships among the boys resulted in mutual support for negative behavior, a condition which impeded learning and fostered poor character development.

The boys, however, continued to express satisfaction with being together, especially in their homeroom section. Even the students who had been encouraged to transfer to various "squad" sections at the beginning of the semester, visited the special section regularly and repeatedly requested to be transferred back. They were not critical of their new sections, but rather wanted to return to old friends and to the mutually supportive atmosphere which characterized the special group.

In only one case was such a transfer effected. The boy, who had been doing well in fourth term, was now failing two subjects. His mother came to school to request the transfer, and reported that her son's work had suffered and that he had lost interest in school. When Dr. K pointed out that the boy would not have any more time for study in the special section than he now had, the mother stated that it was not the extra study time, but rather the teacher, the boys, and the feeling of belonging to the original group that had made the difference in her son's school performance. The boy was reassigned to the special section and passed every subject. His mother reported a marked improvement in his attitude toward school.

But for most of the boys, remaining together in the brief homeroom period was not enough to counteract the growing conflict in their social studies class. Dr. K felt that his contact with the students was perforce too limited to allow for discussion of personal problems or needed help with study skills.

The gains which the special students had made during the tenth year were not sustained in the fifth term. Their final grades no longer exceeded those of the controls, and in social studies fell below with an average drop of sixteen points from the fourth term as compared to a two point drop for the controls.

The evidence did not support the hypothesis that underachievers who had shown improvement as a result of a year's membership in a warm, accepting and flexible situation would sustain their gains when held to uniformly high standards, both of conduct and of achievement. The short period that they had with their homeroom teacher did not provide enough supportive contact. These boys had grown to know each other well and supported each other in various infractions of the rules, uncontrolled behavior and poor effort. It would seem that the fact of being together does not, by itself, produce improvement. On the contrary, it may encourage undesirable behavior. The important element is, apparently, the performance of the teacher in utilizing the group spirit constructively.

Perhaps the fact that they had a woman teacher for fifth term social studies may have failed to meet one of the basic needs of this group–identification with a father figure–a need that was recognized from the tests and interviews and which, as mentioned, has been suggested by other research. Future experimentation was planned with this factor in mind.

Evaluation of Sixth Term

During the sixth term the special group was again retained as a unit for social studies and was programmed with a man teacher, Mr. M.[1] Forewarned by the reports and experiences of the two teachers who had previously handled the special group, Mr. M did not apply, or hold the group to, high academic standards as consistently and formally as was his usual procedure with an honor class.

Mr. M's experience with the group corroborated the impressions of the two previous teachers that the group lacked emotional stability and self-control. He found that any attempt at humor set them off into gales of laughter, and therefore maintained a serious, work-like atmosphere throughout the term, even avoiding an occasional joke.

He was especially interested in the students' great desire to participate in group discussions and recitations. He sensed that this behavior represented a need to gain recognition rather than a desire to move the discussion forward. To solve this problem without injuring feelings required skillful handling on the part of the teacher.

Mr. M found that homework of a factual nature was completed and handed in on time. Any assignment, however, which required independent thought and organization of material was subject to delay, stalling and non-performance. Aware of the dangers of stern rebuke and unacceptance on the one hand and allowing the students to "get away with" inadequate performance on the other, Mr. M followed a middle course. He proceeded to accept assignments that were handed in late, and gave students a chance

[1] Three of the original 31 students had been failed in fifth term social studies. The sixth term social studies class thus had 28 students of the original group.

to rework assignments which had been poorly done, requiring, however, that they incorporate suggestions for improvement. In addition, he devoted several class periods to practical demonstrations of how to do an assignment. Throughout the lessons he paid individual attention to each student and tried to understand him in terms of the particular problems and weaknesses which he presented. While creating a warm and accepting climate in the class, allowing leeway in performance standards and consistently showing an interest in the individual problems of the students, Mr. M also concentrated on teaching the group much needed study skills. He felt that the group could use much more of this sort of help than time and subject matter demands allowed.

At mid-semester (April 1958) on the uniform exams in Economics I, the special group performed at approximately the same level as the highs. Eighty per cent of the class received grades of 80 or above and there were only two failures.

Mr. M believed that the improvement over the previous semester was clearly related to a relaxation of tensions, an attempt to assess the characteristics and problems of the students, and deliberate experimentation with various procedures of helping them improve their learning. However, large class size and shortage of time prevented exploring the many possible techniques in sufficient depth to arrive at an optimum set of procedures.

Improvers and Non-Improvers

Even though at the end of the tenth year the special students, as a group, showed greater improvement than did the controls, there were improvers and non-improvers in both groups. In order to gain some insight into possible factors that are related to improvement, all the available material was reanalyzed comparing students whose grade averages had increased by at least seven points from the end of the ninth year to end of the tenth year, with those who showed no improvement or a drop in grades. It was hoped that such an analysis might provide leads for pre-selecting those junior high school underachievers who would probably become successful students in high school.

A total of 21 improvers was found, 12 from the special group and 9 from the control group; and 21 non-improvers, 10 from the special group and 11 from the control group. The two groups differed significantly on the following items:

a. The improvers were significantly higher on the Iowa Composite and Correctness of Writing scores.

b. On the self-attitudes inventory, the non-improvers showed a greater discrepancy between their perception of their abilities and their wished-for ability status. This score is generally viewed as an index of adjustment and suggests that the non-improvers see their ability to perform in various areas as too far from where they would like it to be to warrant making an effort to improve.

There were several other trends: The incidence of divorces was greater among the parents of the non-improvers. Fewer of the non-improvers had reached a decision on vocational goals; where they did state a preference, it was less often above the level of their father's present occupation. Fewer of the non-improvers were the only or the oldest children, and fewer had older siblings in college who could act as achievement models for them. None of these differences is statistically significant and will be tested again on other groups.

Providing Group Guidance and Study Skills for Underachievers

After two years of experimentation with several approaches,[1] a few lessons stood out most clearly. First, we became increasingly convinced that academic underachievement is a symptom of a wide variety of more basic personal and social problems, and that the depth, seriousness or duration of the underlying problem determines the extent and kind of help a student needs. Furthermore, there are probably some students who by high school age are beyond profiting from any help which can be given directly by the school. Unfortunately, it has not yet become possible to arrive at criteria for making a prognosis on the basis of the kinds of information we have been able to collect.

But for those students for whom it is possible to effect improvement, two factors appear to be crucial: (1) identification with a teacher who is consistently interested and supportive, who views each student as an individual and accepts him as a bright and able person with a need for special help;[2] and (2) assistance in mastering the skills of learning which many of the underachievers failed to acquire in the earlier grades.

To meet these two needs, a program had to be devised which would place underachievers in regular contact with a carefully selected teacher for long enough periods to allow for individual instruction in learning skills. It also seemed advisable to separate the teaching function and the guidance function for these children, so that the person who is working closely and personally with them will not have to grade or evaluate them. It was thought wise not to group these students in a subject class, since they tend to give each other negative support which often cannot be adequately handled within the context of a subject class.

[1] A special mathematics program for failures or near-failures in ninth year mathematics was organized in 1957 and its effects assessed.

[2] For boys, this probably means a male teacher.

❦ 22

The Onset of Academic Underachievement in Bright Children[1]

Merville C. Shaw
University of California, Los Angeles

John T. McCuen
Monterey Peninsula College

The problem of onset of academic underachievement among bright children has been the subject of some speculation, but very little research. After reviewing the findings of their study on able high school underachievers, Shaw and Grubb (1958) hypothesize "that underachievement among bright students is not a problem which has its genesis within the educational framework, but rather one which the underachiever brings with him, at least in embryo form, when he enters high school." In an intensive study of a small number of gifted underachievers Barrett (1957) found an underachievement pattern present by Grade five, but did not investigate the grades below five. No studies specifically attempting to determine whether or not there is any particular grade level at which underachievement begins, or attempting to determine at what level it begins were found in the literature.

Problem

The purposes of the present study were to determine whether there is any specific academic level at which academic underachievement can be

[1] The authors would like to express their sincere thanks to Theron L. McCuen, Superintendent of the Kern County Union High School District, and the administrative staffs of both Bakersfield and East Bakersfield high school for their cooperation in this study.

said to begin and to discover the subsequent pattern of achievement. The information resulting from the study has both practical and theoretical implications. On the practical side, the problems of prevention and remediation of academic underachievement might conceivably be effected by such results. Broedel, Ohlsen, and Proff (1959) confirmed the hypothesis of Shaw and Brown (1957) that underachievement among high school sophomores is not a surface phenomenon which is easily modifiable, but rather is related to the basic personality matrix of the individual. If it is true that academic underachievement is related to basic personality structure then such behavior is likely to occur during the early elementary school years. Specific information regarding the point at which underachievement actually begins has implications both for preventive and remedial measures that may be undertaken.

Such information also has implications from a theoretical point of view. The problem of the genesis of achievement motivation has been a topic of concern to McClelland and his associates (McClelland, Atkinson, Clark, and Lowell, 1953). Hypothesizing that the scores of college males on the McClelland Achievement Motivation Test would be affected by child rearing practices of their parents, they were able to isolate certain differences between subjects who received high scores and those who received low scores. Their criterion of achievement, the MAMT, has not been validated as a predictor of academic achievement, however, and it would not be reasonable to conclude from their results that academic underachievement had its origins in parental child rearing practices. Should it be found that academic underachievement is present in the earliest school years, and is found with some consistency in the same individuals throughout their school careers, more credence could be placed in the general findings of McClelland *et al.* (1953) as they relate to academic underachievement.

Method

The general plan of the study was to select *S*s who were in the upper 25% of the school population with regard to ability and to classify them as achievers or underachievers on the basis of their cumulative grade-point averages in Grades nine, ten, and eleven. The intelligence measure used was the Pintner General Ability Test: Verbal Series, which was administered to all *S*s included in the study at the time they were in Grade eight. A student who achieved an intelligence test score which placed him in the upper 25% of the population (over 110) and who had earned a grade-point average below the mean of the class he was in, was classified as an underachiever. A student who earned a GPA above the average of his class, and whose IQ was over 110, was classified as an achiever. Those who fell exactly at the class average, which was 2.40 on a four point scale, were not included in the study. Only eleventh- and twelfth-graders were included.

A further criterion for the inclusion of a *S* in this study was that he must have attended school only in the school district served by the high schools in the study. All *S*s, then, have had all of their formal education in a single school district. This criterion was established in order to reduce the variability in grades and educational philosophy which would be introduced by the inclusion of *S*s who had moved from one school district to another.

TABLE 1. SIGNIFICANCE OF DIFFERENCES BETWEEN MALE AND FEMALE ACHIEVERS AND UNDERACHIEVERS ON THE PINTNER GENERAL ABILITY TEST

	Pintner Standard Score Means					
Sex	*Achievers*	*Under-achievers*	*F*	*P*	*t*	*P*
Male	81.53	80.14	1.03	*ns**	1.01	*ns**
Female	81.56	80.65	1.54	*ns**	.63	*ns**

* Yields significance below the .05 level.

A single high school district with two large high schools whose combined enrollment was over six thousand was selected for use in the study. In addition to the factor of size and the presence of a fairly representative population from the socioeconomic point of view, it was also important to conduct the study in a school system where specific grades (A, B, C, etc.) were used at both the elementary and high school levels.

One hundred sixty-eight students met all of the criteria for inclusion in the study. This group was divided further into four subgroups of male Achievers, male Underachievers, female Achievers, and female Underachievers for purposes of comparison. Much research has shown the necessity of treating males and females separately in studies of underachievement. In order not to obtain groups whose mean intelligence scores were not significantly different it was necessary to eliminate 8 males and 18 females from the sample. All of those eliminated were from the Achiever groups. The *f* and *t* tests were used to insure that groups compared had both comparable variances and means. These results are reported in Table 1. The final groups consisted of 36 male Achievers, 36 male Underachievers, 45 female Achievers, an 17 female Underachievers.

Following the final selection of *S*s, the academic record for each student from Grades one through eleven was obtained. In the case of elementary school grades it was necessary to convert from letter to number grades. This was done on a four point scale to keep elementary grades comparable to high school grades. Thus, an A became 4.0, a B became 3.0, etc. Each *S*'s grade-point average for each grade (not a cumulative grade point average) was then computed. Mean grade-point averages for each group at each grade level were then computed. Male Achievers were then compared with male Underachievers and female Achievers with female Underachievers on the basis of grade-point average at each grade level by means of the *f* and *t* tests.

TABLE 2. SIGNIFICANCE OF DIFFERENCES BETWEEN MEAN GRADE-POINT AVERAGES OF MALE ACHIEVERS AND UNDERACHIEVERS FROM GRADE ONE THROUGH ELEVEN

Grade	*Mean Grade-Point Average*					
	Achievers	*Under-achievers*	*F*	*P*	*t*	*P*
1	2.81	2.56	1.97	*ns****	1.44	*ns*
2	2.94	2.64	1.94	*ns*	1.77	*ns*
3	3.03	2.58	1.49	*ns*	2.83	.01*
4	3.19	2.72	1.03	*ns*	2.96	.01*
5	3.28	2.75	1.02	*ns*	3.71	.01*
6	3.33	2.67	1.33	*ns*	4.46	.01*
7	3.25	2.56	1.02	*ns*	5.80	.01*
8	3.36	2.50	1.59	*ns*	6.23	.01*
9	3.25	2.14	1.32	*ns*	10.57	.01*
10	3.13	1.87	1.30	*ns*	10.24	.01*
11	2.81	1.85	4.05	.01**	5.46	.01*

* Yields significance beyond the .01 level.
** Yields significance beyond the .02 level but below the .01 level.
*** No significance.

RESULTS

The comparison of male Achievers and Underachievers indicates that a difference significant at the .01 level is found in the GPA of the two groups beginning at the third-grade level, and that this difference increases in significance at each grade level up to Grade ten, where it decreases somewhat. It remains significant at the .01 level, however. A difference in grade-point average in favor of the Achiever group actually exists at Grade one and becomes larger at Grade two, but it is not significant at the .05 level of confidence in either of the first two grades. Results of the *f* and *t* tests are summarized in Table 2.

Graphic presentation renders these results even more striking. Figure 1 indicates that while the general trend of grades in both groups tends to be the same, there is never any overlap. It also shows clearly the decline in mean difference between the two groups at the tenth- and eleventh-grade levels which is due primarily to a drop in the mean grade-point average of the Achievers, rather than a rise in the grades of the Underachievers.

Comparison of the female Achievers and Underachievers presents quite a different picture from that seen in the male groups. Through Grade five the Underachievers actually exceed the Achievers in GPA, although not at a significant level of confidence. At Grade six the Achievers obtain a higher mean GPA for the first time, and from that point until Grade ten this difference increases every year, although it does not reach significance until Grade nine. From Grade nine through eleven the difference is significant at the .01 level. These results are summarized in Table 3.

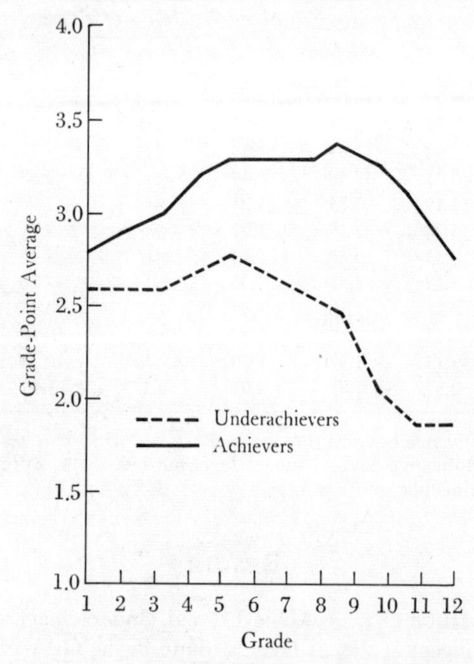

Figure 1. Comparison of the achievement patterns of male achievers and underachievers from Grade one through eleven.

As in the case of the data on males, the data on females is most clearly understood through graphic presentation. Figure 2 contrasts these two groups. As was the case with the male groups, there is again a tendency for the mean grade-point averages of the two groups to diminish slightly in the last year of high school, and again this can be accounted for by a drop in the grade point average of the Achiever group, rather than an increase in the Underachiever group.

With regard to the male Underachievers it would appear reasonable to say that the predisposition to underachieve academically is present when the Underachiever enters school. It is also safe to say that, in comparison to the Achiever controls, the problem becomes steadily more serious until Grade ten, at which time it becomes only slightly less serious, due primarily to a drop in grade-point average on the part of the Achiever group.

Comparison of the female groups does not present nearly so clear-cut a picture. As has been found in other studies of underachievement, there is a great deal of difference between what we find to be true of males and what seems to be true in the case of females. The present study provides no clues which would explain why Underachieving females actually tend to do better than Achieving females in the first five grades, nor do we have any facts which would explain the precipitous drop they take, beginning in Grade six. The fact that actual underachievement among the female group does not show itself until Grade six does not completely rule out the possibility of the presence of a predisposing factor at the time the female Underachiever enters school. The timing of the drop in GPA of female Underachievers is just about right for the start of puberty. We may hypothesize that females do not display their self-directing tendencies to the same extent that males do until they approach adolescence.

Another justifiable conclusion to be drawn is that underachievement is not a temporary phenomenon in the life of these *S*s, but rather is chronic in nature. In comparison to the control group, the male Underachievers have been obtaining grades below their ability level since Grade one. The female Underachievers have been performing below their ability level since Grade nine, and have tended to do so since Grade six. This finding lends weight

TABLE 3. SIGNIFICANCE OF DIFFERENCES BETWEEN MEAN GRADE-POINT AVERAGES OF FEMALE ACHIEVERS AND UNDERACHIEVERS FROM GRADE ONE THROUGH ELEVEN

Grade	*Mean Grade-Point Average*					
	Achievers	*Underachievers*	*F*	*P*	*t*	*P*
1	2.93	3.06	1.19	*ns***	.65	*ns*
2	3.02	3.12	1.33	*ns*	.53	*ns*
3	2.96	3.24	2.37	*ns*	1.59	*ns*
4	3.02	3.18	1.07	*ns*	.87	*ns*
5	3.13	3.18	1.30	*ns*	.25	*ns*
6	3.29	3.18	1.08	*ns*	.59	*ns*
7	3.02	2.76	1.08	*ns*	1.59	*ns*
8	3.13	2.82	1.56	*ns*	1.73	*ns*
9	3.06	2.24	1.40	*ns*	6.46	.01*
10	3.08	2.05	2.22	*ns*	8.66	.01*
11	2.96	2.11	1.33	*ns*	6.69	.01*

* Yields significance beyond the .01 level.
* * No significance.

to the previously stated hypothesis that academic underachievement is not an easily modifiable surface phenomenon.

The most obvious implication of the study is the need for the early identification of Underachievers. At the present time, very little deliberate identification of such students is taking place. The work that is being done tends to be going on at the high school level. Comparison of the studies of Calhoun (1956) and Kirk (1952) at least suggests that while counseling with Underachievers may prove successful at all levels, it requires less time with younger students.

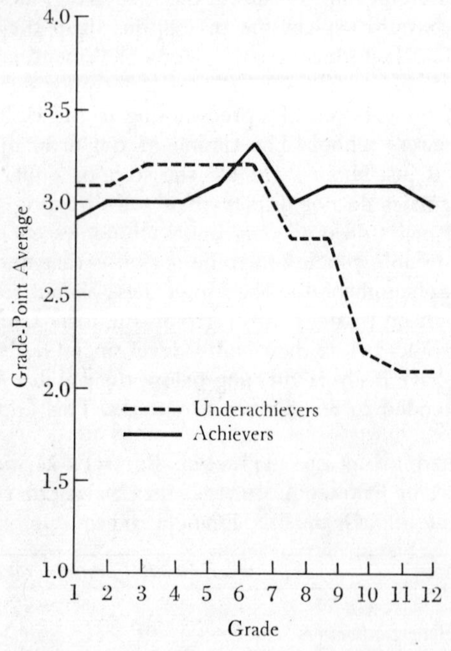

Figure 2. Comparison of the achievement patterns of female achievers and underachievers from Grade one through eleven.

Much more intensive research than has yet been done needs to be done with the parents of Underachievers. McClelland *et al.* (1953) suggest that the parents of Underachievers do not demand a high level of performance from their children. The present study found very many more male than female Underachievers. This would suggest according to McClelland's hypothesis, that a higher level of academic performance is demanded from females than from males. Observation would not appear to support this idea, but certainly it needs intensive study.

What are the factors in the school situation which tend to reinforce the Underachievers predisposition to underachieve; and what are the conditions which might forestall its appearance? These too are important topics for further study.

Summary

Groups of Achievers and Underachievers with IQ's over 110 grouped on the basis of sex were compared on the basis of grade-point average at every grade level from one through eleven. All subjects in the study were from a single school district and had gone all the way through school in that district. Subjects were classified as Achievers or Underachievers on the basis of the cumulative grade-point average they earned in Grades nine, ten, and eleven.

Results for males indicated that the Underachievers tended to receive grades lower than the Achievers beginning in Grade one, and that this difference became significant at the .01 level at Grade three. From Grade three to Grade ten, the difference increased in significance every year. In Grades ten and eleven the difference was reduced somewhat, but remained significant at the .01 level. The decrease in these grades was due to a slight drop in the grades of the Achievers.

Results for females indicated that female Underachievers actually exceeded Achievers in grade-point average for the first five years of school, although not at a significant level of confidence. Beginning in Grade six Underachievers began a precipitous drop in grade-point average and remained below the Achiever group from Grade six through Grade eleven. The difference became significant at Grade nine. The difference became slightly smaller at Grade eleven, due primarily to a drop in the grades of Achievers at that level.

References

Barrett, H. O., An intensive study of 32 gifted children. *Personnel and Guidance J.*, 1957, 36, 192–194.

Broedel, J., Ohlsen, M., & Proff, F., The effects of group counseling on gifted adolescent underachievers. Paper read at American Psychological Association, Washington, D.C., August 29, 1958.

Calhoun, S. R., The effect of counseling on a group of underachievers. *Sch. Rev.*, 1956, 64, 312–316.

Kirk, Barbara A., Test versus academic performance in malfunctioning students. *J. consult. Psychol.*, 1952, 16, 213–216.

McClelland, D. B., Atkinson, J. W., Clark, R. A., & Lowell, E. L., The achievement motive. New York: Appleton-Century-Crofts, 1953.

Shaw, M. C., & Grubb, J., Hostility and able high school underachievers. *J. counsel. Psychol.*, 1958, 5, 263–266.

23

A Comparison of Three Methods of Assisting Underachieving High School Students

Feriha B. Baymur[1]
Ministry of Education, Ankara, Turkey
C. H. Patterson
University of Illinois

ACADEMIC FAILURE is one of the major problems confronting counselors in schools and colleges. Not all failures are a result of lack of academic ability or aptitude. Mental or intellectual ability is not the exclusive determinant of academic achievement. The discrepancy between potential and achievement identifies a group of students who are known as underachievers. Underachievement is both a problem to the individual, who may suffer from the sense of failure, and to society, which loses the full potential contributions of unestimated numbers of its members.

It follows that anything which can be done to reduce the incidence of underachievement will contribute to the individual and social accomplishment and well-being. The present report describes an attempt to reduce underachievement in a group of high school students by three methods, which are compared with each other and with a control situation.

THE PROBLEM

The present study investigates the hypothesis that if emotional factors are involved in underachievement, then therapeutic counseling should be

[1] From a thesis submitted by the senior author for the Ed. D. degree, College of Education, University of Illinois, completed under the direction of the junior author, August 1958. Members of the committee included J. T. Hastings, W. M. Lifton, R. H. Simpson, and W. O. Stanley. Henry Kaiser was helpful in the statistical analysis of the data.

effective in reducing such underachievement. The study further investigates the relative effectiveness of two different methods of counseling, and in addition compares such counseling with an attempt to increase motivation in what might be considered a common or traditional way. The three methods used are individual counseling, group counseling, and what is designated as one-session motivational group counseling. If it were found that group counseling, or one-session motivational counseling, were as effective as individual counseling, this would be important, since these methods are less expensive or time-consuming to use, and thus more students could be reached by the limited number of counselors available.

Design and Procedure of the Study

Subjects

The design of the study called for the identification of a group of underachievers at the high school level. The 220 members of the junior class of a midwest high school were selected as a source for such subjects. Of this group, 209 students had been given the Verbal and Abstract Reasoning tests of the Differential Aptitude Test at the beginning of the school year. Grades for the first semester of the junior year were available at the start of the study.

A student was designated as an underachiever if his percentile rank based on grades was 25 or more points below his percentile rank on the DAT score. In order to obtain a sufficient number of subjects for four matched groups of at least 8 members each, 2 students with differences of 24 percentile points were included.[2] The differences ranged from 24 percentile points to 67 percentile points. There were 9 girls and 23 boys, a sex difference which has frequently been observed among underachievers.

Assignment to Experimental Groups

Since four groups (three experimental and one control) were required, the subjects were matched four at a time on the following variables: discrepancy between grades and DAT score, potential scholastic capacity (DAT score), academic achievement (grades), socio-economic status, chronological age, and sex. Economic status was based upon classification of the subjects by the deans of boys and girls into middle, lower-middle, and upper-lower status. Although this is a rough measure, based on judgments of the deans, it appeared to be sufficient as a control. Three of the four groups consisted of 6 boys and 2 girls, while the fourth included

[2] While percentiles are unequal units, the matching procedure described in the next section assured that the groups were equivalent in degree of underachievement.

5 boys and 3 girls. The success of the matchings on the other variables was indicated by the fact that analyses of variance indicated no significant differences in underachievement, DAT scores, grades, or age among the groups. The ranges within the groups for the first three variables were quite large.

The groups were assigned to the extent possible, randomly to the treatment conditions. It was, however, necessary to select the students for group counseling on the basis of the entire group having the same period free for the counseling session. The resulting groups are designated as follows:

Group I: individually counseled experimentals
Group II: group counseled experimentals
Group III: one-session motivational counseled experimentals
Group IV: noncounseled controls

Treatment Conditions

Group I: This group was provided individual therapeutic counseling at weekly intervals for a maximum of twelve weeks. One student who proved to be rather seriously disturbed was seen twice weekly during the latter part of the period, for a total of 16 interviews for the experimental period. The remainder were seen for from 10 to 12 interviews. Interviews lasted from 35 to 55 minutes. All interviews were conducted by the investigator (the senior author) in a client-centered manner. The counselor had been trained in this approach, including a practicum course under the junior author. Interviews were recorded, and counseling was supervised.

Group II: Group counseling was conducted weekly, but because of holidays and other unavoidable conditions, only nine sessions were held. The counselor attempted to conduct the group sessions in a client-centered manner also. The students in both Group I and Group II were informed of the nature and purpose of the study. This was done to equate the information-motivational factor with Group III. In both situations, however, students were not restricted to discussing academic problems.

Group III: Group III met only once, during the first week of the experiment. Members were informed of the fact that they were underachievers, and were encouraged to work to reduce the gap between potential and achievement. The importance of good grades for further education and employment was pointed out. They were told that some other students would receive special help, but that such help could not be given to all the underachievers in the class.

Members of all three experimental groups were also given copies of *Study Your Way Through School* (Gerken, 1953).

Group IV: The control group had no contact with the counselor. The deans and counselors were given the names of the students in the control group and asked to refrain, if possible, from providing counseling for the duration of the experiment. This they were able to do, limiting their contacts to discussion of curriculum choices for the next year.

Instruments Used

Three different instruments were used to provide criteria for the study since it was anticipated that the outcomes might be related to three different areas: (a) improved personal adjustment, (b) improved study habits and attitudes, and (c) improved academic performance. While the last is the most pertinent area for the evaluation of achievement, the other two might also be affected, and it is possible that results might show here prior to the improvement of academic performance. The following instruments were selected:

1. *Q*-sort. As a measure of personal adjustment a *Q*-sort was used. Fifty statements were selected from Hilden's (1954) pool. A criterion against which the self-perceptions of the students could be compared was developed by having seven experienced counselors and psychologists sort the items into nine piles (yielding a normal distribution of statements) as they thought they should be sorted by a well-adjusted 17-year-old adolescent. Five items were eliminated because of lack of agreement among the judges in their placement. The remaining items were ordered by sums of the placement categories assigned by the judges, and placed in nine categories to form the distribution required in the sorting instructions. Thus a criterion sorting of 45 items was available with which individual student sortings could be correlated. The correlations among the independent sortings of seven judges ranged from .42 to .83, while the range of correlations of each judge with the criterion sort (which included his own data) was from .72 to .91.

2. Study Habits and Attitudes. The Brown–Holtzman Survey of Study Habits and Attitudes was selected to measure the area of study habits and attitudes.

3. Academic Achievement. Grade-point average was used as the measure of academic achievement. The differences between the first semester averages and the second semester averages (the experimental period) constitute the criterion scores.

4. In addition to these instruments, a questionnaire was administered at the conclusion of the experimental period to determine what information and attitudes the students had about the study, etc.

Statistical Analysis and Results

The statistical (null) hypotheses to be tested may be stated as follows:

1. Subsequent to the experimental period, no significant differences will be found among the groups in regard to

a. Positive changes in self concept
b. Improvement in reported study habits and attitudes
c. Increases in grade-point averages.

2. Subsequent to the experimental period there will be no significant differences between the combined individual and group counseled groups and the other two groups.

3. Subsequent to the experimental period there will be no significant gains on the criterion measures in any of the groups.

The hypotheses were tested by analyses of variance and the *t*-test. Prior to the analyses, the subjects in the groups were ranked and paired on the basis of precounseling scores. A two-way analysis of variance was applied. Results will be presented under the three criteria used in the study.

Q-sort

The data for analysis were the correlations of the *Q*-sorts of each student in each group with the criterion sort before and after the experimental period. The differences between these correlations were subjected to analysis of variance. The differences were not significant at the .05 level. While the mean for Group I was the highest, the Group IV (control) mean was next highest, and Group III showed a decrease in relationship to the adjustment criterion.

When the two counseled groups were compared with the other two groups (one-session motivated and control) by means of the *t*-test for matched samples, the resulting t of 2.41 is significant beyond the .05 level. This difference is due to Group I, however, since Group II showed less improvement than the control group in this respect.[3]

A comparison of pretest with posttest scores for the noncounseled groups indicates that the difference (which is slightly negative) is not significant. The pretest and posttest means of the counseled groups are not significantly different ($t = 1.72$); for Group I the difference approaches significance, however ($t = 2.11$, $.10 > p > .05$).

Brown–Holtzman SSHA

The result of the analysis of variance of differences between pretest and posttest scores was not significant. While the means of the two counseled groups were higher than the means of the two noncounseled groups, the *t*-test of the differences was not significant (.20 level).

The pretest and posttest means of the counseled groups do not differ significantly, nor do the means of the noncounseled groups.

[3] While the *t*-test is not ordinarily appropriate following an analysis of variance (even when F is significant), in the present instance it is appropriately used to test an *a priori* hypothesis.

Grade-Point Averages

The analysis of variance of differences in grade-point averages was not significant. A *t*-test of the difference between the two counseled groups and the two noncounseled groups was significant, however ($t = 2.35, p < .05$).

The gain in grades by the counseled groups is significant ($t = 2.25, p < .05$). While most of the gain is apparently in Group II, the gain for this group alone does not reach significance ($t = 1.55$). The difference between pretest and posttest grades for the noncounseled groups is negative.

For Group I, the counselor ranked the students for degree of improvement during individual counseling. This rank order correlated .93 with the ranks of the students on the *Q*-sort ($p < .02$), but the correlations with rankings on the Brown–Holtzman SSHA and grade-point average were insignificant.

Analysis of the posttest questionnaire suggested some possible differences among the groups. Group I students appeared to have clearer ideas about the nature of the study. Approximately equal numbers of students stated that they had worked harder; however, only one or two students in Groups I, II, and III stated they had read the book given them, while none in Group IV had read it. Few students reported that their parents had tried to help them. A question about handedness was included in the questionnaire because of the observation that several were left-handed. Of the 30 students answering the questionnaire, 7 (23 per cent) stated they were left-handed, while another 8 of the remaining 23 stated they could use their left hands equally well in things other than writing. This incidence of left-handedness and ambidexterity suggests further investigation of this characteristic in underachievers.

Discussion*

While the results of the over-all analyses of variance were not significant, the comparisons of the counseled versus noncounseled students yielded positive results on two of the criteria. This occurred as a result of the pooling of consistent trends and increasing the *N*'s in the comparisons. The results are not, however, highly encouraging. There are a number of factors which should be considered in the interpretation and evaluation of the results.

1. The period and extent of counseling were quite limited, particularly for those receiving group counseling.

2. The counselor felt that the group counseling was not a successful experience.

* The Discussion section has been modified by permission of C. H. Patterson.

3. Students in the counseling groups had not volunteered for or requested counseling, or assistance in improving their academic achievement or personal adjustment. Many apparently were not even aware that they were underachievers.

4. It is possible that during counseling which involves deep problems of personal-emotional adjustment, the student's academic achievement might even decline.

5. It is possible that being involved in the experiment to the extent of taking the tests (control group), may have positive effects.

6. The levels of aptitude or ability, and the degree of underachievement, varied greatly within each group. It is possible that different approaches are required for effectiveness with different levels of ability and/or underachievement.

Summary and Conclusions

Thirty-two underachievers were identified in a group of 209 juniors in high school. Four groups of 8 students were matched on aptitude (sum of DAT Verbal and Abstract Reasoning subtests), achievement (grade-point average), underachievement (difference in percentile rank in aptitude and achievement), socio-economic status, age, and sex. Group I received individual counseling, Group II group counseling, Group III a one-session motivational experience, while Group IV constituted the control group. Three measures were obtained prior to and following the 12-week experimental period: (a) a *Q*-sort of 45 items selected from Hilden's (1954) pool; (b) the Brown–Holtzman Survey of Study Habits and Attitudes; (c) grades in the four major courses taken in the first and second semesters. Correlations of individual *Q*-sorts with a criterion *Q*-sort based on sortings by 7 psychologists constituted the *Q*-sort adjustment score.

Two-way analyses of variance indicated that the four groups did not differ significantly on any of the criteria. A comparison of the two counseled groups with the two noncounseled groups indicated that they differed significantly in *Q*-sort adjustment score change (attributed to change in Group I), and in increase in grade-point average.

The results are considered to be encouraging in view of the factors tending to attenuate differences among the groups. While it may be suggested that individual counseling is more effective with personal problems, and group counseling is better with cognitive problems such as improving academic achievement, the nature of the group counseling situation would not make such a conclusion justifiable. The counselor felt that the group did not develop into a therapeutic unit.

Other limitations of the study, some of which have already been pointed out, include the lack of a follow-up beyond the experimental period, limitations of the counselor, the small size of the sample, the brief period of counseling, and the fact that the counseled students had not requested counseling. This last factor is one which perhaps might be present in the usual high school program, however. That underachievers will accept and apparently benefit from counseling is encouraging. However, some of the students would perhaps not have continued with counseling if they had not been aware of, and influenced by, the importance of their continuing for the sake of the experiment.

References

Bradt, K. W., & Duncan, C. P. Degree of personal relationship between instructor and student as a factor in course grade improvement. *Amer. Psychologist*, 1951, 6, 368. (Abstract)

Briggs, L. J., & Roe, R. M. Morale as a function of opportunity to register complaints. Technical Report HRRC-TR-53-4. Human Resources Research Center, Lackland Air Force Base, Texas, 1953.

Brown, W. F., & Holtzman, W. H. Use of the Survey of Study Habits and Attitudes for counseling students. *Personnel and Guidance J.*, 1957, 35, 214–218.

Brown, W. F., & Holtzman, W. H. *Survey of Study Habits and Attitudes.* New York: Psychological Corp., 1956.

Calhoun, S. R. The effects of counseling on a group of underachievers. *Sch. Rev.*, 1956, 64, 312–316.

Drasgow, J. Underachievers. *J. counsel. Psychol.*, 1957, 4, 210–211.

Drews, E. H., & Teahan, J. R. Parental attitudes and academic achievement. *J. clin. Psychol.*, 1957, 13, 328–332.

Feyereisen, K. Eliminating blocks to learning. *Leadership*, 1948, 5, 527–535.

Gerken, C. D'A. *Study Your Way Through School.* Chicago: Science Research Associates, 1953.

Gersten, C. An experimental evaluation of group therapy with juvenile delinquents. *Int. J. group Psychother.*, 1951, 1, 311–318.

Guthrie, G. M., & O'Neil, H. W. Effects of dormitory counseling on academic achievement. *Personnel and Guidance J.*, 1953, 31, 307–309.

Hilden, A. H. *Manual for Q-Sort and Random Set of Personal Concepts.* St. Louis: Veteran Administration Regional Office, 1954.

Hoehn, A. J. & Salts, B. Effects of teacher-student interviews on classroom achievement. *J. educ. Psychol.*, 1956, 47, 434–435.

Kimball, Barbara. The sentence completion technique in a study of scholastic underachievement. *J. consult. Psychol.*, 1952, 16, 353–358.

Kirk, Barbara. Test versus academic performance in malfunctioning students. *J. consult. Psychol.*, 1952, 16, 213–216.

Lecky, P. *Self-consistency, a Theory of Personality.* New York: Island Press, 1945.

RICHARDSON, LAV. H., & PERRY, J. D. Counseling for academic recovery. *J. counsel. Psychol.*, 1956, 3, 136–139.

SERENE, H. F. An experiment in motivational counseling. *Personnel and Guidance J.*, 1953, 31, 319–324.

SHAW, M. C., & BROWN, D. J. Scholastic underachievement of bright college students. *Personnel and Guidance J.*, 1957, 36, 195–199.

SHELDON, M., & LANDSMAN, T. An investigation of nondirective group therapy with students in academic difficulty. *J. consult. Psychol.*, 1950, 14, 210–215.

SHERRIFS, A. C. Modification of academic performance through personal interview. *J. appl. Psychol.*, 1949, 33, 339–346.

SCHOENHARD, G. H. Home visitation put to a test. *Personnel and Guidance J.*, 1950, 36, 480–485.

TYLER, L. E. *The Work of the Counselor*, New York: Appleton-Century-Crofts, 1953.

COMMENT

Since this is an elegant study and report, we can dispense with criticism of its detail. The general results and methods of the article are worthy of additional comment, however.

My colleague, Raymond C. Hummel (who of late has begun to investigate counseling in relation to underachievement), tells me that counseling is not frequently studied in the general operating context of the secondary school. Furthermore, Hummel tells me that the traditional strategy of identifying and admonishing the failing student has seldom been put to the test. These observations lend new significance to this study by Baymur and Patterson. The study surmounts many of the difficulties of research *in situ* and thereby gives us a useful evaluation of one-session motivational counseling so characteristic of secondary school practice. From the results of this study, it seems likely that the "test 'em, tell 'em and loan 'em" formula of the National Defense Education Act of 1958 will likely affect only those of small financial means who have a vision of college as derived at home. If so, what of the others at which the Act aims? This study suggests that fairly intensive counseling contact is necessary to effect motivational change even with the relatively "plastic" adolescent.

Although I congratulate Baymur and Patterson upon relating counseling effort to some of the goals we claim for counseling (e.g., personal adjustment, attitudes toward study, school grades), their study offers opportunity to pose a question Hummel and I have discussed frequently with each other and with our students, namely, have we been using the right method in verifying counseling theory? Let's consider this interesting question a bit more.

Underachievement is probably a condition resulting from a number of causes, e.g., lack of desire, incapabilities of a physical or academic kind, hate of a teacher, or even a teacher's hate of a pupil. Because of this likely multi-causality, the counselor addresses himself to correction of underachievement in a variety of ways. The counseling goals he elects to pursue depend upon his assessment of causes. So does the strategy the counselor elects to adopt in bringing his mind into the relationship for his client's benefit. For these reasons, the counselor in an experiment is likely to have only a small proportion of clients for whom he would consider the goals of the experimenter immediately appropriate. We should not wonder then when "little or no change" attributable to counseling appears in an experiment where a few, long-range effects are expected for everybody.

Because of this condition, perhaps necessary in the present state of the art of counseling, experiments in counseling probably ought to allow the counselor to specify, for each client, the outcome or outcomes he anticipates in the finite period of time in which his art is under test. The counselor might even be given freedom to revise his specifications at appropriate intervals. Verification, the ultimate condition of science, is still possible at the end by assessing the correspondence, for each client, between the results and the counselor's anticipation of them.

When the experimenter elects to test the counselor only within the experimenter's frame of reference, the experimenter should let the counselor, upon assessment of his clients, designate those clients in which he expects none of the changes the experimenter wishes. "Failures" to change are thereby anticipated and represent just as strong a test of counseling theory as do the anticipated "successes." Verification of such *a priori* statements would represent a considerable advance over the present *a posteriori* rationalizations of "failure" so frequently found in conclusions of reports on counseling research. The present rationalizations of "failure" ordinarily note exceptions that might well have been invoked before the experiment was really undertaken.

A science of counseling will eventually permit the counselor to designate what he *cannot* do as well as to indicate what he *can* do. I suspect though that we can better perfect that science of counseling from studies of the variability *within* the results of counseling than from studies *across types* of counseling within a few long-range expectations of counseling as in the present case.

David Tiedeman

Harvard University

24

The Slow Gifted Child

Frank Riessman

IT IS OFTEN CONTENDED that deprived children are non-verbal, that they think in a slow, inadequate manner, and cannot conceptualize. While there are elements of truth in this portrayal, we think that it is a somewhat distorted picture, particularly in the invidious interpretation given the "elements."

How do deprived children learn and think? What are the characteristics of their so-called "cognitive style"? Do they have any creative potential? These are questions to which educators must give serious attention.

POOR OR SLOW?

An interesting confusion prevails in education circles between the "poor learner" and the "slow learner." The two are assumed to be identical. But need this be so? In a pragmatic culture such as ours, oriented toward quantity, speed, and measurement, this error can be fallen into readily. In the classroom it is terribly easy to believe that the child who learns the lesson quickly is a better learner than one who takes a long period of time. And sometimes this is the correct conclusion, as in reading, where studies show that faster readers understand better what they have read. The same thing appears to be true with regard to learning subject matter, such as history or geography. But here the problem is more complicated. The child who learns history more slowly is likely to be ignored and, unwittingly, discouraged by the teacher. Even if she does not ignore him but, on the contrary, gives him special attention, she may reflect to him her implicit assumption that he is a poor student. She may demand less of him, for example. The point is that she never sees the slowness as simply another style of learning with potential strengths of its own; nor does she see potential weaknesses (not *necessary* weaknesses) in the fast learner, who may become glib or impatient with tasks requiring protracted attention. *Because of the treatment he receives in the school system, the slow learner then may become the poor learner.*

It is time to put an end to the negative description of the term "slow" in the learning process. Slowness can reflect many things. It can indicate caution, a desire to be very thorough, great interest that may constrain against rushing through a problem, or a meticulous style. Or it may indicate a desire to mull things over, an emphasis on the concrete and physical. It may also indicate intellectual inadequacy. Extreme slowness probably does connote inadequacy in the absence of counter-indications. Even here we have to be very careful to check all possible blocks, not only the obvious emotional disturbances. There may be many other types of blockage as well, such as auditory blocks, reading difficulties (not of emotional origin), antagonism to the teacher, etc.

The nature of the slowness itself also has to be carefully examined. A delayed end product does not necessarily mean a slow process of thinking. Because a child takes a long time to arrive at an answer does not mean that his thinking is retarded. It may be that his thinking is more circuitous, that he is easily distracted, that he will not venture an answer until he is certain; and there is a host of other possibilities.

While our culture emphasizes speed, there is really no reason to assume that gifted, creative people have to learn rapidly or perform rapidly. Some people take a long time to learn basic concepts, but when they finally do so, they may use these ideas in a thoughtful, penetrating fashion. Others may learn a concept rapidly and then switch to some other area without ever pursuing the concept in depth. There are many slow people who only demonstrate their intellectual power on tasks in which it takes them a long time to get interested, and which have no time requirements. We have seen a fairly large number of college students whose grades and I.Q. scores were low, but who performed quite brilliantly on particular problems or in subjects in which they were deeply immersed. Their poor averages were simply a reflection of the pace required in college that is not attuned to their own style of work. They often fail courses where they could do extremely well if given more time. Actually, an extended college program, say, of five years, would benefit these students immeasurably. Educators tend to think of shortening college to three years for students who supposedly do not require the usual four years. But is there any reason why college could not be lengthened for these students who have a different style and pace of work? Many of these youngsters do, in fact, attend college for five or more years because they have to go to summer school to make up the courses they fail when carrying a schedule that is too heavy for them.

There is little doubt that the deprived child typically works on academic problems in a slower manner. This is shown in many different ways: he requires more examples before seeing a point, arriving at a conclusion, or forming a concept. He is unwilling to jump to conclusions or to generalize quickly (exceptions to the rule bother him). He is a slower reader, slower problem solver, slower at getting down to work, slower in taking tests.

It is important to note that in many areas of life the underprivileged individual is not at all slow; quite the contrary, he is frequently remarkably quick. By way of illustration, in athletic activities and many games he functions rapidly and seems to think quickly. He seems to be both perceptive and quick in judging expressions on people's faces. When verbalizing in his own idiom, he does not appear to be sluggish at all. In figuring out ways of "beating the system" in the factory he is often astoundingly fast. These observations suggest that part of his slowness in the academic sphere is probably due to unfamiliarity with the subjects, limitations with formal language, and insecurity in this setting. But these "defensive" reasons for cautious slowness do not tell the whole story either. It appears at first glance that in the more direct sensory and physical areas, the deprived individual can be fast and acute, while in the middle class settings in which he is unsure, slow caution prevails. The problem gets much more complex, however, once we begin to notice that there are a great many physical activities in which the deprived are notably slow. We had the opportunity of observing over a long period of time a highly skilled mechanic who came from a deprived background. Whenever he built anything in his house such as a cellar or a table, he did so in a meticulous fashion; likewise, when he worked on his car. He seemed to like to work in this manner, mulling things over, taking his time. Most old-time skilled workers like a leisurely pace. The shoemaker does not rush through his work, as a rule, but tends to do it carefully, patiently, at a moderate clip. This is often connected with pride in the product produced. Apparently, then, in things that are taken very seriously, things of deep concern, matters of personal pride, the slow style takes over. Workmanship is not a game or a party, but something enduring. It is also likely that many of the off-the-job pursuits of people like our mechanic—who, incidentally, likes to fish as well as to build furniture—are a reaction against the fast pace of modern industry.

Another source of the slow pace, which is not a sign of inadequacy or insecurity, may lie in the physical, less world-centered approach of the deprived person. It is not as easy to get into a problem or to cope with it as quickly if one has to go through all the steps physically. A word-oriented person can deal with most academic problems facilely, albeit sometimes glibly. A physical individual, on the other hand, likes to *do* as much as he can in thinking through a problem. This is often time-consuming.

While there are various special classes for slow learners, these classes do not really aim at developing advanced conceptual skills. They assume that the slow learner's ability is basically limited, rather than recognizing that he has a different style of learning that may have positive attributes.

They do not envision any potentially gifted children among the slow learners.

Do and See vs. Talk and Hear

In Chapter IV, the physical or motoric style of deprived groups was noted. This style is evidenced in a number of familiar ways:

1. They often appear to do better on performance tests of intelligence.
2. They like to draw.
3. Role-playing is an attractive technique to them.
4. They often use their fingers when counting, and move their lips when reading.
5. They like to participate in sports.
6. They employ physical forms of discipline.
7. They appear to think in spatial terms rather than temporal terms (they often have poor time perspective).

While their more limited temporal perspective undoubtedly produces difficulties, the spatial focus has a positive side to it. Spatial conceptualization permits an entire problem to be seen at once—it does not have temporal restrictions.[1]

The physical learner is, as was noted earlier, usually a slower learner, particularly in the early stages. But it is quite likely that he achieves a different kind of understanding of a problem than the faster, symbolic learner. Unfortunately, because our school system rewards speed, physical learners are discouraged and do not develop, while the symbolic learner is encouraged and moves forward.

While the deprived child does not easily get into problems, and has a short attention span, once he does become involved he is often able to work tenaciously for long stretches at a time. This may be a characteristic of the physical learner, because in order for him to learn he needs to have more of his whole body responding, and this requires a longer "warm-up" period. We are reminded here of the warming-up required in role-playing, which is more "physical." Highly verbal people, who incidentally, often resist role-playing or function in it in a highly intellectual manner, seem to need much less of a warm-up period in studying. Since they use their "muscles" less in thinking, this is perhaps comprehensible.

How Deep Is the Physical Approach?

It is interesting to note that the deprived child's motoric style or approach may not actually be as imbedded as might appear at first glance.

[1] This positive aspect of spatial conceptualization was suggested by Irving Taylor in a personal communication.

There is the possibility that the difference in approach is more of a *set* which is capable of manipulation and change under certain circumstances. This interpretation is suggested by a finding of Miller and Swanson.[2] On one of the tests (the Carl Hollow Square Test) employed to determine whether people tended to be "conceptual" or "motoric," the researchers wanted to see if their subjects could switch their orientations if the instructions were altered slightly. That is, could a physical person perform in a conceptual fashion and vice versa. Miller and Swanson used two sets of instructions. One encouraged the subjects to take a conceptual approach: ". . . it helps to work these problems if you spend some time trying to figure out what is the best way to do them. . . ." Another set of instructions encouraged the subjects to be motoric: ". . . you can solve the problem better by trying all the possible ways to fit these together that you can in the time allowed. . . ." Under these conditions both groups were able to use styles that were not characteristic of them. *Deprived children could perform conceptually about as well as the non-deprived groups.*[3] This is one more example of their hidden intelligence. It is also further evidence that the early environment of the deprived child has not produced irreversible effects.

The Concrete and the Abstract

Abstract thinking is ultimately rooted in concrete sensory phenomena. But most of us in the course of educational experience have come to appreciate abstractions for their own sake. This is true whether we are talking about scientific theories or artistic-literary productions. We do not have to see the concrete applications or origins of Shakespeare in order to appreciate him. But deprived children have a very different attitude toward abstract concepts. They need to have the abstract constantly and intimately pinned to the immediate, the sensory, the topical. This is not to say that they dislike abstract thinking. It is, rather, that they do it differently. Moreover, after they have acquired some feeling for broad generalizations from seeing their derivation and application in practice, then the deprived indi-

[2] Daniel R. Miller and Guy E. Swanson, *Inner Conflict and Defense* (New York: Henry Holt, 1960), p. 346.

[3] Siller found that low-status children do more poorly than high-status children on a variety of tests of conceptual ability and that they are less adequate in handling abstract concepts. In light of Miller and Swanson's findings, there is the possibility that this is due more to a "set" than a basic ability. An interesting residual finding of Siller's is that the differences between the high and low status groups is due to a small number of especially "low scorers" in the deprived groups. "When the groups were examined with these subjects removed, there were no significant status differences." See Jerome Siller, "Socioeconomics Status and Conceptual Thinking," *Journal of Abnormal and Social Psychology*, November, 1957, p. 365–371.

viduals may, to some degree, begin to appreciate abstract formulations per se. This probably comes at a later stage of development, and possibly even then the abstractions will be more firmly connected to things that can be seen, felt, and acted upon.

Since the deprived child approaches abstractions from the concrete, the immediate, the teacher must do likewise. The following is a vivid illustration reported to us recently by a junior high school teacher:[4]

"On the day before the following lesson, the teacher told the class the story of Caliban from Shakespeare's *The Tempest.* The next day, the class walked into a darkened classroom and the teacher, walking around the room and reading by a flickering flashlight, recited the poem by Louis Untermeyer called 'Caliban in the Coal Mines.' It is a plaintive, almost sacrilegious, appeal to the Lord for better conditions in the mines: 'God, if You wish for our love, Fling us a handful of stars.' The lights in the classroom were turned on near the ending of this last line of the poem. Allowing the class to come out of its trance slowly, the teacher distributed copies of the poem and requested, and received, acceptable meanings to certain words. In the discussion that followed the teacher asked why the poet had called his miner Caliban. The answer supplied by a thirteen-year-old girl was: 'They were both in the dark.' "

This same teacher states further:[5]

"Announce a lesson in 'literature'—especially one in poetry—and you will receive an assortment of groans. Announce that you will tell the class a story and you will receive respectful but reserved expectancy. State further that this is the story of two sets of parents who, because of their unwillingness to adapt to the present time, contributed to the destruction of their own children. You will have your audience in the palm of your hand. On the basis of a sympathetic, even empathic approach to the point of view of the adolescent, you have motivated the class to the study of Shakespeare's *Romeo and Juliet.* Will deprived children respond to these techniques? Having used them in my classes, I shall vouch that arguments have started because somebody said that Juliet was a fool to destroy herself for a man. Somebody else wondered if we sometimes learn the truth too late (speaking of the elder Montagues and Capulets). It is not difficult to direct such thinking into the value of having a mind stretched by studying and observing and learning."

THE OUTSIDE VS. THE INSIDE

Deprived children for the most part are not introspective or introverted; nor are they greatly concerned with the self. They respond much

[4] Personal communication from Harold Kirsch, a New York City Junior High School teacher.

[5] *Ibid.*

more to the external, to the outside. They are not given to self-blame or self-criticism, but rather are more likely to see the causes of their problems in external forces. Sometimes this can take the form of scapegoating and projection, but it may also lead to appropriate placement of censure and accompanying anger.

That they are not introspective in focus does not mean that they are incapable of inner thought, imagination, and feeling. But rather, again, as in the case of the concrete and the abstract—the external stimulation must precede the inner development. They are not given to direct enjoyment of introspection qua introspection, but instead require, at least at first, that it be stimulated by external sources.

The Games Format

Anyone who has worked with deprived children knows that one of the surest ways to involve them in an activity is to make it into a game. Now, this is true of all children to some extent, but it is especially true of the underprivileged. Davis and Eells have capitalized on this idea by developing an intelligence test in the form of a game. Cartoon-like personality tests such as the Rosenzweig Picture Frustration Test are much more appealing to underprivileged individuals.

Teachers have told about setting up a mock court in the classroom which enabled the class to discuss discipline, justice, and government in a meaningful way. Originally they had found it difficult to interest the deprived children in these subjects, but the excitement of a make-believe court attracted considerable attention and provided a good beginning for discussion on a higher, more abstract level.

One of the reasons why the new teaching machines are likely to appeal to the deprived child is that they operate pretty much like games. In this connection, we are reminded of the exciting work of O. K. Moore at Yale, where, by using special mechanical devices constructed in the form of games, he has been able to teach three-year-old children to read, write, and type.[6] The use of machines of this kind on a pre-school level with deprived children holds great promise. Perhaps even more important could be their use in special classes for "retarded" children. These game-like devices

[6] The effectiveness of the teaching machines ultimately has to be evaluated in the framework of the long-range learning sets produced by such devices. The present hue and cry concerning their apparent effectiveness has to be weighed in relation to the attitudes toward learning and thinking which eventuate. Also, much of their observed effectiveness may be due to a "gimmick" or novelty (placebo) effect, and not to the intrinsic learning principles presumably involved. Moore's work with small children would not seem to be subject to this effect, but the long-term effects on the child's attitudes toward learning will have to be appraised carefully. See *Time Magazine*, November 7, 1960, p. 103, for a brief presentation of O. K. Moore's methods.

might enable these children to catch up rapidly and return to the main educational "track," and thus reduce the present "two track" character of the educational system.

What is the source of the "games" orientation of the deprived? Apparently, it is related to their down-to-earth, spontaneous approach to things. Their extra-verbal communication (motoric, visual) is usually called forth in games, most of which are not word-bound. Also, most games (not all, by any means), are person-centered and generally are concerned with direct action and visible results. Games are usually sharply defined and structured, with clear-cut goals. The rules are definite and can be readily absorbed. The deprived child enjoys the challenge of the game and feels he can "do" it; this is in sharp contrast to many verbal tasks.

Why Does the Progressive Approach Fail?

Progressive education emphasizes "learning by doing." This fits in with the physical approach of the deprived child. Progressive education emphasizes concrete, experience-centered learning, attuned to the pace of the child. This is exactly what the deprived child needs so much. Why, then, does the progressive approach appear to fail with these children—why do they find it so unappealing on the whole? This is a puzzling problem. Certainly, it must be said, there are a fair number of progressive-minded teachers who, in stressing vivid, example-centered lessons, have been successful with deprived children. But on the average, it is the old-style, strict, highly structured teacher who appears to be most popular and effective with underprivileged children. When this teacher is also lively, and builds concepts from the ground up, and makes an effort to "win the children to learning," she is the model teacher for these youngsters.

The progressive approach by itself, however, does not catch on. It has too many features that are essentially alien to the culture of the deprived: the permissiveness; the accent on self—the internal—the introspective; creativity and growth as central goals of education; the stress on play; the underestimation of discipline and authority. All these values are contradictory to the traditional attitudes and personality characteristics of the deprived.

What is needed is a perfect marriage of the traditional and the progressive. The traditionalist contributes structure, rules, discipline, authority, rote, order, organization, and strong external demands for achievement. He fights to win the child to a high level of conceptual learning. The progressivist places the emphasis on the importance of motivation; the down-to-earth learning by doing; examples drawn from the experience of the child—beginning in the present and moving toward the broad, the abstract, the cultural heritage.

This is the combination that can break through the block which separates the child and the school.

A Different Wave Length

In summary, then, it can be said that the following characteristics are fairly typical of the deprived child's style:

1. Physical and visual rather than aural.
2. Content-centered rather than form-centered.
3. Externally oriented rather than introspective.
4. Problem-centered rather than abstract-centered.
5. Inductive rather than deductive.
6. Spatial rather than temporal.
7. Slow, careful, patient, persevering (in areas of importance), rather than quick, clever, facile, flexible.

It can readily be seen that many of these characteristics overlap. They seem to form a pattern that, according to Irving Taylor, is very similar to that found among one type of highly creative person.[7] Why then does the potential creativity of the underprivileged child fail to materialize? There are a number of reasons, but perhaps the most important is his verbal difficulties. The following chapter is directly concerned with this problem.

[7] Personal communication from Irving Taylor.

25

Individual Classroom Adjustments for Gifted Children in Elementary Schools

James J. Gallagher
Margaret Greenman
Merle Karnes
Alvin King

DURING THE PAST DECADE serious questions have been raised as to the adequacy of existing educational programs to meet the needs of intellectually gifted children. Many special programs have been initiated in the hope of more adequately educating them.

It is of crucial importance that special programs designed to meet the needs of gifted children receive comprehensive evaluation so that future planning and development are based, as much as possible, upon relevant facts. A number of evaluation studies have been carried out testing the adequacy of special class provisions (1, 7, 10), and the effects of acceleration (2, 12). None, to the authors' knowledge, have evaluated the effect of

JAMES J. GALLAGHER is a professor on the staff of the Institute for Research on Exceptional Children, College of Education, University of Illinois, Urbana. MARGARET GREENMAN is director of elementary education in the Champaign Public Schools, Champaign, Illinois. MERLE KARNES is director of special education, Champaign, Illinois, public schools. ALVIN KING is personnel director of Urbana Public Schools.

This project was made possible through the generous cooperation of Superintendent E. H. Mellon, Champaign Public Schools, and Superintendent C. C. Loew, Urbana Public Schools, and their staff and teachers.

Financial support for the conduct of the project was obtained from the Graduate Research Board of the University of Illinois and through the cooperation of Ray Graham, Office of the Superintendent of Public Instruction, Springfield, Illinois.

enrichment programs in the elementary classroom, although "enrichment" is one of the most common recommendations for gifted children.

Problem

The purpose of the present study was to evaluate the effectiveness of a case study approach for adjusting the environment of highly gifted children in an elementary school program. It was hoped that the results of such a study could establish the beneficial limits of such a program and suggest what other special services might be needed for full educational benefit of these children.

Subjects

The present sample of subjects were 29 boys and 25 girls who obtained a Binet IQ score of 150 or over and who were in the second through fifth grade of the elementary school programs in Champaign and Urbana, Illinois (1). Children were referred for study through the observation of teachers and other school personnel or on the basis of superior scores obtained on group achievement and intelligence tests. All of these children, whether nominated by teachers or by their own test performance, were administered an individual intelligence test, the revised Stanford-Binet (L). All students obtaining an IQ score of 150 or over were included in the present study.

Table 1 indicates the father's occupation and mother's educational level of the gifted children in the present sample. Since the major industry of the two communities is a large state university, it was no surprise to find that 40 percent of the families had breadwinners who were college professors or in some way connected with the faculty of the university. Another 25 percent of the children came from professional homes in which

TABLE 1. FAMILY BACKGROUND OF GIFTED CHILDREN

Father's Occupation	*N*	*% of Total Group*	*Educational Level of Mother*	*N*	*% of Total Group*
College Professor	21	40	Graduate Work	4	7
Professional	13	25	College Degree	24	44
Business	9	17	Some College	10	19
Skilled Worker	7	13	H. S. Diploma	10	19
Farm Manager	1	2	Some High School	1	2
Military	1	2	Unknown	5	9
Total	52	100	Total	54	100

the father was a lawyer or a physician, and 17 percent came from homes where the father was engaged in the general business area.

It is interesting to note that a meaningful minority, 13 percent of the children, came from the homes of skilled workers whose occupation does not demand either excellence of verbal skills or college training.

The general educational level of the mothers was, as expected, quite high. Over 50 percent of the mothers had a college degree and seven percent had done graduate work. There was, however, an interesting minority of about 20 percent who did not receive any college work at all. The percentages obtained in Table 1 agree rather closely with the picture of family characteristics of gifted children obtained in other research (11). Although the proportions are weighted in favor of parents of high educational and socio-economic status, an important consideration of the school is that a highly gifted child *still can come from a home of almost any type and character.*

Procedure

The case study approach was chosen as a method that could be used to identify the needs and individualize the program of the child. After identification by the individual intelligence test each of the youngsters were taken through the following steps:

1. The parents were asked if they would approve of the schools instituting a program planned to adapt the curriculum more to the needs of their intellectually superior child. All parents gave permission to have their child participate in the study.

2. The research psychologist on this project administered an extensive test battery to each of the children. It included:

   a. *Mental Ability*
      (1) Stanford-Binet (L)
      (2) Wechsler Intelligence Scale for Children

   b. *Achievement*
      (1) Stanford Achievement test
      (2) Other diagnostic tests as needed

   c. *Social Adjustment*
      (1) Sociometric questionnaire given to the entire class of which the child is a member

   d. *Personality*
      (1) Rorschach Ink Blot Test
      (2) The Michigan Picture Story test
      (3) Self-Ideal Concept test

   e. *Additional Information*
      The parents were interviewed to discover more about the developmental history of the child, and the teacher was interviewed to determine present problems within the classroom.

3. When this information was collected, the Curriculum Adjustment Committee of this project, which included school psychologists, directors of elementary education, directors of special education for each of the school districts and the research staff from the University, met to arrive at some preliminary agreement as to the major problem areas, if any, facing each child.

4. A summary of the relevant information from the meeting of the Curriculum Adjustment Committee was presented in another meeting with the teacher and principal of each particular child. The purpose of these meetings was to ensure agreement on the areas to be given special attention, and to suggest possible avenues of attack by the classroom teacher. At the close of each meeting, it was hoped that a plan would be formulated that could go into operation. The classroom teacher was the focus of this plan although other school personnel were included.

Since the range of needs and problems of the group was great, the range of suggested adjustments was varied also. A short list of some of the suggestions will indicate that variety of the Curriculum Adjustment Committee's recommendations.

a. One child was moved to another school where he could receive more intellectual challenge and stimulation.
b. Three children were accelerated a grade after special planning with present and future teachers.
c. Classroom committee assignments and revised seating assignments were given to some students with a view towards improving their social acceptance.
d. Children were, in a few instances, referred for special treatment of speech and emotional problems.
e. Special projects were given to some children in an area of their known interests in an attempt to stimulate greater motivation and interest in school.
f. Special activities were suggested for children who did not seem to show sufficient creativity or originality. Such activities included completing unfinished poems, creating stories out of imaginative themes (What would have happened if Lincoln had not been assassinated? What would be the feelings of the first man to land on the moon? Suppose there were no more winters, what would happen?).

5. At intervals of from one month to three months, follow-up interviews were conducted by one member of the Advisory Committee in each school district. Each teacher with a child in the project was questioned to determine if the initial recommendations were effective or if other problems had arisen since the study began.

6. In the spring of the second and third years of the project, follow-up interviews were held with parents and teachers of the child and three of the objective test instruments were readministered. These included the Stanford Achievement test, the Self-Ideal Concept rating scale, and the classroom sociometric technique.

As was reported in a previous study (4) the group, as a whole, revealed a wide diversity of adjustment. Upon initial investigation, it was determined generally that these youngsters were not an active irritant to the school. They were not serious academic problems, nor did they manifest marked antisocial behavior. About one out of every four of the children appeared to be making a superior adjustment to the total school situation.

Results

One of the most traditional ways to evaluate a special program is to ask those people who are most closely concerned with the program how they feel it is operating. Such questions, properly phrased and supplemented by other data, can provide important evaluative information.

Teacher and Parent Attitudes

At the end of the third year of the project, rating scales were administered to the teachers and the parents in an effort to determine the scope and direction of changes that occurred in the children. The final rating scales given to parents and to teachers were constructed to be as similar as possible so that some comparison could be drawn between the viewpoint of the home and the school. Both teachers and parents were

Table 2. Parents' Evaluation of Program

Characteristic	*Parent*	*Marked Improvement* N	%	*Mild Improvement* N	%	*No Improvement* N	%	*Loss* N	%
Freedom from Fears	F *N* = 49	3	6	14	29	32	65	0	0
	M *N* = 53	6	11	12	22	34	64	1	2
Motivation	F	9	18	16	33	24	49	0	0
	M	14	11	12	22	26	49	1	2
Creativity	F	5	10	15	31	28	57	1	2
	M	6	11	16	30	30	57	1	2
Social Acceptance	F	3	6	19	39	24	49	3	6
	M	8	15	14	25	29	55	2	4
Academic Performance	F	4	8	10	20	34	69	1	2
	M	8	15	15	28	29	55	1	2

informed that the evaluation that they were making would be kept confidential and not revealed to school administrative staff.

Table 2 indicates parental opinion of the changes which took place in their child as a result of the program. A glance at the Figure will show a marked similarity in parental ratings on the various behavioral characteristics. If the parents of a child tended to see improvement in one area they tended to see improvement in many. As can be seen, fathers were somewhat less inclined to see marked improvement in their children than were the mothers; otherwise, the response trends of the parents were about the same.

The area which seemed to receive most commendation on the part of the parents was *School Motivation.* Interestingly enough, the teachers also felt that the children showed greatest improvement in this category. About 30 to 45 percent of the parents saw either marked or mild improvement in their child on all other characteristics and only a small minority of parents observed any negative effect of the program upon their child's development. There was a tendency to see less change in *Emotional Adjustment* than in most of the other areas, but this was not surprising since a majority of these children did not initially show problems in this area. The parents and teacher ratings were not completely comparable since the teacher ratings were done only on those areas in which recommendations were made for change.

Table 3 shows the teacher ratings on the effect of the recommendations. The teachers saw greatest improvement in the areas of *Motivation, Academic Performance*, and *Social Acceptance* and the least gain in *Emotional Adjustment*, paralleling the parental attitudes. However, a comparison of the ratings of parents and teachers on those children that they rated in common showed them to be in significant agreement on progress in individual children on only two areas, *Academic Performance* and *Creativity*. In other words, the teachers and parents did not agree with each

TABLE 3. TEACHER RATINGS ON CHANGE IN CHILDREN RELATED TO RECOMMENDATIONS

Problem Area	N	*Marked Improvement*		*Mild Improvement*		*No Change*		*Loss*	
		N	%	N	%	N	%	N	%
Freedom from Fears	15	3	20	1	7	11	73	.....	
Motivation	20	7	35	4	20	8	40	1	5
Creativity	17	2	12	5	29	9	53	1	6
Social Acceptance	19	5	26	5	26	7	37	2	11
Academic Performance	9	2	22	5	56	2	22	.....	

other significantly on whether the child in question showed improvement in *Emotional Adjustment, Social Acceptance*, or *School Motivation.*

In addition to being asked about possible changes seen in their child, the parents were requested to identify any changes in their own attitude towards the child or modifications they saw in the behavior of the teacher of their child. The most frequent reaction by the parents was that no change was made from previous practices. The teachers were also asked to respond to parental attitude changes they observed and 34 percent indicated that they saw *No Change* in the parents.

The most frequently mentioned modifications in parental attitude and behavior were that they provided more experiences enriching the child's environment outside of school, and their child's shortcomings were viewed with greater tolerance. This might seem to contradict other responses, often made by the same parents, that "more was being expected" of their child. Actually this was not a contradiction. The parents raised their expected standards of performance for their child in the academic area but were inclined to view certain social and personal characteristics with greater tolerance.

Twenty-four mothers and 17 fathers found change in teacher attitudes towards their child during the program. In many instances these changes were categorized as increased teacher attention given to the child. This attention took the form of extra work and more projects required of the child. The parents, on the whole, seemed rather pleased that higher standards were being set for their children.

Teachers also noted changes in the parental attitude towards school. The teachers felt that about 30 percent or about one-third of the parents showed a more favorable attitude towards school as a result of the program, while none showed a less favorable attitude. Although 50 percent of the parents were viewed as unaffected by the program itself, the total picture was one of a more favorable parent-school climate.

The most frequent parental change noted by the teachers was the increased amount of time parents spent working with their child at home. The teachers also observed 17 percent of the parents encouraging their child to bring materials from home to the classroom. It was found that some gifted children were working on projects of unusual interest and complexity at home who had not mentioned them in school. The teacher had no knowledge of what the child was doing at home. This program helped to integrate some of the children's activities between home and school. Other parental changes took the form of greater teacher contacts, more PTA work, and in four cases, greater contribution of time and materials to the class activities themselves.

One of the clear bonuses of this type of program seemed to be improved parent-school relations in a number of instances.

Do the parental observations of positive change in their children represent what really happened? Were the parents being too kind? Were they just demonstrating the "Hawthorne effect," which suggests that almost any attention paid to people tends to change their perceptions favorably? Parental and teacher observations have to be supported by objective facts before they can be totally accepted as representing the true state of affairs.

Objective Test Findings

Academic Gains

The difficulties involved in evaluating academic growth in children have not been appreciated fully by many teachers and administrators. The usual age and grade norms on standard achievement tests are useful in giving a general estimate of the child's status in relationship to his own age or grade, but these scores cannot be used as measures of growth since they are not equal unit scales. That is, an Equivalent Grade Score increase from 4.0 to 5.0 on Science rarely represents the same amount of growth in knowledge of science as a gain from 5.0 to 6.0.

In order to establish the ratio of the gifted child's growth over a period of time with an equal unit scale, the Stanford Achievement tests were used. Gardner (5) developed a method whereby the growth in a subject area can be measured from one time to another by means of K units. These units are standard scores which are indications of growth in a subject when compared to the performance of an average tenth grade student.

How can we determine the amount of achievement expected of a gifted child? Horn (6) has pointed out that previous attempts to measure academic efficiency by means of an Achievement Quotient were faulty due to theoretical assumptions which could not be met. She therefore proposed a formula based upon theoretical correlations between achievement and intelligence test scores. The prediction of expected level of reading was obtained for the present group by the formula $EA = \frac{2MA + 1\,CA}{3}$. The formula for arithmetic was: $EA = \frac{MA + CA}{2}$.

For each gifted child the expected K score was obtained in four achievement areas: Paragraph Meaning, Word Meaning, Arithmetic Reasoning, and Arithmetic Computation. The group results on expected and obtained achievement before and after the individual planning sessions are shown in Table 4. The time that elapsed between the beginning and the end of the individual programs ranged from 6 months to 32 months, but elapsed time had no relation to amount of improvement.

On Paragraph Meaning the mean *expected* K score obtained by this gifted group was 90.56 or the equivalent of approximately eighth-grade performance. The *obtained* mean K score was 88.65. Thus there was a difference between the mean expected and obtained K scores of −1.9 K units. Translated into more educational terms this result indicated that as a group they were about one-half year below their expected level in the subtests of Paragraph Meaning and Word Meaning. It may be noted that these children were considerably lower in arithmetic skills than in the reading areas. The mean discrepancy between expected and obtained scores on Arithmetic Reasoning was −8.7 K units and for Arithmetic Computation, −20.9 K units.

The group performance was approximately one to three grade levels below expectations in Arithmetic. This would support the general finding that arithmetic skills are more resistant than reading skills to independent vertical gain by gifted children.

The column, *After Planning*, in Table 4 shows the expected and obtained K scores at the end of the experiment. If improvement was found, the discrepancy between obtained and expected should decrease. In Paragraph Meaning the mean difference between expected and obtained K scores was −.46 at Posttest as compared with a −1.91 obtained Before Planning. For each subtest of the Stanford Achievement test the mean discrepancy between expected and obtained K scores was lower at Posttest than it was before planning. In other words, the children were closer, as a group, to their expected achievement scores that they had been prior to the individual planning. This change, however, must be considered *only a tendency* since Mann-Whitney U Tests did not reveal any statistically significant differences between "before planning" and "after planning" scores on the achievement test. It may be noted, in passing, that the arithmetic subtests were as resistant to improvement by this group as were the reading subtests.

The moderate gains obtained on the Achievement test do not necessarily reflect negatively upon the impact of the program. In many instances these children were doing very well in academic work prior to the study and would not be expected to show meaningful gains. The effect of the initiation of academic enrichment procedures by individual teachers could be evaluated more adequately by studying the performance of those children for whom specific academic plans were made.

TABLE 4. CHANGE IN EXPECTED AND OBTAINED ACHIEVEMENT AFTER INDIVIDUAL PLANNING

	Before Planning N = 46			*After Planning N = 46*		
Stanford Achievement	*Mean Expected*	*Mean Obtained*	*Difference*	*Mean Expected*	*Mean Obtained*	*Difference*
	K* Score	K Score	(e–o)	K Score	K Score	(e–o)
Paragraph Meaning	90.56	88.65	−1.91	99.85	99.49	− .46
Word Meaning	86.70	84.07	−2.63	98.19	96.04	−2.15
Arithmetic Reasoning	84.17	75.46	−8.71	95.06	88.44	−6.62
Arithmetic Computation	64.37	43.46	−20.91	82.71	64.79	−17.92

* K scores are standard scores equalizing units of growth in these areas. See reference #5.

Eight children were eliminated from this comparison since they exceeded the ceiling of the examination on their final test.

Nine of the 54 children received some recommendations for improvement of academic work at the time of initial planning. If these plans were effective we should have expected the discrepancy between their expected and obtained scores to decrease. Table 5 shows the median rank of gains obtained by this group as opposed to the total group. Rank in this regard refers to the amount of gain the child made related to his expected achievement. Thus the child who showed the greatest improvement over his standing prior to the initiation of the program would be ranked number one, and the child who received the lowest amount of gain in relation to expected achievement would receive the rank 46. The expected median rank of any subgroup chosen at random from the total would be 23.5.

TABLE 5. CHANGES IN ACADEMIC GAIN RELATED TO SPECIFIC PLANNING AND TYPE OF SCHOOL ENROLLED

		Paragraph Meaning	*Word Meaning*	*Arithmetic Reasoning*	*Arithmetic Computation*
Median Rank Expected by Chance	($N = 46$)*	23.5	23.5	23.5	23.5
Median Rank Obtained by Students Receiving Academic Planning	($N = 9$)	22.0	26.0	24.0	26.0
Median Rank Obtained by Students from Low Referral Schools	($N = 12$)	25.5	29.5	34.5**	30.5

* Eight cases could not be evaluated. They had reached the ceiling of the test at the final testing.
** Significant difference at .01 level of confidence.

The median rank obtained by the children who had received specific academic planning remained remarkably close to chance expectations. On Paragraph Meaning the median rank obtained by the children receiving special planning was 22.0. Similar results close to chance expectancy were obtained for the subtests of Word Meaning, Arithmetic Reasoning, and Arithmetic Computation. These findings seemed to suggest that special planning for these children in academic subject skills did not improve *their* rate of growth over that obtained by the children not involved in such planning.

These negative results can be compared with the median ranks obtained by students who were from Low Referral schools, or schools in which very few gifted children, of the ability level herein studied, were found. In all of the subtests the median rank obtained by these students was higher than chance expectation. The median rank of 34.5 on Arithmetic Reasoning reached a statistically significant difference from chance at the .01 level of confidence on the Mann-Whitney U Test. The differences on the Paragraph Meaning and Arithmetic Computation subtests are in the same direction at a confidence level of .10.

Thus, the academic rate of growth of those gifted children in Low Referral schools was slower than that of the children coming from schools where many more intelligent children were to be found. There are undoubtedly other factors creating difference between the High Referral and Low Referral groups such as family background and enthusiasm for education. The schools should not necessarily be considered the causal agent for this difference. However, these results do suggest that the schools might seriously consider special planning for the academic program of the gifted children in these Low Referral schools.

Social Status

A previous article by the senior author (3) has described in detail the social status of these gifted children prior to program planning instituted by this experiment. The results, briefly summarized, indicated a general high level of social acceptance for this group of gifted children which was not related to sex, socio-economic level, school, or grade level. There was a suggestion that children scoring above Binet IQ 165 were slightly less popular than children who scored a Binet IQ between 150 and 165.

TABLE 6. CHANGES IN PEER ACCEPTANCE BEFORE AND AFTER PLANNING

Social Acceptance in Class	*Before Planning*		*After Planning*	
	N	%	*N*	%
Top Quarter	26	56	21	46
Second Quarter	9	20	11	24
Third Quarter	7	15	5	11
Bottom Quarter	4	9	9	20

$\chi^2 = 1.89$ ($p = .01$ to $.20$)

Table 6 indicates the change in peer acceptance concomitant with program planning. Before planning began, over 50 percent of the group stood in the top quarter of their class in social popularity as measured by the number of nominations for friendship reported by the rest of the class. Only nine percent of this group was found in the bottom quarter. This social popularity trend was statistically significant from chance expectations. After program planning, the sociometric devices were readministered in June of 1957 with the final results indicated in Table 6. The general level of social popularity of the group seemed to diminish slightly.

Only 46 percent of the group were found in the top quarter of their own classroom whereas 20 percent were found in the bottom quarter of their class in social popularity. A comparison between the fore planning and after planning results produced a chi square of 1.89. This meant there was a slight probability that the introduction of the program might have somehow negatively affected the peer acceptance of this group. Further investigation showed that the loss occurred almost entirely at one grade level—the sixth grade—and seemed to be related to those children in Low Referral schools. In those schools, there did seem to be a slight tendency for greater teacher attention to these children to be accompanied by some loss in social status. This is a trend which calls for further investigation.

The teachers of 11 gifted children in our group received special instructions regarding methods by which improvement in peer acceptance might be obtained. Such suggestions involved the manipulation of committee assignments, giving the child a position of leadership in which he would work with other children, and similar gambits. These children could be compared with another group of gifted children who had approximately the same social status at the beginning of the experiment, but for whom no special plans were made concerning their social and peer acceptance.

Of the group that received special planning, four children gained in their social status, three lost, and four remained the same. In the group that received no special planning three children showed gain, four children showed no change, and five indicated a loss in social acceptance. These results indicate that no significant improvement in peer acceptance was forthcoming as a result of special planning, and further, if peer acceptance is to be improved, other and better methods will have to be found rather than the ones used in the present situation.

Self Adjustment

A rating scale patterned after Rogers' Personality test (9) was administered before the individual program was initiated and again after the program had been completed. This scale obtained a measure of the child's self image and self-ideal image in the areas of physical, academic, social, personal, and family adjustment.

Figure 1 shows the median percentage discrepancy between the self and self-ideal ratings of the gifted group before and after program planning. A high discrepancy between self and ideal ratings would be considered indicative of maladjustment and a low discrepancy considered evidence of better self adjustment. If the program had an important influence in a positive direction on these self attitudes it would be expected that the discrepancy scores would be reduced. As Figure 1 shows, the median group discrepancy scores on all subtests remained almost the same from Pretest to Posttest. It can be concluded that no group change of any consequence took place on these self attitudes during the course of the individual programs.

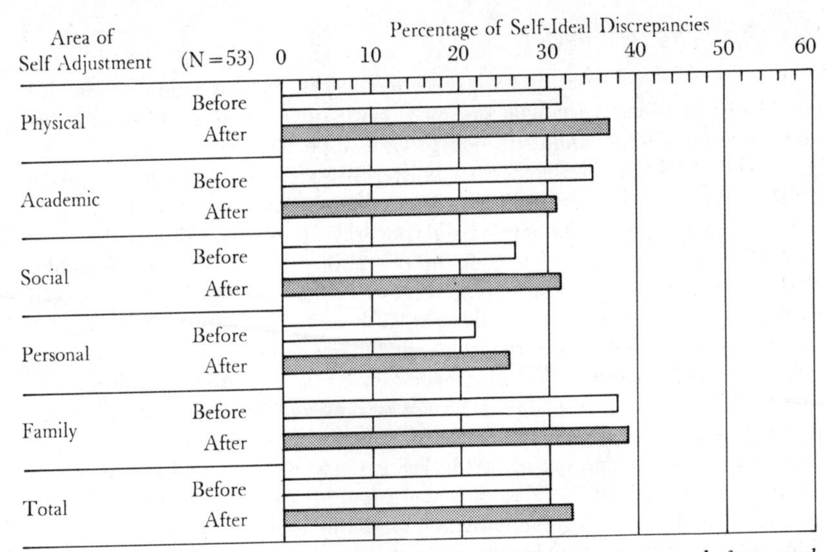

Figure 1. Discrepancy between self and ideal concept scores before and after individual planning.

The 11 children who received special recommendations for aid in personal adjustment showed no deviation from this general trend. It could be concluded that specific planning did not have a meaningful effect upon the self-ideal concepts of these children, as measured by this index.

The Influence of Time

Since this was a three-year study, some of the children were in the study for a much longer period of time than others. Did the length of time in the study have any effect upon changes? There were no relationships found between length of time in the project and improvement on measures of adjustment, peer acceptance, and academic abilities. In practically all instances the children who were in the study for more than a year had different teachers each year. The information obtained the first year was supposed to be passed on to the next teacher. There was the sizable disadvantage that the new teacher had not attended the original meetings.

Individual Changes

The group results can express only imperfectly the findings of this study which was based so much upon individual situations. Therefore, a thumbnail sketch of three of the outstanding successes and non-successes in the group are presented to give a general flavor of what happened in specific instances.

Cases Showing Improvement

Tim. Tim was the most intelligent child in the present study (Binet IQ 205) and was doing very well on initial status in reading achievement. He had many self-doubts about his competence, especially in the area of sports. Tim used his high intelligence to bolster his sagging physical self-image by showing the other students how smart he was. While his academic performance was quite adequate it did not reveal creative thought or the unusual talent expected of a child of this ability level. The recommendations of the case study committee were that the parents should be asked to aid in building his self-confidence in his physical skills. The teacher spent a considerable time strengthening Tim's self-confidence in the classroom so that he would not feel it necessary to belittle other children.

At the end of the project, Tim was reported by the teacher as improving greatly in self-confidence, especially in the physical area. He was more confident and poised in giving reports. He moved from the most unpopular one-fourth of his class in social standing to above average in social standing. Tim showed greater awareness of his own problems by judging himself as less than ideal in all areas of personal adjustment on the self-rating scale. There seemed little doubt that the increased interest in Tim's problems taken by the family, as well as the work of the teacher, played some role in this improvement.

Polly. Polly was one of a number of the youngsters who was adjusting fairly adequately to the school curriculum but was not showing any unusual leadership or creativity. The case study tests and interviews revealed her lack of confidence in herself. This lack of confidence appeared to prevent her from taking imaginative steps in the classroom or in engaging in leadership activity.

The program planned for Polly included specific attempts to place her in positions of leadership under considerable teacher guidance and support.

The results of this added effort on the part of the teacher seemed to pay impressive dividends. Polly was appointed editor-of-chief of the class newspaper and responded extremely well to this challenge. According to the teacher Polly was pleased to be given this responsibility, enjoyed the work, and had done an excellent job.

This change had the added result of improving Polly's social standing in her class. Her own self-ratings had not changed very much but she herself seemed to be a happier person. The parents were extremely pleased with the change they saw in Polly.

Carl. Carl's problem was that, while he was doing moderately well in his school work, he was extremely sensitive to the feelings and attitudes of his classmates. Further, in his home school, his classmates were not interested in high academic achievement beyond their grade level. With the parents' consent, Carl was moved to another school where he received much greater intellectual challenge. The intellectual atmosphere of the home was improved by the purchase of books. The parents had always given Carl, an only child, much attention and affection. This attention took a more intellectual flavor as a result of the study.

At the final rating, Carl was adjusting very well to school. After two years in the new school, he was one of the best achievers in the room, was well liked, and held class offices. Moving Carl into a more adequate and challenging intellectual environment seemed to pay important dividends, as did similar moves in the three or four other cases where such a change in school environment seemed called for by the individual circumstances.

Cases Showing Limited Change

As important as the children who *did* respond to this type of enrichment program are the children who were unable to profit. By studying closely the child who did not respond, insights into the limitations of this type of enrichment program may be obtained.

Alfred. Alfred was a ten-year-old child who was markedly overprotected by his parents. Although his average academic achievement was high, he was slow and languid in accomplishing routine school work. He accepted the parental overprotection without protest and exerted himself only in very restricted areas of intellectual problems. In the beginning of the study he seemed to be fairly well accepted by his particular group.

The program designed for Alfred tried to: (1) encourage him to relate his interest in arithmetic to mechanical devices, inventions and science; (2) encourage responsibility by placing time limits on his work in class rather than allow him to continue indefinitely through procrastination; (3) discuss with the parents the possibility of increasing his responsibilities in the home.

The follow-up teacher interviews revealed that Alfred was manifesting the same types of behavior as had been reported at the beginning of the study. Some of the quotes from the teacher's follow-up a few months after the program began were: "Alfred's work habits have not improved," "He prolongs every assignment 'til he has to be kept after school to get his work finished."

Four months later the comments were much the same, "Alfred has had many opportunities to do creative writing but he continues to do mediocre work." "He continues to be effeminate." The two largest problems remaining at the end of the study according to the teacher were (1) his inability to work to capacity in areas aside from science, and (2) he shies away from physical activity. The recommendations for action did not touch the central problem which would seem to lie within the family interrelationships.

Wanda. Wanda was a conscientious and compliant nine-year-old whose major difficulty seemed to be lack of originality and creativity. She came from a family which adhered closely to rural midwestern values and which did not place a high value upon intellectual excellence in girls. Wanda's mother was a dominant and aggressive woman who was active in community and church affairs and seemed to overshadow her three daughters.

Although Wanda did well on the achievement tests in school her originality and creativity were quite poor and her reading interests were extremely immature. These interests centered around comic books and detective stories. The television programs she watched were typical of those that interest younger children.

The program planned for Wanda attempted to broaden her interests, introduce her to areas of intellectual activities that she had previously been unaware of, and to help her to improve her creative writing. A specific attempt was made to gain the parents' cooperation for this program.

The objective test scores, the parents, and teachers all agreed that Wanda did not show improvement during the time she was observed. The reason for this lack of change seemed to be that the parents were not interested in cooperating with the school's recommendations, and that Wanda was too closely dependent upon the parents' good-will to go against their wishes.

George. George was an eight-year-old only child of superior mental ability, who manifested marked problems in social and personal adjustment. These difficulties included violent temper tantrums coupled with manifestations of strong dependency needs which caused him to be academically ineffective, socially unpopular, and personally miserable. His difficulties seemed to center around disturbances in the family relationships. His history of behavior difficulties extended back into very early childhood.

George's personal problems were obviously interfering with his ability to do his school work and also were making him unpopular with his own age group.

The judgment of the planning committee was that his emotional problems were overshadowing all other difficulties. The recommendation was made that he see the visiting counselor. Plans were also made to lead George out of his immature classroom behavior by gradually giving him more responsibility and commending him for signs of mature behavior. He was placed in the upper reading group as an attempt to show him that the teacher had confidence in his ability. Other activities were planned with a view towards building his self-confidence and his prestige in the group.

These plans did not result in considerable success. Neither parents, nor teacher, nor the test results, were very enthusiastic about George's improvements. In the middle of the second year the teacher said things such as, "George's biggest problem is learning to get along with others."

Later in the year, the teacher was discouraged with his progress, felt he was doing extremely poorly, and found it hard to believe that he was a gifted child. The limited sessions with the school social worker apparently did not yield positive results. At the end of the study the two most outstanding problems George had, according to the teacher, were that (1) he did not work up to his ability and (2) he had become a show-off and engaged in much attention-seeking behavior.

Summary and Discussion

Fifty-four highly gifted children (Binet IQ 150 and over) in the elementary grades (two through five) were examined by the case study method. Each child had an adjusted program planned on the basis of the individual needs revealed during the case study. This program was primarily the responsibility of the classroom teacher although she had available supplementary services such as speech correction, counseling, curriculum advice, etc.

Evaluation reports were obtained from parents and teachers at the end of the program concerning the progress of the children and objective tests were administered at the beginning and at the end of the program.

The subjective reports of parents and teachers suggested that they had observed considerable gains in their children in all areas of development during the program. The objective test reports revealed little, if any, benefit obtained by the group in areas of academic achievement, self-concept, or social status.

Since the objective tests did not measure such characteristics as motivation and creativity it seems possible that there *was* a meaningful change in attitude toward school work in many of the children. This was one of the few areas of agreement on individual children between parents' and teachers' ratings. About one-fourth of these children were making a close to maximum adjustment prior to the initiation of the program and substantial growth was not to be expected from these children.

Educational Implications

The success of these individual planning sessions for highly gifted children was limited although the sessions did prove useful with certain individuals. The most obvious advantage obtained through this procedure was a greater understanding by the teacher and other school personnel of the needs and characteristics of each child. Specific action based upon that understanding, however, was limited by three major factors:

1. *The inability of the teacher to carry out suggestions due to deficiencies in her own curriculum skills.* A teacher who is markedly deficient in her own knowledge of mathematics could hardly stimulate a highly gifted child in this area even if she knew that this was a potentially fruitful area of attack. No one was more vocal about their own limitations than the teachers, and any recommendations for action would have to take into account this important problem. A closer look at the teacher training curriculum seems called for. Unless the teacher has greater content kowledge in many areas than now seems to be the case, "enrichment of gifted children" means little or nothing in actual operation.

2. *Limited available auxiliary facilities.* In some instances it would have been useful to have available, to a greater extent, the services of a psychologist, a school social worker, a speech correctionist, or a reading specialist. The psychologist who tested the children was attached to the research project and not available to the schools once the project had been completed. The demands of the problem children in the school systems were too great to allow the unlimited use of the auxiliary facilities available.

3. *The inability of the school to deal with basic problems.* In this study, and in actual practice, the schools have often been reduced to dealing with secondary problems or symptoms of problems in children. If the poor motivation of the gifted child is due to severe father-child conflict, for example, then the school is not likely to improve the child's motivation by introducing new and more stimulating books. If the parents do not accept the idea that a problem exists, or if the school is reluctant to face the parents with the problem, then limited improvement could be expected.

The relatively poor showing, academically and socially, of gifted children from low referral schools (schools where there were few gifted children) raises the question as to whether special measures should be taken to more effectively meet their needs. One specific recommendation would be to group these intellectually superior children together so that they would not remain in a relatively isolated intellectual environment. The few children for whom this recommendation was executed seemed to thrive academically and were not seriously affected socially and emotionally by their environmental change.

Another important educational implication was based on the contacts with the parents of these gifted children. The generally enthusiastic response of the parents to this program and their strong desire to assist in whatever way possible suggested that the schools have a powerful and potentially useful ally in the home. While it is not always clear as to how the parents could best aid these children it would certainly be within the realm of possibility for the school to (a) spend more effort in informing the parents as to the nature and scope of the school program as it is related to their child, and (b) consider ways in which parental activity could positively supplement this school program.

The general recommendations to the school systems was based upon the conclusion that adjustments for gifted children in the regular classroom are likely to be nebulous and unproductive approaches *unless* there are sufficient psychological services available to diagnose the child's individual needs and *unless* the teacher has sufficient curriculum skills available to carry out an enriched program for these children. Most school systems have neither service in sufficient supply nor do they provide enrichment for their intellectually superior in the classroom.

Thus the specific recommendations to the schools included:

1. Additional psychological help be employed to give necessary diagnostic services.
2. A curriculum specialist be employed who can help supplement the skills of the teacher in certain content areas.
3. A program of grouping be instituted to aid those children who are in positions of relative intellectual isolation.
4. Plans be developed to enlist more effective aid from the parents in relation to the total school program.

Both of the cooperating school systems responded to these recommendations by employing a curriculum specialist to aid in the content areas and in reviewing their policies of pupil placement on an ability basis. The psychological personnel required for other purposes was too great to allow staff assignments to gifted children at this time.

For many years "adjustments within the regular classroom" has been an accepted answer to the education of the gifted child in the elementary grades. It seems apparent that sizable retooling in the teacher training institutions, and more auxiliary personnel need to be provided before anything approaching the theoretical ideal can be obtained. Under the existing circumstances, other attempts at providing a more enriched environment for gifted children should be given careful consideration.

Selected Research References

1. Barbe, W. B., "Evaluation of special classes for gifted children," *Except. Child.*, 1955, 22, p. 60–62.
2. Birch, J. W., "Early school admission for mentally advanced children." *Except. Child.*, 1954, 21, p. 84–87.
3. Gallagher, J. J., "The peer acceptance of gifted children in elementary school." *Elementary School Journal*, 1958, 58, p. 465–70.
4. Gallagher, J. J., and Crowder, Thora, "The adjustment of gifted children in the regular classroom." *Except. Child.*, 1957, 23, p. 306–12, p. 317–19.

5. GARDNER, E. F., "Comments on selected scaling techniques with a description of a new type of scale." *J. clin. Psychol.*, 1950, 6, p. 38–43.

6. HORN, ALICE, "Uneven distribution of the effects of specific factors." *Educational Monographs*, U. of Southern California, 12, 1941.

7. PASSOW, A. H., "The talented youth project: a report on research underway." *Educ. Res. Bull.*, 1957, 36, p. 199–206.

8. PRESSEY, S. L., *Educational acceleration, appraisals and basic problems.* Columbus: Ohio State U., 1949.

9. ROGERS, C. R., "Measuring personality adjustment in children nine to 13 years of age." *Teachers College Contributions to Education #458*, New York: 1931.

10. SUMPTION, M. R., *Three hundred gifted children.* Yonkers-on-Hudson, N.Y.: World Book Co., 1941.

11. TERMAN, L. M., and ODEN, MELITA H., *The gifted child grows up. Genetic Studies of Genius, Vol. IV.* Stanford, Calif., Stanford U. Press, 1947.

12. WORCESTER, D. A., *The education of children of above-average mentality.* Lincoln, Nebr.: U. of Nebraska Press, 1956.

26

Review of Research on Early Admission

Maynard C. Reynolds
Jack W. Birch
Alice A. Tuseth

IF ADMISSION TO SCHOOL based upon factors besides chronological age is to be considered, a first task is to specify what these other factors might be. In this chapter a review of selected research on readiness for school will be provided. Some of the factors or variables to be considered are: chronological age, mental age, physical maturity, emotional and social maturity, and sex. It is now widely agreed that no single criterion is adequate as the determinant of school admission. The orientation should be to multiple criteria.

This chapter will also review research evaluations of early admission programs as conducted in a number of communities. Consideration is given to the long-range implications of early admission as well as to the immediate adjustment of early-entering children in kindergarten or first grade.

An exhaustive review of studies on these topics is beyond the scope of the present bulletin. Only literature judged to be especially relevant to the early admission issue is summarized. Readers wishing to have a comprehensive review of research on acceleration are urged to read Keys' (1938) summary of research up to 1938 and the Pressey monograph (1949) which covers research up to 1949. Reviews of more recent research may be had from a number of sources. Worcester's book (1956) probably provides the most extensive reports of research on the early admission issue of any recent volume. The bibliography included in the final pages of the bulletin will be useful to those who wish to make a full review of the relevant research.

Factors of School Readiness

Chronological Age

Chronological age (CA), now virtually the only factor considered in admitting children to school in most school districts, is obviously one variable to be considered in setting school admission policies. Programs as now conducted in most kindergartens are adjusted to four and five year old children and would be inappropriate for most older or younger children.

Among unselected children entering kindergarten and first grade, the younger ones generally do not achieve or adjust as well as those who are older. Carter's study (1956), for example, contrasted 50 underage and 50 normal age children in grades two through six. The underage children did not equal the scholastic achievement of normal age children. Studies by Hamalaenin (1952) and King (1955) produced similar findings.

A somewhat more complex study, which involved comparisons of groups formed according to combinations of CA and MA, has been reported by Forester (1955). Forester studied records of 500 pupils in the kindergarten through high school. For purposes of his study, children were grouped into six CA segments and six MA segments, according to relative standing in CA and MA for grade placement. He concluded that very old-very dull pupils did not do well in school, that the very old-very bright excelled throughout the school years and that the very bright-very young pupils had difficulty from junior high on. The latter finding is one of the exceedingly few research findings which might be considered negative to early admission for bright pupils.

Studies such as those of Carter and Forester, which show CA to be an important variable in school admission procedures, should not obviate consideration of other variables. Since CA shows a substantial correlation with many other variables, such as physical and social maturity, in any broad group of children, its chief merit may be its somewhat indirect reflection of a child's general maturity level. When one considers a relatively narrow range in CA, however, the correlation with other variables is not high and we may do much better by going directly to other variables in setting admission standards. It is also important to note that studies of retrospective design which compare children of various CAs in school adjustment and achievement have not touched the really central issue of early admission for children *carefully selected* on variables other than CA.

Most children now admitted to kindergarten vary in CA from about 4-8 to 5-8. Holding strictly to such a range has the advantage of being convenient, objective, and easily understood. It is the present thesis that exceptions should be made to accommodate certain children who are below the standard age for school admission. The means for selecting these exceptional cases is the principal topic of discussion for the remainder of this bulletin.

Some states have established statewide minimum CA standards for admission to school. The present writers see no objection to such action, but it is considered most unfortunate if the standards fail to provide for exceptions when appropriate procedures for early admission are applied. Worcester's reports (1956) on Nebraska show extraodinary success in a carefully developed early admission program in a state having a general statewide "cut-off" date.

Although not immediately relevant to the early admission issue, it is of interest that in some English-speaking nations–including Scotland, England, New Zealand, and Australia–children are admitted to formal school programs, which include instruction in reading, at ages up to a full year younger than in the United States. It is possible that further research and changes in instructional methods will make a general change in school-entering age advisable in this nation.

Mental Age

Mental age (MA), measured by individual intelligence tests, is more closely related to school achievement at all grade levels than CA. Kazienko (1954), for example, found MA was a better predictor of success in school than either IQ or CA. Hobson (1956, 1948) has established that MA is a workable criterion for admission to school. Stake (1960) has developed actuarial tables showing the very substantial relationships between pre-school MAs and achievement levels in elementary grades.

In most communities which have flexible admission programs the major evidence required for early admission is relatively high MA. The minimum MA for early admission to kindergarten varies from 4-10 in some schools to as high as 6-10 in others. Sometimes a lower limit in CA is set along with a minimum MA requirement. For example, one school district allows children to be up to six months underage in CA, but sets a minimum MA of 5-2 for admission to kindergarten.

Administering an early admission program puts heavy emphasis upon individual psychological examinations and requires the employment of well-trained school psychologists. Fortunately the schools are rapidly becoming employers of psychologists who are prepared for this special work. Most school psychologists welcome the opportunity to participate in early admission programs. They are often helpful in interpreting the program in the community and in conducting evaluations of the programs as well as in the testing and related activities with individual children.

The test most commonly used by school psychologists in assessing intelligence of children is the Stanford–Binet Intelligent Test (Terman and

Merrill, 1960). Although results on this tend to be more reliable at later ages, they are sufficiently reliable at school-entering ages to be highly useful (Bayley, 1955). It is unlikely that a child who receives a high score in testing for early admission will prove to be significantly lower in relative intelligence in later testing. Enough experience has been cumulated in many communities to establish the reliability and usefulness of individual psychological test results given at pre-kindergarten ages when interpreted by well-trained psychologists.

Physical Maturity

One of the variables about which there are often expressions of concern in early admission programs in physical development. Since early admission is proposed only for bright children, it is relevant to consider the relationship between giftedness and physical development.

In general, gifted children tend to be heavier, taller, and more mature physically than average children. Olson and Hughes studied a series of children's records which had been collected in a laboratory school. In describing growth patterns of gifted children, they observed that: "Their physical attributes tend, on the whole, to lie above the average typical of children in general but tend to be less highly developed than the intellect which so often constitutes the chief basis for the identification of the gifted" (1950, p. 62).

Hollingworth, after considerable investigation of the physical and motor development of children, comes to these conclusions about intellectually gifted children: "They tend to be tall and heavy, and to maintain a high ratio between height and weight" (1926, p. 110). She found that gifted children with an IQ of about 150 at 10 years of age are on the average as large, strong, and swift as average unselected 11½ year olds, while intellectually they can do the work of 15 year olds.

In the Stanford University *Genetic Studies of Genius*, physical superiority was found to be one characteristic of gifted children. In 1923, 37 anthropometric measures were made of 594 gifted subjects, most of whom were between the ages of seven and 14 at the time. The findings of the study were summarized as follows: "The gifted children as a group were above the best standards for American-born children in growth status as indicated by both height and weight; they were also above the established norms for unselected children in California. In lung capacity, considered in relation to height, weight, and age, the means for the gifted subjects were above the Baldwin norms. The gifted subjects on the average exceeded the norm groups in breadth of shoulders and hips and in muscular strength. In all respects the results of the measurements showed that the gifted group was slightly superior physically to the various groups used for comparison" (Terman and Oden, 1947, p. 20).

Hobson (1948) reported that the underage superior children admitted early in Brookline Schools over a period of many years could not be distinguished physically from their older classmates after the kindergarten year, if then. Similar observations have been reported from the Nebraska studies (see Chapter VI) and from a number of communities in which early admission has been tried. The Nebraska studies have been conducted on a broad group of bright children, many of them below the "gifted" category. It is to be noted, of course, that excellent health and physical maturity are usually included among criteria of admission.

The notion that bright and gifted children are physically immature and susceptible to disease has been refuted by careful studies. Not all bright children are physically mature enough to enter kindergarten or first grade at ages younger than normal, but many of them meet this criterion quite adequately. The tendency in communities having early admission programs is to evaluate the physical development of individual children, rather than to prescribe definite criteria such as minimum height or weight standards. A few communities require examinations by physicians of all early-entry candidates.

Actually, there is no evidence that physical development is a relevant variable in determining whether or not children should enter school early. It may be more important to ascertain that the child is in good general health than to learn whether he is tall or short, stocky, or thin, well coordinated or awkward. Attention to problems of health is always important, whether or not early admission procedures are followed.

Social and Emotional Adjustment

Teachers frequently express concern that underage children may have difficulties in emotional and social adjustment, i.e., in adjusting to standards of group behavior, forming friendships with older children, tolerating long periods away from home, and meeting work standards. Adequate social and emotional maturity should always be a consideration in making early admission decisions.

Admission policies based upon CA offer no assurance that children will show adequate maturity in social and emotional adjustment. Social maturity shows higher correlation with MA than with CA. Studies of gifted children have shown that they tend to be ahead of their agemates in social and emotional development, as well as in intellectual ability. Studies in which only bright, generally mature children were entered early show that such children do not have difficulties in social and emotional adjustment any more frequently than equally bright children who delay school entrance until the normal age.

Psychologists, teachers, and school principals usually want to meet with early entry candidates and judge for themselves which children appear mature enough to start school. The psychologist may use the Vineland Social Maturity Scale and other tests, in addition to his informal observations of a child, in forming his judgments.

Sex

Because boys more frequently than girls have difficulties in school adjustment and achievement in early years, it has sometimes been suggested that admissions standards should be different for the sexes. Pauly (1951 and 1952), for example, has argued that boys should be admitted at a more advanced age than girls. Such a procedure must be judged to be crude, at best, since many boys are ready for school at ages considered satisfactory for girls. Our attention must be given to individual determinants of school readiness rather than to base rates for sex groups. The suggestion of a simple age differential for school admission of sex groups should be rejected.

Other Variables

Other variables related to success in school and useful in judging readiness for early entry may be listed, such as personality factors, motivation, richness and extent of preschool experiences, attitudes of parents, creativity, reading readiness, and socio-economic status. The judgments made by school personnel about individual children presented for decisions regarding early entry should take into account all such variables. If the question refers to early entry to first grade, reading readiness assumes major importance and formal testing in this area would ordinarily be a part of the assessment procedure.

A question sometimes raised concerns possible harmful effects of acceleration through production of eye strain. Wester (in Keys, 1938) attempted to answer this question by analyzing health records of accelerated students and equally bright nonaccelerated students in high school and found that 13 percent of the accelerants wore glasses compared to 24 percent of the nonaccelerated group. The number of serious eye conditions was about equal for the two groups. It is noteworthy that no evidence of acceleration causing vision problems was produced.

Ophthalmologists have stressed recently that there is no great danger in using what vision a person has. This has led to vastly increased instruction of children with partial sight using ordinary instructional materials. The notion that eye strain results from early education has now largely disappeared. It is normal for preschool children to be somewhat farsighted. Unless the condition is extreme, no adverse effect because of early education need be anticipated.

STUDIES OF EARLY ADMISSION TO SCHOOL USING MULTIPLE CRITERIA

Research on acceleration through early admission to school is overwhelmingly favorable to early admission procedure. Studies by Hobson (1948), Smith (1951), Monderer (1954), Birch (1954), Kazienko (1954), Mueller (1955), Cutts and Moseley (1957), Miller (1957), and Stake (1960), for example, all support carefully administered early admission procedures. Reviews of research have consistently pointed favorably to early admission (see Keys, 1938; Pressey, 1949; Worcester, 1956; McCandless, 1955; Norris, 1958; Fliegler and Bish, 1959; and Reynolds, 1960). Through all the years of his monumental *Genetic Studies of Genius*, Terman (1947) consistently recommended moderate acceleration of gifted children.

In all studies cited above early admission was allowed only following individual psychological testing and careful judgments about other facets of school readiness. No studies are known which are unfavorable to this form of acceleration when such selective procedures were applied, but at least one program is reported to have been discontinued on the basis of administrative difficulties. Reported in *Time* (1955) under the title, "Hopping Like a Bunny," is the experience of one school district in moving back to a strict CA admission standard after trying a flexible admissions procedure. Apparently parental objection was the reason for the policy reversal. Successful operation of early entrance programs in many communities demonstrates that parents will usually support the program.

Some of the most comprehensive programs of early admission and evaluations of such programs are summarized in succeeding portions of the present bulletin. Included are Hobson's studies of the Brookline, Massachusetts program which dates back to 1932. In 1956, Hobson described the status of 550 underage children who graduated from high school between 1946 and 1955. Results, given in some detail in the following chapter, are entirely favorable to early admission. It is especially noteworthy that the advantages shown by accelerants were evident in early years and increased regularly throughout their full public school program.

The Brookline data show no reason for fear that accelerants will become socially maladjusted when they reach secondary school levels. Hobson compared the extracurricular activity participation throughout the four years of high school of the underage and the other graduates in the 1946 and 1947 senior classes. After-school employment was counted as an extracurricular activity. The underage girls and boys averaged 18.8 different activities; the others averaged 12.1 activities. An informal analysis of activity participation of all boys graduating in the ten years from 1946 to 1955 revealed "that the underaged boys seldom achieved eminence in the contact sports although there was a hockey goalie and a football quarterback among them." Except for this one type of activity, there seemed to be no difference in the kinds of activities participated in by the underage and other students. Compared with their older classmates, the accelerated boys and girls were less often referred to school officials for emotional, social, and other personality maladjustments.

The effects of acceleration as shown in high school and college have been carefully studied by Keys (1938). In one study, Keys and Wester (1938) were concerned with the adjustment of 70 high school pupils having IQs of 120 or over and in line for graduation at 16-8 or younger. Forty-six of these were matched on the basis of sex, grade, IQ, race, and socio-economic status with a group who were graduated at 17-6 or older. These two groups were called experimental and control, respectively. The remaining 24 accelerants had IQs of 136 or above and were treated as a separate high IQ group. A low IQ group of 43 accelerants was also included in this study for comparison purposes. The IQ range for this latter group was 93 to 119 and the age range, at graduation, was from 15-1 to 16-8. The four groups were compared in regard to their scholastic attainment, participation in athletics and other student activities, physical condition, personality adjustment, and attitude. Findings definitely favored acceleration of the high IQ group. Participation in athletics favored the experimental group with 44 percent of the boys playing on the football team compared with 11 percent of the controls. In the tenth grade, however, participation of the older boys was slightly higher than the others. For the girls, athletic participation and honors increased with the IQ of the group. In leadership and extracurricular activities, the high IQ group definitely excelled and the experimental group was somewhat superior to the control group. Bright accelerated students were characterized by counselors as timid, shy, reserved, too studious, or not good mixers, less than half as often as bright *un*accelerated students.

Early admission to kindergarten or first grade usually means the children involved will become underage college students. A comprehensive study of the effects of acceleration at the college level has been provided by Pressey (1949). He, along with other close observers of the effects of acceleration, reports that the risks of social maladjustment have been greatly exaggerated and that not to accelerate superior students could cause maladjustment. He reports that the findings of more than 30 years of experimentation and research on acceleration have been almost universally favorable to moderate acceleration of gifted students.

Gifted boys and girls tend to reach puberty at earlier ages than other children. The Stanford studies have also shown that social and emotional maturity correlate more closely with MA than with CA. Terman and his associates concluded that "the influence of school acceleration in causing social maladjustment has been greatly exaggerated" (Terman and Oden, 1947, p. 275).

Several studies have been reported from Nebraska, where Worcester's students conducted a number of related investigations between 1951 and 1955 (Worcester, 1956). A summary of additional work in Nebraska is provided by Hiskey in Chapter VI of the present volume. Smith (1951), in the Lincoln, Nebraska schools, compared the records of 175 early kindergarten entrants when they were in grades one to five with the records of children admitted at the usual age. The younger ones received equal or higher academic marks and equal or higher ratings on social and emotional adjustment than their older classmates. In the Fairbury, Nebraska schools, Monderer (1954) followed early admitted children through kindergarten and primary grades. Early entering children proved as far advanced as the others in their classes in intellectual, social, and physical maturity. Kazienko (1954) assessed the relative importance of mental age, chronological age, and intelligence quotient with respect to determination of fourth grade achievement. He found mental age to be significantly more influential than the other two separately or in combination.

Mueller (1955) investigated the proposition that younger bright pupils, even though able to do well in school upon early admission, might do even better if they entered school when they were older. He was able to compare groups of children who had received differential treatment in Grand Island, Hastings, and a number of rural communities in Nebraska. Teachers rated 4275 children on achievement, health, coordination, acceptance by other children, leadership, attitude toward school, and emotional adjustment. A small number of the children had been tested and approved for early admission and for various reasons had not started early. No trend appeared which would suggest that waiting had benefited them, and the results from the overall study were in strong support of the generalization that it is to the advantage of children to enter school at younger ages if they are mentally ready.

In summarizing the early Nebraska studies, Worcester says:

"[the children] who were admitted to kindergarten on the basis of individual mental tests were, on the average, approximately eight months younger than those admitted regularly. There were no statistical differences in physical development. In academic work, the younger did as well or better than their older classmates. Judged by their peers or by teachers' ratings, they are socially and emotionally as well or better adjusted. They have as good or better coordination. They are accepted by their peers. They like school. They do as well or better than those of the same age who were a year later in getting started in school. Indeed, no negative effects have been discerned. As compared with those who took the test but did not pass it, the younger ones had gained a year of school life without loss in social adjustment" (1956, p. 28).

An analysis of the school adjustment of 43 mentally advanced children admitted early to the first grade in the Pittsburgh, Pennsylvania public schools was reported by Birch (1954). The follow-up after one to three years indicated that in the overwhelming majority of instances the children were making satisfactory or better adjustment in the academic, social, emotional, and physical areas. Birch reports that there were very few difficulties with parents whose children were not admitted early, perhaps because all parents had been fully informed about the early admission procedure and given opportunities for individual consultation with psychologists.

Cutts and Moseley (1957) described an experiment in early admission to first grade for mentally advanced children begun in New Haven, Connecticut in 1922. In this instance, the New Haven public schools were in the process of raising the age of admission to first grade for children in general from 5-0 to 5-8 as of the first of September. In October of 1922 eight children who were below the new age requirement were recommended for admission by the school psychologist. All were assigned to first grade, completed the work satisfactorily and moved on to higher grades with increasing success. The plan grew rapidly. Parents proved cooperative, even when their children were not among those admitted early. Follow-up studies through the high school years showed favorable results. This early study indicates that an increase in the age of admission to school for children in general should be accompanied by special provisions for that small but important group of mentally advanced children who are best served by earlier admission.

Sweden has a plan of entrance testing for all children. The test is made up of twelve parts: comparisons, memory span, similarities, knowledge, missing parts, absurdities, classification, patterns, counting, direction, deduction and drawing. The test, called *Skolmogmad Sprovning*, literally, "school-rightness test," is given in May to seven year olds and exceptional six year olds. Total possible score is 100; average scores range from 22 to 30. All those scoring over 20 are passed. Others wait another year. Parents have a right of appeal if they feel the test was in any way unfair.

Edlund (1955) published results of a study done in Karlskrona, Sweden concerning success of early entrance in Swedish schools. Compulsory school age in Sweden is seven years attained January through December. Special regulations issued in 1946 permitted mature and intellectually capable children, as shown by a testing program, to begin school in the year they reach six provided they attain six before July 1. Exceptional cases could start even if birthdays fell after July 1. Slower children, as shown by test, could wait until age eight for school entrance. Since Swedish schools begin at the end of August, children tested and showing the required amount of readiness could begin school at 6-2—exceptional cases even at 5-8. Late developers could wait until 8-8.

Edlund's study showed a tendency for normal age children to receive higher academic grades in school than early entrants, but, he contends, the differences were due to inconsistencies in grading practices and that actually little is gained by having brighter, more mature children wait a year to enter school.*

Conclusions and Implications

It may be concluded, from the research cited above and that to be summarized in succeeding chapters, that early admission to school of mentally advanced children who are within a year of the ordinary school-entrance age and who are generally mature is to their advantage. Although there are needs for further research, there are few issues in education on which the research evidence now available is so clear and so universally favorable to a particular solution. The chapters which follow offer a practical guide to school officials who wish to accept this challenge.

Bibliography

Bayley, Nancy. On the growth of intelligence. *Amer. Psychologist*, 1955, 10, 805–818.

Birch, J. W. Early school admissions for mentally advanced children. *Except. Child.*, 1954, 21, 84–87.

Carter, L. B. Effect of early school entrance on the scholastic achievement of elementary school children in the Austin public schools. *J. educ. Res.*, 1956, 50 (10), 91–103.

Cutts, N. E., & Moseley, N. *Teaching the bright and gifted*. New York: Prentice-Hall, 1957.

Edlund, S. Under Sokniggar Rorande Kalmarprovets Prognosvarde Betraffande Underariga Elevers Skolmognad, Publications of the New Society of Letters at Lund, *Vetenskaps Societen*, Vol. 47. Lund, Sweden: C. W. K. Gleerup, 1955.

Forester, J. J. At what age should a child start school? *Sch. Exec.*, 1955, 74, (3), 80–81.

Fliegler, L. A., & Bish, C. E. The gifted and talented, in the education of exceptional children. *Rev. educ. Res.*, 1959, 24 (12), 5.

Hamalaenin, A. E. Kindergarten-primary entrance age in relation to later school adjustment. *Elem. Sch. J.*, 1952, 52, 406–411.

Hobson, J. R. *Scholastic standing and activity participation of underage high school pupils originally admitted to kindergarten on the basis of physical and psychological examination*, Presidential Address, Div. 16 (School Psychology). Amer. Psych. Assn., (Sept.) 1956, (Mimeo.). See also *Educ. psychol. Measmt.*, 1962, (Winter).

* For research relating to Swedish practices, the authors are indebted to Mrs. Margaret H. Pascoe, Teacher, Minneapolis Public Schools.

HOBSON, J. R. Mental age as a workable criterion for school admission. *Elem. Sch. J.*, 1948, 48, 312–321.

HOLLINGWORTH, LETA S. *Gifted children: their nature and nurture*. New York: Macmillan, 1926.

KAZIENKO, L. W. Beginner grade influence on school progress. *Educ. Admin. & Supervis.*, 1954, 40, 219–228.

KEYS, N. *The underage student in high school and college*. Berkeley: Univer. of California Press, 1938.

KING, I. B. Effect of age of entrance into grade 1 upon achievement in elementary school. *Elem. Sch. J.*, 1955, 55, 331–336.

MCCANDLESS, B. R. Should a bright child start school before he's five? *Education*, 1955, 77, 370–375

MILLER, VERA V. Academic achievement and social adjustment of children young for their grade placement. *Elem. Sch. J.*, 1957, 62, 257–263.

MONDERER, J. H. An evaluation of the Nebraska program of early entrance to elementary school. *Dissertation Abstr.*, 1954, 14, 633.

MUELLER, K. Success of elementary students admitted to public schools under the requirements of the Nebraska program of early entrance. *Dissertation Abstr.*, 1955, 15, 2103.

NORRIS, DOROTHY, & OTHERS. Programs in the elementary schools. *Yearb. nat. Soc. Stud. Educ.*, 1958, 57, Part II, Chicago: Univer. of Chicago Press, 1958, 222–262.

OLSON, W. C., & HUGHES, B. O. Growth patterns of exceptional children. *Yearb. nat. Soc. Stud. Educ.*, 1950, 49, Part II, Chicago: Univer. of Chicago Press, 1950.

PAULY, F. R. Sex differences and legal school entrance age. *J. educ. Res.*, 1951, 45 (9), 1–9.

PAULY, F. R. Should boys enter school later than girls? *Nat. Educ. Assn. J.*, 1952, 41, 29–31.

PAULY, F. R. Let's give boys a break. *Phi Delta Kappan*, 1959, 40 (4).

PRESSEY, S. L. Educational acceleration: appraisals and basic problems. *Bureau of Educ. Monogr.*, Columbus, Ohio: Ohio State Univer., 1949, No. 31.

REYNOLDS, M. C. Acceleration. In E. P. Torrance (Ed.), *Talent and education*. Minneapolis: Univer. of Minnesota Press, 1960, 106–125.

SMITH, J. The success of some young children in the Lincoln, Nebraska public schools. Unpublished master's thesis, Univer. of Nebraska, 1951.

STAKE, R. E. Predicting success of the early starter. *Overview*, 1960, (Nov.), 32–34.

TERMAN, L. M., & MERRILL, MAUDE A. *Stanford-Binet Intelligence Scale, manual for the third revision, Form L-M*. Boston: Houghton Mifflin, 1960.

TERMAN, L. M., & ODEN, MELITA H. *Genetic studies of genius.* Vol. 4. *The gifted child grows up.* Palo Alto, Calif.: Stanford Univer. Press, 1947.

WORCESTER, D. A. *The education of children of above-average mentality.* Lincoln: Univer. of Nebraska Press, 1956.

EPILOGUE

Who Pays the Bills?

It should be clear from the articles included here that improving the education of gifted children, to say nothing of the educational problems of the rest of American youth, is no small task. It requires many more well-trained professionals with a variety of skills and, consequently, a large increment in financing over present custom. "But there is no money available," people will cry. Of course there isn't. There never is.

We learned from Senesh's article on economics that man's unlimited wants are always in conflict with his limited resources. It is the decision as to what one does with such limited resources that counts. Even as wealthy a country as the United States cannot finance everything that is useful or enjoyable or profitable. What is called for then is a system of priorities. It is in these priorities, not in the speeches of its leaders, that a nation reveals its true character.

Warren Weaver (1962) has described some alternative decision making that might have been with the budget necessary for the race to the moon, *if* education had received a higher priority. It makes for interesting reading.

> . . . it may cost 30 billion dollars to "put a man on the moon."
>
> "It is sobering to think of an alternative set of projects that might be financed with this sum. We could:
>
> 1. Give a ten percent raise in salary, over a ten-year period, to every teacher in the United States from kindergarten through universities, in both public and private institutions (about 9.8 billion dollars);
> 2. Give ten million dollars each to 200 of the best smaller colleges (two billion dollars);

3. Finance seven-year fellowships (freshman through Ph.D.) at $4,000 per person per year for 50,000 new scientists and engineers (1.4 billion dollars);

4. Contribute 200 million dollars each toward the creation of ten new medical schools (two billion dollars);

5. Build and largely endow complete universities with medical, engineering and agricultural facilities for all fifty-three of the nations which have been added to the United Nations since its original founding (13.2 billion dollars);

6. Create three more permanent Rockefeller Foundations (1.5 billion dollars); and still have 100 million dollars left over to popularize science.[1]

It has been said that a person when thinking in terms of his country makes the common assumption that his nation is immortal and will go on forever. A man must face his own limited life span and ask, "What will be said about it?" when it is all, too soon, over. And this is a good thing because it helps us order our values. It is, perhaps, too bad that we cannot think in these terms as a nation and say "What will be said about America?" when, all too soon, it is over. Perhaps "too soon" is five hundred years, or a thousand years, but it will come and if we can believe history, it comes sooner than we think.

What image will we leave? Some critics believe it will be that of a materialistic orgy, others say a tasteless culture of the common man, still others maintain it will be that of a generous, but foolish, dupe. But it is within our power to mold the image that we leave, and it is through education that we can best improve ourselves.

We have had enough of speeches supporting and eulogizing education. What is required is the honesty to see our needs clearly and the courage to act on that knowledge.

[1] Weaver, Warren. What a moon ticket will buy. *Saturday Review,* August 4, 1962, p. 38.

INDEX

A

B

C

R

S

T

U

V

W

Y

Z